CHUTZPAH

Other Books by Alan M. Dershowitz

THE BEST DEFENSE

REVERSAL OF FORTUNE: Inside the von Bülow Case

TAKING LIBERTIES: A Decade of Hard Cases, Bad Laws, and Bum Raps

CHUTZPAH

ALAN M. DERSHOWITZ

Little, Brown and Company
Boston   Toronto   London

First Edition

Excerpts from "The Pollards and Rosenbergs" by Alan Dershowitz, March 18, 1987, and "About Men: Collective Adolescence" by Alan Dershowitz, February 1987 (Mag). Copyright © 1987 by The New York Times Company. Reprinted by permission.

Lenny Bruce monologue originally published by Ballantine Books in *The Essential Lenny Bruce* by Lenny Bruce.

Cartoon on page 19 from *Totally U.S.* by Simon Bond. Reprinted by permission of Methuen, London.

Library of Congress Cataloging-in-Publication Data

Dershowitz, Alan M.
   Chutzpah / Alan M. Dershowitz. — 1st ed.
      p. cm.
   Includes bibliographical references and index.
   ISBN 0-316-18137-4
    1. Dershowitz, Alan M.   2. Jews — United States — Biography.
3. Lawyers — United States — Biography.   4. Jews — United States —
Politics and government.   5. Jews — Politics and government — 1948–
6. Jews — Identity.   7. Antisemitism — United States.   8. United
States — Ethnic relations.   I. Title.
E184.J5D39   1991
973'.04924 — dc20   91-6443

20 19 18 17 16 15 14 13 12

MV NY

Published simultaneously in Canada
by Little, Brown & Company (Canada) Limited

Printed in the United States of America

To Carolyn, who inspired me to write this book
from the first day we met

Contents

Acknowledgments   ix

Introduction   3

I   A Polish Jew Comes to America:
The Jewish Century of American Life   21

II   Leaving Brooklyn:
Learning About Anti-Semitism in the Real World   35

III   At Harvard:
Quotas, Conflicts, and Honors   63

IV   Going on Television:
The Pervasiveness of Anti-Jewish Attitudes   93

V   Auschwitz:
The Holocaust, Justice, and Faith   130

VI   Visiting Synagogues Around the World:
Exploring the Different Meanings of Jewishness   181

VII   Israel:
An American Jewish Civil Libertarian Goes to Israel   209

VIII   In the Soviet Union:
Are We Our Brothers' and Sisters' Keepers?   250

IX   In Marion Prison:
     The Pollard Case and the Crisis
     in American Jewish Leadership   284

  X   Jews in a "Christian America":
     The Separation of Church and State   313

Epilogue   The Past and the Future   343

     Notes   355

     Index   367

Acknowledgments

WRITING THIS BOOK has been a truly ecumenical experience. Research was done by Rozella Oliver, Norman Eisen, Ann Goglia, and Claudia Marbach. My legal associates, Jack Zaremski and Joseph Lipner, provided invaluable assistance as both participants in and researchers on some of the events in the book. The manuscript was typed by Maura Kelley and production of the manuscript was overseen by my secretary, Peggy Conant. Without the help and encouragement of my literary agent, Helen Rees, and my editor at Little, Brown, Fredrica S. Friedman, it could not have been done. Thanks also to Peggy Leith Anderson for her editorial assistance.

Various chapters were read and critiqued by my sons, Elon and Jamin, my nephew Adam, my niece Rana, my brother Nathan, and my sister-in-law Marilyn. Special thanks to Elon for his perceptive suggestions. My mother also read those parts I was willing to show her. My baby daughter, Ella, kept me up at night and inspired me to think about the Jewish future.

A word of acknowledgment also goes to my lecture audiences throughout the country, especially to those persons who asked the probing questions to which this book tries to respond.

Finally, profound appreciation to my Jewish mentors and role models who showed me — by their example — how to live as a proud American Jew.

CHUTZPAH

Introduction

AMERICAN JEWS need more chutzpah. Notwithstanding the stereotype, we are not pushy or assertive enough for our own good and for the good of our more vulnerable brothers and sisters in other parts of the world. Despite our apparent success, deep down we see ourselves as second-class citizens — as guests in another people's land. We worry about charges of dual loyalty, of being too rich, too smart, and too powerful. Our cautious leaders obsess about what the "real" Americans will think of us. We don't appreciate how much we have contributed to the greatness of this country and don't accept that we are entitled to first-class status in this diverse and heterogeneous democracy.

As we approach the close of the most cataclysmic century of Jewish history — a century that has witnessed the death of European Jewry, the birth of Israel, and the ongoing relocation of world Jewry to the United States and Israel — the time is ripe for a major reassessment of the situation of Jews in America and in the world. The goal of this book is to contribute to that reassessment by raising and trying to respond to a number of perplexing questions, and by sharing my perspective as an observer of, and sometime participant in, recent events that have helped shape the contemporary Jewish experience.

The list of pressing questions is virtually endless. Among them: Are American Jews truly first-class citizens of this nation to which we have contributed so much? Or have we merely managed to achieve a greater degree of toleration than Jews have been accorded by other "host nations" throughout history? Indeed, is it possible for Jews to achieve normalcy in a "Christian country" like America, or can that happen only in the Jewish state of Israel?

If we are first-class Americans, then why do we obsess about what our "hosts" will think of us? Why do anti-Jewish attitudes persist in America? Why does it seem so unlikely that our country will have a Jewish president? Why is it harder even today for a qualified Jew to get certain jobs and to gain admission to some universities than it is for an equally qualified non-Jew?

If we are indeed first-class citizens, why are we singled out for the accusation of dual loyalty when we support Israel? And why is Israel singled out for super-scrutiny and double-standard criticism, expected to maintain a level of moral behavior not demanded of anyone else? Is it because Israel is the Jewish nation and the Jew among nations?

Has the material success of Jews in America, coupled with the military success of the Jews in Israel, changed the nature of what is perhaps history's most persistent bigotry? Are we experiencing a new strain of the old anti-Semitism virus, different from medieval anti-Judaism, different from nineteenth- and mid-twentieth-century racial anti-Semitism, different also from twentieth-century political anti-Zionism? And what shall we call this new phenomenon, which we cannot even yet define with precision?

Should a people who survived genocide respond to subtle bigotry it feels but cannot clearly identify? Can it afford to risk the charge of collective paranoia and the dangers of crying wolf? Can it afford not to? What does the coming century have in store for a people that has struggled against millennia of oppression but now seems relatively successful, if not entirely secure?

Sometimes my "responses" to these questions will — in the Talmudic as well as Socratic tradition — take the form of even more vexing questions. At other times I will offer tentative answers of my own or of others in my generation of American Jews.

This book reflects my concern that despite the unmistakable contributions of Jews to the American success story, we seem willing to accept less than first-class status. We still seem fearful of offending the "real" Americans — in the face of the reality that we are no longer guests in someone else's America. Jews are still regarded as pariahs in many other parts of the world, and Israel remains an outcast nation within much of the third world. It is for these reasons, among others, that American Jews must insist on first-class treatment, as Americans and as Jews. We must not accept the status of second-class Americans, just because we are Jewish rather than Protestant or Catholic. And we must not accept the status of second-class Jews, just because we are

Americans rather than Israelis. We need not compromise either our Americanism or our Jewishness. Nor can anyone else define our Americanism or our Jewishness for us.

The past century has brought so much change, it is almost as if we have not had a collective moment to reflect on where we are and where we are likely to be going. This book is a call for such reflection at this watershed in our history. It is a demand for change in our own attitude toward ourselves, in the attitude of others toward us, and in our attitude toward others. It is a call for us to seize control over our own destiny in order to assure that the changes we experience in the future will not mirror our past.

Change has been a constant throughout Jewish history. Just a little more than a hundred years ago, few Jews lived in the United States and even fewer in what is now Israel. Today these two nations are home to most of the world's Jews.

Near the end of the nineteenth century, the world's Jewish populations were centered in eastern and central Europe and in the Islamic nations of North Africa and Asia, where they had lived for a millennium. A half-century later, everything had changed. European Jewry was destroyed in the space of five years. The establishment of Israel brought most of Europe's survivors as well as most Sephardic Jews from the Islamic countries to the new Jewish state. Now, large numbers of Soviet Jews are emigrating to Israel and the United States, as a result of ongoing changes in Communist nations that no one could have anticipated even two years ago.

The eternal "wandering Jew" has now settled into two *goldeneh medinas* — golden nations.* Perhaps we have finally stopped wandering. Perhaps not. Who really knows *where* the Jewish world will be at the close of the twenty-first century? Who knows *what* the Jewish world will look like a hundred years from now? In light of what has happened to us in just one brief century, only a fool would try to prophesy our future.

---

* The concept of the "wandering Jew" gave rise to the old joke about the nineteenth-century Polish Jew from Warsaw, who tells his friend that he is moving to America. The friend exclaims: "But that's so far away." To which the rootless Jew responds: "From what?"

Leonard Fein, in his remarkable book *Where Are We?* (New York: Harper & Row, 1988), recounts a somewhat more contemporary version of that joke. Fein writes in his book primarily about what he calls "the inner life of American Jews." Although what I write in this book deals primarily with our "outer life" — our actions, reactions, politics, and passions — it reflects the same generational attitudes as Fein's book. We do, after all, come from roughly the same generation and share roughly the same politics. Though some of our questions are similar, many of our answers are quite different.

Who in the nineteenth century could have foreseen the fundamental changes in the nature of Jewish demography, Judaism, and Jewish daily life that have overtaken us? Who could have imagined back in 1890 that instead of Jews cowering in fear of a pogrom threatened by local Ukrainian thugs, there would be a Jewish state with a fearsome military machine capable of defeating the combined armies of all the Arab nations? Who would have predicted that instead of being excluded from the great American universities, corporations, and law firms founded by Protestants, Jews would be selected as their presidents, CEOs, and managing partners? Who would have believed the current rates of Jewish intermarriage and assimilation, coupled with the recent increases in Jewish orthodoxy and fundamentalism?

A century ago, Viennese journalist Theodor Herzl sought "normalcy" for the Jewish people through political Zionism. The history of European Jewry, with its millennia of anti-Semitism, had persuaded him that Jews could never be accepted into European societies. The only solution was a Jewish homeland. Herzl believed that anti-Semitism would hinder Jews everywhere, forever, in whatever land they might live:

> The Jewish question exists wherever Jews live in perceptible numbers: where it does not exist, it is carried by Jews in the course of their migrations. We naturally move to those places where we are not persecuted, and there our presence produces persecution. This is the case in every country, and will remain so, even in those highly civilized — for instance, France — until the Jewish question finds a solution on a political basis. The unfortunate Jews are now carrying the seeds of anti-Semitism into England; they have already introduced it in America.[1]

Herzl argued that Jews could avoid enmity only by working their own land, speaking their own language, and collecting their own garbage.

Theodor Herzl was right about Europe, but the Jewish century of American history seems to have proved his prescription incomplete. American Jews have achieved a modicum of normalcy. Although the Jewish immigration of the late nineteenth and early twentieth centuries did introduce the seeds of anti-Semitism into America, these seeds have never sprouted into the poisonous weed of institutional bigotry experienced in many European countries. Jews have been extraordinarily successful in America. We have not melted into anyone else's pot. Instead, we have reshaped the pot to accommodate our unusual dimensions. In the process we too have reshaped ourselves somewhat to fit into our environment.

Some Israeli Zionists still smugly assure us that while American Jews *appear* to have achieved normalcy, if we scratch beneath the placid surface of our acceptability, our status as second-class Americans as well as second-class Jews becomes apparent. When, in 1985, Jonathan Jay Pollard, an American Jew, was caught spying for Israel within the United States, the discovery sent shock waves through the American Jewish community. Jewish leaders rushed to condemn Pollard and distance themselves from his actions. The charge of dual loyalty — at least in the minds of some Jews — reared its ugly head.

In analyzing this situation, Shlomo Avineri, a professor of political science at Hebrew University in Jerusalem, argued that the Pollard affair showed just how insecure American Jews really are.

> In the Pollard case, something more profound is now surfacing: a degree of nervousness, insecurity and even cringing on the part of the American Jewish community which runs counter to the conventional wisdom of American Jewry feeling free, secure and unmolested in an open and pluralistic society. . . .
>
> But the truth of the matter is simple: you, in America, are no different from French, German, Polish, Soviet and Egyptian Jews. Your exile is different — comfortable, padded with success and renown. It is exile nonetheless. . . .
>
> America, it now evidently appears, may not be your promised land.[2]

With all due respect, Professor Avineri misunderstands America. We are nervous, insecure, and "even cringing." But we are also different from French, German, Polish, Soviet, and Egyptian Jews. The source of *their* nervousness, insecurity, and cringing was largely *external*. They really were second-class citizens, guests in someone else's country. The source of *our* nervousness is largely *internal*. We may think of ourselves as guests in America, and some bigots may seek to impose that status upon us, but the reality is different.

A central message of this book is that a century after the arrival of Jews in significant numbers to America's shores, the time has come for us to shed our self-imposed second-class status, drop our defensiveness, and rid ourselves of our pathological fear of offending our "hosts." We must strike from our vocabulary the offensive concept of *shanda fur de goyim* — an embarrassment in front of the gentiles.[3]

America *is* different. It is not the original property of any particular ethnic or religious group. American nationalism is not at all like Russian nationalism, or Polish nationalism, or French or German nationalism. There are, sadly, very few original Americans — the descendants of the Native Americans whom we decimated and subjugated. The rest of us are *all* immigrants; the recentness of our arrival here is merely a matter of degree, and is becoming more so as the generations pass. That is why the Statue of Liberty and Ellis Island are symbols as important to American history as Independence Hall or the battlefield at Gettysburg. Because the U.S. Constitution requires the separation of church and state, no particular sect has achieved the status of the official American faith. Thus, Judaism is as authentically American as is Protestantism, Catholicism, or Islam. We are not a "Christian nation" or even a "Judeo-Christian nation." Nor are we an Anglo-Saxon people or a white people. A majority does not a national character make, as evidenced by the obvious fact that we are not a woman's nation, just because a majority of our citizens are female. We are truly a diverse nation of immigrants, where all are equal under law. That is what makes America different for Jews.

But Jews have not always insisted that they are just as fully American as the *Mayflower* descendants or the Daughters of the American Revolution. It is as though we are repeating the cry of the European Jews quoted by Herzl: "We depend for sustenance on the nations who are our hosts, and if we had no hosts to support us we should die of starvation." Too often we act as if we are satisfied to be tolerated. Too often, as Professor Avineri notes, we seem to fear that if we displease our hosts, they will ask us to leave *their* country.[4]

This should not be surprising, in light of our millennia of experience as tenants at will in other people's homelands, when we did live in other countries at the sufferance of the *real* owners of the land. Over the centuries, we were expelled, pogromed, crusaded, inquisitioned, jihaded, and holocausted out of countries that we helped to make great.

Even if our fears are understandable in light of our collective experiences over the centuries and the misguided perceptions of some who regard themselves as "hosts," these fears do not serve us well as we begin our second Jewish century in America. Just as we no longer accept exclusion from the legal, medical, banking, and other professions — an exclusion that earlier generations took for granted — we must no longer accept as inevitable that American presidents must all be Christians, that anchorpersons on the network news may not "look Jewish," or that there will always be ceilings on the proportion of Jews in our great universities, on our courts, and in our corporations.

There is nothing that Jews cannot accomplish in America, unless we choose not to strive for it. This is not to say that there is no external anti-Semitism directed at Jews. Indeed, it is because of our long history of victimization by others that many Jews — particularly those who were alive during the 1930s and 1940s — hold back from assertively demanding equality. They worry about rocking the boat — a boat whose owner, they fear, may ask them to disembark. A representative story from that generation is about the two Russian Jews who were sentenced to death by the czar. As they stood before the firing squad awaiting their certain execution, they were offered blindfolds. The first Jew bravely turned down the blindfold. The second Jew turned to the first and implored: "Please, take the blindfold. Don't make any trouble."

We are at a generational crossroads. The Jews who were the American pioneers — our first generation of immigrants — were indeed guests in other people's land. They had to prove their worth, and they did so beyond anyone's wildest dreams. Subsequent generations, who lived through anti-immigrant bigotry, the Depression, and the Holocaust, were understandably fearful of demanding equality. They produced a Jewish leadership that was cautious, conservative, and generally efficient. The generation that reached political maturity after the establishment of Israel and the elimination of most barriers to Jewish economic, educational, residential, and social acceptability, was also afraid — but not in the same way as its predecessors. It was fearful of endangering the status it had achieved so quickly in the post–World War II era. It had too much to lose to risk offending the "real" establishment.

The byword of past generations of Jewish Americans has been *shanda* — fear of embarrassment in front of our hosts. The byword of the next generation should be *chutzpah* — assertive insistence on first-class status among our peers.

In addition to being a call for change, this book describes my half-century journey as a Jew from the working-class Brooklyn ghetto in which I was born and raised into the current world in which my generation of Jews and non-Jews lives. We are the generation that grew up after the Holocaust and the establishment of Israel, that has lived through the movements for civil rights and gender equality, and whose members are struggling with their identities as Jews, as Americans, and as Jewish Americans.

Though it is about Jewish experiences and concerns, the book has been written for the non-Jewish and Jewish reader alike. It tries to understand and explain the mind-set of my generation of Jewish Americans by juxtaposing our Jewish roots and experiences with our American roots and experiences. I do not pretend that my life is typical of my generation, but the conflicts I write about are representative of those experienced by many of my contemporaries.

I hope, of course, that my journey will continue for many more years — I'll settle for a lot less than the biblical 120* — but this midcentury mark in my life is an appropriate point for pausing and taking stock.

My personal midcentury point also happens to coincide with the end of the first Jewish century of American history — one hundred years of unprecedented Jewish achievement, and substantial contribution toward this country's greatness as a world leader. The beginning of America's second Jewish century marks an appropriate occasion for reflection.

My Jewishness is a very important part of my life. Indeed, though I live and participate quite actively in the secular world, my Jewishness is always with me, both consciously and unconsciously. It is not with me in the way that religion guides the lives of believers and practitioners of orthodox religions. My Jewishness provides few unambiguous rules of belief or action. There is no *Guide to the Perplexed* or other single book to which I can turn for answers.

Sometimes, particularly during my younger years, my Jewishness was most in evidence as the authority against which I rebelled. Occasionally, my Jewishness, and the history of persecution it represents, is the source of my anger — what some have called the permanent chip on my shoulder. More often, it provides the basis for my "Holocaust mentality" — my constant state of preparedness for potential persecution. Sometimes it is a source of vicarious pride, despite my belief that no one should take pride in the accomplishments of others — even ancestors — over whom they had no influence.

Finally, my Jewishness is always with me as a reminder of where I

* The biblical life span of 120 years gives rise to the story of the old man who wished for his best friend, "You should live to 120 and a few weeks." When the friend asked why the extra few weeks, the well-wisher replied, "God forbid you should drop dead on your birthday!"

came from, and of the unpayable debt I owe my parents and grand-parents and other predecessors who have left me not only a legacy of Jewishness, but also a legacy of family devotion and closeness.

I cannot leave my progeny any legacy comparable to the Orthodox commitment to, and intimate knowledge of, Jewish tradition and practice that my predecessors left me. Though I have not abandoned my Jewishness — far from it — I have also not carried on the tradition of daily religious observance and total immersion in the sources of the tradition. Sometimes I regret not having done so. If a person could lead several lives and then compare them at the end of the journey, I think I might have chosen the Orthodox as one. I have often specu-lated about the "road not taken," as Robert Frost called it, especially since I was among the first in my family to have taken a road not traveled by my forebears.

I chose a more secular road. Some of my contemporaries have com-bined the roads — remaining strictly observant while entering the American mainstream — and with notable success. This option was available to me, and indeed, I followed it for the first half of my life. In my generation — as distinguished from our parents' — it is not difficult to accommodate one's professional and personal life to fit the structures of Orthodox practices. There are, to be sure, inconveniences and sacrifices. But no one goes hungry in our America because he or she will not work on the Sabbath or eat unkosher food.*

I did not abandon the ritual — or as much of it as I did — because of practical difficulties. I changed because my Jewishness is both too important to me and not important enough. It is too important in the sense that I could not continue to live — and to impose upon my children — practices, rituals, and authorities in which I did not ac-tively believe. These daily acts had become so routinized that I felt uncomfortable performing them as part of a set of religious beliefs. My religious mentors urged me to continue to perform the rituals, even if they ceased to have meaning. That is the Orthodox way: Act and it will produce belief. (The tradition has it that when God offered the Torah to the Jews at Sinai, the Jews responded, "We will do and we will listen." Doing before listening is thus said to be part of the tradition.)

But principle is as important to me as practice. That too was part

---

* The challenge of simultaneously living an "outside" secular life and an "inside" religiously observant life is captured sensitively by Herman Wouk in his wonderful novel *Inside, Outside* (Boston: Little, Brown, 1985).

of my Jewish heritage. And if I could not believe in the principle underlying a particular practice, I found it difficult to carry through on the actions.

There will be those who read this and say: "Aha, you are truly an ignoramus" — *am ha-aretz*, in the somewhat elitist Hebrew phrase (loosely translated as "a person of the soil"). "You do not understand the true principle underlying the prohibitions." I spent years hearing this kind of religious one-upmanship from my Hebrew teachers. "You must learn a lifetime," they admonished, "before you have the right to challenge." The editor of an Orthodox Jewish newspaper put it this way: "Unless you have completed the study of the entire Talmud (over 60 volumes) and its many commentaries, you are not capable of discussing our religion."[5]

I recall proudly announcing to a high school teacher that I had become an *apikoros*. In the Hebrew-Yiddish idiom, *apikoros* — a Hebrew variant of the Greek term for a follower of Epicurus — means "disbeliever" or "heretic." My teacher immediately put me down by responding, "You're not educated enough to be an *apikoros*; you're just an ignoramus. Only after you learn enough of the Talmud to be considered a Talmud *chachem* [a brilliant student] can you know enough to choose to become an *apikoros* — and by then you'll know enough not to choose that path of unrighteousness." Pretty clever! They get you to learn for years, and by the time you're prepared to challenge, you've committed yourself to the system.

I have always rejected that approach, whether it was tried by law teachers, Hebrew teachers, or philosophy teachers. The burden of proof is on those who would have me behave in a certain manner. I do not mean empirical proof, of course. A principled argument will do just fine. I do, therefore, precisely what orthodox religions say you can't do: I pick and choose — hopefully on some principled basis — among the religious practices and select those with which I wish to comply. It's *my* religion, after all, and I don't see why I can't be the final arbiter when it comes to its content. In this respect, at least, my attitudes are similar to those of many in my generation who are struggling to adapt traditional religious values and practices to contemporary world views.

It is partly because I cannot leave my children the Jewish legacy that is to be found in the existing tradition — with its literary and oral tradition that goes back thousands of years — that I wanted to write a book that documents my journey as a Jew.

It is a journey that many men and women of my generation have taken. I suspect that a considerable number of Jews and non-Jews as well have shared similar reflections and analogous experiences. They struggle with some of the same conflicts, conundrums, and inconsistencies that I have encountered since departing from the path — the Halakah — that was so well traveled by the Jews who came before us. Left without a well-demarked alternate path, or even a compass or a road map to guide us, we are groping our way in the darkness of unexplored terrain.

Having in mind the aspirations and fears of any voyage of discovery, I begin this dialogue between generations — and within my generation — by focusing on a series of recurring images that remind me of the contradictions of being a half-century-old American Jew near the close of the twentieth century.

The first image is imaginary. I am standing in the middle of Harvard Yard. On one side of the yard is the then-president of Harvard University, Derek Bok. On the other side is my mother, from Brooklyn — a formidable match for any president. They both gaze at me with a mixture of pride and disapproval. Though they are both looking at the same me, the images they see are completely different. The Harvard president sees a *shtetl* Yid, a small village Jew, in a black coat with sidelocks and a prayer shawl. My breath smells of herring, and when I am not singing a Yiddish song, I am speaking with a thick accent and vigorous gestures about Israel.

My mother sees an assimilated Wasp dressed in a tweed jacket with patches at the elbows, wearing Docksider loafers, and carrying a polo mallet. My mother can almost smell the gin and vermouth on my breath, and she can hear me whistling — my grandmother always told me never to whistle because it was a *goyisher* thing to do. When I speak I sound like George Plimpton and my mother doesn't understand a word I say.

I run away from both of them to look in a mirror. What I see is a middle-aged man dressed a bit too much like a hippie with the characteristically uncomfortable nervousness of my generation that Woody Allen made famous. The smell on my breath might be from a glass of red Bordeaux — not quite as sweet as the Manischewitz of my youth, nor nearly as dry as the martinis of my colleagues — and the shoes on my feet are Rockports bought at a bargain price in Filene's Basement. I own an expensive, though aging, BMW — I told my mother it stands for British Motor Works — but I save my tea bags for a second or third use. I speak quickly with many Brooklynisms, an occasional Yiddishism, and a faint touch of Boston. My mother corrects my Brooklynisms and berates me every time I say "can't" or "ain't."

I know I am neither the Yid that I imagine Bok sees or the Wasp that my mother fears I have become. That I know for sure. What I indeed am — and what others of my generation with similar identity conflicts are — is a more difficult question.

The next image is a nightmare I sometimes have. The central character used to be Dr. Joseph Mengele. Now it is any Jew-hater, ranging from Palestinian terrorist Abu Nidal, to neo-Nazis, to "Ivan the Terrible" of Treblinka. The phone rings. It is Mengele calling from Paraguay: "The Israelis are about to capture me and I want you to be my lawyer." I pause. He continues: "I thought you were supposed to be this big-shot civil libertarian! Will you take my case, or are you the world's biggest phony?" In the dream, I tell him to come to my office the next day. But I am undecided about whether I will represent him, turn him in, or kill him with my bare hands.

The third image — an actual occurrence — is of my immigrant grandmother sitting in my mother's living room in Brooklyn, trying to talk the late Supreme Court justice Arthur Goldberg out of running for governor of New York. "You'll be a lightning rod for anti-Semitism. Everything you do wrong will be blamed on the Jews. You're so Jewish — not like the Lehmans or the Morgenthaus. You're Arthur Goldberg, one of *us*. The country isn't yet ready for a Governor Goldberg." I sat there embarrassed at my grandma's old world attitudes.

The fourth imagines a time when American foreign policy turns against Israel and Israel's very survival is at stake. As an American, I see myself opposing our policy toward Israel as strongly as I did our policy in Vietnam. But because I am a Jew, my motives are questioned when I speak out. Among those leading the attack on my loyalty are other Jews — the image is too blurred for me to make out whether they come from the extreme right or extreme left — who fear that the opposition of Jews like me will engender questions about their loyalties.

The fifth image is utopian: anti-Semitism in all of its forms comes to an abrupt end. It was Ilya Ehrenburg who once said, "So long as there is a single anti-Semite in the world, I shall declare with pride that I am a Jew." This negative raison d'être for the continuation of

Judaism is profoundly disturbing. Yet for many Jews it rings at least partly true. Some of the most influential Jewish organizations in America and throughout the world were established in reaction to anti-Jewish actions. As I imagine a world in which no one hates Jews, Israel, or indeed anything Jewish, I wonder whether and how my life as a Jew would change. I know that I do not share Ehrenburg's exclusively negative reason for declaring with pride that I am a Jew (and a Zionist, which Ehrenburg was not), but I am not certain how much of my commitment to Jewish values and survival is energized by our enemies.

The sixth image is a recent vignette — a true story. My mother is vacationing at a Jewish hotel in the Catskill Mountains, and is sitting around with a group of older women. One of them hears my mother's name and, without realizing that she is my mother, launches into a discussion of that other Dershowitz, the Harvard professor. "Such a wonderful boy he is, but why did he have to go off and marry that shiksa [non-Jewish woman]? All the smart and successful ones do it, Henry Kissinger, Ted Koppel, Arthur Schlesinger. Why?" My mother, playing dumb, strings along the know-it-all: "How do you know that Dershowitz married a shiksa?" Mrs. Know-it-all knows: "My son's cousin is his best friend. He was at the church where they had the wedding." My mother responds: "Well, I heard that he married a Jewish woman." "So you heard wrong," Mrs. K.I.A. assures my mother. "That's the story his family is putting out, can you blame them?" At this point, my mother can't hold back: "Alan Dershowitz is my son. I was at the shul where he married Carolyn Cohen, whose father's name is Mordechai and whose mother speaks fluent Yiddish. So what do you say about that?" "Oh, I'm so glad it wasn't true!" Mrs. K.I.A. says in obvious relief, but quickly adding: "Now what about Henry Kissinger, is his wife Jewish too?"

The final set of images is part of an ongoing theme: I — and my generation of American Jews — as spectators to the most dramatic events in modern Jewish history. The variations on this theme began for me in the spring of 1945, listening with my father to the radio as the Allied armies advanced on Berlin. My father, who was a reluctant spectator to the war because of a medical deferment, would tell me how the speed of the Allied forces would determine how many of our relatives might survive. He had a map of Europe on the wall, and we would put up thumbtacks to mark the positions of the armies com-

manded by Eisenhower and Zhukov. We listened and talked as others
fought and died.

The theme continued as my father, my younger brother, and I
watched Abba Eban on television defending Israel's right to become
and remain a nation. Later there were the wars — the Six-Day, Yom
Kippur, and Iraqi wars. By then I was an adult, teaching at Harvard.
Again I was a spectator, this time watching with my own children.
Many of us thought about volunteering, but we quickly realized that
was fantasy, and we contented ourselves with raising money and writing op-ed pieces — the ultimate spectator activities for American Jewish intellectuals.*

Then there was the struggle of Soviet Jewry. Once again, we could
not participate, except vicariously. We marched, wrote, contributed,
even took trips to Moscow (with our American passports safely in our
pockets). We could feel the anguish of our brothers and sisters of
silence. But it was their anguish. We were spectators.

While the Jewish world around us was experiencing the most tu-
multuous epoch in modern times, we were blessed — and cursed —
with an enclosed, heated, and overstuffed box seat to history. My
generation of Jews was too young to fight against Nazism or for Israeli
independence, too American to make *aliyah* (emigrate to Israel), too
comfortable to put our bodies on the line for anything Jewish. Instead,
we observed, contributed, grieved, cheered, evaluated, criticized, supported, prayed, and worried. We read every book and article, watched
every television program, and objected to every negative stereotype.
We became part of what is perhaps the most effective lobbying and
fund-raising effort in the history of democracy. We did a truly great
job, as far as we allowed ourselves, and were allowed, to go. But at
bottom we were — and continue to be — spectators to history.

And because of the combination of *our* affluence, success, and com-
fort, on the one hand, and *their* suffering, destruction, rebirth, and
daily danger, we cannot help feeling enormously guilty over our relative passivity, insulation, and distance.

Being a spectator gives one plenty of time to reflect on how, but for
the grace of God, the foresight of our grandparents, or simple dumb

---

* Woody Allen, in his film *Manhattan*, is asked whether he has read the "devastating" op-ed
piece on a proposed Nazi march. Woody responds: "Well, a satirical piece in the *Times* is one
thing, but bricks and baseball bats really gets right to the point." Another character argues
that "biting satire is always better than physical force." But Woody gets the last word: "But
physical force is always better with Nazis, uh . . . because it's hard to satirize a guy with, uh,
shiny boots on." *Four Films of Woody Allen* (New York: Random House, 1982), p. 203.

luck, there go we. And I have done more than my share of reflecting. I have also shared my reflections over a quarter century with the best and the brightest students, with lecture audiences around the world, and with friends and colleagues of my generation, and those older and younger.

It takes a certain amount of chutzpah to try to generalize from one's personal experiences. But I feel secure in the knowledge that my feelings, perceptions, attitudes, beliefs — even practices — are widely, if silently, shared by a large number of Jewish Americans who were brought up after World War II and reached maturity during the period of the great Jewish success story of the past few decades.

I am fortunate in having available a unique resource to help me understand the changes I have undergone over the past five decades, especially since I moved from Brooklyn to Cambridge more than a quarter-century ago. This resource is a close-knit group of friends with whom I grew up in the Borough Park section of Brooklyn. We started out together in almost identical circumstances: we attended the same religious schools; we observed the same degree of orthodoxy in our religious practices; we are all third- or fourth-generation Americans, whose grandparents spoke Yiddish and whose parents spoke English; we all came from working-class or small-store economic backgrounds; we all married our Jewish teenage sweethearts. Six of the eight original marriages are — *kineahora*, as our grandmothers would say (without provoking the evil eye) — thriving. None of the group still lives in Brooklyn. Only two or three are as Orthodox as we had been in Borough Park. We are all very Jewish in our rather different ways. We all want our children (there are nineteen of those) and grandchildren (there are four of those) to be brought up "Jewishly" — though each of us defines that term somewhat differently.

We eight Borough Park boys and our wives get together several times each year. We have watched each other change — and stay the same — for nearly forty-five years. Throughout this book, I will make reference to this group, because they serve as both a mirror by which I can see myself more perceptively and a lens through which I can see the world, especially my Jewish generation, more clearly.

And now, a word about the title of this book. Chutzpah is a concept more easily demonstrated than defined. As Justice Potter Stewart once quipped about the meaning of pornography: "I can't define it, but I know it when I see it." We immediately recognize a chutzpahnik — a person manifesting the quality of chutzpah — when we observe him or her in action, despite the inadequacy of single-word definitions. Indeed, the word *chutzpah* has both a positive and a negative connotation. To the perpetrator of chutzpah it means boldness, assertiveness, a willingness to demand what is due, to defy tradition, to challenge authority, to raise eyebrows.

To the victim of chutzpah, it means unmitigated gall, nerve, uppityness, arrogance, hypocritical demanding. It is truly in the eye of the beholder.

The classic illustration — the youth who murders his parents and then pleads for mercy on the grounds that he is an orphan — has been supplemented in my own experiences: A client convicted of selling false antiques who tries to pay me in — you guessed it — antiques. The woman whose criminal case I won but who sued me for malpractice because she was unable to continue to defraud the government. The anti-Semite who sent me a letter castigating Jews for being cheap — and the letter had ten cents postage due. The neo-Nazi accused of disturbing the peace by demanding that Jews be "sent back to Israel" who pleaded with me to defend him because "you Jews control the American legal system." Iraqi dictator Saddam Hussein, who, after holding foreigners hostage in Iraqi hotels, sent them bills for room and board. The Palestinian terrorist who blinded himself while making a bomb and then, when subsequently charged with a terrorist murder, demanded mercy on the ground that he was blind. (The ploy worked, at least with some media. The *Boston Globe* headline read: "Israelis Convict Blind Palestinian.")[6]

Finally, on the next page, there's the cartoon my nephew Adam found hanging in a bookstore in Woodstock, New York.*

On occasion, I myself have been described as having chutzpah. It is a characterization I welcome, for I choose to accept it in all its positive connotations. I consider myself assertive on Jewish issues — as I am on civil liberties issues — though not in the violent sense of the Jewish Defense League. But I am secure enough about my Jewishness to criticize Israel and Jewish leaders when I think they are wrong. I am also secure enough in my Americanism to criticize American leaders when I think they are wrong on Jewish (and other) matters.

---

* If you come across any other definitions or illustrations of chutzpah, please send them to me (c/o Harvard Law School, Cambridge, Massachusetts 02138) for inclusion in the next printing. Talk about chutzpah!

'I'd like to buy a book on chutzpah
and I'd like you to pay for it.'

I am a proud and assertive Jew, and a proud and assertive American. Many in my generation no longer feel like guests in anyone else's land. It is not enough for us, as it was for our grandparents and parents, that we be tolerated as a minority in a country where only the majority are first-class citizens. We insist on being treated as equals. We have no qualms about seeing a Goldberg, a Shapiro, or a Cohen run for governor or even president. We need not *sh'a shtill* (be quiet) as my grandmother constantly warned. We don't have to worry about *shanda fur de goyim*, or being "lightning rods" for anti-Semitism if we are too visible or successful. Maybe we are overconfident. Maybe we are no more secure than the Jews of Germany thought they were in 1929.

Maybe we are tempting fate — and history — by our assertiveness. Again as my grandmother would say, *"Kineahora*, I hope not." And I don't think so.

Whether we are right or wrong, this is how a lot of us feel today. I think it is a perception worth sharing.

A Polish Jew
Comes to America

The Jewish Century of American Life

IT WAS one hundred years earlier that the first Dershowitz had set foot on American soil. Our family was celebrating this centennial event with a gala Chanukah gathering on Long Island. We were honoring the memory of our pioneering ancestor, who had made the crossing from Galicia in 1888. His name was Zecharia and he spelled our last name with an extra *c* — Derschowitz — which mysteriously dropped out over time. He was my great-grandfather, which makes me a fourth-generation American. I never met Reb Zecharia, as everyone called him. (He was not a rabbi; the title *Reb* was the Yiddish equivalent of Sir.) But I remember my great-grandmother, Leah, his wife, who died when I was a young child.

One of my treasured possessions — my only material inheritance — is a wonderful family portrait taken on the stoop of my great-grandparents' home and *shteeble* — small synagogue — on South Tenth Street in the Williamsburg section of Brooklyn.* The brown-and-white photograph contains four generations of Dershowitzes. At the base of the stoop, sitting in an old chair, is my great-grandmother Leah. Four of her seven children, including Louis, my grandfather, surround her. Her grandson Harry, my father, stands on the top of the stoop. Below

---

* The name of our neighborhood was not pronounced like that of the colonial Virginia town with the same spelling; ours was "Villiamsboig," as Houston Street on the lower East Side is pronounced "How-stin." I recall a friend of my grandfather's who made vests in a shop on West Broadway. He would always say, "I make wests on Vest Broadvay." I could never understand why he couldn't simply shift the *w* and *v* sounds, so they would come out right.

him is my mother, Claire, holding her two-year-old son — me — in her arms. Various uncles, cousins, and aunts surround us.

The family has grown in numbers over the century. At last count, Reb Zecharia's direct descendants numbered nearly 500. He was blessed with 7 children, 27 grandchildren, more than 100 great-grandchildren, and over 300 great-great-grandchildren — and still going strong. My grandfather Louis alone had more than 70 great-grandchildren. His younger brother Hymie — who was born in America in the early 1890s and died just recently — was blessed with 176 descendants at last count. The great-great-great-grandchildren — the sixth generation — are just beginning to be born, and if family trends continue, they promise to number in the thousands.

Most of Reb Zecharia's descendants live in the New York area, but others have spread across the continent from California, to Illinois, to Maryland, to Toronto, to Connecticut and Massachusetts. A growing number have emigrated to Israel over the past several years, following my father's two youngest brothers, who moved there in 1950 and 1969, respectively.

More than 250 family members attended the centennial celebration. As I looked around the large hall, bedecked with old photographs of the early days, I reflected on the history of Jews in America. The hundred years of my family's presence in America represented the most significant era of the Jewish-American experience.

There were Jews in America, of course, before 1888, but their numbers were insignificant and their impact on American life — though profound in a few individual instances — was nowhere near as great as it was to become in the twentieth century.[1] The Jews who participated in America's first century — roughly from the time of the Revolution to the post–Civil War period — were primarily German and Spanish and Portuguese in national origin. The first ordained rabbi did not even reach American shores until 1840. And what he observed — "Most people eat foul food and desecrate the Sabbath" — led him to give up the rabbinate and open up a dry goods store (what else!). Other rabbis followed him, introducing Reform Judaism from Germany and Americanizing it.[2] But beginning in the mid-1880s a whole new type of European Jew — different in national origin, in religious practice, in education, and in politics — passed through Castle Garden or, later, Ellis Island.[3] These Jews were Eastern Europeans. They came from the *shtetlach* (plural of *shtetl*, "small town") of

Galicia, Latvia, Lithuania, Ukrainia, and other areas within the Pale of Settlement, the territory within the borders of czarist Russia where Jews were legally allowed to reside. The Pale of Settlement covered an area of some 386,100 square miles from the Baltic Sea to the Black Sea. According to the 1897 census, 4,899,300 Jews lived there, forming 94 percent of the total Jewish population of Russia. It was, however, not only the limitation of their residential area that oppressed the Jews. By force of historical circumstances they were also restricted in their occupations, often limited to work that paid little and led to pauperization. This, together with incessant anti-Jewish decrees and waves of pogroms, especially during the years 1881–1884 and 1903–1906, resulted in a constant stream of Jewish immigration from the Pale of Settlement to Western Europe and the United States.[4]

The arrival here of these peasants, tradesmen, tailors, shoemakers, jewelers, and rabbis marked the beginning of the Jewish century of American history. The leader of Reform Jewry in America, Rabbi Isaac Mayer Wise, worried that these Jews would be a *shanda fur de goyim*: their primitive religious practices would, in his words, make American Jews appear "ridiculous before the world." Wise insisted that his Reform German Jews were "real Americans," while the newly arrived Eastern European Jews "are not." Wise and his colleagues warned of the dangers of continued Jewish immigration into America, while another rabbi predicted that the new Jews "will either be the fame or shame of American Judaism." In fact, as one study of this period concludes, it was these Eastern European Jews "whose culture became virtually synonymous with that of American Jewry and eventually formed the Jewish community in the United States."[5]

The vast majority of Jews now living in the United States trace their roots to Eastern European immigrants who came here between the 1880s and the 1920s, after which the gates were shut on most Jewish (and other non–Western European) immigration by exclusionary laws.[6] Although we have traveled in different directions, most of our ancestors began their journey to the *goldeneh medina* in the steerage compartments of transatlantic steamers.

Reb Zecharia Dershowitz arrived at Castle Garden, New York, in January 1888. With him were his wife, Leah, their sons Louis (age five), Sol (age four), and Sam (age two), and their daughter Sadie (an infant). They had left the Galician *shtetl* of Pilsner several months earlier on their way to a new life. On his citizenship papers filed in the district court in Brooklyn, he listed his occupation as tailor and his country of origin as the Austro-Hungarian Empire. In his affidavit, he renounced all loyalty to the king of Hungary and the emperor of Austria. The small town he came from was near what is now the Polish-Soviet border in the Galician region of the Carpathian Mountains.

It is difficult to imagine the courage it must have taken my great-grandfather, then twenty-three years old, to cut his own roots so drastically by leaving the comforts — familial and religious, if not material — of the *shtetl* for the uncertainty of a new life in America. A few other townsfolk, but not many, had come before him. These *landsleit*, as they were called, formed benevolent organizations that made the transition a bit easier. They provided sick benefits, interest-free loans, burial rights, and other necessities. Reb Zecharia soon became president of a *landsleit* group — called in Yiddish a *chevra*, or "friendship circle." His *chevra* was called One Hundred Canon Street, apparently for the lower East Side building in which it met. One of the first items of business for any *chevra* was to purchase burial plots for the members and their families so that they could be assured eternal rest in sanctified ground. Reb Zecharia's name is among those engraved into the pillars that flank the entrance gate to the Mount Hebron cemetery in Queens, New York.

Dying as a Jew would be easy in America. But what about living as a Jew? That would prove more of a challenge. Could a strictly Orthodox Jew, easily identified by his full beard and sidelocks, find a job that did not require him to work on the Sabbath? Could he maintain his kosher observance? Could he educate his children in the Talmudic tradition, which emphasized dedication to religious study?

My great-grandfather did find work, as a pocketbook maker. Although he never made a good living, he did earn enough to provide a crowded home for his growing family.

Reb Zecharia's proudest accomplishment in America was the founding of a small *shteeble* — a local prayer house — in the Williamsburg section of Brooklyn. The Dershowitz family moved to Williamsburg in 1910, a year after my father's birth, and shortly after the completion of the Williamsburg Bridge, connecting the lower East Side to Brooklyn. The entire family moved en masse and nearly all of them moved into a single four-level house on South Tenth Street, between Bedford Avenue and Berry Street. The ground level housed the *shteeble* in front and the pocketbook workshop in the back; the "parlor floor" was the home of Reb Zecharia and his wife and their as yet unmarried children; other floors became home to the married daughters and their families. The married sons — including my grandfather — all lived within a block or two, and considered the South Tenth Street homestead as the family gathering place and religious center.

An article in the English-language newspaper *Der Yid*, entitled "The First Yiddish Communities in America," described the origin of the Dershowitz *shteeble*:

> In those days Sabbath observance was very difficult, [since] for one who did not work on Saturdays, it was almost impossible to acquire a job. . . .
>
> Reb Zecharia . . . made for himself, in the house, a little factory from which he drew forth for himself a meager sustenance. In the same place, in the basement, Reb Zecharia made a "Bais Hamedrach" [a house of prayer], the first chassidische shtiebel in Williamsburg.[7]

The *shteeble* was very much a family enterprise. Louis, the eldest son, who had a beautiful tenor voice, was the cantor. Louis's seven sons and several nephews constituted the choir. Louis sang the traditional Galician liturgy and composed numerous melodies of his own, some of which we still sing at family gatherings — including the 1988 Chanukah centennial.

The more than 250 family members in attendance at our centennial were not completely representative of the current Jewish-American population. But then again, I'm not certain that any single family can be representative of the incredible diversity within the current array of Jewish families in America. Very few in my family have achieved the kind of financial success stereotypically associated with Jewish immigrants. The family joke is that we have the lowest wealth–to–time-in-America ratio of any Jewish family. The vast majority of my family has remained religiously observant. Some have become *more* Orthodox than were Reb Zecharia and his children. In that respect, my family is somewhat different from most other Jewish families in America, which have experienced greater assimilation and more religious diversity within Judaism. But in a larger sense, the changes in religiosity within my own family do reflect a more general phenomenon: many children of assimilated Jews have become more religious than their parents, or at least more closely identified with their religious heritage. My son Jamin calls this process "reJewvenation."

I recall my own grandfather Louis as very American. Though strictly Orthodox, he did not affect any obvious religious garb. In the family portrait on the stoop, he is dressed in the street clothes of the time, sporting a straw hat and flowery tie and holding a large cigar. He could be Italian American, Irish American, or German American. He spoke with a Brooklyn accent and was proud of his American patriotism. He rooted for the Brooklyn Dodgers and always bragged to his friends that I made my high school varsity basketball team. His message to me was always the same: "Be a good American. This is a wonderful country for the Jews."

Several of Louis's grandchildren and great-grandchildren — my cousins — wear black coats, long *payess* (sidelocks), and external *tzitzit* (fringed prayer garment). I'm not sure he would have approved, since these are European rather than American in appearance.

Our family also includes a number of somewhat more secular Jews, who attend synagogue occasionally, more out of ethnic solidarity or nostalgia than religious devotion. Virtually every descendant of Reb Zecharia is a committed Jew in his or her own way.

Reb Zecharia, like so many of his contemporaries, worked for a time in a sweatshop. The shop he worked in, making pocketbooks, was located in a building just east of Washington Square, site of the ill-fated Triangle Shirtwaist Company. On the Saturday of the great fire in 1911 that engulfed the building and killed 145 workers, Reb Zecharia was at home. It was the Jewish Sabbath. He learned two lessons from this: he vowed that his children would never become factory workers and he vowed they would never work on the Sabbath. Reb Zecharia's son Louis, who began selling matches on street corners when he was eight years old, eventually worked as a printer and box maker. He met Ida Maultasch, an immigrant from Zhikov, Poland, at the turn of the century. They soon married, and my father, Harry, was born in 1909.

My maternal grandfather's move to America was every bit as courageous as Reb Zecharia's. Naftuli Ringel arrived with the second wave of Polish émigrés, in 1907. Unwilling to serve in the Polish army, he fled the small Galician city of Przemyśl, which is now in Poland, adjacent to the Soviet border. Przemyśl, a center of Jewish learning and Hasidism, was one of several such towns with thriving Jewish culture and trade. My grandfather left behind three brothers, dozens of nieces and nephews, and scores of close relatives. More than three decades later, all but one brother would be murdered along with seventeen thousand other Jewish townsfolk when the SS reached the city. The remaining brother fled the approaching Nazi troops and made his way to Siberia and eventually to Israel. (In 1987, my son and I "returned" to Przemyśl and found no evidence that a single Jew had ever lived there.)

My grandfather escaped the Polish army, and ultimately the Holocaust, by seeking sanctuary in Scranton, Pennsylvania, where a previously emigrated relative had settled. The only job available in Scranton was that of a *shochet* — a ritual slaughterer of kosher animals. As unable to take the knife to their throats as he was to fire a gun at faceless targets, he quickly found his way back to lower Manhattan, where he worked as a customer peddler to earn passage for his second wife and three babies still back in the old country. This wife, Blima Newman — my grandmother — was the sister of his first wife, who had died in childbirth. Under Jewish tradition, an unmarried younger sister is obliged to marry a widowed brother-in-law, and my grandmother, then a sixteen-year-old, obeyed that commandment without question — a decision she never regretted during her long life. (She died recently, at the age of ninety-two.) After their arrival in America — and the death by diphtheria of two of the babies — the family moved into an apartment on Rivington Street and settled into the Orthodox life of lower Manhattan until they, in turn, were able to afford the move across the East River to Williamsburg.

Soon after that move, my two grandfathers met and became friends. Together they helped to establish the first Orthodox yeshiva in Brooklyn, Torah V'Daas, which, loosely translated, means "religion and wisdom." Before the establishment of Torah V'Daas, my father, Harry, had attended public school, where he was taught Americanism by stern Irish schoolmarms whose idea of secular punishment was the recitation of Hail Marys and whose concept of American music was "Silent Night." My mother, Claire, can still recite "Ah stendey nobilay missa recordum tuom," her pronunciation of the words of the Mass, *Ostende nobis misericordiam tuam* (Show us your mercy), though she has no idea what it is her public school teachers made her memorize. Once the all-male yeshiva was in operation, all the boys in my father's and mother's families attended; the girls remained in public schools under the watchful eyes of their distrusting parents.

After several years of public high school — there was no local yeshiva beyond the eighth grade — my father went to work as a salesman on the lower East Side of Manhattan, where he and a partner soon opened a small store that sold men's work clothes, wholesale during the week and retail on Sundays.

My mother, an excellent student, graduated from high school in the summer of 1929, at the age of sixteen. Her career at City College was cut short — she wanted to be a schoolteacher — when she had to get a job to help support her family, which was hard hit by the Depression. She never returned to school, in part because my grandmother had heard that schoolteachers had to work on Shabbes, the Sabbath. My mother has worked as a bookkeeper ever since.

The Depression of the 1930s shaped the lives of my parents' generation. Many were not able to finish school and become professionals. Some became civil servants. Others opened small businesses and eventually benefited from the expanding economy that followed World War II.

My parents — my father died in 1984 — made heroic efforts to combine Orthodox adherence to Jewish law with relatively full participation in American life. But our way — the more secular way of my particular branch of the family — is not good enough for some of the proselytizers among us. At every opportunity, they try to get us to change our ways and become more like them. "Why can't your children be just a little more religious?" complained a cousin to my mother at the centennial gathering, as if my mother could still control the level of her middle-aged children's religious observance.

The speeches at the centennial reflected the diversity as well as the relative homogeneity within the family. They began with a rabbinical invocation by an uncle, replete with biblical references, Talmudic homilies, and *musser* (a plea for greater religious devotion). It ended with a rip-roaring, hellfire-and-brimstone oration by one of my cousins which reminded me that TV evangelists do not have a monopoly on religious fervor.

One speaker speculated on the derivation of our family name, suggesting that it comes from the Hebrew word for "itinerant preacher," which is *darshan*. Another suggested that it might reflect a town in which our family once lived, such as Dershov on the German-Polish border.

This discussion of family names reminded me of an interesting exchange I once had with Isaac Bashevis Singer, following the PBS dramatization of his story "The Cafeteria." A character in the play had referred to "that lawyer from Kraków named Dershowitz." I was intrigued by the possibility that Singer had actually known a lawyer in Poland with my last name. I managed to reach Singer on the phone and asked.

Singer laughed and in his heavily accented voice responded: "The joke's on you, Professor. There is no such person. But the television people asked me to come up with the name of a lawyer that sounded Polish but would not be too difficult for an American audience. So I thought of you. *You're* the lawyer from Kraków!"

My own brief talk tried to bridge the gaps among the religious subgroups within the family. I emphasized to the assembled descendants of Reb Zecharia that but for their pioneering ancestor's willingness to make a change — to leave his *shtetl* and come to America — we would all have been casualties of the Holocaust. I reminded them of the pressures the young Reb Zecharia must have felt from his parents, peers, and other relatives to conform to the religious mores of his *shtetl*. America may have been a land whose streets were paved with gold — a land of *material* opportunity. But it was regarded by most European Orthodox Jews as a *spiritual* Sodom and Gomorrah, whose cities were lined with temptations to stray from the religious orthodoxy of the *shtetl*. Beards were shaven, earlocks cut, and *tzitzit* worn under the modern stylish street garb of the day. There were stories of men forced to desecrate the Sabbath in order to make a living. And even before the film *Hester Street*, it was widely known that many a young man who left his wife and children behind "for a few months until I get settled" was seduced by American women and never sent money to bring over his abandoned family.

Coming to America was not the safe way, not the old way, not the road taken by those to whom religious observance was the all-consuming passion of life. It was not like going to Palestine in those days, or Israel today. Making *aliyah* — going up to Zion — fulfilled a religious commandment, a mitzvah. Coming to America was making a new *secular* life, hopefully within the constraints of religion, but not in pursuance of any of its commands.

At the time, leaving the *shtetl* and moving to America was a one-way, permanent, and total commitment. There were no phones, airplanes, or other efficient means of communication or transportation. For Reb Zecharia, and for many others, the move meant never again seeing — or speaking to — parents, siblings, friends, and community.

As I looked out upon those of my relatives who refused to break with the past — indeed who had returned to a past well beyond that in which Reb Zecharia had lived — I wondered what he would think of their black coats, *payess*, and beards. I wondered if he would approve of their decision to wear garb calculated to separate them visually from other Americans. I wondered if he would approve of their total immersion into religion — of their willingness to allow religion and custom to dominate their lives so totally. I wondered what he, and my grandfather, would say about those descendants who refused to allow their children to receive a secular education precisely in order to deny them the opportunity to choose a life-style somewhat different from that of their parents, an opportunity we had been given by our mixed religious and secular education. To this day, my mother wonders whether she "did the right thing," by exposing my younger brother and me to choices and options about our religious and secular lives. She has concluded that *she* did the right thing in letting us choose, but that *we* did the wrong thing by choosing the more secular life.

Orthodox Judaism — even its most liberal branches — has developed protective mechanisms against assimilation. The requirement of Sabbath attendance at synagogue, coupled with the prohibition against driving on the Sabbath, assures the continuity of Orthodox Jewish neighborhoods, centered around — and within walking distance of — an Orthodox synagogue.

These neighborhood synagogues become the social as well as religious centers for the surrounding community and increase the odds that Orthodox children will meet and socialize with "one of their own." The Orthodox schools — day schools, yeshivas, Talmud Torahs (after-school religious programs) — also provide the propinquity that so often leads to permanent coupling. Even prohibitions against eating unkosher food have led, especially in the recent years of increased affluence within the Orthodox community, to the establishment of numerous kosher restaurants, where the Orthodox meet and eat together.*

But protective insularity is very much a matter of degree. Modern Orthodox Jews mix freely with non-Orthodox Jews and non-Jews at the workplace, in universities, at health clubs, and in "mixed" neighborhoods. Hasidim and other insular extremists forbid — in practice if not by religious edict — all but the most formal contact with out-

---

* Shakespeare's Shylock, upon being invited to dine with a Christian business associate, replied: "I will buy with you, sell with you, talk with you, walk with you, . . . but I will not eat with you, drink with you, nor pray with you."

siders. I have a Hasidic friend who loves baseball and attends New York Yankee games. (He is prohibited from watching them on television, lest he be influenced by a "sexy" commercial.) In order to ensure against prohibited physical contact with members of the opposite sex, he buys four extra seats: one on each side of him and one in front and in back. He keeps the four seats empty to protect against prohibited contact. He does not go to very crowded games, to avoid the resentment of preventing others from using the empty seats.

Some of these insular mechanisms are mandated by the Halakah, the Orthodox rules of ritual. Others are derived from a narrow, somewhat pedantic construction of these religious rules. Still others have no religious basis whatever. For example, the wearing of black clothing and fur hats, characteristic of some Hasidic sects, simply reflects a tradition harking back to the secular dress worn in Europe generations ago. But their very anachronism serves a religious purpose, by isolating the wearers from others outside their religious circle. A part of the Dershowitz family — called the *Malachim* (angels, or messengers of God) — affect this garb. Most of them stayed away from the family gathering, but a few showed up "in uniform."

The extremely Orthodox family members who did attend regard themselves as the spiritual descendants of my great-grandfather's legacy. They tell a family story calculated to show Reb Zecharia's devotion to religion, and the rewards he reaped for his devotion. During the first Succoth holiday he celebrated in America, my great-grandfather built a *succah* — a ritual hut to commemorate the huts built by the Jews during the exodus from Egypt. He went to considerable expense to make sure that the roof was covered with bamboo reeds of high quality — called *schach*. The newspaper *Der Yid* recounts the denouement as follows:

> In the middle of the holiday meal they heard a strong crack on the succah just above Reb Zecharia's head. They went up to look and saw a . . . heavy rock which anti-semitic . . . neighbors had thrown down. The strong, hard bamboo had, however, prevented the rock from falling further. Thus, he was saved, thanks to buying the expensive "schach," and fulfilling the commandment of succah, completely with all extra glorification.[8]

As I continued to reflect out loud on my great-grandfather's heritage, and his gift to us of life in America, I began to realize that *we* — the more secular branch of the family — were his true spiritual heirs. Like him, we had adapted to change while preserving much of our heritage. We were partaking of a full American life and a full Jewish life. We had taken something from our new nation and given something back to it. We were living *in* America, while some of his other descendants were living in tiny self-contained enclaves that were *surrounded by* America — *shtetlach* located in Munsey, Williamsburg, Lakewood, and Borough Park. (Though my mother and other members of my family still live in Borough Park, they do not live within the enclosed communities created by the Hasidim.) They had, in effect, made the return trip back to the *shtetl* he had left. But now the *shtetlach* were no longer located in Poland — those had all been destroyed. The new *shtetlach* happened to be located in an alien land called America, against whose assimilationist influences the insularity of the new *shtetl* and the old garb protected.

It occurred to me that these *shtetl* Dershowitzes were celebrating the wrong ancestor. They should have been honoring the Dershowitzes who stayed behind, those who refused to change and adapt, those for whom religion was the all-consuming passion of their lives, those who would make no move unless it was dictated by Halakah. But there would have been no Dershowitzes left to honor our ancestors if they had all followed that static path and not moved part of the family — even if inadvertently — out of harm's way before the Holocaust.

There also would have been fewer Dershowitzes — indeed fewer Jews — if my grandfather Louis had not taken extraordinary steps during the late thirties to rescue endangered relatives in Poland and Czechoslovakia. The first step involved the family *shteeble*, which had never had a formal rabbi.

During the late 1930s it was decided to hire a professional rabbi to conduct services. One was brought over from Europe, but the congregants were not satisfied; after two weeks the newly hired rabbi was fired, given a small amount of severance pay, and sent on his way. A new rabbi was brought over from Europe, but he, too, was unceremoniously fired in a matter of weeks. This process continued until dozens of rabbis had passed through the "turnstile *shteeble*" or the Rabbi-of-the-Month Club, as it began to be called. Everybody in the neighborhood soon understood this charade for what it was: a small-scale rescue operation designed to save European rabbis who were endangered by Nazism. For nearly a decade it succeeded in circumventing the restrictive immigration laws, by claiming a "need" for imported rabbis to lead the fickle congregation.

The second step was recently described by one of its grateful beneficiaries, a cousin named Tsvi Dershowitz, who is now a prominent Conservative rabbi in Los Angeles. Once, in introducing me to his congregation for a talk, he reminded me of this story about my grandfather's incredible efforts on behalf of our cousins trapped in Czechoslovakia just before the outbreak of World War II:

"Louie Dershowitz — who was as poor as a church mouse — undertook to beg and borrow to plead the cause of a family he had never known and never met, and eventually my family and those of my four uncles all received the necessary affidavits financially guaranteeing that the immigrant would not become a public charge that enabled us to escape to America in 1939, just thirty-six days before Hitler marched into our native Czechoslovakia. So Louie saved all five families from certain death, and that's why I can be here to tell you this story."

I wondered whether the ultraorthodox Dershowitzes, for whom categorical adherence to the letter of law was all-consuming, realized how different they were from their politically active forebears. I thought these somewhat critical thoughts, but I dared not express them publicly.

Instead I ended the talk with the story of the old inner-city synagogue that had just moved to the suburbs and acquired both a modern building and a modern rabbi. At the first Sabbath service, when the congregation recited the *Shma Yisrael* prayer ("Hear, O Israel, the Lord our God, the Lord is One . . ."), half the congregation stood up while half remained seated. The standing half yelled, "Stand up!" to the seated half, while the seated half yelled, "Sit down!" to the standing half.

The new rabbi was upset at the boisterous commotion, and after the service he asked representatives of both groups to meet with him and the old rabbi to ascertain the tradition of the congregation. At the meeting, the sit-down group asked the old rabbi whether it wasn't the tradition to sit down. The old man pondered and then shook his head. "No, my children, that is not the tradition." The stand-up group was exultant as it said, "Then it must be the tradition that we stand up." Again the old rabbi pondered and again he shook his head in the negative. "No, my children, that is not the tradition."

At this point, the new rabbi's patience snapped and he thundered, "Rabbi, I can't take it — half of them stand, half of them sit, they all yell at each other, and I can't even hear myself think." The old rabbi pondered and nodded his head in the affirmative. "*That*, my children, is the tradition."

As I finished this story, my mother — who always gets the last word — stood up in the audience and added: "The important thing is that they all say the *Shma Yisrael*." And, of course, my mother is right. Traditions change. Customs surpass beliefs in importance. Politics and religion overlap. Neighborhood mores determine specific levels of religious observance. Externalities assume psychological significance beyond their original religious meaning. But at the core, there is a commonality of shared historical experience and shared beliefs. For some, these are summed up in the *Shma Yisrael*. For others, they are epitomized by the commandment "Thou shalt love thy neighbor as thyself," or in the Hebrew-Yiddish term *rachmones* (compassion). And for still others, it is *Ahavat Yisrael*, a love for Israel. For all of us, the shared historical memories of the Holocaust and the pogroms that preceded it over millennia form an unbreakable bond — and common fear of recurrence, albeit in different form. In January 1991, hardly a Jew anywhere in the world — regardless of religious observance — did not think of the gas chambers when Iraqi missiles rained down upon Israel and television flashed pictures of Israeli children being fitted with gas masks. The core of our common heritage may be difficult to define, but it is easy to recognize, especially during times of danger.

I surely recognized it in the diversity and commonality of Reb Zecharia's descendants who attended the centennial celebration on Chanukah in Long Island. I saw in them — in us — the diversity and commonality of the Jewish experience in America.

Several months after our centennial, I read a news account about other Jewish families that were gathering to celebrate their arrival in this land of opportunity. I am certain that although the words were different for each family, the music was similar. So were the tears, reflecting the sadness of our common history and the joy of our current status as first-class citizens in this land of opportunity.

Leaving Brooklyn

Learning About Anti-Semitism
in the Real World

MY JOURNEY across the Brooklyn Bridge after college was not nearly as long as my great-grandfather's transatlantic voyage from Galicia to the lower East Side of New York, but in some ways it was almost as traumatic. Reb Zecharia could expect to be greeted by a few *landsleit* upon his disembarkation at Castle Garden. My classmates at Yale Law School also included a small number of *landsleit,* from Brooklyn, but they had begun the transition four years earlier, when they moved into the dormitories of colleges such as Columbia, Princeton, and Cornell. They had also attended public high schools and lived in somewhat more mixed neighborhoods than Borough Park, where I grew up. I made the journey from my Brooklyn *shtetl* to Yale Law School in one step, without the transition through an Ivy League college or a dormitory experience.

I was born in Williamsburg in 1938 — in a hospital, the first in my family to be delivered outside the house. My grandfather Ringel was so worried that I might be stolen by another family — apparently a real concern in the Poland of his birth — that he remained on guard outside the baby room until it was time for me to go home. (In later years, whenever I misbehaved, my grandmother would wonder whether someone hadn't managed to switch me for a better-behaved baby.)

Shortly before my brother, Nathan, was born in 1942, we moved to Borough Park, a more modern Orthodox neighborhood. Borough Park was not quite the suburbs, but it was farther away from the lower East Side and there were more trees and open spaces.

The Borough Park in which we grew up is an amoebalike area with ever-shifting and imprecise boundaries. Its central core is the one square mile within which nearly 100,000 Jews, most of them Orthodox, make their homes. At the periphery, both geographically and politically, live several thousand Italian, Puerto Rican, and Scandinavian families.

The people of Borough Park were an amalgam of Eastern European Jews, reflecting the overlapping waves of immigration that had begun near the end of the nineteenth century and continue to this day (Soviet and Iranian Jews being the most recent wavelets). Borough Park is unique among American Jewish neighborhoods in that it has always been a Jewish enclave, unlike, say, the lower East Side of Manhattan, which was Irish before it was Jewish and has since become heavily Puerto Rican. The first occupants of the small tract houses built on the site of rural farms were Jewish immigrants seeking to escape the crowded ghettos of Manhattan to the new frontier opened up by construction of the Brooklyn Bridge in 1883. The Jewish suburbanites of the first wave were relatively affluent and progressively Orthodox. They built several majestic houses of worship and community centers that still dominate the neighborhood's low skyline.

For generations, the high-domed shuls echoed the resounding voices of the world's most renowned cantors and male a cappella choirs intoning the traditional melodies of Eastern European Jewry. Cantors such as Yoselle Rosenblatt, Moshe Kusevitsky, and Berela Chagi were regarded as the Carusos, Bjoerlings, and Pavarottis of their art and competed for the affection — and dues-paying membership — of the local congregants. My own introduction to music took the form of participation in the choir that accompanied Chagi and Kusevitsky during their final years. To this day, I will travel long distances to listen to a great cantor and I have a considerable collection of cantorial recordings.

Although by the time I was growing up, Brooklynites had started to abandon the "duhs," "dats," and "toids," our accent was still quite distinct. We referred to it as "duh King's English," since Brooklyn was in Kings County. The neighboring "Queen's" English was slightly more refined; but Bronx English — a term that some regard as an oxymoron — was incomprehensible even to us. Our bodily functions were performed at the "terlit"; our heat was provided by "earl" (which could heat water to a "berl"); and our cameras were loaded with "filum." (I recall vividly my first recitation at Yale Law School, during which my accent was openly laughed at by several students, until, a few days later, they met Professor Abraham Goldstein — from Williamsburg by way of City College — whose accent made mine sound almost midwestern). Perhaps in reaction to the Brooklyn stereotype, our parents, especially those who prided themselves on their American birth and did not want to be confused with the "greenies" — the new immigrants — took special pains to correct our "ain'ts" at every opportunity. Even today, whenever my mother pays one of her frequent visits to court to hear me or my brother argue a case, she invariably keeps a list of Brooklynisms that have unconsciously — quite consciously, if I am before a Brooklyn judge — crept into my speech. (Her favorites are "keyant," which I often substitute for the contraction of "cannot," and "eyask," which I use as a synonym for "request.")

Most important for my parents, the move to Borough Park represented, if not a sharp break with their upbringing, at least a transition to a somewhat different life-style — a life-style that was theirs rather than their parents' or grandparents'. There were few beards or black coats, and the street language was English, not Yiddish.

There was, to be sure, a considerable degree of continuity. We joined a different branch of the same synagogue — the Young Israel of Borough Park. I attended a yeshiva built on the model of the one my grandparents had helped to establish in Williamsburg. Indeed, my eighth-grade teacher in Etz Chaim (The Tree of Life) Yeshiva was to be the same excellent teacher — Mr. Abraham Kien — who had taught my father at the Torah V'Daas Yeshiva a generation earlier.

Eventually my grandparents followed us to Borough Park, but they were living on my parents' home turf, and that made all the difference even in a family where devotion to parents was the highest commandment. Though the traditions of religious observance continued, my parents had to define their own Jewishness, for themselves and for their children. I recall my grandmother's shaking her head in critical bemusement whenever my parents did anything different — less traditional — from the way it was done in Williamsburg. My parents' move paralleled that of many Jews of their generation — to Long Island, to New Jersey, and to other suburbs throughout the nation. These moves from homogeneous American *shtetlach* to somewhat more "mixed" neighborhoods precipitated significant changes in religious observance, marriage patterns, and Jewish identification.

Shortly after our move to Borough Park, my parents bought a tiny two-family house on Forty-eighth Street between Fifteenth Avenue and Sixteenth Avenue. My uncle Hedgie and his family lived upstairs. My cousin Sheindie and her new husband moved into the basement. My cousin Leybie rented the garage as the "warehouse" for the goods he peddled. My brother and I maintained an "easement" on the front of the garage for our basketball hoop and stickball backstop.

Our block was soon to become famous, as Sandy Koufax and Jackie Mason moved onto it. Later — after we moved — it would become the world center for the Bobover Hasidic dynasty. Indeed, even its name has now been changed to Bobover Promenade. But while we were growing up, Forty-eighth Street was a tree-lined thoroughfare with few cars. Most of its residents were modern Orthodox Jews, with a handful of what we called "frumies" — ultraorthodox — and another handful of what we called "goyim" — Conservative, Reform, or unaffiliated Jews. We even had one self-declared atheist, whom everybody regarded as something of a kook. The only authentic non-Jew was the superintendent of the apartment house on the corner — and he spoke a serviceable Yiddish.

Borough Park was free of any real violence though not of an occasional street fight between members of social-athletic clubs. Our club, called the Shields, sported chartreuse-and-black jackets that were promptly banned by our yeshiva. But we circumvented this primitive censorship by keeping our jackets at the home of a member who lived near the yeshiva and proudly flaunting them the moment school was out. Our fights tended to be with fists, and no one ever got hurt, except for the occasional chipped tooth or bruised face suffered at the hands of an Italian gang from the other side of New Utrecht Avenue.

Real crime — robbery, rape, murder — was nonexistent, and when an occasional burglary occurred, it was invariably attributed to "outsiders." Several years ago my mother called me in hysterics. Her apartment had been broken into. They took her Chanukah menorah, her Shabbes candles, and other silver religious items. I sympathized with her and then observed, "See, Mom, there *are* Jewish burglars." Without hesitating an instant, my mother snapped back, "The burglars weren't Jews; they were *Israelis!*" To her, the newly arrived immigrants from Israel — mostly Sephardim — were no more Jewish than the Italians who lived a few blocks away. To my mother, the current population of Borough Park consists of Russians, Hasidim, Israelis, Hungarians (all of whom are, of course, Jewish) — and "real

Jews" like her. When we were growing up, it consisted entirely of "Jews" — like us.

My earliest friends from Borough Park included the seven boys who, along with their wives, constitute the group that I have remained close to for nearly half a century.

I first met Carl Meshenberg even before we began elementary school. Our grandmothers were friends from the old neighborhood, and we played in the same playground as toddlers. We were inseparable throughout our youth and adolescence. Every Friday night, following the Sabbath meal, I would walk around the corner to Carl's home, where his family — which ate at a more leisurely pace — was eating dessert. While enjoying my second serving of strudel, I would join their family discussion and the singing of their traditional family *zemiros* (Sabbath songs). Carl's father, Herman, like my father, had been born in this country on the lower East Side. His grandfather, like mine, had emigrated to this country from Galicia. As was the case with my family, nearly all his family who had remained in the old country were murdered during the Holocaust. The one survivor went to Israel after the war, where he raised a family. Carl's father had a small trimmings business in the garment district, which generated a modest income until it went bankrupt in 1961. After that, Herman became the executive director of a small synagogue in Rumpson, New Jersey.

Carl's family was somewhat more political than mine, and the Friday evening discussions around their table tended to center around current events. Everyone joined in the debate, and no deference was paid on account of age or gender. After about a half-hour of back and forth, Carl and I would excuse ourselves and move on to the next house. Barry Zimmerman's family went to a synagogue that had a cantor, and so they finished their services later than we did. If we timed our movements accurately, we would arrive at the Zimmermans in time for my third dessert and yet another brief family discussion.

Barry's parents were old Borough Parkers. His father, Sam, who moved to Borough Park from Hell's Kitchen (a tough Manhattan neighborhood), where he was born, managed a men's clothing store that had been owned by Barry's maternal grandfather, who had moved to Borough Park from Poland at the beginning of the twentieth century. Barry's grandfather had been a tailor and had opened a basement shop in Borough Park, which had gradually developed into a retail clothing store. Barry's father ran it until the Hasidim began to take over the neighborhood in the 1970s. Hasidim have a special style of clothing and they insist on buying from a fellow Hasid. Sam finally sold out to a Hasid, and the store now sells the special black garb of one particular Hasidic sect.

From Barry's house, we would go to our prearranged meeting place with our "gang." On warm nights, it was a street corner frequented by groups of neighborhood girls with whom we would flirt. On winter nights, it was the home of one of our group members. Sometimes it was Bernie Beck's house, where his artsy mother would discuss current trends in theater or film. Or it was Zollie Eisenstadt's house, where his father would regale us with his imitations of Groucho Marx. When we went to Hal Jacobs's apartment, his quiet parents would generally leave us alone, while they talked to each other. Josh Weisberger's parents, on the other hand, wanted to know about everything we were doing.

The remarkable similarity of our backgrounds — which, of course, we never thought about while we were growing up — reflected the shared experiences of our entire generation of contemporaries. Most of our parents were born in this country of parents who had emigrated from Poland near the close of the nineteenth century. All of our parents struggled through the Depression and into the war and postwar years. None was rich, but none lacked bread for the table. All lost family in the Holocaust and all have relatives in Israel.

We all went to yeshiva elementary school and most of us went on to yeshiva high schools. We were observant of Orthodox Jewish rules. None of us was deeply religious in the theological sense. We rarely talked about God or religion. Our discussions focused on baseball, girls, jokes, parents, and other areas of interest that we shared with teenagers throughout America. We took our religious obligations and restrictions for granted, as part of the social structure in which we lived.

Our girlfriends came from the same background. I met Carl's wife, Joan, before he did. Joan was a cheerleader and I was on the basketball team. I was the first boy she ever danced with, at a postgame dance, when she was a high school freshman and I a junior. Carl and Joan have been married for nearly thirty years and are grandparents three times over. Joan still looks like a cheerleader.

Barry's wife of twenty-eight years grew up around the corner from me, and her father sold us our smoked fish. Bernie's wife's father fitted me for my first pair of glasses. Josh's wife was on my color-war team at camp. Zollie's wife grew up in a displaced persons camp in Germany, and moved to Borough Park from the lower East Side, where she was part of my brother's crowd. Murray married an out-of-towner from Massachusetts. Hal and I were both divorced from our first wives and are married to women we met later in our lives.

As adolescents, we were a rowdy, macho, and somewhat undisciplined lot. We were all wise guys, quick with a quip and more interested in being respected by our peers than our teachers. Josh was the great athlete of the group, excelling in basketball, soccer, punchball, stickball, and bowling. Carl was our scientist, capable of making a small remote-controlled bomb out of some firecrackers and an electronic toy. Barry was the biggest and toughest guy when we were growing up, protecting us by his sheer size. Zollie was the brain, always getting A-pluses in all his subjects. Bernie was the clown, capable of cracking us up with a funny gesture or sound. His chief competitor was Murray, who specialized in off-color stories. Murray also knew more obscure facts than anyone except the contestants on "The $64,000 Question." Hal was the best-behaved boy in the group, always getting A's in conduct and sitting quietly in class, while the rest of us cut up.

We rebelled against the authority of our rabbis, teachers, and principals, but not so much against our parents, who seemed more vulnerable and less authoritarian. We always traveled in packs and were closer to — and more dependent on — each other than we would have been willing to admit. None of us could have foreseen that we would remain such good friends over so long a period of time, especially after all of us moved out of the old neighborhood and into such different lives and occupations.

I was a terrible student in elementary school and at Yeshiva University High School, especially in the religious subjects. I simply couldn't pay attention to the rote manner by which we were "taught" to memorize and recite portions of the Torah, prophets, and Talmud. My teachers told me I lacked *sitzfleisch* — literally, enough meat on my rear end to allow me to sit for long periods of time. Critical questions that challenged the relatively closed system of hermeneutics and interpretation were frowned upon. Whenever I asked what I thought was a difficult question, I was reminded that "if the question is good, then the great rabbis have asked it before you; and if the great rabbis didn't ask it, it is obviously a *klutz-kasheh*" — the question of a stupid person.

I was a real troublemaker, challenging the rabbis and mocking their old-fashioned ways. I also cut class frequently to attend Brooklyn Dodger games and movie openings at Radio City Music Hall and the Roxy with Carl and Barry. My mother — who was mortified by my poor grades — was called to school so frequently that one of my friends thought she worked there. I was suspended from attending religious classes for my last six months of high school because of "lack of respect." When people ask me whether a good Jewish education, with its mastery of Talmudic dialectic, contributes to making a good lawyer, I respond that I don't know, since I didn't have a particularly good Jewish education!

Most of my attention was focused on sports, both as a participant and spectator. I was a good athlete, though not nearly in Josh's league. But I was a formidable fighter. (I'm reminded of Woody Allen's quip about swimming not being a sport: "It's just *not* drowning." The same was true about fighting: it was *not* getting beat up. And running was not getting caught.) When I graduated Yeshiva University High School, my parents got me a baseball encyclopedia, which they inscribed, "You should know your Talmud like you know your baseball." The only academic activity I excelled at was debating, which led the editor of my high school yearbook to draft an entry for me which read: "He has a mouth of Webster and a head of Clay." (My mother made him change it.)

My principal, who was an Orthodox rabbi, called me in one day to give me career advice: "You've got a good mouth, but not much of a *yiddisher kup*" (a Jewish mind). "You should do something where you use your mouth, not your brains." His recommendation: "You should become either a lawyer or a Conservative rabbi."

Many of our teachers — especially in our religious subjects — were right off the boat from the European displaced persons camps. Several of our classmates had also experienced Hitler's concentration camps. But I do not remember any classroom or street-corner discussion about the Holocaust. It was in the air; it was part of the experiences of many of our friends and neighbors; almost everyone had lost relatives. But it was not discussed. The reminders were all around us: in the tattooed numbers we could see on the wrist of a classmate when he rolled up his sleeve to punch the pink rubber ball we called a "Spaldeen"; in the fatherless or motherless families; in the "extra brother" some kids had; in the memorial prayers on specified holidays. We all knew, but we did not ask.

Nor were we particularly sensitive or sympathetic. Cruelly, we exploited the fears of our "greenie" teachers in our mischief making. When one particular teacher, who had survived aerial bombardment, turned to write on the blackboard, we would let go with a low whistle that built to an explosive crescendo simulating a dropping bomb, and wait in giggling anticipation to watch his frightened reaction. When a teacher hit us — a common form of discipline — we would threaten to report him to the Black Hundreds, the cossacks, or the SS.

I couldn't wait to get out of the Yeshiva system and into a school where everything could be questioned — where there were no absolutes. I knew how stimulating that kind of environment could be, because our Shabbes tables — Friday night dinner and Saturday afternoon lunch — were a kind of Socratic dialogue. These discussions were mostly about family or neighborhood matters, rarely about politics or world affairs. My father, a quiet man, always encouraged dialogue and debate. He rarely injected himself into the conversation, except to ask "Is it fair?" or "How would that help the underdog?" or "Would that be the right thing to do?" My father, in his own quiet way, had an exquisite sense of justice. Later in my life, the man who most reminded me of him was Earl Warren, who was chief justice when I served as a law clerk to the Supreme Court.

My friends and I also engaged in wonderfully stimulating discussions outside the classroom — over lunch or on the basketball court. A major subject was the reconcilability of the Bible with science. All morning we studied religious subjects, which were premised on creation. All afternoon we studied secular subjects, which were premised on evolution and other scientific insights. We never tried to reconcile these world views in the classroom, but outside we fought the old battles with enthusiasm. Carl, the scientist, was always on the side of evolution. Bernie was more of a believer in the irrational. Zollie knew all the arguments on both sides. Barry was cynical about everything. Murray always knew a fact that undercut any theory put forward. Hal sided with whoever seemed to be losing the argument. Josh usually listened until the very end.

Despite my desire for a change from the intellectually stifling atmosphere of the Yeshiva classroom, a part of me was frightened of change. My parents were similarly ambivalent. They had me apply to

Yeshiva University, where most of my high school classmates would enroll. I was rejected, however, after a personal intercession against me by my high school principal. A few years ago, a fund-raiser from Yeshiva called to inform me that I had been designated alumnus of the year by the high school that had suspended me and prevented my admission to its parent university. When I reminded him of my experiences in high school, he quickly responded: "We selected you as *alumnus* of *this* year, not *graduate* of 1955." The president of Yeshiva University, in presenting the award to me, acknowledged that I had graduated from the high school *"summa cum tsuris"* (with a maximum of problems). Several years later, when I was awarded an honorary doctorate of laws by Yeshiva University, the president said that it was in compensation for their rejection of me as a student some thirty-five years earlier.

After my rejection by Yeshiva, my mother decided to submit an application to Brooklyn College. I wanted to go to City College in Manhattan, but my parents did not want me to "go away" to an "out-of-town" school. Admission to Brooklyn College was far from automatic for someone with my high school grades. I had to take a competitive examination and was admitted by the skin of my teeth.

As was typical of New York City college students, I lived at home while attending school. Brooklyn College was a forty-five-minute walk or ten-minute drive from our house in Borough Park. As Orthodox yeshiva boys, my friends and I could not become full participants in the life of even a commuter college like Brooklyn. Our religious observances precluded us from partaking in social functions on Friday nights or Saturdays — the most important times for parties and athletic events. Nor could we eat with the other students, because of our kosher dietary restrictions.

But a group of us — graduates of Yeshiva University High School, which I had attended, and Flatbush Yeshiva, where several of my friends had gone — were determined to live college lives as full as our religious constraints permitted. Accordingly, we founded the first Orthodox house plan in Brooklyn College's history. A house plan was a cross between a fraternity, a social-athletic club of the kind that ethnic street kids used to operate out of neighborhood storefronts, and a gang. It had no "house" or national affiliation, but it conducted meetings, arranged parties, and fielded various intramural sports teams. We named our group Knight House. All house plans had to be named after prominent educators, and following the rejection of our initial application to name the house after Leonard Hoar, we found an educator named Sarah Knight. Our boastful motto read *Semel Equis Satis,* which, loosely translated, means "Once a Knight Is Enough." We held our dances on Sundays and petitioned the intramural committee to avoid scheduling our basketball, soccer, and touch-football games on late Fridays or Saturdays. We had our own table in the college cafeteria, to which we brought our kosher sandwiches from home.

Among members of our Orthodox house plan were five of us from the Borough Park group: Barry, Josh, Zollie, Hal, and me. The three other Borough Park boys, who attended different colleges in the New York area, became honorary members and attended many of our functions.

The fact that my entire group went to local colleges was partly a function of economics, convenience, and the availability of good colleges in New York City. But it was also a function of persistent anti-Semitism in the Ivy League and other elite schools. None of these schools ever came to recruit at the yeshivas. The few superstar students who applied on their own were almost always rejected. And the one or two yeshiva graduates per decade who were admitted to places like Princeton, Harvard, Dartmouth, and Yale had generally unhappy experiences. All of my friends are smart enough to have done well at any Ivy League college — as each did in the school he attended. But a subtle message of exclusion was being sent by the admissions offices in Princeton, Cambridge, Hanover, and New Haven. Perhaps not against all Jews, but certainly against our kind of Jews. We knew that our "place" was at one of the New York City colleges and we would make the best of it — always with a bit of envy of our contemporaries who lived in the Ivy League dormitories and took courses from famous professors.

In establishing the first Orthodox Jewish house plan at Brooklyn College, we had two goals in mind. First, we very much wanted to enjoy a well-rounded college life. Prior generations of Orthodox students viewed college as a series of classes to attend while continuing to live life at home and in the yeshivas and synagogues. We wanted to live a full college life on the campus while merely sleeping at home. Predecessor generations of Orthodox students did not have time for full participation in college life, since many had to work, while others continued their rabbinical studies. We were the first generation of Orthodox Brooklyn College students freed of those responsibilities.

Our second goal was somewhat chauvinistic. We wanted to prove that Orthodox Jewish boys were not wimps or weirdos. We were every bit as good — athletically, socially, politically, and in every other way — as the non-Orthodox Jews. There were very few non-Jews among the student body at Brooklyn College in those days, and we had little contact, except in class, with the small number of Catholic and black students. I don't think I ever met a white Protestant student in my four years at Brooklyn, though the administration — president, deans, department chairmen — was primarily Midwest white, Anglo-Saxon, and Protestant. We called the hall in which President Gideonese, Dean Stroup, and the other assistant deans were located the Wasp Wing.

Our house plan was determined to destroy the somewhat negative stereotype of the clannish Orthodox student. And we succeeded beyond our wildest expectations. Our athletic team won several intramural championships, thanks largely to Josh's heroics. A few of our members were elected student-body officers, including two of us who became president of the student government. It wasn't quite *The Revenge of the Nerds,* but we certainly made our mark on the life of the college.

But even while partaking fully in campus activities, we did remain socially isolated from non-Orthodox Jews and non-Jews in many important respects. We did not date, or even party, beyond our Orthodox circles. In this respect, we were different, but only in degree, from the other house plans or fraternities. They too were organized along ethnic lines: there were Jewish, Irish, Italian, and black fraternities and house plans. The same held true for other colleges in those days.

Our interaction with outsiders took the form primarily of competition between us and them. Our teams played their teams. Our candidates ran against their candidates. Our group studied together and tried to get better grades than "they" did. We were out to prove a point, not to become assimilated into a different world. And we had a membership of sufficient size — our house plan, which started with eight, numbered about sixty by the time we graduated, and an Orthodox woman's house plan had also been established — to give us a relatively full social life without leaving the confines of our Orthodox community.

By my senior year at Brooklyn, I had decided to go to law school. That path seemed natural in light of my success in debate and school politics. I had no idea what the practice of law was, except what I had read about the careers of such legal luminaries as Clarence Darrow, Thurgood Marshall, and Louis Brandeis. My uncle Morris was a lawyer, but he specialized in contract cases, which held no interest for me. I asked Grandma Ringel to introduce me to an old friend of hers, whom she always called "Judge Berenkoff." I had no idea what kind of judge he was, but he was the only judge I knew. My grandmother wondered why I wanted to meet Judge Berenkoff. I told her that since he was a judge, he might have some good career advice for an aspiring lawyer. My grandmother laughed and said: "Berenkoff's no judge, he's a butcher." She explained that "his first name is Judge," and then she spelled it out: "G-E-O-R-G-E," which she, with her Yiddish accent, pronounced "Judge."

Despite my lack of career advice, I was determined to go to an "elite" law school like Harvard or Yale. Though I didn't acknowledge it to myself at the time, it was important for me to leave the world of my Orthodox Jewish parents and try to make it in the "other" world. That other world was a complete mystery to me. Although I had encountered it superficially during debate tournaments, I needed to know whether I could compete with these well-dressed and self-assured Wasps who had used words like "balderdash" and "poppycock" in rebutting my debate arguments.

Yale was my first choice for law school because of its somewhat broader approach to law in those days. My chances for admission seemed fairly positive, since I had gotten very good grades and had been elected president of the student government as well as several other organizations. I had even excelled at intramural athletics. My parents were pessimistic about my prospects, since they had heard from friends that Yale had a small Jewish quota. While that was still the case at the undergraduate level, the law school admitted a significant number of Jewish students and my application was accepted (after a short time on the waiting list).

I had still never been away from home — except for Jewish summer camp — and I was a bit fearful of moving to so "distant" a location as New Haven. My parents made it plain to me that I would not be going alone. If I wanted to go to an out-of-town law school, I would have to be married. The idea of trusting me not to meet an unacceptable woman — which meant a non-Orthodox Jew — was out of the question. My family, indeed the entire socio-religious structure of the community, had worked so hard to make certain we could never socialize with girls who did not come from Orthodox Jewish families, that they would never tolerate the risk of a chance meeting with the wrong kind of marriage mate. (I am, of course, deliberately using the language of the period.)

In my case, there was no problem. All through college I had been dating an Orthodox Jewish girl named Sue Barlach, whom I had met at a camp that specialized in making appropriate matches. Several of my group members were also dating their soon-to-be brides, whom they had met in similar structured situations. These were not the arranged marriages of our grandparents' generation. We had complete choice — within the closed group we were permitted to date.

The decision was made that Sue and I would get married before I enrolled in law school. I was not yet twenty-one years old, and so my parents had to sign the marriage license. Although Sue was younger than I, she was not a minor, since the age at which a female could marry without parental consent was eighteen.

One consequence — if not purpose — of the marriage was that, once again, I would not be participating fully in the social life of the institution I was attending. But this time, it didn't quite work out that way. The life of Yale Law School in the early sixties was centered around classes, the *Law Journal,* and other academically related activities. Though I did not sleep or eat in the dorms, I virtually lived at the law school. Both my academic and social life were focused around its enclosed courtyard. It was at Yale that I met and befriended my first Wasps, blacks, and even non-Orthodox Jews.

I recall my first day as a law student at Yale. I read a Supreme Court decision involving a compulsory flag salute during World War II, to which some Jehovah's Witnesses objected on religious grounds. The majority agreed with the religious objectors, but Justice Felix Frankfurter dissented essentially on the ground that patriotism during wartime is more important than religious liberty. Frankfurter, a Jew, began his dissent with a remarkable self-characterization: "One who belongs to the most vilified and persecuted minority in history is not likely to be insensible to the freedoms guaranteed by our Constitution."[1] (He, of course, proceeded to be quite "insensible" to the religious freedoms of the Jehovah's Witnesses!)

I read the Frankfurter characterization in astonishment. As a twenty-one-year-old student, I simply couldn't identify with it. I didn't feel "vilified," or "persecuted," or even as part of a "minority." I wasn't black, Hispanic, Native American, or a woman. I was a white male Yale law student — a member of a privileged elite. (Indeed, it was not until I met my Yale classmates that I realized I was relatively poor! In my working-class neighborhood of Brooklyn, I was middle class.)

In 1959, I found it difficult to understand how Jews could feel vilified. I was on top of the world, both individually and Jewishly. The Holocaust was not part of my personal memory. Although I recalled my father's map and the influx of displaced persons into my neighborhood, the Jewish community of my school years had experienced a collective amnesia about the Holocaust. It was never mentioned in yeshiva, in Jewish camp, in discussions among my friends, or even at the synagogue. The word itself — Holocaust — was not part of our vocabulary. The tragedy was too recent, too painful, too evocative of guilt.

Israel had not yet become an object of vilification at the United Nations and throughout many parts of the world. It was a universally popular showplace in which bronzed kibbutz youths had miraculously turned a desert into a garden paradise. Zionism was moderate socialism, not pernicious "racism." To be sure, the Arabs hated Israel and the Jews, but the whole world (with the exception of a few stuffy Englishmen and Anglophile State Department anti-Semites) seemed to hate the Arabs.

The Jews of Silence (as novelist and essayist Elie Wiesel had called Soviet Jewry) were silent and so were we about their plight. We knew nothing about Jewish suffering in Ethiopia, Syria, Argentina, or other far-flung corners of the world.

As American Jews, we were in our golden age. It was actually "in" to be Jewish during the sixties. It was certainly not anything to be "vilified" about. It never occurred to me to devote my time and attention to Jewish rights. In the tradition of my family and background, I was determined to fight for the rights of the real underdogs, and Jews were clearly not in that category. Or so I thought.

Yale Law School in the early 1960s was regarded as a true meritocracy. Though my fellow classmates numbered among them children of presidents, Supreme Court justices, and multimillionaire industrialists, the only hierarchy I ever saw at Yale Law School was based on grades, *Law Journal* writing, moot court competition, and classroom performance. I later learned that there existed a number of "exclusive" clubs among the students from which Jews — certainly Eastern European Jews from New York City colleges — were excluded. But these clubs were so secret that I didn't learn of their existence until after I had graduated. I had experienced no overt anti-Semitism among my fellow students and absolutely no hint of it among the faculty. A large percentage of the professors were Jewish, some overtly and proudly so. The dean was Jewish, as was his predecessor. I felt like a first-class citizen as a Jew at Yale Law School.

Two representative stories stand out in my mind from my early days at Yale. The first involves Professor Abraham Goldstein. During the course of the semester, he called on some of the students with famous names — Taft, Brennan, Marshall, Danforth — without comment. When he came to my name he asked: "Dershowitz, from the well-known Dershowitz family in Williamsburg?" At first I thought he was mocking my humble origins, but I soon realized that with his background — he had grown up in the same neighborhood as my parents — the name Dershowitz had a more personal meaning than the famous names.

My other story involves Professor Guido Calabresi, who taught me torts during my first semester. When I went home for the Jewish holidays, I told my parents about the brilliant teachers at Yale: Goldstein, Pollack, Bickel, Skolnick, Schwartz. Then I told them about the most brilliant of my then teachers: Calabresi. Without missing a beat, my mother asked: "Is he an Italian Jew?" Angrily I said: "Don't be so parochial. He's an Italian Catholic. Not all smart people have to have Jewish blood." Several months later, I learned that Guido Calabresi was in fact descended from Italian Jews. To this day, I have never told my mother. I didn't want to encourage her ethnocentricity. (This is a good test of whether my mother will read this far in the book!)

Class rank and position on the *Law Journal* determined status. I was fortunate in both regards, ranking at the top of the class and having been elected editor in chief of the *Yale Law Journal.* That made me something of a celebrity in the small world in which we lived. Professors called me Chief, directed the hardest questions at me in class, and asked me to work as their research assistant. I had also published two well-received *Law Journal* articles and had excellent faculty references. In fact, Harvard Law School had already expressed interest in recruiting me for its faculty. Students regarded me as something between a student and a junior faculty member. I mention this privileged status in the Yale hierarchy only to make a point about the rude awakening that came with my first quest for a job.

It was an absolute shock to me when I learned that there was an entirely different hierarchy that operated within the legal profession, especially — though not exclusively — in the Wall Street firms to which most Yale law students aspired.

The summer between the second and third years in law school is job time. In the spring, the students don their "lawyer suits" and line up for interviews with the big firms. I had my heart set on the Washington firm of Covington and Burling or the New York firms of Cravath, Swaine, and Moore, or Paul, Weiss, Rifkind, Wharton, and Garrison. I was interviewed by these and a few dozen other "white shoe" firms. The interviewers were polite and the interviews seemed to go well. I was surprised at the questions about high school and college, however, since I was applying for a law job and thought my law school record was what counted. To my chagrin, I began to get a few rejection notices. At first I thought the competition for the few jobs was just too keen. Then I began to learn who had been offered the jobs for which I had been turned down. Some were students at the middle or bottom of the class, the ones who generally got the answers wrong and came to me and my *Law Journal* colleagues after class for the right answers.

Soon a pattern began to emerge. The students who got the best jobs were the white Anglo-Saxon Protestants. Of course, the Wasps with higher grades got better jobs than the Wasps with lower grades, but the lowest-ranking Wasps got better job offers than the higher-ranking Jews. Some Jewish students — a very few — near the top of the class did receive job offers from the elite firms, and I simply didn't understand this apparent break in the pattern.

I began to ask around and finally was "initiated" into the "facts of life" by a third-year student, in much the same whispered way that an elementary school kid learns about sex from an upperclassman in the schoolyard. My initiator, a Jewish *Law Journal* editor, told me about the different types of firms and the kinds of students they were looking for.

"First there are the 'white shoe' firms. All the partners and associates are Wasps, except for maybe one real estate or tax partner. They don't have any Jews, unless their names are Lehman or Morgenthau. Don't even bother to apply.

"Then there are the 'quota firms.' They'll take a Jew or two every year, but you have to have gone through the 'Waspification' process of attending Yale, Princeton, or Harvard, and preferably a prep school like Exeter or Groton. Even then, they probably will skip over the Jew when it comes to partnership decisions, but they'll help him get a partnership with a good Jewish firm.

"After the quota firms come the 'balanced firms.' These are firms with a balance between Jewish and Wasp partners, and they want to keep it that way. Since these firms are very popular with Jewish applicants and not so popular with Wasp applicants, it's much more difficult for a Jew than for a Wasp to get an offer. In fact, the only Wasps who apply to mixed firms are those who can't make it to the Wasp firms. You've got a real shot at one of these firms.

"Finally, there are the Jewish firms. Even they prefer Wasps when they can get them — these firms are always trying to become elevated to the status of balanced firms, but hardly any Wasps apply. They also prefer Wasp-looking and Wasp-sounding Jews, but they'll grab a smart Yid like you." As an afterthought, my coach told me that none of the firms that came to recruit at Yale hired blacks or women, except for an occasional token, and that ethnic Catholics — Irish and Italian American — had problems of their own, as well as firms of their own.

That, in a nutshell, was my introduction to the world of bigotry, discrimination, racism, and anti-Semitism called the American bar. Its distinguished leaders — who are still honored by law school scholarships, in paintings in law libraries, and in the mastheads of the great firms — were operating an apartheid-like system of law practice, nearly a decade after *Brown v. Board of Education* and nearly two decades after the Nuremberg trials.

Nor was this apparent phenomenon — discrimination against all except white Protestant males — unique to law firms to which Yale students applied. It was true of law practice in virtually every major city in America, as well as to professions such as banking, accounting, architecture, insurance, and medicine.[2] It had also been true, at least until after World War II, of many elite colleges and universities, including law schools and especially medical schools.

Several of my Brooklyn friends had experienced similar rejections in other professions, such as engineering, insurance, and finance. Even in our quest for part-time jobs as teenagers, we knew that certain companies excluded Jews. It was simply the way the real world worked, and we were supposed to accept it and gratefully take what "they" left over for us. Since our parents' generation had it so much worse, it seemed unbecoming of us to complain about our lot.

Still, I was shocked to learn that this practice extended even to alumni of so egalitarian an institution as Yale Law School. I recall speaking to the dean of Yale Law School, Eugene V. Rostow, a Jew who had worked at Cravath, Swaine, and Moore many years earlier. He confirmed the general pattern of law firm hirings, but emphasized that there could be exceptions, citing his own example. He acknowledged that "German Jews who came from money" had a better chance than "Jews like us." And that "Jews like us" had a better chance if they went to an Ivy League college and a prep school. When I described my background — Yeshiva University High School and Brooklyn College — he did not respond, except to suggest that I improve my wardrobe.

Upon learning of the way law was practiced in American firms, I resolved never to become part of that system. But I did want to see it in operation at first hand. I decided, therefore, to persist with my applications to the major firms in each of the categories described by my student mentor. It was clear that had I been a Wasp, I would have received an offer from every firm to which I applied. It was quite amusing to watch the law firm interviewers squirm as they tried to come up with excuses as to why I might not get an offer of summer employment. The best came from a lawyer at Sullivan and Cromwell (I later learned he was one of their token closet Jews), who pointed to the one poor grade I had gotten in a single course and said with a straight face that they didn't hire C-plus students. He then proceeded to hire a student with significantly lower grades than mine.

In the end, I was turned down by all the firms in the white shoe and quota categories. One balanced firm — Paul, Weiss, Rifkind, Wharton, and Garrison — offered me a summer job, but then it withdrew the offer when the senior litigation partner learned that I was an Orthodox Jew, since my Sabbath observance would make me unavailable to the firm on Friday nights and Saturdays. Covington and Burling said they were full for that summer, but encouraged me to apply at a future time. It turned out that this balanced firm had already picked its Jew (and picked well; he was James Freedman, a Harvard College graduate who was just behind me in ranking at Yale and who is now the president of Dartmouth College).

Eventually, I went to work for Kaye, Scholar, Feirman, Hays, and Handler, which was a predominantly Jewish firm with a small number of non-Jewish partners (and a considerable number of Jewish partners with non-Jewish names such as Livingston and Robinson). I worked at Kaye, Scholar for about six weeks and loved every minute of it. It was — and still is — a great firm. But I was determined never to enter that world. Discrimination was far too central to the American law firm for me to be comfortable within its structure. Indeed, I was determined to fight such discrimination from without.

Several years later — when I was teaching at Harvard and occasionally litigating cases — I was to get my chance. In 1975, a young lawyer who had been working as an associate at Cravath, Swaine, and Moore called and asked me to assist him in his lawsuit against that firm. He had been passed over for partner after eight years of high-quality work. He told me that the reason he was not made a partner was that he was an Italian American, and that his venerable firm had never promoted an ethnic Catholic to partnership.

By the time this man asked me to take his case, Cravath and most of the other Wall Street firms had stopped discriminating against Jews, but if this man's story was to be believed — and it seemed perfectly plausible, especially in light of Cravath's long history of discrimination — they were still discriminating on the basis of ethnic and religious background. I agreed to take the case without fee.

My student assistants and I conducted some research which disclosed that many of the partners in the firm were now opposed to discrimination, but that there were still some holdovers from the old regime. One man in particular was well known for his anti-Catholic bias and had reportedly declared that no Catholic would become a partner in his section of the firm while he could still cast a blackball.

Cravath hired the firm of Paul, Weiss, Rifkind, Wharton, and Garrison to defend it in court. The selection was interesting for several reasons. First, Paul, Weiss was always a predominantly Jewish firm, one of those that tried to maintain a balance. Its senior litigator, Simon Rifkind, a former federal judge, was responsible for the policy against hiring Orthodox Jews under which my offer of a summer job with the firm had been withdrawn. Finally, Judge Rifkind's son was a partner in the Cravath firm, a Jew hired during the period when they were still discriminating against Jews, though hiring an occasional token, especially one whose father had been a federal judge and was the leading commercial litigator in New York.[3]

Cravath took the legal position that as a partnership it was lawfully entitled to discriminate on any basis it desired, including race, religion, sex, and ethnicity. (It publicly denied that it had, in fact, discriminated on any of these bases, and that factual issue was never resolved in the lawsuit.) The lawyers it chose to present that argument in court were Simon Rifkind, who was active in many Jewish philanthropic organizations, and Morris Abram, who would eventually become the chairman of Presidents of Major Jewish Organizations and who had recently ended a brief term as president of Brandeis University. Nor were Rifkind and Abrams alone in supporting the legal right of law firms to discriminate. None of the major Jewish organizations — which are dominated by big law firm lawyers — took a public position in relation to the Cravath case. Indeed, several prominent Jewish lawyers called to urge me to drop the case. As one of them put it: "Cravath has been good to Jews lately, so don't rock the boat." I responded angrily that discrimination against Italian Americans was every bit as pernicious as discrimination against Jews and that legitimating discrimination against anybody was legitimating it against everybody.

The court rejected Cravath's argument, agreeing with our contention that it was unlawful for a large law firm to discriminate on the basis of religion, race, sex, or ethnicity. Eventually the U.S. Supreme Court — in a case brought by a woman who was denied a partnership in an Atlanta firm — accepted our position in a definitive ruling that cited our case.[4] At long last, the legal profession itself was subject to the same rules it had helped to impose on other institutions in our society. Never again would a law student — whether Jewish, Catholic, female, black, or Hispanic — have to confront the kind of discrimination I had encountered during the time I was at Yale. It would still exist in practice — and in legal theory against gays in some states — but it was no longer permissible in the eyes of the law.

But in my day discrimination was not only acceptable, it was the rule — the way of life in the major American law firms. And everyone involved had to know it. I recall being interviewed by Supreme Court Justice John Harlan for a possible clerkship. He looked at my résumé and declared it to be impressive. But, he wondered out loud, why had I not worked for one of the great Wall Street firms? The patrician Harlan had himself been a senior partner at Dewey, Ballantine, Bushby, Palmer, and Wood. I looked him straight in the eye and responded, "Mr. Justice, you must know that the great Wall Street firms, including Dewey, Ballantine, discriminate against Jewish lawyers." He appeared genuinely surprised, and he passed politely to a different subject. I did not get his clerkship. Several years later, when I related this story to a Jewish colleague who had clerked for Justice Harlan, he assured me that Harlan, who hired many Jewish law clerks when he was a judge, was precisely the kind of patrician who might well have been oblivious to discrimination in his own firm. At one level of awareness perhaps, but at another level never!

My experience with discrimination — especially at the hands of the Paul, Weiss firm over my Sabbath observance — caused me an embarrassing moment during my interview for the Supreme Court clerkship I did get. My first choice among the justices was newly appointed justice Arthur Goldberg. When I went for my interview with him, he simply tossed a petition for a writ of certiorari — a request for Supreme Court review of a case — across the desk and asked me to read it quickly. When I finished perusing the ten-page document, he asked for my "considered judgment" about whether it should be granted or denied and why. A heated discussion ensued and, to my amazement, he offered me the job on the spot. But I hesitated. I had to tell him about my "problem" — that I couldn't work on Friday nights or Saturdays. I blurted it out: "Mr. Justice, I hope you won't withdraw your kind offer when I tell you that I'm Sabbath observant — that means I can't —"

Justice Goldberg cut me off. "I know what that means, and I'm insulted that you would even suggest that it might cause me to withdraw my offer. I know how it feels to be discriminated against. How could I possibly discriminate against anyone on account of their religion?"

I apologized and explained how my offer from the Paul, Weiss firm had been withdrawn. Justice Goldberg was surprised. "Does Sy Rifkind know about what his firm did?" the justice asked. "Sy is quite active in Jewish causes, you know."

I looked at Justice Goldberg sheepishly and said, "I'm sorry to tell you this, but it was Mr. Rifkind himself who withdrew the offer after learning of my Sabbath observance. He has a policy of wanting his people available to him seven days a week, twenty-four hours a day." The justice shook his head in bemusement, but he never forgot the story.[5]

Indeed, several years later, after he left the Supreme Court, Justice Goldberg was being courted by the major New York law firms. At his meeting with Paul, Weiss, he raised the issue of discrimination against Orthodox Jews and was assured that the policy would end. It did, and now Paul, Weiss has a kosher kitchen, daily Talmud class, and a significant complement of Orthodox lawyers and paralegals. And it is a more diverse and better firm for it.

During my three years at Yale Law School, I remained strictly Orthodox. I never attended classes on the Sabbath or on major Jewish holidays. On some holidays, I walked to class but did not take notes (because of the Orthodox prohibition against writing on these days). I prayed each morning while wearing my *tefillin* and *tallis* (phylacteries and prayer shawl). My parents had conveniently arranged for my wife and me to rent an apartment directly across the street from the Young Israel Orthodox synagogue, and the rabbi had no hesitation in calling me at 7:00 A.M. when the congregation was one man short for a minyan (ten Jewish men).

I ate only kosher food and therefore could not eat lunch with my classmates in the common dining room. My wife packed me a sandwich each morning and I ate with a few married friends who also brown-bagged it. I did not wear a yarmulke to class, but everyone knew I was Orthodox. I was an active participant in the class at Yale Law School, and yet as an Orthodox Jew I remained apart from its social fabric. In that respect, I was like other Jews who were succeeding in the workplace but remained outside the social fabric of American life. Several of my childhood friends, who were working in non-Jewish environments, were experiencing similar dichotomies in their lives. This was especially true of Bernie Beck, whose business it was — I kid you not — to import and sell Christian religious items, including statues of the various saints. (He recently sent me a statue of Saint Jude, the saint of desperate causes, after *Time* magazine dubbed me the Saint Jude of the legal profession.) Bernie worked in the most non-Jewish of businesses but he continued to live a Jewish life, always reminding us that the biblical patriarch Abraham's father was in the business of making idols for people who worshiped them.

When the time came for nomination of editor in chief of the *Yale Law Journal,* my Sabbath observance became an issue. The *Law Journal* was regarded as a twenty-four-hour, seven-day-a-week job. We turned out, after all, a major legal periodical, averaging 150 heavily footnoted pages each month. It was entirely student run and required incredibly long hours, especially for the editor in chief, who had responsibility for every word that was published. Could a six-day-a-week student be trusted with that responsibility? What would happen if a crisis developed during the Sabbath? In the end, my supporters prevailed with the argument that since I had already succeeded in writing two articles and getting good grades on my six-day schedule, there was no reason to believe that I would be hindered in my new job.

At the end of my tenure as editor in chief, the staff roasted me by presenting me with a mock copy of the *Law Journal* with every seventh page blank!

Although I was an observant Jew during my years at Yale Law School, I was not very Jewish minded. I had no real interest in Israel, in oppressed Jews, in the Holocaust, in anti-Semitism (except as it minimally affected my career choices). It was as if my observance filled my quota of Jewish concern. I was so busy conforming to the ritual that I had no room in my life for more political Jewish issues. As I became somewhat less observant, after leaving Yale, I found myself becoming more Jewishly involved. The same was true for my boyhood friends, who have all become more active in Jewish political and communal affairs even as most have reduced the degree of their ritualistic observance.

Part of my transition process was attributable to my two clerkships following law school. I clerked for two very Jewish, but not very observant, judges. My first clerkship was with David Bazelon, who was the chief judge of the U.S. Court of Appeals for the District of Columbia, the second most important court in the nation.

Judge Bazelon was a remarkably innovative judge. He first came to public attention in 1954, when he wrote the *Durham* decision, which revolutionized the law of insanity. Judge Bazelon opened up the insanity defense to the urban poor whose crimes were the product of their upbringing, social conditions, and other deprivations. He was also a pioneer in bringing legal services to the poor and the disadvantaged. As a judge, he saw the enormous disparities between how the wealthy are treated in court and how the poor are mistreated.

In addition to his influence on the law, Judge Bazelon had great personal influence on most of his law clerks, including me. We have remained friends and I owe much of what I have become to his guidance and example.

Judge Bazelon rarely went to synagogue, but he was a Jewish judge in every sense. He saw the world through his Jewish background. His humor was frequently in Yiddish. His speeches referred to the rabbinic literature. He described himself as a secular American with a "Jewish soul." If a defendant deserved compassion but no writ of habeas corpus — or other formal legal remedy — was technically available to him, Bazelon would wink at me and order that I find some ground for issuing a "writ of *rachmones*." *Rachmones* is the Hebrew-Yiddish word for "compassion." Even his non-Jewish clerks had to know what that alien world meant if they were to do Bazelon-style justice.

Bazelon was always an outsider, a questioner, even as one of the most influential jurists of his time. For him, the greatest quality of a judge — indeed of any human being — was *rachmones*. Though quite wealthy and powerful, he always remembered his roots as the youngest of nine children of a poor Chicago family. He had little respect for his Jewish contemporary, Justice Felix Frankfurter, whom he regarded as "all brain, no heart" and who he believed was trying to hide his Jewishness behind a facade of Anglophilia. Bazelon was fond of quoting Shakespeare's Shylock: "The brain may devise laws for the blood, but a hot temper leaps o'er a cold decree." For Bazelon, the law had to come from the heart as well as the brain and it must understand the hot temper as well as the cold calculation.

The Jewish justice with whom he most closely identified was Arthur J. Goldberg, who beat him out for what was then regarded as "the Jewish seat" on the Supreme Court. Upon Justice Frankfurter's resignation, the names of both Chief Judge Bazelon and Secretary of Labor Goldberg were prominently mentioned as replacements. I was clerking for Bazelon at the time, and I can recall his mixed emotions at the appointment of his old friend to the seat to which he also aspired. Bazelon knew that it was extremely unlikely that a second Jew would be appointed to the high court (despite the precedent of simultaneous service by Justices Louis Brandeis and Benjamin Cardozo for a brief period). Yet he was delighted at Goldberg's appointment and was effusive in his praise of his old Chicago buddy.

Both Bazelon and Goldberg had come out of similar backgrounds. Goldberg was born into poverty, the youngest of eight children. His father died when Goldberg was three. He worked his way through school and graduated first in his class from Northwestern University Law School, where he tutored the slightly younger Bazelon.

Goldberg quickly became the nation's leading labor lawyer, virtually developing that fledgling area of practice. He engineered the merger between the American Federation of Labor and the Congress of Industrial Organizations.

During World War II, Goldberg was appointed head of the labor division of the Office of Strategic Services (the predecessor to the Central Intelligence Agency) and helped to establish secret operations with antifascist labor groups behind the Nazi lines.

When President John F. Kennedy was elected in 1960, he appointed Goldberg as his secretary of labor. Goldberg proceeded to revolutionize the job, becoming an active negotiator who brought an end to several strikes. Kennedy's only hesitation in appointing him to the Supreme Court so "early" in his term — 1962 — was that he would be losing his most effective cabinet member. Kennedy told a friend that Goldberg was "the smartest man I ever met."[6] Goldberg expressed a willingness to remain on as Secretary of Labor for a few more years. "There will be more vacancies," he commented to the president. "No one can be sure of that," responded Kennedy. "I'm putting you on the Court now," he insisted. It would, as it tragically turned out, be President Kennedy's final appointment to the Supreme Court.

Justice Goldberg had a remarkable, if brief, career on the Supreme Court. He quickly became one of the Court's dominant forces, and the swing vote on many issues. I was privileged to be his law clerk during the middle of his three years on the Court. In that year, he wrote seminal decisions on capital punishment, the exclusionary rule, reapportionment, freedom of speech, right to trial by jury, separation of church and state, and other important areas. I worked closely with him in each of these areas, especially capital punishment and the Escobedo case, which outlawed police interrogation of suspects held in custody without access to their lawyer.

As his law clerk, I was privileged to attend private lunches in his chambers with dignitaries, including high-ranking Israeli officials. One of Arthur and Dorothy Goldberg's closest personal friends was Golda Meir, whom they knew from their early Zionist days in Chicago and whom they always called Goldie. Once, when I traveled to Israel, the Goldbergs asked me to smuggle a carton of unfiltered Chesterfields past her security guards, so she could enjoy a few puffs of her favorite cigarette, which her doctor had banned. When I produced them, Golda grabbed them in glee and said, "I bet I know who they're from." Goldberg took a passionate, if not always uncritical, interest in matters Israeli and Jewish.

Bazelon and Goldberg showed me how to maintain — indeed increase — my involvement in Jewish affairs without being a fundamentalist about religious observances. They showed me what it meant to have a Jewish sense of compassion. They lived their Jewishness every day, without the ritual. And their Jewishness — their *rachmones* — resonated in me more powerfully than the Jewishness of ritual.

I recall a weekend visit my maternal grandmother made to my home while I was clerking for Judge Bazelon. Grandma Ringel came into the office and asked if she could meet with the judge alone. He welcomed her into his chambers where they conversed — he later told me — in Yiddish. My grandmother had a complaint. She noticed that I had rushed through my morning prayers in fifteen minutes, obviously finding them less important. "He used to *daven* for a full half hour," she informed the judge. "Can't you let him be a little late in the morning?" she importuned. "It will do you both some good," she assured the judge, "if you let him *daven* the extra fifteen minutes." Judge Bazelon assured my grandmother that he would not stand in the way of my religious obligations. He repeated this story — in Yiddish with appropriate accent — to every Jew he knew over the next several months.

My Justice Goldberg story is also about my transition from strict orthodoxy. Arthur and Dorothy Goldberg always gave a wonderful Passover seder, with government officials — especially non-Jewish ones — in attendance. George Meany would sing Irish ballads; Hubert Humphrey would tell stories; and Dorothy Goldberg would sing Yiddish labor union songs. He invited me to one, and without even asking, made sure the entire event was kosher. He and Dorothy firmly believed that people who kept kosher should not be treated as second-class citizens, with "special kosher" meals. If there was one kosher person, the entire affair would be kosher. The vice president, several Supreme Court justices, cabinet members, and foreign diplomats were all invited to the one I was to attend. I had no idea of the efforts and expense they had undertaken just for me. At the last minute, my parents prevailed on me not to break the tradition of attending the seders in Brooklyn. The option of one seder with the Goldbergs and the other with my family was not possible, since we did not travel on Passover. I politely told the Goldbergs that I could not attend their seder, and they did not say a word. It was only years later that Justice Goldberg first told me how angry I had made them by bowing out of their seder after all the effort they had gone through. "The vice president had to eat kosher catered food rather than Dorothy's wonderful kosher-style cooking because of you. And you went to your parents'." He also chided me about how stringent my observance had been during my clerkship with him — once he had even had to drive to my apartment in suburban Maryland on a Saturday to confer with me on an emergency case — and how it had seemed to slacken after I left him.

*   *   *

I did, in fact, maintain my Orthodox ways through both my clerk-ships, though it was becoming clear to me that my strong commitment to Judaism would have to manifest itself in ways other than strict adherence to rules in which I had no abiding belief. My move from Washington, D.C., to Cambridge, Massachusetts — and the raising of my two constantly questioning children — would provide the impetus to my gradual transition from passive observance of ritual to active participation in causes.

The process of change that I was going through paralleled that which several of my boyhood friends were experiencing as they moved into mixed neighborhoods and workplaces. It was a process, with variations, that every Jewish generation has been through as its members move to new locations and new occupations. It is always traumatic, because there is no map for a road never before trodden. Every generation — indeed every person — has to work change through anew, as if it had never happened before and will never happen again. Historically, change is a constant. But for those who are experiencing it, it is a bit like a game we used to play as kids: we would be blindfolded, spun around, and then told to find familiar landmarks. I felt like that when I set out for Harvard Law School to begin my career as a teacher.

I decided to teach at Harvard not because I expected it to provide a Jewish environment. I wanted to teach at a university with an excellent law school, as well as first-rate departments in other areas, since I was interested in interdisciplinary work in the areas of criminal law, psychology, and psychiatry. I also wanted to live in a large metropolitan area, where I could visit courtrooms and gain some practical experience about the law in action. I knew that by moving to Cambridge I would be entering a far less Jewish world than the ones in which I had previously lived. But I had no idea just how alien it would be.

At Harvard

Quotas, Conflicts, and Honors

WHEN I ARRIVED at Harvard in the fall of 1964, it was as un-Jewish an institution as I could imagine. The comedian Lenny Bruce had a routine about what and who were "Jewish" and "goyish." *Goyish* is a Yiddish word for "not Jewish." *Goy* in Hebrew simply means "nation," but it has come to mean (demean?) nations or peoples other than the Jews. Here is Bruce's routine:

Dig: I'm Jewish. Count Basie's Jewish. Ray Charles is Jewish. Eddie Cantor's goyish. B'nai B'rith is goyish; Hadassah, Jewish.

If you live in New York or any other big city, you are Jewish. It doesn't matter even if you're Catholic; if you live in New York, you're Jewish. If you live in Butte, Montana, you're going to be goyish even if you're Jewish.

Kool-Aid is goyish. Evaporated milk is goyish even if the Jews invented it. Chocolate is Jewish and fudge is goyish. Fruit salad is Jewish. Lime jello is goyish. Lime soda is *very* goyish.

All Drake's Cakes are goyish. Pumpernickel is Jewish and, as you know, white bread is very goyish. Instant potatoes, goyish. Black cherry soda's very Jewish, macaroons are *very* Jewish.

Negroes are all Jews. Italians are all Jews. Irishmen who have rejected their religion are Jews. Mouths are very Jewish. And bosoms. Baton-twirling is very goyish.

Underwear is definitely goyish. Balls are goyish. Titties are Jewish.

Celebrate is a goyish word. Observe is a Jewish word. Mr. and Mrs. Walsh are *celebrating* Christmas with Major Thomas Moreland, USAF (ret.), while Mr. and Mrs. Bromberg *observed* Hanukkah with Goldie and Arthur Schindler from Kiamesha, New York.[1]

The quickest way to tell whether a place is inherently goyish is to look at the Jews who are prominent there. The Jewish professors at Harvard in 1964 were — with some exceptions — the most goyish group I had ever encountered, far more so than the Yale law professors I had known, and certainly more so than the two very Jewish Jews I had worked for in Washington.

It was not only their goyish dress — some of them looked like they were probably wearing tweed underpants beneath their British-tailored slacks. Nor did they "dress British and think Yiddish." They thought British too. Their Anglophilia — copied from Felix Frankfurter's — affected their mannerisms, their attitudes, their style of speech, their choice of metaphors, even their jokes. Lenny Bruce would have characterized Yale Law School as Jewish and Harvard Law School as goyish.

I vividly recall my first dinner party at the home of Dean Erwin Griswold. His wife served roast beef and vegetables. I ate the vegetables but left the meat. I never expected my plate to be inspected, but the next day the dean asked me why I had left the meat. I told him I was kosher, and he quickly responded that none of the other Jewish professors kept kosher. He reminded me that even the Catholics had changed their rules about meat on Fridays and asked whether I didn't think it was time for "your people" to adapt the old rules to modern times. I think that the dean's well-intentioned remark kept me kosher for an extra year.

I also recall my first confrontation over my Jewishness. Saturday morning classes had been a long tradition at Harvard Law School, and it was assumed that they would be taught by the junior faculty members. As the most junior of the faculty, I was assigned a Saturday class. I told the dean that I didn't work on Saturdays. He said I had to. I described how Justice Goldberg had accommodated his schedule to my preferences, and asked why Harvard wouldn't do the same.

The dean — who was an extremely fair man — explained that it would be inequitable to allow me to avoid the Saturday burden while others had to bear it. I asked why Saturday morning classes were so important. He acknowledged that they were largely a holdover from the past. A few days later, he informed me that I would not have to teach on Saturdays and that in the future there would be no more Saturday classes.

Jewish professors (and students) at the Harvard Law School of the early 1960s were expected to behave like grateful guests in someone else's home, and most of them seemed to feel most comfortable in that role.

It was almost as if nothing had changed since 1922, when Professor Harry A. Wolfson, Harvard's first Jewish professor of Judaic studies, told his students that being born Jewish was like being "born blind, . . . deaf, [or] lame," and that their "common lot as Jews" was to be "isolated, to be deprived of many social goods and advantages." He urged them to "submit to fate" rather than "foolishly struggle against it," because "there are certain problems of life for which no solution is possible."[2]

This was all understandable, if not particularly prescient, in light of Harvard's history and policy toward Jewish faculty. Prior to World War II, the number of Jewish professors at Harvard Law School could be counted on one hand. And the law school was considered progressive on these matters. The university itself, particularly the college, was worse. In all of its history, there had never been a Jewish dean at Harvard. University Hall, where the president had his office, was virtually *Judenrein* (Jew-free).

Nor was Harvard all that different from other Ivy League and non-Ivy elite schools such as Stanford. There were — and I believe there still are, though with radically different figures — *numerus clausus* (literally, "closed number") systems in operation, designed to limit the percentage of Jewish students. These numerical restrictions had their origins in Eastern Europe as part of overtly anti-Semitic government policies.

The limitations, which applied to students and even more stringently to faculty members, were often so low as to qualify as tokenism. Today the word in vogue is "quota," but current quotas are very different — in intent and in operation — from the *numerus clausus,* which was directed against Jews. The *numerus clausus* restrictions were ceilings without floors: they were not designed to assure *at least* a certain number of Jewish admittees; they were designed to assure *no more than* that number.

Todays' benign quotas are floors without ceilings: they are designed affirmatively to assure that at least a certain number of minority applicants are accepted; there is no limit — at least in theory — on the number of applicants above that minimum who will be accepted.

Harvard's history of discrimination against Jews is fairly typical of that of other major universities. Indeed, it reflects the condition of Jews in elite American institutions and professions during the first half of this century — a condition in whose shadow my generation of Jewish Americans came of age, and which continues to have a profound impact on our world view. It would be difficult for anyone to have a full appreciation of the ambivalence of many Jews toward current benign quotas (and other perceived threats to their hard-earned status) without being aware of this history.

I focus on Harvard's story because I know it best and because it provided a model for subtle discrimination that was emulated by other universities, businesses, professions, and institutions. The Harvard model is also important because it is the model widely in effect today, having been expressly legitimated by the 1978 Supreme Court decision in the famous *Bakke* case.

In 1909, the presidency of Harvard passed from Charles Eliot to A. Lawrence Lowell, who would hold the post for the next twenty-four years. Until the accession of Lowell, who was an overt racist (he supported racist immigration laws, and was overtly anti-Irish, anti-Italian, antiblack, and anti-Oriental, as well as anti-Jewish), Harvard's admissions policy was relatively standardized.[3] Since there were few nonwhite, non-Protestant applicants, there was no reason to deviate from academic criteria. But as Jewish applicants increased over the years, Lowell and others in the university administration became more and more dissatisfied with an admissions system that was accepting a growing number of "undesirables" — particularly immigrant Jews.

In January 1922, the dean's office noted that "Mr. Lowell feels pretty strongly" that Harvard should limit the percentage of total available scholarship aid that could be awarded to Jewish students to the percentage of such students in the class.[4] Because Jewish students (especially those from Eastern Europe) were often financially needy, a limitation on aid would inevitably curtail their numbers.

On April 14, 1922, Lowell sent two proposals concerning Jews to the committee on admissions. One suggested that "all doubtful . . . cases shall be investigated with the nicest care, and that such of this number as belong to the Hebrew race shall be rejected except in unusual and special cases." The other called for the rejection of all Hebrews applying for admission by transfer from other colleges "except such applicants be possessed of extraordinary intellectual capacity together with character above criticism."[5]

Much of the rhetoric bandied about concerning the Jews focused on their allegedly unrefined immigrant manners. "The colleges have been identified for years with a certain product — 'Harvard men,' 'Princeton men' being supposedly recognizable types — and they wish to continue delivering the kind expected of them. They do not consider the Jewish applicant good raw material." In a 1926 article, admissions chairman Henry Pennypacker railed against smart applicants with "extreme racial characteristics" who did not pass "the test of character, personality and promise."[6]

It was vintage Harvard claptrap covered with the elitist language of "character" — a concept devoid of specific content and impossible to challenge in a particular case, especially since the admissions office conducted its investigation into an applicant's Jewishness "with the nicest care."

The old Harvard types who administered this pretextual procedure certainly could not have passed their own test — fairly administered — of "character above criticism." They didn't even have the honesty to acknowledge publicly what they were doing. In some instances, they were breaking the law by discriminating against Jews.[7]

Throughout May of 1922, the Harvard faculty, in meetings and memoranda, debated the Jewish question. Lowell, in correspondence with William Hocking, professor of moral philosophy, rejected the notion of a psychological test of the type used successfully at the time by Columbia, "because not enough Jews could be excluded by objective tests of any kind." He proposed a percentage system that could be

> applied to any group of men who did not mingle indistinguishably with the general stream — let us say Orientals, colored men, and perhaps I can imagine French Canadians, if they did not speak English and kept themselves apart. . . . This would apply to almost all, but not all, Jews; possibly, not probably, to other people. . . .

Lowell told an alumnus that he did not want any Jews who were unwilling to give up their "peculiar practices."[8]

Lest he be charged with advocating quotas in order to hurt Jews, Lowell quickly assured the public that what he had in mind was a benign quota designed to "help" the Jews:

> The anti-Semitic feeling among the students is increasing, and it grows in proportion to the increase in the number of Jews.
> If their number should become 40 percent of the student body, the

race feeling would become intense. When, on the other hand, the number of Jews was small, the race antagonism was small also. . . .[9]

Lowell apparently never considered imposing a ceiling on the number of anti-Semites admitted to Harvard. That would have struck too close to home.

If there was indeed any discernible increase in anti-Jewish feelings among the students, it was obviously being encouraged by those at the top — like Lowell and his appointees — who missed no opportunity to pronounce the Jewish "character" deficient. On one occasion Lowell told an alumnus that "50 percent" of the students caught stealing books from the library that year "were Jewish." When Professor Felix Frankfurter learned of this and demanded specifics, Lowell acknowledged that his 50 percent figure translated into one student.[10]

Judge Learned Hand's response to Lowell's proposed quota was among the most memorable:

> I cannot agree that a limitation based upon race will in the end work out any good purpose. If the Jew does not mix well with the Christian it is no answer to segregate him. Most of these qualities which the Christian dislikes in him are, I believe, the direct result of that very policy in the past. . . .
>
> If anyone could devise an honest test for character, perhaps it would serve well. I doubt its feasibility except to detect formal and obvious delinquencies. Short of it, it seems to me that students can only be chosen by tests of scholarship, unsatisfactory as those no doubt are. . . .
>
> A college may gather together men of a common tradition, or it may put its faith in learning. If so, it will I suppose take its chance that in learning lies the best hope, and that a company of scholars will prove better than any other company.[11]

The report of the committee, when finally issued in 1923, repudiated quotas as inconsistent with Harvard's tradition of "equal opportunity for all, regardless of race and religion." Instead of quotas, it adopted a system of "geographic distribution" designed to "attract more applicants from the South and West."[12]

It was Harvard hypocrisy at its worst: out of one side of its mouth it repudiated an anti-Jewish quota, while out of the other side it established geographic preferences expressly designed to limit the number of Jews. That year, an article in the *Harvard Graduates' Mag-*

azine informed alumni that the new policies of geographic distribution "will keep out a group of students in which many are certainly unfit. Of these, at present, a considerable proportion are Jews, but they will not be excluded, either in name or in fact, on racial grounds."[13]

But the goal of reducing "Jewish representation" by means of geographic distribution did not succeed, at least in the short run. After Harvard's well-publicized rejection of religious quotas, the number of qualified Jewish applicants rose and the percentage of Jewish students actually increased slightly. President Lowell was furious. He became convinced that unless the admissions officers were given total discretion, the numbers would continue to rise. Wary of starting another public fiasco, Lowell proceeded quietly this time by writing the chairman of the admissions committee, in 1925: "To prevent a dangerous increase in the proportion of Jews, I know at present only one way which is, at the same time, straightforward and effective, and that is a selection by a personal estimate of character on the part of the Admissions authorities."[14]

In January 1926, a committee report recommended that the total number of freshmen be limited to one thousand, that admissions, even within the group of academically acceptable candidates, be made highly discretionary, and that a greater emphasis be placed on qualities of "character and fitness." Soon after, a photograph was required with all applications.

In 1926, Clarence Mendell, the new dean of Yale College, was told by Harvard's admissions chairman Pennypacker that Harvard was "going to reduce their 25% Hebrew total to 15% or less by simply rejecting without detailed explanation."[15] This new effort was successful; the percentage of Jews at Harvard dropped significantly. Harvard administrators, of questionable character themselves, were using the pretext of "character" to mask their outright religious discrimination.

The "great" men who administered this systematic discrimination today have buildings named after them in Harvard Yard. Their names are honored by students who have no idea that these men were a pack of dishonest bigots unworthy of respect or emulation. Whenever I am asked to speak in any of these buildings, I go out of my way to educate the students about the awful men whose names are memorialized by these edifices. I remind them that Harvard has refused to name a house after Leonard Hoar, Harvard's third president, lest the unfortunate pun tarnish Harvard's image. It would be far better for a house to be named after Hoar, who was a Puritan minister, than after Lowell, whose name may sound more suited to Harvard's image, but who should be honored by no one other than the Ku Klux Klan.

Harvard, of course, was not the only university that was searching for ways to perpetuate the white Protestant homogeneity of its student body. Other institutions, particularly those with large Jewish applicant pools, followed President Lowell's successful misuse of "character" to establish ceilings for Jews. (Dartmouth was more direct. Even as late as 1945, its president declared Dartmouth to be "a Christian college founded for the Christianization of its students.")[16]

One of the inescapable conclusions to be drawn from this history is that Harvard's pretended quest for increased "diversity" was, in fact, designed to achieve the opposite of a diverse student body. It was a desperate attempt to increase the homogeneity of its student population in the face of incursions by disturbingly diverse elements from the ghettos of Eastern Europe via the slums of New York and other urban centers of the East Coast. What the xenophobic college officials feared most was the kind of diversity that Jews and other minorities threatened to bring.

Thus, the midwestern farm boy and the southern lawyer's son were admitted not so much because of the diversity they might provide, but primarily because they were seen as far more *similar* to typical Harvard students than was the first-generation immigrant from New York. In order to continue the dominance of native-born white Protestant students in the overall college population, the admissions committees had to "diversify" at a relatively superficial level: they had to extend the search for white Protestants to other geographic areas of the country, and to white Protestant public school students, precisely in order to stem the influx of certain other diversifying "elements" — who were congregated in the urban Northeast. The mechanism they resorted to was the phony and insulting test of "character," administered in a discretionary manner by a homogeneous group of frightened bigots who were committed to the racist proposition that Jews, as a group, lacked character.

By the end of the period, Harvard, under President Lowell, had solved its "Jewish problem" by developing precisely the kind of discretionary admissions process legitimated — indeed, praised — fifty years later by Justice Lewis Powell in the case *Regents of the University of California v. Bakke*. That decision lent the Supreme Court's imprimatur specifically to Harvard's admissions system, and most particularly to its approach to affirmative action, based on the need for "diversity" and the "discretion" of the admissions committee. Then, as now, Harvard purported to be seeking a diverse student body by having its admissions officers consider a variety of both subjective and objective data about each applicant. Both then and now, however, such unlimited discretion makes it possible to target a specific religious or racial group — for decrease or for increase — and to apply what is in effect a different standard of admissions to that group without expressly acknowledging the difference. In both cases, everyone knows what is going on, but no one has to acknowledge the specific influence of religion or race on the decision to admit or reject.

It should not be at all surprising that many Jews would be sensitive to concepts such as "diversity," "discretion," and "character," since they came into being as code words for anti-Jewish quotas. Nor should it be surprising that the likes of Justice Lewis Powell — whose professional life was spent in the segregated world of law firms and bar associations — would feel comfortable with these code words. The legal profession in which Justice Powell and his contemporaries had come of age had behaved just like Harvard and other elite universities in confronting its "Jewish problem."

Leaders of the bar, including future chief justices Harlan Stone and William Howard Taft, made no bones about their dislike of Jewish and other immigrant lawyers who, in Stone's words, "exhibit racial tendencies toward study by memorization" and "a mind almost Oriental in its fidelity to the minutiae of the subject without regard to any controlling rule or reason." Others complained of the influx of Eastern European immigrants "with little inherited sense of fairness, justice and honor as we understand them." Paul Cravath, founder of one of the great law firms in America — himself a lawyer with highly questionable legal ethics — berated lawyers with "too much imagination, too much wit, too great cleverness, too facile fluency" — qualities of which "the best clients are apt to be afraid."[17]

Henry S. Drinker — who was chairman of the American Bar Association's ethics committee for many years and whose treatise on legal ethics is still among the most widely relied upon by bar associations — berated the ethics of "Russian Jew boys who came up out of the gutter [and] were merely following the methods their fathers had been using in selling shoe strings and other merchandise."[18]

The attempt to equate Jewish "racial" traits with unethical behavior reached its nadir in 1916 when President Woodrow Wilson nominated Louis Brandeis to the Supreme Court. The leaders of the American Bar Association lined up solidly against the nomination, invoking the code word "character." Six former association presidents, at the instigation of incumbent Elihu Root, declared that Brandeis was "not a fit person to sit on the Court." Former president and future chief justice Taft dipped his "pen in vitriol [dispatching] letter after letter of calumny to friends and family, berating Brandeis for his ethics, politics and his religion." Numerous local bar associations and individual elite lawyers alleged that Brandeis had a "defective standard of professional ethics." Harvard president Lowell, one of the more vocal among the elite, believed Brandeis to be unscrupulous in his legal practice and "untrustworthy."[19] He signed a petition attacking Brandeis's — you guessed it — "character."

Brandeis's eventual confirmation only strengthened the resolve of the Anglo-Saxon legal establishment to preserve its hegemony. As James Beck, former solicitor general of the United States, wrote in 1922: "If the old American stock can be organized, we can still avert the threatened decay of constitutionalism in this country." Not surprisingly, the tack taken by the elite lawyers was to increase the power of the bar association to impose its own conception of legal ethics on all lawyers, practicing and prospective. This was far better designed to achieve the intended goal than an increase in educational requirements which, as one bar association lawyer observed, might "keep *our own* possibly out." Accordingly, "character" committees sprang up throughout the country, charged with the function of screening prospective lawyers. It is not surprising that these committees, manned by the likes of Root, Drinker, and other lawyers with a distinct prejudice against outsiders, would disqualify a high percentage of "Russian Jew boys," blacks, and other ethnic "undesirables." They also imposed restrictions against women.[20]

Pennsylvania in particular made "heroic" efforts to "cleanse" its bar of Jews. The number of successful Jewish applicants declined more than 20 percent after the establishment of screening mechanisms, and not a single black was admitted to practice between 1933 and 1943. The emphasis upon "character" — by bar associations, universities, and other elite institutions — served to hide overt bigotry from public view. But nobody was really fooled. Only deliberate self-deception —

such as that reflected by Justice Harlan in his interview of me — allowed some to deny the obvious.

Though matters had certainly improved since the end of World War II, they hadn't improved enough. There was still a discriminatory hierarchy both at Harvard and in the elite bar. This legacy of second-class citizenship was all around us as my generation of Harvard professors came into its own.

In 1971, when Derek Bok was promoted from dean of the law school — a post to which he had been appointed without Jewish competition by the anti-Semitic president of Harvard Nathan Pusey — to president of Harvard, I decided that the time had come to confront the issue of anti-Semitism at Harvard directly and personally. If a Jew could not become dean (or president) of a great school, that was not a school at which I would spend my professional life — just as I would not spend my life at a law firm that discriminated. More was at stake, of course, than my own discomfort with my chosen employer or profession. Harvard was a symbol, a leader in higher education. Its bigotry reflected a widespread legacy of bigotry throughout American life. Many barriers had fallen, but some still stood, and they had to be assailed.

The word around the law school was that Bok's replacement as dean would be made by the outgoing president, Pusey, and not by Bok, the incoming president. In light of Pusey's well-known bias, this would assure the continuation of the ignoble tradition of selecting deans by their religion — or at least by the absence of any Jewish background.

Along with another faculty member, I went to see Derek Bok and told him of my expectation that Pusey would act on his prejudices in selecting our new dean. Bok told us that the appointment of the new dean was Pusey's responsibility. I countered that the new dean would be serving under Bok, not Pusey, and that the responsibility for assuring that the selection was not influenced by religion was his.

I hinted broadly that I would not feel comfortable at an institution that continued its bigotry in the 1970s, and that the time had come — once and for all — to put an end to applying religious criteria in selecting deans. Bok seemed to agree, but he appeared nervous about taking the decision away from Pusey. As we left, however, he assured us that the choice of the new dean of the law school would not be based on religion.

We were convinced that this meant that Bok had decided to make the selection himself. Several weeks later, it was announced that Albert Sacks, a Jew, would serve as dean of the law school. This was followed in quick succession by the appointments of several Jewish deans throughout the university.

Derek Bok had broken the tradition against Jewish deans. It seems ironic — though it was, of course, inevitable — that Derek Bok, who was probably the last president of Harvard selected under a system in which only non-Jews were deemed eligible, would be the one to end Harvard's administrative apartheid.*

Shortly thereafter, religious barriers began to crumble at other universities as well. At about the same time, my friends in other professions and businesses were reporting similar progress to me. Barry became a sales manager at Union Carbide; Carl became an engineer with a company that used to discriminate against Jews. Jews were on the way to becoming first-class citizens in the workplace, at least for most jobs.

But ending barriers to deanships did not mean ending all discrimination against Jews at Harvard and other universities. It continues today against Jewish applicants at many elite schools where the number of qualified Jewish applicants exceeds the "desired" number of Jewish students in the "ideal" student population. It is somewhat reminiscent of the "balanced" law firms that discriminated against Jews during my law school days. The problems are not the same as they were in the bad old days of A. Lawrence Lowell. Nor are the motives underlying Jewish ceilings the same. And certainly the numbers are different. But this does not mean that a person's Jewishness — more precisely, his visible identity as being Jewish, such as his name, hometown, or high school — is not sometimes a negative factor in the admissions process. I am convinced that it is, though university officials continue to deny it. Consider, for example, the *combined effect* on Jewish applicants of affirmative action for racial minorities *and* "geographic distribution" policies.

Geographical criteria allow admissions officers to preserve an artificially high representation of white Protestants in a student body. Whether or not this is one of the *purposes* — conscious or uncon-

---

* I regret in retrospect not protesting the appointment of Bok as president. Although Bok put an end to anti-Jewish discrimination in the selection of deans, he himself was selected by a bigoted committee in a bigoted manner, since all Jews — and probably other non-Wasp males — were automatically excluded from consideration. The *process* by which he was selected was thus illegitimate.

scious — of some current admissions officers is not the critical point. This is the undeniable *effect* of geographic distribution. White Protestants are distributed more evenly around the country than others, and they are less likely to live in metropolitan areas than are blacks, Jews, Asians, and Catholics. It follows that these latter groups are relegated, under a geographic distribution approach, to fighting among themselves for the smaller pieces of the pie allotted to them.

Geographic distribution imposes, in effect, a ceiling on the number of students taken from the various northeastern metropolitan areas, such as New York City, Boston, Philadelphia, and Washington. These metropolitan areas contain very heavy concentrations of black, Jewish, and Catholic applicants. Accordingly, if black students are given a preference in admissions, and if geographic considerations are kept constant, then the black preference is obtained disproportionately at the expense of Jewish and Catholic applicants. Thus, while all white applicants are affected by any race-specific affirmative action program, Jews and Catholics appear to be affected disproportionately, while leaving many white Protestants disproportionately less affected.

It should not be surprising to learn, therefore, that when Harvard College finally began to accept significant numbers of black students — as well it should — the concern among Jewish faculty was that there would be a concomitant reduction in the number of Jewish students. This phenomenon led to the famous "doughnut" exchange:

> Dr. Chase N. Peterson, dean of admissions at Harvard, recently addressed a group of Jewish faculty members suspicious that Harvard had decided to reduce the number of Jews it would admit. Peterson averred that there is no particular "docket" or area of the country whose quota of admissions has been reduced. Rather, he said, it is "the doughnuts around the big cities" which are not as successful with the Harvard Admissions Committee as they used to be. . . . "But now we have to be terribly hard on people with good grades from the good suburban high schools, good, solid clean-nosed kids who really don't have enough else going for them." The doughnuts, said Peterson, included such areas as Westchester County and Long Island, New York, suburban New Jersey, and Shaker Heights, Ohio. When he described these areas to the Jewish faculty members, the *Crimson* reports, one stood up and said, "Dr. Peterson, those aren't doughnuts, they're bagels."[21]

Whatever its current purpose, there can be no question that geographic distribution has the effect of artificially increasing the number of white Protestant students while artificially decreasing the number of black, Jewish, Asian, and Catholic students.

During my years at Harvard, I have fought against basing admissions decisions on race alone. I am very much in favor of aggressive affirmative action in all areas of life, but I do not regard as fair an admissions process that gives dispositive weight to the race of the candidate. And I am fundamentally opposed to the hypocritical face that Harvard and other elite institutions have put on their admissions process in order to hide the dispositive nature of race from public view.

What do I mean, then, when I say that I am in favor of affirmative action? I strongly believe that in admitting students to a university, it is appropriate to look at the distance the applicant has traveled to get to where he or she is. For example, consider two applicants who are competing for one place. Mr. Poor was born in poverty to uneducated parents. He worked his way through high school and college. His grade score is 3.4 on a scale of 4.0 and his scholastic aptitude score is 1,400 on a scale of 1,600. Mr. Rich was born with a silver spoon in his mouth, to college-educated parents who provided special tutors and test-preparation courses. His grade scores are 3.6 and 1,450.

There are two arguments, in my view, that may favor Poor over Rich, despite his lower scores. The simple empirical argument is that Poor may be smarter and have better academic potential than Rich; their "objective" scores may have been skewed by Poor's underpreparation and Rich's overpreparation. In the parlance of the profession, Poor's scores may underpredict his performance, while Rich's scores may overpredict his performance. Any good admissions system will try to account for this.

The second argument is more controversial. Even if Rich will be a marginally better performer, Poor *deserves* consideration for his efforts and for the barriers he has had to overcome.* But it does not follow from this moral argument that race alone should be dispositive in admissions decisions.

Although there are powerful arguments in favor of racial floors — such as the need for racial diversity and racial role models — there can be no doubt that significant costs inhere in allowing a university to consider race in and of itself in admissions decisions. At the most fundamental level, it is simply wrong to do so. To reward some

* There is no moral argument for preferring a Mr. Rich with *lower* grades and scores to a Mr. Poor with higher ones. Yet such preference is common. See the *Boston Herald*, August 30, 1988: "Merit Has Nothing to Do with Quayle's Rise."

persons for the accident of their race is inevitably to punish others for the accident of theirs.

Also important, however, is the impact that race-specific affirmative action programs have on racial stereotyping. If persons of any given race are admitted to a particular school with significantly lower test scores and grades than persons of other races, it will follow with near certainty that many persons in the preferentially admitted racial group will perform less well than other persons whose scores and grades had to be higher for them to be admitted.

The corollary to this is that if any particular group is discriminated *against* — by which I mean nothing more than that higher scores are generally required of them for admission — it will follow that admitted persons from that group will perform better than admitted members of other groups.

This probably explains two disturbing phenomena that have been observed over the years: first, that minority applicants admitted under race-specific affirmative action programs (and subsequently evaluated on a race-blind grading system) appear to be performing less well, on the whole, than persons from other groups; and second, that during the period when Jews were being significantly discriminated against in elite college admissions, they tended, on the whole, to do better than average once admitted.

The problem is that these observations seem to reify invidious racial stereotypes, at least in the short run. So long as it is significantly easier for minority applicants to be admitted to a particular school, these groups, on average, will tend to perform less well. And there is a danger that this may confirm the racial stereotyping. It may be argued, of course, that it is better to have significant numbers of minority elite professional school graduates with somewhat lower grades than fewer minority graduates — or none at all. This is especially so because many of the students admitted with lower grades will, in fact, do extremely well at the elite schools, thus disproving the racial stereotyping. The real question here is a matter of degree, depending on how far a school is willing to go in reducing the scores required for members of preferred groups and elevating the scores required for members of nonpreferred groups.

I have long advocated the development and vigorous application of affirmative action programs that are not based on race alone. But these are harder to implement, because they must be individualized rather than based on group criteria. Despite this difficulty, several progressive jurists, including the late William O. Douglas, agree with this approach. Said Douglas: "The key to the problem is consideration of such applications in a racially neutral way. . . . Such a program might be less convenient administratively than simply sorting students by race, but we have never held administrative convenience to justify racial discrimination."[22]

The issue of affirmative action has contributed significantly to racial tensions between the Jewish and black communities, despite the fact that Jews tend to support affirmative action programs — of every type — to a significantly greater degree than do whites from other ethnic groups.[23] There are, of course, many Jews who — recalling the way "quotas," "diversity," and "discretion" were used against them — are wary of *specific types* of affirmative action programs, especially those that discriminate against Jews today. This is entirely understandable, in light of our history, and should be taken into account by those who jump too quickly to single out Jews for criticism on the affirmative action issue. Indeed, singling out Jews — from among other white ethnic groups — for *special* criticism over affirmative action is, itself, a subtle manifestation of anti-Semitism, especially in light of Jews' greater support for even race-specific affirmative action.

Over the past several years, I have been engaged in an ongoing debate with my younger son, Jamin, about these concerns. My son, who recently graduated from Yale Law School, is a strong supporter of affirmative action programs of all kind. Like me, he prefers those that do not focus exclusively on race and do not give undue advantage to elite blacks from wealthy families. But he is prepared to give substantial weight to the race of an applicant, since race alone is often a factor in discrimination, subtle and overt.

His argument — which has persuaded me to a degree — is that in light of America's unique history of racism and its continuing impact today, it is better to err on the side of giving some blacks who have not suffered from discrimination a measure of undeserved benefit than to risk denying benefits to some blacks who have suffered discrimination. He has also persuaded me that there is an enormous difference between the white majority imposing racially motivated discrimination on a black minority, and the white majority imposing discrimination against other whites (on an equal basis) in a positive effort to undo the effects of past discrimination. The person discriminated against — whether black or white — is undoubtedly hurt, but there is a real difference between the institutional impact and intensity of the hurt suffered as part of an invidious pattern of racial *subordination* and as part of a benevolent pattern of racial *equalization*. As Oliver Wendell Holmes once put it: "Even a dog understands the difference between being stumbled over and being kicked."

I have learned a great deal from my debates with Jamin, but I still insist that it is indefensible for any program of affirmative action to do what Harvard's continues to do: namely, hold relatively constant the white, Anglo-Saxon, Protestant "quota" of admittees through the discriminatory vehicles of "geographic distribution" and "alumni preference" (i.e., giving preference to descendants and relatives of alumni), while adjusting for the black affirmative action quota largely by reducing the number of Jewish, Catholic, and now Asian-American admittees. Jamin and I are in full agreement that the "burdens" of any fair affirmative action program must be spread equitably throughout the entire applicant pool and not imposed most disproportionately on groups that were relatively recent victims of Harvard discrimination. Indeed, if the burdens must fall disproportionately on some group, it would be fairer if the groups historically *favored* by discrimination were to bear a heavier burden of current efforts to achieve equality.

Over my years at Harvard, I have become a sort of unofficial advocate for Jewish concerns. My colleague Alan Stone, who has been associated with Harvard for more than forty years, probably overstated it when he called me "Harvard's first Jewish Jew."* He describes me as his first colleague to "wear his Jewishness on his sleeve," and he once joked with me that some of my colleagues worry that "someday you're gonna open a kosher delicatessen in Harvard Square!" (In 1988, several friends and I did open a short-lived kosher deli there, called Mavens Kosher Court.)

When I came to Harvard in 1964, I had no expectation of assuming the role of defender of the faith in Harvard Yard. During my initial years on the faculty, I experienced some ambivalence about my Jewish identity. Despite my early encounters with the dean over kosher food and Saturday teaching, there was a part of me that wanted to become John Harvard. Had the university not been as overt about its bigotry

---

* Felix Frankfurter, who was the first Jew to become a professor at Harvard Law School, went out of his way to describe himself as "a Harvard Law School Professor who happened to be a Jew," and not as "a Jewish professor at the Harvard Law School." In a somewhat perverse recognition of his background, he always boasted that he demanded "higher standards" from students who were Jews. See Jerold Auerbach, *Rabbis and Lawyers* (Bloomington: Indiana University Press, 1990), p. 155.

under President Pusey (highlighted by his refusal to allow Jews to marry in Harvard's Memorial Church), I doubt that I would have become involved in Jewish issues as intensively as I did. But I felt my second-class citizenship as a Jew quite palpably, especially during the crisis leading up to the Six-Day War, between Israel and the Arab states, in 1967. I felt pressure not to express my strong support for Israel, lest my Americanism and my Harvardism be called into question. Nobody suggested that I support the Arab side or even that I not support Israel, though it was pointed out to me that several of Harvard's most prominent professors of Jewish background were anti-Zionist. It was a matter of degree. If my support for Israel were perceived as too strong, too emotional, I would be seen as the kind of Jew who placed his parochial Jewishness before his other, more universal values. In the days just before the Six-Day War, my Jewishness *was* my most important value. I really feared another Holocaust, as President Gamal Abdel Nasser of Egypt threatened to drive the Jews into the sea. And I decided not to try to hide my feelings. I organized students and faculty in support of Israel. I provided legal services to several students who wanted to fight for Israel. I helped raise money for the Israeli army.

I recall one non-Jewish faculty member — who was rumored to have a Jewish ancestor — berating me for acting as if *my own* country were under siege. I responded that my own *people* were under siege and I would not sit by while Jews anywhere were in danger. He politely pretended not to understand what I was talking about and walked away.*

It felt good to express my Jewishness fully and openly in a Harvard context. I never stepped back into the closet or even the shadows.

Over the next several years, a number of other events occurred that solidified my Jewish activism. Between 1969 and 1970, I worked on a pro bono basis on the defense of the Chicago Seven, first as a consultant in pretrial issues and then on the appeal from the contempt convictions. During the course of the trial, one of the defendants, radical activist Abbie Hoffman, came to speak at Harvard. He publicly thanked me for donating my legal services to his cause. With his typical humor, he said that he was considering making a contribution of $10,000 — the fee he would have expected to pay — in my honor

---

* Another non-Jewish faculty member, Livingston Hall, was among the leaders in the effort to help Israel. He had no fear of being considered "too Jewish."

to the Palestine Liberation Organization. The Harvard audience laughed. I wondered out loud to several friends whether, if I had been a black lawyer, Hoffman would have joked about making a contribution to the Ku Klux Klan.

During the course of the Chicago Seven defense and in the years immediately thereafter, I experienced at first hand my first exposure to left-wing anti-Zionism. Several of the defendants and lawyers — most especially attorney William Kunstler — were virulently anti-Israel. They agreed with their guru Daniel Berrigan, the priest-writer-activist, who characterized Israel as "a criminal Jewish community" that "manufactures human waste." He also accused "American Jews" of ignoring the "Asian holocaust" in Vietnam "in favor of economic and military aid" to "racist" Israel.[24] This was all before the notorious "Zionism is a form of racism" declaration by the United Nations General Assembly in 1975, before Israel's invasion of Lebanon in 1982, and before the Intifada, the general Palestinian uprising that began in late 1987. Berrigan's anti-Semitic diatribe was worthy of *Der Stürmer,* but because of his popularity among knee-jerk radicals, it drew surprisingly little criticism from the left. I immediately circulated a letter of condemnation that was signed by several of his former lawyers.

Shortly thereafter, I experienced the natural extension of this thoughtless brand of Israel-bashing. I also worked as an unpaid consultant on an aspect of the Angela Davis case in California. Davis, who was one of the leaders of the American Communist party, was charged with murder in connection with a 1970 shoot-out at the Marin County courthouse. She claimed that as a black, a woman, and a Communist, she could not receive a fair trial in any American court. She was acquitted, so maybe she was right! After her acquittal, she announced that she would be devoting the remainder of her life to defending political prisoners like herself. A short time later, I read that she was going to Moscow to receive some human rights prize from the Soviet Union. I called her office and gave them a list of Jewish prisoners of conscience in the Soviet Union — Jews who had been imprisoned because they wanted to emigrate to Israel or to learn about their heritage. I asked if she would be willing to speak up on behalf of these political prisoners. Several days later, I received a call back from Ms. Davis's secretary informing me that Davis had looked into the people on my list and none of them were political prisoners. "They are all

Zionist fascists and opponents of socialism." Davis would urge that they be kept in prison where they belonged.

These experiences — and others — persuaded me that if I was going to be true to my belief in defending the underdog and in seeking a single standard of justice, I would have to become as active in defense of *Jewish* human rights as I had been active in defense of other people's human rights. I began to devote more and more of my time to Jewish issues, without reducing my commitment to other causes.

Whether or not I was Harvard's first Jewish Jew, I have certainly become one of its most outspoken advocates of Jewish causes. Students, faculty, and members of the community call me when they perceive that Harvard is being insensitive to Jewish issues. Whether it be holding graduation on the Jewish holiday of Shevuoth, giving Jew-baiters a platform, failing to consider Jewish concerns in the admissions process, or honoring a particular person.

These issues, which I have confronted in the Harvard context, are a microcosm of issues faced by the Jewish community in general. For example, the issue of Jewish-black relations has assumed crisis proportions throughout the United States, not only in universities, but in the schools and streets of Brooklyn neighborhoods like Brownsville and Crown Heights, in the factories of Shreveport, Louisiana, and in the suburbs of Chicago. My Brooklyn friends and I — all of whom were active in or supportive of the desegregation movement of the 1950s and 1960s — were taken by surprise when former allies turned into adversaries. We could not understand why some of the most vitriolic anti-Semitic and anti-Zionist rhetoric seemed to be emanating from those with whom we had marched hand in hand, promising to "overcome" racism and religious bigotry. Inevitably, these pervasive conflicts have had an important Harvard dimension as well.

During the late 1970s and 1980s, tensions began to build between some Jewish students and some third world students. Though the concerns tended to focus most particularly on affirmative action and the Israeli-Arab dispute, they sometimes seemed to transcend specific issues. As the faculty adviser to the Harvard Jewish Law Students Association, an organization I helped to establish in the 1970s, I was thrown into the vortex of this conflict.

It came to a head several years ago when a coalition of black and third world students convened a weekend conference called Third World Communities and Human Rights. There was, of course, much to discuss on the subject, such as the massacres in Uganda by Idi

Amin, the killing of schoolchildren in central Africa, the mass murders committed by Syrian and Iraqi dictators, and the virtual lack of press freedom and due process in most third world countries. None of these subjects was on the agenda. The sole human rights discussion consisted of a tribunal convened to judge the "so-called nation of Israel, for its 'terrorism and genocide.' "

The main panelist and guest of honor at this tribunal, subsidized in part by Harvard Law School, was the third secretary to the Libyan mission of the United Nations. He wasn't invited by name; the Libyan mission was simply asked to send an emissary, and whoever showed up would be given guest-of-honor status. The sole purpose of this obvious provocation was to "stick it to the Jews," as one of the student sponsors acknowledged to me.

No supporter of Israel was permitted to participate in the panel. When the Harvard Jewish Law Students Association peacefully protested the honoring of the Libyan, comparing the selection to a white law school group's honoring a representative of the South African government, members were threatened with violence by some third world students. More important, they were made to feel guilty by some members of the law school and university administrations, who spoke at the conference.

Mayor A. J. Cooper of Pritchard, Alabama, another honored guest, denounced the Jewish Law Students Association and me, as its faculty adviser; then he turned to the Libyan and said, "I believe that what you have to say represents the best for which this nation stands." He was cheered loudly by the audience, as were other speakers who made overtly anti-Jewish statements.

When Jews complain about anti-Semitism or anti-Zionism, they are often made to feel that they are oversensitive. Blacks are expected to speak and react strongly about any manifestation of antiblack attitudes, as well they should. We, too, should feel proud to vigorously defend Jewish rights.

The end result is a psychological sense of defensiveness on the part of Jews for doing what they ought to be doing. Indeed, no Jew should have *had* to speak out on this issue at all. We should have been defended by advocates of human rights who were not Jewish. This should not have been an issue of Jews against others, but that's the way it was perceived.

Over the next several years — almost as if it were on a schedule — third world organizations at Harvard staged an annual spring event that seemed calculated to exacerbate tensions with the Jewish community. The culmination came in the late 1980s when the Black Law Students Association, then under the domination of a radical provocateur named Mohammed Kenyatta, invited a PLO speaker and announced that the organization was "officially" recognizing the Palestine Liberation Organization and embracing its program, which included the destruction of Israel. During the question-and-answer period, Kenyatta explicitly refused to recognize any Jewish questioners, an act for which he was ultimately chastised by the president of the university.

Jewish students were frightened to speak out publicly, though private resentments were obvious. Finally, after a half-dozen provocations, I gave an interview to "CBS Evening News." In it I said: "Every spring at Harvard there is an event . . . where some third world and black communities say this is 'Stick it to the Jews' week.

"They bring a PLO speaker or they bring some other opponent of Jewish values and they conduct an event in which they have very little inherent interest except that it really riles up the Jewish community. And we never see it in reverse.

"It's widely known in the Harvard community. The administration is aware of it and has acknowledged it to me."

I amplified my views in an interview with one of the Harvard newspapers:

> I think that Jewish scapegoating just has to end, and it's about time Jews started fighting back. I feel a responsibility as a faculty member and as a strongly identified Jew to not remain silent in the face of these provocations. I will continue to speak out on them as they occur. I would like to see greater bridges built, because I think Jews and blacks have far more in common than they have differences. But the bridges have to be in both directions.[25]

The response was immediate and angry. This is what the head of the Harvard Black Law Students Association said:

> Dershowitz's comments typify his ignorance of the fact that black and Third World students . . . have recognized the PLO as a legitimate representative of the Palestinian people. His statement, that there's no reason for an alliance between Third World Americans and Palestinians . . . ignores a number of realities, not the least of which [is] that Israel is one of the largest, if not the largest, arms supplier to apartheid South Africa.[26]

Another black leader argued that anti-Israel speakers were necessary to offset the "slanted viewpoint from the national media." Another black student, who was working for me at the time, confided that for at least some of the black students "this flirtation with anti-Zionism is seen as revenge over perceived Jewish opposition to racial quotas."

Despite the criticism over my blunt remarks, they apparently had an effect. The annual cycle of anti-Jewish events ended, and relationships between Jewish and black students at Harvard have improved considerably.

Anti-Jewish speech persists at other colleges and universities, ranging from New York City College to Dartmouth. The student newspaper at the University of Massachusetts ran an op-ed article by a black student leader entitled "The Jewish Race Should Learn." It warned that the Jews, as a race, would be held accountable for Israel's "colonialist" actions. On other campuses a pamphlet began to be widely circulated by Stokely Carmichael's "All African People's Revolutionary Party." It called for the destruction of "racist" Israel and blamed the problems of blacks on "Jewish mercantile capitalism," which controlled "the banks, businesses and financial institutions in [the black community], selling us rotten meat in the corner store, dry rotted clothes and charging high rent for slum buildings."

This pamphlet and others were old-fashioned, primitive anti-Semitism. Sometimes they used the cover of anti-Zionism, but one did not have to scratch too deeply to uncover the anti-Jewish message.

These experiences at Harvard and elsewhere persuaded me that in the world at large, Jews were underdogs to a far greater extent than I had realized in my student days at Yale, when I could not identify with Justice Felix Frankfurter's characterization of Jews as a "vilified and persecuted minority." I was coming to realize that although Jews are not the only group that is despised and condemned throughout the world today, opposition to us is unique in several respects: We are the only group against whom discrimination and hatred has been officially sanctioned by international law. The General Assembly's 1975 resolution equating Zionism with racism is an official invitation to discrimination against Jewish national self-determination — an invitation that has been gladly accepted by many nations and groups around the world. We are also the only group equally despised by the extreme right and left. Every other group, even the racist regime of South Africa, has its supporters on one extreme. But the extremes on both sides of the political spectrum hate the Jews and Israel.

The fact that Jews are condemned from the right and the left is nothing new. Over the years, we have grown accustomed to anti-Jewish propaganda from the extreme right and, more recently, from the extreme left. What is relatively new is the growing acceptability of anti-Jewish bigotry among some intellectuals, university students, and moderate black and third world leaders.

I was slow in realizing how quickly the world was changing. During the first decade of my professional life, I worked on the causes of the downtrodden, the underdog, the unrepresented. But it was always other people's causes: the civil rights struggle, the antiwar movement, the campaign against capital punishment, the litigation for freedom of expression, and the fight for gender equality. My clients and causes were not Jewish. (Indeed, the only client whom I remember as being Jewish was porn star Harry Reems, and he certainly wasn't being prosecuted for doing anything particularly Jewish.) Being a Jewish participant in other people's causes was the most natural feeling in the world. It was expected of us, and we were appreciated for it.

Then, in the 1970s, things began to change, at first imperceptibly and then quite palpably. University campuses are often the bellwether of change, and yet I did not believe that what I was experiencing at Harvard necessarily reflected trends in the outside world. I soon learned from my friends and others that it did, at least to some degree. It was no longer "in" to be Jewish, either at Harvard or outside. Third world causes were meeting with greater receptivity. While antiapartheid rallies were being attended by thousands (including large numbers of Jews), Soviet Jewry rallies attracted only a handful of students, nearly all of them Jewish. Pro-PLO speakers were more popular by far than pro-Israel speakers. Although the lie of Holocaust denial was receiving no legitimacy among established scholars, some schools were welcoming "revisionist" speakers.

By the beginning of the 1980s, my old friends from Brooklyn were enrolling their children — as I was mine — in colleges around the country. I was receiving reports of how difficult it was to be a committed Jew on college campuses from Berkeley to New York City College. Jewish students no longer experienced social exclusion on account of their heritage, but politically involved Jews — those active in Israeli or Soviet Jewry causes — were made to feel as if they were reactionary defenders of colonialism. Jewishness on college campuses was plainly on the defensive.

I felt that the time had come for Harvard to put its considerable prestige behind Jewish values and aspirations, the way it had done, for example, in regard to black and third world concerns. In recent years, Harvard had bestowed honorary degrees on important symbols of other people's aspirations: Bishop Desmond Tutu of South Africa, humanitarian Mother Teresa, civil rights figure Bayard Rustin, jurist Barbara Jordan, and others. I began to urge the powers that be to do the same for Jews. Over a several-year period, I suggested Elie Wiesel, Anatoly Shcharansky, Ida Nudel, Simon Wiesenthal, and others who represented Jewish values, aspirations, and suffering.

The decision to grant this high honor is shrouded in mystery. Discreet campaigns are conducted on behalf of potential honorees, and the decision is ultimately made by a group of about twelve alumni, professors, and members of the governing boards who are handpicked by the seven-man governing corporation. Jewish students and faculty had recommended Jewish heroes, but to no avail. It has been particularly galling that no recent honorees have been singled out in remembrance of the Jewish suffering during the Holocaust. Yet during the same period of time, several German officials — including some who fought for the Nazis — have been honored in various ways.*

To further exacerbate matters, in 1983 Harvard University named a major scholarship program after John J. McCloy, the American high commissioner to Germany after the war, who had pardoned Nazi war criminals and returned confiscated Nazi property to these criminals. McCloy had also played a leading role in the relocation and confinement of 110,000 innocent Japanese Americans during World War II. Moreover, he advised President Franklin Roosevelt to deny refuge to European Jews seeking to escape the Holocaust, and near the end of the war he advised against accepting the pleas of American Jewish leaders to bomb the rail lines leading to the death camps. He played an important role in rescuing Klaus Barbie, the Butcher of Lyon, from French justice. And finally, he presided over one of the most discriminatory law firms in the country.

In light of this history, it is not surprising that many Americans of Jewish and Japanese heritage did not regard John J. McCloy as a man deserving to be honored for his deeds. It is also not surprising that many German industrialists, especially those who did business as usual during the Hitler barbarities, regarded McCloy as some kind of hero.

---

* When Teddy Kollek, the mayor of Jerusalem, was honored in 1984, the university went out of its way not to mention Israel, but rather to focus on the city of Jerusalem as a kind of ecumenical capital whose "precious heritage" Kollek had "preserved."

Accordingly, the Volkswagen Foundation funded the new Harvard program honoring him.

When a number of students complained to me about the McCloy honor, I recommended that they speak to the dean of the John F. Kennedy School of Government, Graham Allison, who had recently acceded to the demands of black and other students to change the name of the library, which had been named after a family who had business interests in South Africa.

When a group of students went to see Allison about the McCloy scholarship, he made them feel — as the students, who left the meeting in tears, told me — "like moral lepers," who "did not understand anything about how the world or Harvard operates."[27]

He told the Jewish students that if they wanted to learn, they should speak to Professor Guido Goldmann — the son of Nahum Goldmann, late president of the World Jewish Congress — who had recommended to the Volkswagen Foundation that the scholarship be named after McCloy, a family friend.

Harvard had covered its Jewish rear by having one of its "house Jews" behind the proposal. During the postwar period, Goldmann's family had close personal, political, and business ties to McCloy. I had experienced this "house Jew" technique early in my years at Harvard. Whenever the university did anything that had the potential for creating tensions with Jewish students or faculty, the administration made sure that it had at least one house Jew on its side. It would then argue that the Jews were divided over the issue.

The house Jew phenomenon transcends Harvard. It is used widely by other institutions — corporate, governmental, social. I saw it first-hand while I worked in the nation's capital. In fact, Arthur Goldberg first alerted me to it. The role was one he adamantly refused to play. He was always an inside advocate for Jewish causes within the administrations he served; but he was never a house Jew who allowed his Jewish identity to be used to justify actions against what he perceived to be the Jewish interest. Goldberg always encouraged me to stand up against Harvard's house Jews.

It is not clear to me whether those who employ this technique realize how offensive it is. I recall receiving a letter once from President Derek Bok, who has generally been very sensitive to Jewish concerns, in which he responded to certain criticisms I had made of Harvard's admissions policies. He ended his letter with the following handwritten postscript: "I do not feel that anti-Semitic policies under

President Lowell provide much of a basis for attacking the current policies of our admissions committee. If you really feel that current policies may simply mask a deeper desire to exclude Jews, I suggest that you pursue this matter further with Al Sacks and Henry Rosovsky." Bok was thus inviting me to air my criticisms with two Jewish deans, who were more institutionally loyal than I was.

It was against this background that my phone began to ring off the hook on June 8, 1987. In that morning's *Boston Globe,* an article appeared under the heading "A Son Who Tries to Explain Away the Sins of His Nazi Father." The thrust of the article, by a Rice University history professor named Francis L. Lowenheim, was that Harvard was about to confer an honorary degree on a man who had actively and continuously attempted to cover up — and lie about — his father's role in Nazi crimes. The honoree was Richard von Weizsäcker, the president of the Federal Republic of Germany. His father, Baron Ernst von Weizsäcker, was convicted of war crimes at Nuremberg and sentenced to seven years' imprisonment. John McCloy had commuted his sentence to one year. The baron had been Hitler's state secretary, a member of the Nazi party and the SS, and on the personal staff of Heinrich Himmler, head of the SS and Gestapo. He was the man who informed Adolf Eichmann, the official in charge of Jewish extermination, that there were no objections on the part of the German foreign ministry to the deportation of thousands of French and stateless Jews to Auschwitz. He was also the man who rejected Sweden's offer to accept Norwegian Jews about to be sent to Nazi death camps, and he refused to intervene on behalf of Catholic priests who were sent to the camps.

The Nazi war criminal's son, President Richard von Weizsäcker, was certainly no conscientious objector to Nazi aggression. He was a soldier who participated in the brutal invasion of Poland, which commenced Hitler's genocidal program. After the war, he helped his father construct a perjurious and unsuccessful defense before the Nuremberg Tribunal, which included the outrageous claim that even the Jews had no "misgivings against Auschwitz." As recently as 1985, Richard von Weizsäcker said, "I really believe that [my father] did not know about the existence of the gas chambers and the systematic mass killing."[28]

But the evidence was overwhelmingly to the contrary. The prosecutor who brought charges against the father has pointed to letters to Eichmann and other documents that prove that "he worked together with the butchers." The prosecutor said that it must have been horrible for the son "discovering all these signatures and letters to Eichmann." But still the son persisted in trying — according to a *New York Times* reporter — to "rehabilitate his family name."[29]

Those who supported the Harvard honor pointed to a speech Weizsäcker gave in 1985 in which he appeared to acknowledge the guilt of his generation. "Who could remain unsuspecting after the burning of the synagogues . . . ? Whoever opened his eyes and ears and sought information could not fail to notice that Jews were being deported. . . . When the unspeakable truth of the Holocaust then became known at the end of the war all too many of us claimed that they had not known anything about it or even suspected anything."[30]

Yet while blaming others he persisted in claiming that his own father — who was no ordinary citizen or even mere Nazi party member — did not know. Perhaps a son should not be condemned for blinding himself to his father's guilt, but neither should he be honored for his mendacity and aided in his ignoble goal to "rehabilitate his family name."

Several of the calls I received that morning came from Holocaust survivors — Baron von Weizsäcker's victims. They did not want the Harvard honor to be understood as helping Richard von Weizsäcker to rehabilitate the deservedly disgraced name of his criminal father.

After reviewing Weizsäcker's record, I wrote him the following letter:

> In your speech to the Bundestag of May 8, 1985, you declared that "anyone who closes his eyes to the past is blind to the present."
>
> Many of us on the Harvard faculty, student body, and community believe that you have closed your eyes to your father's criminal past. We believe that you assisted your father in constructing a perjurious defense at the Nuremberg trials, and continue to deny that he knew of the Holocaust.
>
> A great university should be a place of discourse, not denial. I challenge you, therefore, to debate me about the role *you* have played — and continue to play — in covering up your father's ignoble past.

I received no reply from him, but I did get an immediate response from the Harvard police advising me that the "Secret Service had expressed concern about" any protests and warning me that "if something unexpected happens, they will act in the manner they deem fit." This seemed a bit disproportionate, since I had announced that all I planned to do was hand out a leaflet at the entrance to Harvard Yard. The leaflet, entitled "The Other Side of Richard von Weizsäcker's Honor," described his role in denying his father's guilt and posed a series of questions such as "Do you believe a Harvard honor should be used to help 'rehabilitate' a family name which has been deservedly disgraced by a war criminal?"

At the ceremony itself, when the honor was conferred, Weizsäcker was described as having been born to a "distinguished family." He had succeeded in having Harvard rehabilitate his family name.

Within weeks of receiving the honor, Weizsäcker felt comfortable enough with his past to become the first European head of state to meet with Austrian president Kurt Waldheim, who had just been placed on our Justice Department watch list as a suspected Nazi war criminal. A few years later, Weizsäcker was instrumental in obtaining Dutch pardons for two major Nazi war criminals who had originally been sentenced to die for actively causing the murders of more than ten thousand Jews living in Holland, including Anne Frank. Their sentences were first commuted to life imprisonment, and then they were freed and given a hero's welcome by German compatriots. President Weizsäcker "praised" the Dutch decision, calling it a "humanitarian act."[31]

During the course of my protests, the Harvard administration again turned to its house Jews. They hastily convened a lunch in Weizsäcker's honor at which the Jewish dean of the faculty pointedly presided. Rabbi Ben Zion Gold — the head of Harvard Hillel — wrote a letter to the local Jewish newspaper which not only defended Harvard and Weizsäcker (many of the facts he pointed to had obviously been provided by the administration), but condemned those who were criticizing the honor. He characterized the newspaper articles that had opposed the honor as "gross mischief" and analogized their publication to "throwing a stink bomb into a giant party."[32] You can imagine how I felt reading this from the pen of my own rabbi, whom I admired — and continue to admire — so much. But I have long believed that even rabbis can be wrong. And Rabbi Gold was wrong in condemning critics of the Weizsäcker honor in such inappropriate terms.

Another recent event demonstrates how embarrassed some professors of Jewish background feel about their Jewishness. In the fall of 1989, an official delegation of Soviet prosecutors and judges — several of whom had personally participated in the persecutions of Jewish dissidents — was invited to meet with members of the Harvard Law School faculty. After a few moments of polite casual exchanges, I was called on and asked a question about recent anti-Semitic demonstrations near the Kremlin. I inquired how the authorities were planning to strike a balance between the new freedoms and the old anti-Semitism. The head of the delegation responded by denying that any such demonstrations had taken place. When I gave them the date, the place, and the name of the official who had greeted the anti-Semitic organization Pamyat, one of my colleagues — a man of Jewish background — interrupted and tried to apologize for my rudeness in asking so divisive a question. He made it clear that he wanted to disassociate himself from my "agenda." The Soviet delegate then went back to explaining why "Zionism is a form of racism."

In a subsequent memo to the faculty, I suggested an analogy to a meeting with law enforcement officials from South Africa, and I wondered whether a faculty member would feel comfortable trying to stop a black colleague from asking a hard question about apartheid.

Jewish life at Harvard remains vibrant despite subtle efforts by some house Jews to impose a *sh'a shtill* (keep quiet) mentality when it comes to criticizing our "benefactors." It is easier these days than it was in earlier generations to be a Jewish Harvard student or professor. There is no overt anti-Semitism. Nor are there explicit Jewish ceilings on admission or faculty appointments — though being Jewish is still a relative disadvantage. It is somewhat more challenging to be a Jewish Jew who happens to be at Harvard, though that, too, is easier than when I arrived in Cambridge a quarter-century ago. I feel perfectly comfortable with my Jewishness at Harvard, because I refuse to feel or act like a guest in someone else's world, as some of my Jewish colleagues still do. I guess I'm fortunate in not viewing Harvard's beneficence toward Jews as a one-way street. Jewish students and professors have become an important part of Harvard's greatness, just as Jewish citizens have become an important part of America's greatness. We must insist on being treated as first-class members of every institution we belong to, whether it be the nation, our workplace, or our social clubs. We have earned that status, and we endanger it every time we allow ourselves to be treated as anything less.

Going on Television

The Pervasiveness
of Anti-Jewish Attitudes

DURING my first decade at Harvard, I devoted my professional
life primarily to my scholarly work — teaching and writing articles,
textbooks, and reviews. Over the past decade or so, however, I have
become involved in high-visibility legal cases and have appeared more
frequently in the media. These public appearances have exposed me to
an underside of American life that few Jews ever experience.

Every time I appear on television or in the press, I get letters by the
dozens. Most respond to the subject matter of my appearance. But in
every batch of mail, there are sure to be at least a few overtly anti-
Semitic missives. Some of them are from the "regulars": professional
anti-Semites who seem to spend their pathetic days writing anonymous poison-pen letters. I can recognize them from their handwriting,
their postmark, or a pet phrase. Some are from nuts, the kind who see
the entire world through paranoid lenses. The most disturbing ones
come from apparently normal Americans who truly seem to believe
that Jews are the personification of evil. A considerable number of
these letter writers proudly sign their names and give their addresses.

The most remarkable aspect of my anti-Semitic mail is that it is
rarely stimulated by the content of my remarks. It is generated by the
very fact that I have appeared on television or radio or in print.
Regardless of the subject, these correspondents manage to see a Jewish
angle. If I am defending the right of free speech, it is because "Jews
are loudmouths" or because "Yids run the pornography business." If I
am speaking about racial equality, it is because "kikes are nigger-
lovers." If I am representing an indigent defendant without any fee, it

is because "Bolshevik equality is a Jewish idea." If I am representing a wealthy defendant for a large fee, it is because "Jews are money-hungry capitalists." If my topic is criminal justice, it is because "Jews are against the right of real Americans to own guns" or because "you Jews are a bunch of fag-loving liberals." When I spoke out against our involvement in Vietnam it was because "yellow-bellied Jew cowards don't like to fight for America," or because "Jews take their orders from the Kremlin."

Very few decent Americans ever read or hear what overtly anti-Jewish Americans think about "the Jews." When I showed some of these letters to my Brooklyn friends, they were shocked; they had absolutely no conception that the feelings reflected persist among some elements of the American public. My friends urged me to share some representative samplings of my correspondence with the readers of this book. Here are some recent letters:*

> Every time I see you on national TV for the past 15 years . . . espousing your ultra-liberal views on the death penalty, abortion, civil rights — which rend the social fabric of this nation, I better understand the social conditions which caused Hitler to eradicate the virus which infected Germany in the 1930s.
>
> The bug has been assimilated into the life blood of America: Jews in the very top positions of government: the F.D.I.C., The Bureau of Labor Statistics, the federal judiciary, the porn entertainment industry — Hollywood, the TV industry — all three networks, etc.
>
> With all your vast pseudo-sophistication and erudition, have you got the guts to read this letter to your classes at Harvard?
>
> I thought not, *kyke*.†
>
> > Yours truly,
> > William Orr
> > Slidell, Louisiana

After an appearance on "Nightline," I received the following letter:

> From watching you over a period of time on Nightline with Ted Kopple [*sic*] is was my opinion and conclusion that you are a commie assed pinko . . . Shyster.
>
> You should be tarred and feathered and tied to an ox cart to be

---

* I cannot vouch for the fact that the signatures on the letters cited in this chapter are those of the actual letter writers, but these are the names that appear on the letters received.
† I did.

kicked and stomped and spit on while you are draged down to the port docks to be deported back to soviet Russia. . . . I hope somebody spits chew tobacco in your face while you are laying in the gutter dieing from Aids.

> Yours for 100% Americanism,
> Theodore W. Bradshaw
> Sequim, Washington

Another "Nightline" appearance stimulated one viewer to complain that "you and your ilk are brutally self-centered Jewish fanatics with no concern for the plight of other people. . . . Your race has paid a heavy price in the past for this maniacal ethnocenterism. . . . The enormous cunning etched in your repulsive eyes, the primordial symptoms of a Jew."

Following an appearance on the "Morton Downey Show," I received a long neatly typed letter that concluded: "Perhaps you people have a genetic deficit from too much interbreeding. . . . The shit is going to start to hit the fan."

After a discussion of church envoy Terry Waite's capture by terrorists in the Mideast, this was a signed letter sent to me by George T. Shaheen:

> If you "Jews" are such honorable people, *"WHY"* were six million of you fed into the "ovens"???????
>
> Alan, let me predict a calculated fact. *Much Before* the end of this century, a "holocaust" will take place in A-M-E-R-I*K-A The like of which will make "Hitler" appear as innocent as a little "altar" boy during Mass!

When I appeared with former New York mayor Ed Koch on a show moderated by Ted Koppel discussing drugs, this was one response: "Just a reminder, this is the United States of America — This show has been devoted to the propaganda interests of a foreign power. . . . No one will accuse you of *dual* loyalty — it is obvious where your loyalty lies."

A discussion of capital punishment led one fan to comment:

> I don't want to support even half the prison population in this country and wish to fuck they were executed tomorrow morning. Ever thought of relocating in Israel? I'd pay your passage for Christs sake. While your leaving could you take half the Mexicans and niggers out with you? . . .

An appearance on the Phil Donahue show provoked this postscript to a letter about legalized prostitution: "You give Jews a bad name, as if Jews aren't hated enough."

A TV appearance about the Claus von Bülow case generated this thoughtful response from a Boston woman named Mrs. J. M. Ransfor:

> My brother — a Harvard Grad — is a famous judge in another State and he says he is appalled at the quality of the lawyers now being turned out at Harvard. I work for a very prestigious law firm & all the men are laughing at you. You are simply a kike jew from the Bronx. . . .

A *New York Times* op-ed article led to the following: "Sadly, you people are asking for another pogrom, for you are increasingly behaving as the Jews of Germany did. You are all vile and will deserve whatever pogrom overtakes you."

A four-page letter written jointly to me and Congressman Barney Frank of Massachusetts by Roger M. Rush of Portland, Maine, included these words:

> There are no people on the face of the earth more racist, more Nazi (Nationalist) more bigoted than these so-called Jews who "absorbed" the name Israel.
>
> It was pseudo Jews who formed the N.A.A.C.P. and all other hate groups to stir up trouble between the blacks and whites. The reason we don't find out the truth about AIDS is because so many pseudo Jews have it and there are so many queers in government.
>
> The United Nations was right on the button when they said that Zionism is Racism. The Jews financed Adolph Hitler as a means of getting the pseudo Jews as "God's chosen people" (bunch of shit) to return to Israel. . . .
>
> Jewish elements provide the driving power for both Capitalism and Communism. . . .

One common theme seems to be that since I am merely "a guest" in someone else's country, I should not be telling the host "how to run his house." An article I wrote about the rights of nonsmokers provoked this: "I hope you do realize Mr. Dershowitz that We the original Americans were here a wee bit before the 12 inch hot dog and 1 inch high constitutional experts who hawk their oskar meyer's." A recent letter expressed a similar thought somewhat differently:

After our fore-fathers had founded a Protestant Christian Republic and established a thriving economy, the Jewish immigrants came to the United States, to get in on the gravy train. . . . The Jews have roamed the earth for 2000 years, to all nations of the world. In most of these nations they were not welcome (as far as I am concerned they are not welcome here, that makes me anti-Semitic, to hell with the Jews). . . . I do not know what the rest of the American people are going to do, but I am not going to take it without a fight. . . . The Jews are Communist. They are the sons of Satan. The Jews are a mixed conglomeration of Asiatic *Pagan* races, of mixed bloods, breeds, reared on the Jewish Talmud written 2500 years ago. This letter was written after 20 years of research.

> Yours in Christ,
> John M. Rector
> Tulia, Texas

A letter postmarked Skokie, Illinois (with the words "Jew Haven" added), closed with the demand that Jews "should all go back to the African Jungle and bring your Black brothers. Who needs you crooks? Madmen. . . . Jew kids are mostly nuts. . . . Yiddish lies!! Kill! Kill! Kill! Money! Money! Money! (Other peoples). Greed! Greed! Greed! Busy bodying in others affairs!" It was signed "anti-Semetic."

One diatribe ended with this wish: "Do I wish I could make you experience the Nazi period in Europe, how do I wish."

My involvement as defense counsel for Jonathan Pollard, accused of spying for Israel, provoked this gem:

Many of us who only acknowledge loyalty to the United States alone finally have the smoking gun proving where you are coming from. It is not news to me because I have been on to you for some time now. But your intervention in the case of traitor Pollard and his conspirator wife puts the final stamp on you for all Americans to now see.

Another letter complained about the influx of Soviet Jews into America:

Further, you want to bring all the Russian Jews here — send them to Israel. Give us Palestinians & Arabs; they become loyal Americans & would fight (combat is not a word familiar to American Jews) for this country. . . .

Shoving that Holocaust down our throats so we won't dare be "anti-

Semetic." Let me tell you, young man, among most Americans it is
perfectly OK — just like being anti communist, equals pro American. . . .

A newspaper column in which I pointed out that the anti-Jewish
views expressed by conservative columnist Patrick Buchanan were not
reflective of mainstream America provoked a flurry of responses. The
first was this:

> Hymie!
> Why do you think [Buchanan's] views are not American Main-
> stream? I know many many people like myself even tho Catholic, hate
> all niggers and jews. We are a silent majority. All you have is the press,
> congress and money. We are ex-democrats and 100% for the Arabs.
> Your people and the niggers are the butt of all our jokes.

Of all the letters I have received — and the anti-Semitic ones now
number in the thousands — the correspondence that disturbs me most
comes from frightened Jews. I recall one particularly poignant letter
from an elderly couple who had survived the Holocaust. It was written
in a combination of broken English and Yiddish and it urged me to
please "stay off television" because "most Americans don't like what
you say," and they will "make another Holocaust" if they don't like the
Jews. The couple made it clear that they agreed with most of what I
was saying, but their opinion didn't "count," only "they" — the non-
Jews — counted. And "they see you as a Jew," and unless "they" liked
what I was saying "it will be bad for the rest of the Jews." So either
"change what you are saying" or "stop being on television." The letter
writers were very respectful — and very frightened.

These letters make it crystal clear that some Americans see me first
as a Jew, regardless of what I happen to be saying. My face, my name,
my attitudes, all have Jew written on them. Regardless of the lyrics,
the music is Jewish. I don't know that I object to this perception. I *am*
very Jewish, and I'm proud of it. Obviously I am appalled that my
anti-Semitic correspondents are so hateful and wrongheaded about
Jews and Jewish values. But they are entitled to view me as a Jew, and
to conclude that my ideas do derive, at least in part, from my Jewish
heritage.

What obligations do these realities impose on me as a Jewish American who speaks out frequently on a wide range of public issues?

Surely on the one hand I cannot accept the *sh'a shtill* attitude of my grandmother's generation — the fear that any Jewish visibility will inevitably create resentment and anti-Semitism. Not that my grandmother was wrong, as a matter of fact. Visibility does indeed enhance some of the existing resentment. So does Jewish success, and indeed Jewish survival. For some, the very idea that the Jews, who did not accept Jesus as the Messiah, can continue to thrive, is a rejection of their theology. For others, even without a theology, Jewish success — particularly when it is seen as out of proportion to our numbers — is a gnawing discomfort.

I recall a question following a speech I once gave in Los Angeles, in which a woman who identified herself as Jewish asked whether she should stop her daughter from applying to Harvard. She wondered whether the large number of Jews in elite universities didn't foster anti-Semitism. I responded that anti-Semitism thrives best *in the absence* of Jews. I pointed to the places with the most virulent anti-Semitism: Poland, the Ukraine, Arab countries, and now even Japan. Anti-Semitism prevails in these places without there even being significant numbers of Jews. I told her that the postmarks on my own anti-Semitic mail come primarily from small, rural towns with few or no Jews, and from members of insular groups that have little or no contact with Jews. Then I pointed to Harvard itself, which was far more anti-Semitic before the Jews arrived than it is now that potential anti-Semites have the opportunity to meet and interact with real people who are Jewish.

I related the story of a slightly eccentric Brahmin woman from Boston who came to see me about a legal problem. I concluded that her problem was not within the area of my expertise, so I recommended another lawyer. She asked whether he was Jewish, and I responded, "What difference does that make?" She said that she didn't "get along very well with Jews" and didn't know whether she could "trust them." I asked her why she had come to me, since I was obviously Jewish. I'll never forget her answer: "The Jews *I know* are all fine. I have a Jewish doctor and a Jewish pharmacist whom I trust with my life. It's those other Jews — the money-grubbing ones, the dishonest ones — that I'm not comfortable with."

I pressed the Brahmin woman about whether she had actually ever encountered one of "those" Jews, and she responded, "Heavens, no. I would never allow myself to have any contact with such a person." The lawyer I recommended happened to be Jewish, and the two of them got along famously.

The best antidote to anti-Semitism is Jews. The more the better, since the smaller any sampling, the greater the likelihood of a statistical anomaly that might appear to confirm the stereotype, such as President Lowell's infamous accusation that 50 percent of Harvard library thefts had been perpetrated by Jewish students.

To be sure, the actions of some individual Jews may well engender anti-Semitism in bigots who are predisposed to generalize about an entire people from one individual. But positive actions are as likely to provoke such bigotry as negative ones. Indeed, it is probably fair to say that Hank Greenberg's quest for Babe Ruth's home run record back in the 1930s provoked as much anti-Semitism as Bugsy Siegel's control over Las Vegas; that Henry Kissinger's domination over American foreign policy during the early 1970s — for better or worse — generated as much anti-Semitism as Rabbi Bernard Bergman's nursing home "scandal"; that Barry Goldwater's run for president — even though he was only partly Jewish by background* — generated as much anti-Semitism as Stanley Friedman's corruption conviction in New York; that Israel's spectacular victories in the Six-Day and Yom Kippur wars resulted in as much anti-Semitism as its later failures in Lebanon and on the West Bank.

Indeed, American Jewish success as a whole — as manifested by "disproportionate" Jewish representation in the media, academia, Congress, business, and other high-visibility occupations (excluding sports, at least as players)† — has plainly contributed to resentment by some. And Jewish failure is welcomed, even gloated over, by those who resent our success.

The important point is that *Jews* are not to blame for anti-Semitism. Anti-Semitism is the problem of the bigots who feel, express, and practice it. Nothing *we* do can profoundly affect the twisted mind of the anti-Semite. We should never take — or refrain from taking — any action just because of its anticipated impact on anti-Semites.

Getting back to the woman's question about whether she should

---

* I have noticed that Jews have an interesting way of dealing with what one of my sons calls fractional Jews. When a person whose father was Jewish but whose mother was not, does *good*, we quickly claim him as a half Jew; but when such a person does *bad* we quickly point out that there is no such thing as a half Jew, and that because the malefactor's mother was not Jewish, he is not Jewish. When a person with a Jewish mother and non-Jewish father does *bad*, we are quick to point out, however, that he is only half Jewish.

† A friend of mine who is a sports agent recently told me that Bar Mitzvah is the age when a Jewish boy realizes that his chances of playing on a major league sports team are considerably less than his chances of owning one.

keep her daughter from applying to Harvard, I told her that once a Jew forbears from seeking maximum success in order to placate the anti-Semite, he accepts second-class status and rewards the anti-Semite for his bigotry.

When I told my Brooklyn friends about the California woman's question, they could not identify with it. Our generation of Jews had been brought up with the need to succeed — to show "them" that we were as good as they were. Perhaps our attitude also reflected a subtle self-perception that we were starting out as second-class citizens. But at least it placed no limits on our aspirations. It recognized the reality of anti-Semitism without accepting its legitimacy and intractability.

In order to know how to react to the ever-present reality of anti-Semitism, it is important to place the problem in its historic perspective. Without this history, it is impossible to comprehend the largely irrational nature of the phenomenon.

Felix Frankfurter's characterization of the Jews as "the most vilified and persecuted minority in history" may or may not be accurate. Comparative assessments of vilification and persecution are not testable by any scientific standards. But no objective observer can doubt that the Jewish people *have* been vilified and persecuted over millennia.

During the Old Testament period, anti-Jewish attitudes and actions were primarily a function of traditional tribal antagonisms. But even back then, there were instances of specifically anti-Jewish attitudes and actions by such tyrants as Antiochus Sidetes, Haman, and other biblical villains, who invoked negative stereotypes of Jewish "uncleanliness," "disloyalty," and "separateness."

Until the advent of Christianity, however, there was no ideological justification for singling out Jews for special vilification and persecution. The Gospels, especially Matthew and John, contain the theological basis for Christian anti-Jewish doctrine. According to Matthew, the Jews admit their collective guilt for the killing of Christ: "Then answered all the People and said, His blood be on us, and on our children." And John declares that the Jews are the personification of evil: "Ye are of your father the devil, and your will is to do your father's desires." Moreover, the Jews, by rejecting the true religion, had broken their covenant with God. Jewish punishment and failure were thus as much a fulfillment of biblical prophecy as were Christian reward and success. Such punishment and failure had to be collective as well as individual. The Jewish nation could never again be restored, at least not until its members accepted the true faith. The sons and daughters of the devil were destined to wander the earth, nationless, despised, destitute, and powerless.

When Christianity became the official religion of the Roman Empire in the fourth century, the church achieved the political power to assure that its prophecy of Jewish failure was fulfilled. Jews were excluded from positions of influence, and their rights — political, economic, social, and religious — were taken away. It became a civic virtue, as well as a religious obligation, to contribute to the vilification of the Jews. Thus, theological anti-Judaism devolved into more generalized economic, political, and social stigmatization and discrimination against Jews. The Code of Justinian, enacted in 534 A.D., curtailed Jewish freedom of worship, banned Jews from holding public office, and divested them of most property rights.

These civic deprivations and discriminations spread throughout Europe during the Middle Ages. Wherever Jews wandered throughout Christendom, they were burdened with theological and civil discrimination and vilification. They were segregated into ghettos, disqualified from engaging in "Christian" occupations, denied the right to work the land, and forced into trades and professions that were perceived as exploitative.

During the second millennium of Christianity, Jews were also massacred in large numbers by religious crusaders and inquisitors purporting to act in the name of their God. In 1096, French and German Jews were subjected to mass murder by the first Crusaders, men who have been glorified in literature, art, and history. It has always amazed me that some decent Christians still honor the memory of these genocidal killers of women, babies, and men — mass murderers who provided a precedent for the Holocaust. In my own state of Massachusetts, Holy Cross University calls its athletic teams the Crusaders. That seems about as sensitive as if a Lutheran university were to name its football team the Storm Troopers. At least, to my knowledge, no college has glorified the Inquisitors.

The Crusades were followed by outbreaks of religiously inspired mass murder against the Jews for several centuries. The period of the Black Death, during the middle of the fourteenth century, led to the scapegoating of the Jews for the epidemic and the destruction of more than two hundred Jewish communities throughout Europe. The Spanish Inquisition, at the end of the fifteenth century, marked the expulsion of Jews from Spain and the movement of Jews eastward toward Poland, the Ukraine, and Russia. Jews were similarly expelled from other Christian nations — for example, England in 1290, France in 1306, Austria in 1421, and Portugal in 1497.

The Middle Ages also witnessed the development of one of the most persistent and pernicious historical lies in the history of Christianity, namely the "blood libel." The blood libel was a clerical invention charging the Jews with murdering Christian children in order to use their blood for religious rituals. Although its origins are shrouded in obscurity, it seems to have been strengthened by a corruption of a tenet that emerged from the Fourth Lateran Council (1215), in which the eucharistic doctrine of transubstantiation — the bread and wine of the eucharist as Christ's body and blood — was formulated. Jews were occasionally accused of stealing a consecrated host and subjecting it to mistreatment. The Fourth Lateran Council also enacted a canon requiring Jews to wear a distinguishing badge — a precedent for the yellow star of Nazism.

The blood libel was preached from the pulpit, written in holy books, and passed down from generation to generation. It provoked — and justified — religious pogroms from as early as 1298, when an estimated 100,000 Jews were murdered in Germany and Austria, and has persisted into the twentieth century.

In 1876, a leading Russian writer wrote a pamphlet "concerning the use of Christian blood by Jewish sects for religious purposes."[1] This pamphlet was quite popular in czarist Russia and was reprinted numerous times. Between 1911 and 1913, a Jewish superintendent of a brick kiln in Kiev stood charged with murdering a twelve-year-old Christian boy in order to use his blood in a religious ritual. Although the evidence was overwhelming that a gang of thieves had committed the murder, the Jew — Menachem Mendel Beilis — was framed by the anti-Semitic minister of justice and charged with the crime. The trial became an international event (and eventually the subject of Bernard Malamud's prize-winning novel *The Fixer*). Among the prosecution witnesses was a Catholic priest named Father Justin Paranaitis, who swore that the murder of the boy bore all the hallmarks of a ritual killing as required by Jewish tradition. His testimony was refuted by several experts on Jewish law, who testified that there was absolutely no basis in Jewish sources for the use of Christian blood in ritual. The jury, composed of local Christian peasants, unanimously acquitted Beilis.

But even this trial did not put an end to the blood libel. Hitler used it extensively in his propaganda campaign against the Jews. Esteemed German scientists lent their credibility to the preposterous claim in a special issue of *Der Stürmer* published in 1934, and in articles published thereafter.

Even after World War II, the bishop of Lublin, Stefan Wyszynski — soon to become Primate of all Poland and a cardinal of the Catholic church — declared that it was still "undetermined" whether Jews engaged in "ritual murder" of Christians. He claimed to have studied the testimony in the Beilis trial and said he was still left in doubt about the truth.[2] Bishop Wyszynski's agnosticism over the blood libel followed the 1946 Kielce pogrom in which more than forty Jews were murdered by Polish Christians amidst rumors of a bloodletting by Jews against a Christian youngster.

One great Jewish writer, Achad Ha-Am, who was born in the Ukraine in 1856, found ironic consolation in the persistence of the blood libel throughout history. He argued, with a touch of cynicism, that even the acceptance of an idea by the entire world "does not make us doubt whether all the world can be wrong and we right." He used the blood libel to explain Jewish unwillingness to bow to the pressure of consensus — Jewish stiff-neckedness. "But, you ask, is it possible that everybody can be wrong, and the Jews right? Yes, it is possible: the blood accusation proves it possible. Here, you see, the Jews are right and perfectly innocent."[3]

If it is true that there is, in fact, a Jewish quality of stiff-neckedness, and if it is also true that some of this quality derives from false charges that have been leveled against us throughout history, then we may be observing an interesting and more general phenomenon at work. Christian theology has generated certain attitudes and actions against Jews. These in turn have generated certain responses by Jews. The responses then confirm the original prejudices. In the context of the blood libel, it operates in the way that Achad Ha-Am suggested: Christians falsely accuse Jews of murdering Christian children for blood. The Jews persist in denying the false charges and come to understand that just because the whole world believes an idea, that does not make it true. This skepticism and obdurateness become a generalized quality among some Jews and leads many non-Jews to dislike them because they are so stubborn and aloof.

In other contexts, the phenomenon is even more apparent. Christian discrimination disqualifies Jews from certain occupations, thus relegating them to "non-Christian" work, such as moneylending and commerce. Jews are then despised because they are moneylenders and tradesmen, rather than "productive" citizens who work the land. Shakespeare captured this phenomenon brilliantly in his portrayal of the Jew Shylock and the Christian reactions to his occupation and attitudes.

Christian theology forces Jews to live apart from true believers and to wear identifying marks. Jews are then condemned for their aloofness and separateness. Christian theology denies Jews the right to their own homeland, and expels them from nation after nation. Jews are then condemned as rootless wanderers, who sap the national wealth of their host nations.

In the course of a debate in the British House of Commons in 1833 over whether the Jews should have their legal and political disabilities removed by law, two great parliamentarians, Robert Peel and Thomas B. Macaulay, referred to this phenomenon. Historian Macaulay put it this way:

> We treat them as slaves, and wonder why they do not regard us as brethren. We drive them to mean occupations, and then reproach them for not embracing honorable professions. We long forbade them to possess land; and we complain that they chiefly occupy themselves in trade. . . . During many ages we have, in all our dealings with them, abused our immense superiority of force; and then we are disgusted because they have recourse to that cunning which is the natural and universal defense of the weak against the violence of the strong.

Arguing that "bigotry will never want a pretense," Macaulay then went on to praise the history of the Jewish people:

> In the infancy of civilization, when our island was as savage as New Guinea, when letters and arts were still unknown to Athens, when scarcely a thatched hut stood on what was afterwards the site of Rome, this condemned people had their fenced cities and cedar palaces, their splendid temple, . . . their schools of sacred learning, their great statesmen and soldiers, their natural philosophers, their historians and their poets.

Macaulay implored his fellow Parliamentarians to consider whether "if, while excluded from the blessings of the law, and bowed down under the yoke of slavery, they have contracted some of the vices of outlaws and slaves, shall we consider this as a matter of reproach to *them?* Shall we not rather consider it as a matter of shame and remorse to *ourselves?*"[4]

The arguments of Peel and Macaulay prevailed over the anti-Semitic bigotry invoked by other "honorable members," who had proposed that the Jews are "naturally a mean race" and that it "has been prophesied that the Jews are to be wanderers on the face of the earth, and that they are not to mix on terms of equality with the people of the countries in which they sojourn."[5] Parliament finally removed all legal disabilities against the Jews and granted them full equality under the law.

Perhaps the best example of this circular phenomenon can be found in the writings of Martin Luther, the father of the Protestant Reformation. Ironically, Luther began his career as a reformer by praising the Jews and condemning the "passion preachers [who] do nothing else but exaggerate the Jews' misdeeds against Christ and thus embitter the hearts of the faithful against them." But after his efforts to convert the Jews failed, he began to attack them as "the stiff-necked Jews, iron-hearted and stubborn as the devil." As he grew older his attacks became more vicious. He dehumanized the Jews by referring to them as "disgusting vermin," as well as "venomous and virulent." Toward the end of his life — and at the height of his influence — Luther articulated a specific program against the Jews which served as a bible of anti-Jewish actions over the next four centuries, culminating in the Holocaust.[6]

In many ways, Luther can be viewed as the spiritual predecessor of Adolf Hitler. Indeed, virtually all the themes that eventually found their way into Hitler's genocidal writings, rantings, and actions are adumbrated in Martin Luther's infamous essay "Concerning the Jews and Their Lies," written in 1542. Here are some excerpts (emphasis added):

First, *their synagogues or churches should be set on fire. . . .*

Secondly, *their homes should likewise be broken down and destroyed. They ought to be put under one roof or in a stable, like Gypsies,* in order that they may realize that they are not masters in our land, as they boast, but miserable captives. . . .

Thirdly, they should be *deprived of their prayerbooks and Talmuds* in which such idolatry, lies, cursing, and blasphemy are taught.

Fourthly, *their rabbis must be forbidden under threat of death to teach* any more. . . .

Fifthly, *passport and traveling privileges should be absolutely forbidden* to the Jews.

Sixthly, they ought to be stopped from usury. All their *cash and valuables of silver and gold ought to be taken from them* and put aside for safekeeping. For this reason, as said before, everything that they possess they stole and robbed from us through their usury, for they have no other means of support. . . .

Seventhly, let the *young and strong Jews and Jewesses be given the flail, the ax, the hoe, the spade, the distaff, and spindle.* . . .[7]

It is remarkable — though probably not coincidental — that Hitler followed Luther's blueprint so closely, from the concentration of Jews and Gypsies, to the denial of passports for Jews, to the creation of forced work camps for "young and strong Jews."

Nor did Luther engage merely in rhetoric. He successfully urged actions against the Jewish populations in various parts of Germany. Luther's anti-Jewish actions earned him the epithet Lo-Tahor, the Hebrew term for "unclean," which is also a play on the German pronunciation of his name.

Though many Protestant sects have renounced Luther's anti-Jewish writings, they are still widely published and are included in neo-Nazi catalogs alongside the writings of Hitler, Goebbels, and contemporary Holocaust-deniers. It is shocking that Luther's ignoble name is still honored rather than forever cursed by mainstream Protestant churches. The continued honoring of Luther conveys a dangerous message, a message that was not lost on Hitler: namely, that a person's other accomplishments will earn him a position of respect in history, even if he has called for the destruction of world Jewry. (This justification is frequently offered today in defense of Black Muslim leader Louis Farrakhan.)

By the sixteenth century, the time of the Reformation, the negative stereotype of the Jew had become firmly established in Christian theology. Religiously based prejudice had relegated the European Jew to the status of pariah. Jews were excluded from certain forms of livelihood, from certain geographical areas, from most governmental positions.

Because these exclusions were generally not total, a few industrious Jews managed to overcome the barriers. Some excelled at the trades in which they were permitted to engage, especially banking, commerce, and the professions, building networks throughout Europe. Because it was so much harder for Jews to secure admission into universities, those few who were admitted tended to do better than the average. Because Jews were discriminated against in the civil service, those who managed to enter government were likely to be more talented than the run-of-the-mill incumbents.

The opposite side of this coin was far less shiny. Because of these same barriers, the vast majority of Jews were denied educational and occupational opportunities. These Jews were relegated to the most undesirable work and living situations.

The result was an entirely unnatural dichotomy within the Jewish communities of Europe. Jews would overachieve in small but visible numbers; and they would underachieve in large and also visible numbers.*

This historically imposed dichotomy led to the classic motifs of European anti-Jewish bigotry. The Jews were looked down on because they did not work the land or produce wealth. At the same time, they were seen as part of an international conspiracy of wealth and power. The poorest Ukrainian *shtetl* dweller was in league with the financial dynasties of the Rothschilds and Oppenheimers. This bizarre combination of powerlessness and power — of being both looked down at with disdain and looked up to with envy — produced the literature and actions of classic anti-Jewish bigotry: the mockery of the bearded *shtetl* Jew and the fear of the moneyed cosmopolitan Jew. The most obvious manifestations of classic anti-Semitism were the ghetto and the pogrom; its most deadly extensions were the concentration camps and the Holocaust.

The conspiracy theory of Judaism was given considerable impetus by the publication of various forgeries, culminating in the issuing by the czarist police of *The Protocols of the Elders of Zion* in 1903. Earlier versions were published in France and seem to have been based on a novel written in the 1860s. The common theme of these fictional works is that a group of Jewish elders met to plan the destruction of the gentile world and its replacement by a Jewish empire. The *Protocols* purported to be an actual transcript of two dozen secret meetings of these elders. It was circulated throughout Europe after the Russian Revolution as a truthful account of the Jewish conspiracy, and con-

---

* This absence of "normalcy" was acutely perceived by journalist and Zionist Theodor Herzl, and its elimination became one of his most powerful arguments for a Jewish state in which Jews would engage in every occupation.

tributed greatly to the development of political anti-Semitism in the early twentieth century.

The term "anti-Semitism" — which is the current all-inclusive nomenclature for the wide variety of anti-Jewish attitudes and expressions — is of relatively recent vintage and served a particular historic role in the transition from a theologically based bigotry to a more nationalistically premised form of racism. "Anti-Semitism" was coined not by Jews, as a term of censure against those who practiced this form of bigotry, but rather by those who approved of anti-Jewish attitudes, as a term of pride. Wilhelm Marr, a German racist politician, is "credited" with coining the term. He established the "Anti-Semitism League" in 1879. The term quickly caught on, though it did not aptly capture the essence of the bigotry or its religious origins.

The new term "anti-Semitism" did, however, correspond to a relatively new development in European politics: namely, the phenomenon of anti-Jewish political parties in Germany, France, Austria, Hungary, Poland, Romania, and Russia. "Christian-Social," "Catholic People's Party," "Christian Democratic Movement," and "United Christians" became euphemisms for "no Jews allowed," and "anti-Jewish platforms." Though these parties retained, through their pseudo-religious names, a tie to their religiously bigoted predecessors, their anti-Jewish programs were based more on notions of nationalism, ethnicity, and *volk*. Other parties took on even more specifically programmatic names, such as Anti-Semitic People's Party, French National Anti-Semitic League, Universal Anti-Semitic League, and National Anti-Jewish Party.

These overtly anti-Semitic parties played an important role in European politics for approximately seventy years, beginning in the 1870s and ending with the destruction of the Third Reich. They preached a more "racial," "biological," and "nationalistic" brand of anti-Jewish bigotry — Jewish racial enmity — than did their religiously driven predecessors. The Enlightenment had made theological anti-Judaism somewhat anachronistic. But there was still a large residue of anti-Jewish feeling in search of a justification or theory. The new, more racial anti-Semitism provided that. In at least one respect the racial bigotry was even worse than the theologically based vilification: Jewish racial inferiority was deemed to be inherent and not subject to change through religious conversion or assimilation.

In the waning years of the nineteenth century, the trial and conviction of Alfred Dreyfus on espionage charges contributed to the strength of the new anti-Semitic parties, especially in France. There is no doubt now that Alfred Dreyfus was, in fact, framed for a crime committed by someone else. But at the time, there was a widespread belief that the Jewish colonel had betrayed his native France and that his betrayal was typical of Jews' disloyalty to their host nations. The Dreyfus Affair is a sordid tale of judicial corruption at the highest levels. Such injustice could not have been accomplished without the active complicity of the military, the prosecution, the judiciary, and others within the government. Nor could it have prevailed for so long without the acquiescence of the mainstream press, many intellectuals and large elements of the populace, and the French Catholic church.

In the beginning, the evidence of Dreyfus's guilt seemed overwhelming, consisting largely of documents written in a hand bearing some resemblance to his. The fact that Dreyfus was Jewish made him the perfect suspect at a time of rampant anti-Semitism, especially in the French military. Though the evidence was questioned by some within the general staff, the honor of the military was at stake. Accordingly, a secret file — far more persuasive than the public file — was assembled and clandestinely turned over to the court-martial. The secret file included a damning document purportedly written by Dreyfus. But unbeknownst to the court-martial, that document was a forgery.

Dreyfus was found guilty in 1894 and was sentenced to Devil's Island. But a devoted brother, a few skeptical journalists, and a handful of honest military men kept the case alive, even as its victim barely survived. Over the years, the truth slowly came to light and the prosecution's case began to crumble. However, not until 1906 was public opinion turned around and Dreyfus vindicated, officially declared innocent, and restored to his rank in the army.

For Jews throughout the world the Dreyfus case and its accompanying anti-Semitic hysteria constituted a turning point. The seeds of Hitler's Holocaust could be sensed in the French cries for "extermination" of the Jewish "parasites." A military physician proposed "vivisection of Jews rather than harmless rabbits," and there were calls for "all the kikes and kikettes and their kiddy-kikes [to be placed] in glass furnaces."[8] It was while covering the Dreyfus Affair that Theodor Herzl, then a young Viennese journalist, was stimulated to write a pamphlet called *The Jewish State* (1896). He gave voice to an idea that became known as political Zionism and led to the establishment of Israel some fifty years later.

Though weakened by Dreyfus's pardon, the anti-Semitic movement in Western Europe remained an influential minority constituency to be reckoned with until Adolf Hitler came to power. At that point, the dynamics of anti-Semitism changed dramatically. The forces of Nazism had a receptive audience for their genocidal anti-Semitism, an audience that had been exposed to a steady diet of Christian anti-Jewish theology for nearly two millennia and then to racial anti-Semitism for half a century.

Christian anti-Jewish attitudes are explainable, even if incompletely, by the historical developments outlined above. But how does one explain anti-Jewish attitudes expressed by non-Christians, indeed often by anti-Christians, particularly leftists? Although Zionism and Israel have become the focus of recent anti-Jewish expressions by some, left-wing anti-Jewishness predates the emergence of modern Zionism.

It is revealing to catalog well-known historical, literary, artistic, and intellectual figures who have expressed strong anti-Jewish attitudes that do not directly reflect Christian theological prejudice.

Some left-wing anti-Jewish attitudes, such as those expressed by Karl Marx, are simply bigoted overgeneralizations against the tiny percentage of Jews who — along with a much larger number of Christians — were involved in capitalistic practices that were exploitative of working people. This is some of what Marx — who himself was the son of Jews — said about "the Jews":

> What is the object of the Jew's worship in this world? Usury. What is his world god? Money. . . .
>
> Thus we find every tyrant backed by a Jew, as is every Pope by a Jesuit.
>
> As soon as society succeeds in abolishing the empirical essence of Judaism, which is the huckster and the conditions that produce him, the Jew will become impossible, because his consciousness will no longer have a corresponding object.[9]

Ironically, one of Marx's competitors for the mantle of father of communism, Mikhail Bakunin, described Marx as "a Jew [who] is surrounded by a crowd of little, more or less intelligent, scheming, agile, speculating Jews." He described the "Jewish world" as an "exploiting sect, a people of leeches, a voracious parasite, closely and intimately connected with one another." And he said that "this Jewish world is today largely at the disposal of Marx or Rothschild." He saw Marx and Rothschild as two sides of the same Jewish coin, both seeking "strong state centralization" for the benefit of "the Jewish nation."[10]

Equally bigoted is the common right-wing claim that all (or most) Jews are Communists or that all (or most) Communists are Jews. The essence of bigotry is overgeneralization.* Those who oppose capitalism should criticize capitalists, rather than Jews who happen to be capitalists. And those who oppose communism should criticize Communists, rather than Jews who happen to be Communists.

Other left-wing anti-Jewishness may be understood as part of a more generalized antireligious bias. Voltaire, for example, writing in the eighteenth century, directed his most vituperative antireligious comments against the Old Testament and its adherents, the Jews, using the most vulnerable religion as a surrogate for all organized religion. Of course, he did not limit his anti-Jewish statements to *religious* beliefs. He overgeneralized against Jews, calling them "an ignorant and barbarous people," who might someday "become deadly to the human race."[11] Voltaire's more generalized bigotry is confirmed by his perverse view of blacks as racially inferior and of separate origin from other human beings. Although Voltaire's philosophical writings contributed to the Enlightenment, and indirectly to the emancipation of Jews in some parts of Europe, this allegedly egalitarian writer is viewed by many today as one of the intellectual godfathers of modern anti-Semitism and racism.

Most non-Christian-based anti-Semitism cannot be explained, however, as part of a more generalized opposition to capitalism, communism, religion, or any other broadly defined phenomenon of which Jews are but a small part.

How then does one understand — not even forgive, simply understand! — the virulently anti-Jewish statements of intellectuals throughout history? Their number includes H. L. Mencken ("The Jews could be put down very plausibly as the most unpleasant race ever heard of"); George Bernard Shaw ("Stop being Jews and start being human beings"); Henry Adams ("The whole carcase is rotten with Jew worms"); H. G. Wells ("A careful study of anti-Semitism, prejudice and accusations might be of great value to many Jews, who do not

---

* Jackie Mason jokes that being an anti-Semitic bigot deprives one of the opportunity to find *particular* faults in *specific* Jews.

adequately realize the irritation they inflict"); Edgar Degas (characterized as "a wild anti-Semite"); Denis Diderot ("Brutish people, vile and vulgar men"); Theodore Dreiser (New York is "a kyke's dream of a ghetto," and Jews are not "pure Americans" and lack "integrity"); T. S. Eliot (a social as well as literary anti-Semite, even after the Holocaust); Immanuel Kant ("The Jews still cannot claim any true genius, any truly great man. All their talents and skills revolve around stratagems and low cunning. . . . They are a nation of swindlers"). Other "famous" anti-Semites include Tacitus, Cicero, Aleksandr Pushkin, Pierre Renoir, Thomas Edison, Henry Ford, and, of course, Richard Wagner.[12]

This dishonor roll of anti-Jewish bigotry goes on, and includes people of every race, religion, geographic area, political leaning, gender, and age. The answer to the question Why? probably lies more in the realm of abnormal psychology than in any rational attempt to find understandable causes in history, politics, or economics. Anti-Semitism is a disease of the soul, and diseases are best diagnosed by examining those infected with them.

We retain the term "anti-Semitism" today even though it does not describe or capture the varieties of anti-Jewish attitudes that we are experiencing. It is as if to keep reminding ourselves that no matter how different these current manifestations seem, they are all — or nearly all — rooted in the classic, primitive strain that is ingrained so deeply and painfully into our memory and consciousness.

These primitive manifestations of anti-Jewish attitudes are still prevalent in the United States, as evidenced by the annual census of swastika graffiti and other overt "incidents" of right-wing anti-Semitism compiled by the Anti-Defamation League of B'nai B'rith (ADL). I am personally reminded how little has changed every time I open one of my almost daily anti-Semitic missives.

The perception of how much anti-Semitism exists is highly generational. My parents' and grandparents' generations — which have personal memories of the pogroms, *Kristallnacht*, and the Holocaust — tend to read a great deal into even a single anti-Semitic incident. My children's generation — which has not personally experienced institutionalized anti-Semitism — tends to minimize even a discernible pattern of anti-Semitic incidents. My generation — which has seen both institutionalized anti-Semitism and the perceptible shift away from it, at least in America — tends to share some of the attitudes of our elders and youngers. We look for patterns, for signs of official legitimacy, and for changes. We study the ADL's annual audit of anti-Semitic incidents, but we also look at the bigger picture of decreasing official anti-Semitism in our major institutions.

When my Brooklyn friends and I get together for our periodic discussions, we compare notes on our perceptions of anti-Semitism. Carl, who is an engineer with a firm that has a great number of government contracts, is particularly sensitive to governmental suspicions of "dual loyalty" by Jews with security clearance. Barry, who has worked for and with Fortune 500 companies, tells us about anti-Jewish trends in big business. Bernie, who sells religious items to Christians, is always up on the latest in theological attitudes toward Jews. The others report on their experiences and those of their friends and children.

We do not allow fear of anti-Semitism to stop us from doing what we believe is right. We do not spend our days and nights worrying about what "they" will think of us. But we remain on our guard for any recurrence of the old poison, especially in new bottles. We do not accept the attitude burlesqued by Woody Allen in his film *Annie Hall,* where Alvy Singer tells his friend that he was a victim of anti-Semitism because someone had invited him to lunch with the question "D'ju eat?" (The Brooklyn contraction of "Did you eat?") "I distinctly heard him say," Singer insists, "*Jew* eat!" But we also do not ignore "Jewish American Princess" jokes, recognizing in them a combination of sexism, anti-Semitism, and simple insensitivity.

We understand that the true situation may be more like another scene in Woody Allen's classic movie, in which both Alvy and his girlfriend Annie Hall are talking to their psychiatrists on a split screen. Each is asked how frequently they make love. Singer replies: "Hardly ever . . . three times a week." Hall replies: "Constantly . . . three times a week." I can easily imagine my mother and my sons both reading the same ADL audit of anti-Semitic acts and my mother saying, "Twenty-five acts of synagogue vandalism in *one* year is so high," while my sons might say "Only twenty-five acts in a whole year is nothing."

My friends and I would be more likely to wonder how quickly the police responded to these incidents, how forcefully they were condemned by non-Jewish politicians and religious leaders, and how seriously the prosecutor and judge regarded these manifestations of anti-Semitism.

The differences in our attitudes reflect — at least in part — the very different histories of European and American anti-Jewish attitudes and actions.

Thankfully, American anti-Semitism has at no point been comparable to the vicious European variety, but neither has this country been free of prejudice against its Jewish citizens. The religious freedom established by Roger Williams in 1636 must be balanced against the "welcome" given to twenty-three Sephardic Jews in 1654 by Peter Stuyvesant. Governor Stuyvesant of New Amsterdam, whose name is still honored in contemporary New York, fought to stop these "hateful enemies and blasphemers" from "infecting" his colony. In some states, laws prohibiting Jews from voting, holding office, or serving as witnesses in trials endured until well after the adoption of the Constitution in 1787.[13]

By the 1870s, the ranks of American Jewry had swelled by a quarter of a million immigrants: Christian society responded with a policy of polite exclusion. In the decades that followed, exclusionary measures expanded in response to the upward mobility of Jews and the great influx of Russian and Polish Jewry. Vacation resorts openly proclaimed that they permitted "No dogs, No Jews." Even Brooklyn's Coney Island was "restricted," because — as a hotelier put it — "We must have a good place for society to patronize [and] we cannot do so and have Jews. They are a detestable and vulgar people."[14] (Even as late as 1968, my family and I were excluded from a resort town named Point of Woods on New York's Fire Island.* Homes were sold with restrictive covenants barring resale to "Hebrews," as we were recently reminded when it was disclosed that Chief Justice William Rehnquist had purchased a home with a restrictive covenant against Jews.) Employment advertisements stated that "Christians only need apply." Events reached a prewar low point in 1913 when, in an atmosphere poisoned by anti-Semitism, a Georgia Jew, Leo Frank, was wrongfully convicted of murdering a young Christian girl. The hate that polluted Frank's trial led to the lynching of Frank and later to the election of a principal anti-Jewish agitator, Thomas E. Watson, to the U.S. Senate.

The post–World War I period saw the steady spread of anti-Semitic feeling. Jewish immigration was limited; colleges and universities established quotas; the Ku Klux Klan enjoyed a rebirth; and Henry Ford's *Dearborn Independent* gave new voice to all the traditional anti-

* In response, we organized a protest march of Jews, blacks, Hispanics, and others against whom the restriction applied.

Jewish canards, circulating countless copies of *The Protocols of the Elders of Zion* in a reworked "American" version. Ford ultimately recanted, but the damage was long since done; indeed, his publications are still sold by hate groups. In the thirties, dozens of nativist and pro-Nazi organizations sprang up, eager to blame U.S. economic woes on the Jews. American Jews who lived through the period vividly remember the Silver Shirt Legion, modeled after Hitler's storm troopers; the German-American Bund, whose public rallies were presided over by Führer Fritz Kuhn; and radio priest Father Charles Coughlin, who preached anti-Semitism to an audience of well over three million.[15]

When America joined the war against Hitler, overt anti-Semitism lost its popular audience, and has never regained it. Blatant animosity to Jews was discredited to a great extent among Americans by the horrors of the Holocaust. However, discrimination in employment, housing, the professions, and social clubs did not begin to drop sharply until the sixties.

Even today, organizations like the Anti-Defamation League annually receive thousands of complaints of discrimination in a wide variety of settings. Furthermore, as my hate mail attests, a substantial number of individual anti-Semites remain a part of our society. Nor have anti-Semitic organizations died out: the Liberty Lobby publishes its *Spotlight* weekly for tens of thousands of subscribers; White American Resistance (WAR) leader Tom Metzger has succeeded in placing his television program, "Race and Reason," on public-access cable around the country; the neo-Nazi skinheads have hundreds, perhaps thousands, of adherents across the country.

Of greater concern today are new varieties of anti-Semitism, which are sometimes more subtle but seldom any less virulent than the traditional brand. Some commentators have refused to acknowledge the possibility that old prejudices persist in an undercover or reformulated manifestation.

The leading advocate of this position is journalist and scholar Charles Silberman. In *A Certain People* (1985), Silberman emphasizes the insignificance of the anti-Semitism which remains, denying the existence of "any 'new anti-Semitism' or any significant increase in the old."[16] He paints a rosy picture of an America that has made dramatic progress in reducing anti-Semitism since the days when he was a young man. Acknowledging that the glass is only part full, he focuses — gratefully — on the full part, and discounts the empty part. It is largely a difference in generational perspective, since Silberman came of age a generation before my friends and I did, and he thus experienced far more anti-Semitism than we did. We have come a long way since the 1930s, and it is important to acknowledge the distance we have traveled, even if there is still a long way to go.

Silberman argues that Jews have achieved full access to — and notable success in — the worlds of business, the professions, and education. He points to the close ties between Israel and the United States. He cites polls showing anti-Semitic attitudes on the decline. While recognizing the existence of hate groups and of such "isolated pockets of discrimination" as some black anti-Semitism, Silberman concludes that certainly a residue of anti-Semitism remains, but it "declines significantly from one generation to the next." "If there is a danger," he writes, "it comes from within — from a new parochialism that leads many communal leaders to turn inward and focus exclusively on Jewish concerns."[17]

My perceptions and those of my friends are quite different, and more in accord with those Jews who report, Silberman says, "that they have had a direct personal experience of anti-Semitism in the last twelve months."[18] Silberman attempts to explain these statistics away as the result of "hypersensitivity" or "misinterpretation," but I believe that they reflect both a persistence in the old forms of anti-Semitism and the emergence of new forms, some of which have become more manifest since the publication of Silberman's book. There is less of the former and more of the latter.

Among the new strains of the old virus is a form of what purports to be anti-Zionism but is actually an old tree with right-wing roots and left-wing branches. I am referring to Communist-inspired anti-Zionism, which has had a profound impact in this country — especially in university communities — and throughout the world. Between the time of Joseph Stalin's accession to power and the recent changes under Mikhail Gorbachev, the Soviet Union was the chief producer and purveyor of this anti-Jewish media blitz. Thousands of books, pamphlets, articles, and videotapes were printed, reproduced, distributed and redistributed, broadcast and rebroadcast.

Much of this mid-twentieth-century anti-Jewish propaganda was simply the traditional poison of nineteenth-century anti-Semitism decanted from the old czarist bottles and recanted into new bottles of anticosmopolitanism and anti-Zionism. Systematic monitoring of Soviet publications during the 1970s and early 1980s compiled by the

Institute of Jewish Affairs in London revealed the classic recurrent themes of anti-Zionism: Zionist moneylenders, Zionists as the chosen people who despise all non-Zionists, Zionist rabbis who preach biblical genocide against all goyim, Zionists with long hooked noses and grasping hands, Zionist collaboration with Hitler, Zionist barbaric practices such as circumcision and ritual slaughter of animals.

In 1979, a distinguished group of leading lawyers from throughout the world, many of them non-Jewish, participated in an international colloquium on Soviet Jewry. After examining massive amounts of evidence, they concluded that "a wave of anti-Semitism is inspired officially by the USSR which employs to this end books and all possible media facilities, including the distribution of Soviet anti-Semitic publications in foreign countries."[19]

Although the publication of anti-Jewish materials within what is now the Soviet Union goes back to the czarist period, its recent, more open proliferation dates roughly from the UN General Assembly's resolution condemning Zionism as a form of racism and encouraging member nations to do everything in their power to combat Zionism. This resolution provided a legal cover for systematic state attacks on Zionism and Zionists.*

Since the establishment of new freedoms in the Soviet Union and Eastern Europe, new problems of anti-Semitism have developed. The first group to hold a mass demonstration in the center of Moscow was Pamyat, a notoriously anti-Jewish, ultranationalist organization that blames all of Russia's problems on the Jews. Similar manifestations of Soviet-style anti-Semitism have been observed in Eastern European countries as well, as they begin to throw off totalitarianism.

Another ancient form of anti-Jewish bigotry — this one difficult to label anti-Semitism — is Islamic in origin. The Koran and subsequent holy books of Islam contain theological attacks on the Jews for refusing to recognize the true messenger of God. But there is also some theological praise for Jews as fellow People of the Book. Though there have been historical episodes of Jewish persecution — particularly at the hands of Shiites — they pale by comparison with Christian persecutions. Indeed, there has been a relatively long history of benign tolerance of Jewish minorities in the Arab and Muslim world.

---

* Recently the Vatican recognized that anti-Semitism often wears the mask of anti-Zionism. Martin Luther King had made a similar observation years earlier: "When people criticize Zionism, they mean Jews; you're talking anti-Semitism."

Much of this changed with the advent of Zionism. Islamic anti-Jewishness became — and still is — a staple of the political rhetoric of the region. The grand mufti of Jerusalem, in addition to becoming Hitler's ally during World War II, adapted Nazi genocidal theory to an Islamic theology. He called on his "Muslim brothers" to "Murder the Jews! Murder them all." Other Islamic leaders used Nazi words like "extermination" in referring to the goals of Arab victory.

The rhetoric continues today from organizations such as Hamas. A recent leaflet of Hamas, the Islamic Resistance Movement, lists "the traitorousness of the Jews, their lies, their hatred and torture for us and all humanity." It calls for the Palestinians to "Islamicize" and "destroy the Jews."[20]

Nor is this kind of anti-Jewish rhetoric limited to the Middle East. A Swedish radio station called Radio Islam expounds the major themes of traditional anti-Semitism. It quotes from the *Protocols* and claims that "Judaism, the Torah, and the Talmud stink of racism and contempt for other peoples." It denies the Holocaust, while praising the Nazis and regretting that Hitler did not finish his job. Ironically, little was heard about Islamic insensitivity toward Jews during the flap over Salman Rushdie's novel *Satanic Verses*. Some of the very individuals, organizations, and even nations most vocal in condemnation of Rushdie's "insensitivity" toward Islam are in the forefront of promoting Islamic insensitivity toward the Jews.[21]

There is yet a third strain of the current virus of anti-Semitism, this one even more difficult to diagnose. Its danger lies in its subtlety, its pervasiveness, and its acceptability at all levels of our society. This is a phenomenon familiar to all of us, yet difficult to articulate and expose: the singling out of Jewish institutions and especially Israel for special scrutiny, and the application of a double standard to Jewish things and persons. The phenomenon, which currently has no accepted name, assumes a variety of forms, but its most obvious manifestation is the special and often gloating attention paid by the media, by intellectuals, and by the government to any deviation by Israel, no matter how trivial, from the highest norms of human rights, civility, and sacrifice. Though Israel may often be deserving of criticism, what is missing is the comparable criticism of equal or greater violations by other countries and other groups. This constant, often legitimate criticism of Israel for every one of its deviations, when coupled with the absence of legitimate criticism of others, creates the impression currently prevalent on university campuses and in the press that Israel is among the worst human rights violators in the world. We have all heard that phrase repeated many times. It is not true, but if it is repeated often enough, it takes on a reality of its own.

Another reflection of this new virus is a growing acceptance of intellectual criticism directed against Jews which would never be tolerated against other minorities. For example, when the *Nation* recently ran its fiftieth-anniversary issue, it invited Gore Vidal to contribute an article. Vidal wrote a crass, ignorant piece of anti-Semitism called "The Empire Lovers Strike Back," in which he described Jews in Israel as a "predatory people" with "an alien theocracy," and Jews in America as "a fifth column."[22] Suppose the piece had been about blacks in America and had accused blacks who support South African liberation of dual loyalty; no decent magazine in this country, surely not the *Nation,* would have published it. But the *Nation* has a Jewish readership and a Jewish editor, and perhaps there is a feeling that a "Jewish" magazine can tolerate this kind of crude anti-Semitism. I am obviously not for censorship. I am focusing on the factors that influence a newspaper or a magazine to print what it chooses to print, and the fact that the *Nation* chose to print this is significant.

The Jewish community has other double standards imposed upon it as well. Jews are expected, because of their reputation as civil libertarians, always to defend their enemies — and generally they do. No other group is expected to defend its enemies in comparable fashion. Whether it be Jewish victims of the Holocaust who are supposed to be defending the rights of Nazis to march through the Jewish community of Skokie, Illinois, or Jewish victims of terrorism being expected to defend the PLO's right to open an information office in Washington! I happen to defend both those rights, but I cannot ask every Jewish victim to agree with me, as the media often seem to, while rarely demanding that level of perfection from other groups. For example, when black students disrupted a white South African speaker at Harvard — and a prominent black professor justified the disruption* — the story received little attention, and the censorial actions generated virtually no criticism. Yet, as I related in Chapter III, Jewish students who protested the honoring of a Libyan at a human rights conference were publicly berated.

* Professor Randall Kennedy stated that disruption of a speaker can be justified if there are those in the audience who "feel it is a stain on humanity if certain persons speak without disruption" (*Washington Post,* June 6, 1987).

This, then, is the newest form of anti-Jewishness. It is neither medieval anti-Judaism, nor nineteenth- and twentieth-century anti-Semitism, nor contemporary anti-Zionism. It is something different and more subtle. Anti-Judaism is religious; while anti-Semitism is racial and regional. They are both primitive, discredited, and dated, at least as mainstream attitudes. It is far too easy for the new anti-Jews to disclaim anti-Semitism: "How can you accuse me of being an anti-Semite? I support the Palestinians, and they're Semites. I'm anti-Zionist, not anti-Semitic." Even the *New York Times* has used the term "anti-Semitism" to describe anti-Arab expressions.[23]

We need a new term to describe this phenomenon, this double standard, this super-scrutiny of things Jewish, this singling out of Israel. "Anti-Judaism" does not quite capture it, because it is no longer completely directed against the religion or theology of the Jews. Nor does "Judeophobia," since it suggests fear — rather than resentment — of Jews. The essence of the new phenomenon is anti-*Jewishness*, an assault on Jewish values and attitudes, on things Jewish and on persons who reflect Jewishness.

Moreover the label "anti-Semite," invented by anti-Semites as a proud epithet, is an inherently neutral term. It simply means those who are against Jews. It does not necessarily connote the sickness and evil inherent in such bigotry. The term "Judeopath" would seem far more fitting. It suggests a pathological hatred of Jews and clearly puts the onus on those who hate rather than on those who are hated. No one would be proud of being labeled Judeopathic, as some claim pride in the label anti-Semitic. No one could talk about "objective Judeopathy" in the way that some sociologists casually talk about "objective anti-Semitism," as if it were somehow the fault of the Jews.*

Whatever it is called, this assault on Jewishness must be placed high on our agenda. The world, especially the Western world, perceives Jews as comfortable, powerful, and not in need of help. We no longer suffer from the kind of social, economic, educational, and residential anti-Semitism that characterized my parents' generation and the experiences of my own generation when seeking jobs in the

---

* Sociologists sometimes contrast "objective" with "abstract" (or "subjective") anti-Semitism. Whereas the "objective" variety is said to arise from real conflicts with flesh-and-blood Jews, "abstract" anti-Semitism is defined as being directed against the abstract idea of the conspiratorial Jew (see Silberman, p. 341). These terms are themselves loaded with anti-Semitic implications, since they suggest that Jews are in some way responsible for "objective" anti-Semitism.

professions. We are comfortable enough and powerful enough to provide domestically for our own needs, but we do not today have the
power, and we have not been using the power we have effectively, to
prevent this proliferation of the new anti-Jewishness. We are today
both a powerful and a powerless people, a permanent minority living
by our wits, by our accomplishments, and to some degree by our
acceptance by shifting majorities. But as we add to our accomplishments, the envy grows.

Those who argue that anti-Semitism is a thing of the past are, in
some respects, absolutely correct. Political anti-Semitism does not
formally exist in this country. No mainstream American politician
nowadays would endorse swastika-painting or Jew-baiting. Occasionally a neo-Nazi or KKK leader seeks a major party nomination in some
obscure part of the country, and on a few occasions an overt anti-
Semite has even won a local primary, only to be defeated in the general
election. In one recent case, a man who claimed that his KKK ties
were behind him — David Duke — was elected to the Louisiana legislature from a suburb of New Orleans but was unsuccessful in a bid
for a U.S. Senate seat. (He received 40 percent of the total vote and 60
percent of the white vote.) This is in sharp contrast to some parts of
Europe, where anti-Semites still win, or to the 1930s in this country,
when overtly anti-Semitic (as well as antiblack and anti-Catholic)
politicians won seats in the Senate and Congress.*

Nonetheless, although overt anti-Semitism is, fortunately, no
longer the blight it once was on the American political scene, anti-
Jewish attitudes are still quite prevalent throughout the country. My
letters reflect one persistent strain of the virus. The continued, if
lessened, discrimination against Jewish aspirants to high office reflects another. The perceived need to keep the number of Jewish
students at elite universities below some undefined but all-too-real
number is yet another. And the acceptance of the continued double
standard of judgment relating to Israel and Jewish values is the apparent wave of the future.

Each of these strains of the anti-Jewish virus — of Judeopathy —
must be responded to vigorously. But the treatment should be directed
to the sick person, the Judeopath, and not to the innocent target, the
Jew.

---

* Of course, our winner-take-all electoral system generally prevents fringe elements from
being elected. If we had a system of proportional representation of the kind Israel or France
does, there would probably be Nazis and Communists in some of our legislatures.

I was appalled during a recent Yom Kippur service at Harvard Hillel when a student asked the rabbi what he, as a post-Holocaust American, should make of the spray-painting of swastikas and anti-Jewish graffiti in the town of Wellesley on the eve of Yom Kippur. The rabbi, after a few remarks downplaying the significance of such incidents, said: "You know that some of these swastikas are painted by Jews. I know of more than one instance where Jews have done this." When the perpetrators were arrested, they turned out to be anti-Semitic non-Jews. Yet, the message conveyed by the rabbi to the largest gathering of Jewish students during the year was that Jews might have been the culprits.

The *old* anti-Semitism is waning; but the *new* Judeopathy is alive and well. It is a product of our successes, rather than our failures. (A major paradox of the Jewish condition today is that our success contributes to the hatred of us; or as my grandmother would have put it, the world does not *fagin* — indulge or allow — us our successes. My Brooklyn friends refer to this jealousy of Jewish accomplishments as "Jewlousy.") Its goal seems to be to keep us in our place as less than first-class citizens — to remind us that we are still guests in our host's country, that our religion is merely tolerated in a Christian world, that Israel's survival is dependent on the continued support of the American treasury. My anti-Semitic letters say this directly. The mainstream media, some politicians, and many student leaders send the same message more subtly.

There is no reason we Jews should accept the subordinate status this new form of anti-Jewishness seeks to impose on us. Yes, we have received much from America, but we have given back much in return. America's Jews have contributed as much to the success and vibrancy of this country as any other group, including the *Mayflower* descendants. This is every bit as much *our* country as it is "theirs." Our "immigrant status" as compared with that of other religious, ethnic, and national groups is merely a matter of degree. That, thankfully, is what distinguishes America from other nations in which Jews have lived as a minority.

The Jewish century of American history includes the period of this country's greatest successes — with no small indebtedness to its Jewish immigrant population. The United States, during its first century as a nation, was a young backwater of unrealized potential, rich in material resources but poor in achievements. The collective infusions of many immigrant and native groups were required to turn America into the most powerful, dynamic, progressive, and compassionate nation in history. And Jews played no small role — indeed, it would not be unduly boastful to say that we played a "disproportionally" large role — in this transformation. We have earned a prominent place in the pantheon of our country.

We do not have to justify ourselves as Jewish Americans. My white Anglo-Saxon Protestant friends never think about whether their actions will "reflect badly" on Wasps. There is no Wasp concept of *shanda fur de yidden* — an embarrassment in front of the Jews. Nor should we worry about what others will think of us *as Jews*. Of course, we should be concerned of what people we respect will think of us *as individuals*. But the time has come for us to feel completely free to be ourselves. No Jew should have to worry about becoming active in politics — even unpopular politics. The anti-Semites will condemn liberal Jews because they are liberal, conservative Jews because they are conservative, and moderate Jews because they are moderate. Indeed, I myself have been condemned on *all three* grounds by those looking for reasons to condemn. Most of my overtly anti-Semitic mail condemns me for my liberalism. But I have also been attacked from the left by radicals who are appalled by my support for "fascist Israel" and my lack of enthusiasm for some race-specific quotas. Indeed, the Boston chapter of the National Lawyers Guild once established a subcommittee just to attack me for my "Zionist reactionary Red-baiting," after I had criticized the Soviet "trial" of Jewish refusenik Anatoly Shcharansky.

A recent incident at Harvard Law School demonstrated that anti-Semitism can come from unlikely sources. A Jewish student, active in the conservative Federalist Society, received these two letters from fellow students. The first, which came from a Jew, included the following "lawyerlike" logic:

Racist, right-wing Jews are an anathema to me.

Do you now identify so strongly with your class interests that you've forgotten that it was these very people (money, power, etc.) who sent twelve million human beings to the gas chambers of Auschwitz and Buchenwald? . . .

I would have thought that you lost enough of your people to anti-semitic, homophobic, red-bashing Nazis to engage in such repugnant, dangerous behavior.

I know I did.

The second, from a non-Jew, was more direct: "I think you and your untermenschen are full of it. Kindly fuck off."[24]

The fact that the first student was Jewish does not make his sentiments any less racist or offensive. The second student's reference to "untermenschen" — a Nazi term used to identify Jews, blacks, and other racially undesirable groups — is beneath contempt.*

I report this incident to demonstrate that it is not the liberal or conservative *content* of remarks made by a Jew that provokes epithets directed at his or her Jewishness. It is the fact of Jewishness coupled with any degree of controversiality surrounding the remarks.

It is foolish — and self-defeating — for Jews to try to tailor their remarks or actions so as to avoid anti-Semitic responses. Only the blandest comments by the blandest Jews hold the prospect of stimulating no anti-Semitic reactions. And being bland is not a Jewish characteristic. As Harry Golden used to put it: "Jews are just like everyone else — except more so!" I recall a class in which I was discussing the Canadian concept of a "visible minority," which means a minority capable of being recognized easily, such as blacks or Native Americans. A student raised her hand and asked whether Jews were a visible minority. I responded: "No, we are an *audible* minority."

A recent incident in Massachusetts illustrates that negative Jewish stereotypes are still close to the surface. In December 1990 my friend Harvey Silverglate and I opposed a local judicial nominee named Paul Mahoney. Our opposition was based on published reports that he had acted improperly when he was an assistant district attorney. It was also based on reports from a *Boston Globe* journalist that during an investigation of a man named William Bulger, who was president of the Massachusetts senate, Mahoney — then his assistant — had appealed to ethnic favoritism in an effort to kill a negative *Globe* story about Bulger that was based in part on information provided by Silverglate. Mahoney had reportedly asked the reporter, whose name was O'Neil, why a man with a name like O'Neil would believe a man with a name like Silverglate over men with names like Bulger and Mahoney.

I requested permission to appear at Mahoney's confirmation hearing to ask the Governor's Council — which must approve all judicial nominations — to conduct a thorough investigation of these and other charges that had led several editorial writers and columnists to oppose

* In the early days of the Gulf War, while Israel was under attack by Iraqi Scud missiles, the following telling headline appeared in the *Boston Globe:* "Peace Activists Express Concern About Anti-Semitism in Movement" (January 22, 1991, p. 6).

the nomination. Before I could even begin my presentation, Bulger, the president of the senate, attacked both Silverglate and me as "crafty," as "connivers" and "manipulators." He accused us of controlling "the media" and of having "no moral constraints." Invoking an Old Testament reference, he cited the story of how Jacob had tricked Esau. Then in a dramatic gesture, he pointed to our faces and hissed: "Look at them, look at them," as if our "craftiness" could be seen on our obviously Jewish faces.

Most of the press recognized the code words for what they were and condemned the senate president for his "savage and venomous display of name-calling," as well as for his indecent use of code words that "if not anti-Semitic [were] close to it." An editor of the *Boston Globe* characterized Bulger's statements as "soft-core anti-Semitism."[25]

But some Jews put the blame on me for stirring up anti-Semitism. I was advised that as a visible Jew, I have a responsibility not to provoke the kind of outburst that Bulger engaged in. The message implicit in such advice is clear: don't get involved in political disputes with people who may harbor anti-Jewish feelings, lest your involvement bring those feelings out into the open. Accepting that advice would be tantamount to accepting second-class status, which I will not do and which no Jew should be asked to do in America.

I plan to continue — as a proud Jew and a proud American — to speak out on every issue of importance. *Sh'a shtill* has never served us well. It did not save us from the Nazis. It did not help Soviet refuseniks. And it will not protect our interests as Jewish Americans. We cannot accept one standard of freedom of expression for Jewish Americans on the one hand and a different standard for "real" Americans on the other. I know that I will never accept the status of guest in America, at Harvard, or in the world at large. We are full citizens, and as such we have an obligation to speak our minds.

As usual, Mark Twain got it just about right. In 1898, Twain received a letter from an American Jewish lawyer. The lawyer's letter was prompted by an article Twain had published about a visit to Austria in which he had observed that in recent demonstrations and riots precipitated by a language proposition, "all classes of people were unanimous only on one thing — *vis* in being against the Jews."[26]

The lawyer wondered why this was so, especially since "no Jewish question was involved," and "*the Jews were the only ones of the nineteen different races [sic] in Austria which did not have a party — they are abso-*

lutely non-participants" (emphasis added). The lawyer went on to say that Jews were well behaved and yet were "the butt of baseless, vicious animosities."[27]

Mark Twain agreed with the claim that the Jew was well behaved. "His race is entitled to be called the most benevolent of all the races of men." An exaggeration, certainly. But Twain was surely correct that whatever faults Jews may have — individually or even stereotypically — these do not explain their status as historical victims of worldwide persecution. To explain this phenomenon, Twain turned to one of the factors singled out by the lawyer as "a credit" to Jews: namely that the Jews had no party, that they were nonparticipants in government. Here Twain is at his rapier-wit best:

> Who gives the Jew the right . . . to sit still, in a free country, and let somebody else look after its safety? The oppressed Jew was entitled to all pity in the former times under brutal autocracies, for he was weak and friendless, and had no way to help his case. But he has ways now, and he has had them for a century, but I do not see that he has tried to make serious use of them.[28]

Twain recognized that the small number of Jews in the United States at the time would not make it easy for them to exercise significant power. (He doubted, by the way, the *Encyclopaedia Britannica's* estimate of the American Jewish population as 250,000 — having written to the editor that he "was personally acquainted with more Jews than that in my country!") But he proposed the quintessential American approach to maximizing power:

> In our days we have learned the value of combination. We apply it everywhere — in railway systems, in trusts, in trade-unions, in Salvation Armies, in minor politics, in major politics, in European Concerts. Whatever our strength may be, big or little, we organize it.

He admonished the Jews to do likewise:

> In politics, organize your strength, band together and deliver the casting vote where you can, and, where you can't compel as good terms as possible. You huddle to yourselves already in all countries, but you huddle in no sufficient purpose, politically speaking. You do not seem to be organized, except for your charities. There you are omnipotent; there you compel your due of recognition — you do not have to beg for it. It shows what you can do when you band together for a definite purpose.[29]

Twain urged the American Jews to learn from the example of Irish Americans.*

In his conclusion, Twain reminded the lawyer that since the Jew constituted but one percent of the human race, he

> ought hardly be heard of; but he is heard of, has always been heard of. He is as prominent on the planet as any other people. . . . His contributions to the world's list of great names in literature, science, art, music, finance, medicine, and abstruse learning are also away out of proportion to the weakness of his numbers. He has made a marvelous fight in this world, in all the ages; and has done it with his hands tied behind him. All things are mortal but the Jew; all other forces pass, but he remains. What is the secret of his immortality?[30]

Well, his "immortality" almost came to an end during the Second World War. Indeed, the "immortality" of entire Jewish families, clans, villages, sects, and other sub-groups did come to a final end. But we have survived and we have followed Twain's all-American advice.

We have organized and combined. American Jews, who comprise barely 2.5 percent of our nation's population, have *earned* power — economic, educational, political, informational, charitable, moral — disproportionate to their numbers. No one gave us this power. If today we own more newspapers, TV stations, movie studios, and investment banks than our numbers would suggest, it is because individual Jews — often immigrants with little money — saw opportunities where others did not. If we have succeeded in law, medicine, and academia, it was despite quotas, not because of them. We did have some advantages — for example, an emphasis on education and family stability — but these advantages were not bestowed by any government, but rather by our traditions and values.

We need not apologize about our successes. We earned them, the hard way. (Certainly not "the old-fashioned way," of bigotry, discrimination, and exclusion.)

We need not be apologetic or defensive about our power in America. For we have seen what can, and will, happen if we abdicate our

---

* Twain asked his correspondent whether he had ever heard of the "plan" of a journalist named Hertzl. "He wishes to gather the Jews of the world together in Palestine, with a government of their own." Although he had no personal objection to the idea, Twain doubted that the world would ever allow "that concentration of the cunningest brains . . . in a free country." He wondered what would happen if "that race finds out its strength. If the horses knew theirs, we should not ride any more." Mark Twain, *Concerning the Jews* (New York: Harper and Brothers, 1934), p. 23.

power. Our history as a people demonstrates that we *need* more power than others to survive. That is one of the important lessons to be learned from thousands of years of anti-Jewish bigotry. I am reminded of it every time I open one of my poison-pen letters. We are not the Swiss and our history is not one of being left alone. It is one of constant victimization and repression. Without power — indeed, without power disproportionate to our numbers — we will continue to be victimized. We should strive to enhance our power on every front.

We were powerless for two thousand years. We have become powerful only in the very recent past. Israel has been strong for only a few decades. It takes time to adjust to power and strength, especially after a long history of weakness. It is far easier to adapt to weakness, because the alternatives are limited. Power and strength bring with them greater options and more opportunities — to do both good and bad.

When the "Jewish Lobby" defeats an enemy of Israel or of the Jews, we should proudly proclaim the victory of justice over injustice. When "Jewish contributors" influence the outcome of a media campaign, we should declare a victory of truth over falsity. When "Jewish wisdom" outsmarts those who would destroy us, we should sing the praises of "brains over brawn." When "Jewish ethics" persuade disinterested others to support our moral high ground over the hypocrisy of those who would apply a double standard, we should glory in the vindication of right over wrong.

That is the American way. That was Mark Twain's way. That is also the Jewish way. There is no virtue in the kind of disproportionate weakness of which Twain's correspondent boasted and for which Twain rightly castigated him. There is virtue in winning, especially when right is on your side. There is morality in power, when that power is used to prevent the emergence of the kind of base evil that has so often victimized us (and others) in the absence of power.

The philosopher George Santayana tells us that "those who cannot remember the past are condemned to repeat it." As survivors of the most thorough genocidal plot ever devised — and every living Jew is a survivor of Hitler's Holocaust — we cannot afford to have the lessons of our history repeated on us. The most important lesson of our history is the need of, and justification for, moral power to prevent immoral deeds.

Auschwitz

The Holocaust, Justice, and Faith

THOUGH I WAS only a child living a safe distance from the European killing fields, the Holocaust remains the most formative event in my experience. I cannot escape — nor do I try — its continuing influence on my life, my religion, my ideas, my perceptions, my sense of justice, and my psyche.

The Holocaust changed the nature of Judaism and of Jews forever. It changed the way Jews look at non-Jews, and vice versa. It changed the way every compassionate person views justice and injustice. It should challenge the faith of every thinking being. My friend Robert Nozick argues that the Holocaust makes it possible now to contemplate, without welcoming, the destruction of the human species as a "satisfying close" to the history of our epoch. "That species, the one that committed *that,* has lost its worthy status. Humanity has desanctified itself."[1]

To Nozick, a brilliant and creative philosopher, the desanctifying event was the Holocaust itself — the deliberate and often sadistic mass murder of two-thirds of European Jewry, nearly six million persons, in a genocidal attempt to rid the world of the Jewish "race." To me, as a person who has spent his life in the pursuit of justice, the ultimate desanctification has been humankind's *response* to that indescribably horrible event. I was not a responsible adult during the years of the actual killings, but I was — and am — a responsible adult in the aftermath of the Holocaust. While I attended yeshiva, then law school, and pursued my career as a lawyer, thousands of Hitler's assistant and associate genocidal killers — ranging from high-ranking Nazi politicians, to SS officers, to death camp guards — continued to live happy, guilt-free lives. Every time I look at the photographs of Nazi soldiers, with their mocking smiles, taking aim at the babies and women they are about to machine-gun into anonymous mass graves, I imagine those soldiers — now honored businessmen, grandfathers, church leaders — living out their lives in peace. And I think about a world that allowed both the Holocaust and its aftermath to happen.

I experience a haunting guilt for not having devoted my career to hunting down these killers of my people and bringing them to justice. But I also realize that there was no "justice" to which to bring them. In the years after the war, no one really wanted to try all, or even most, of the surviving Nazi war criminals. (A terrible misnomer, since their brutal crimes had nothing to do with achieving military ends.) Everyone — the United States, Israel, the international business community, the United Nations — wanted to get on with the pressing job of building the future. There was little time, energy, or resource for bringing to justice those who were responsible for the past, even so horrible a past as the Holocaust.

Of course, there were the few symbolic trials — at Nuremberg, in Jerusalem, in several American courtrooms. But the reality for the vast majority of willing mass murderers is that injustice has prevailed. The innocent were punished. The guilty were rewarded.

I have never understood why a Jewish revenge movement did not emerge after the Holocaust. There was, in fact, a limited revenge movement, documented in Michael Elkins's book *Forged in Fury* (1981). The birth of Israel deflected energy away from revenge and into defending the new state. And then there were those like Elie Wiesel, winner of the 1986 Nobel Peace Prize, who, while urging us never to forget the deadly past, pointed us toward a living future.[2]

From the time I was in elementary school, I recited in Hebrew the following verse from the Thirty-seventh Psalm several times each day, as part of the prayer after meals: "I was a child and then grew old, but I never saw a righteous person abandoned or his children asking for food." I recall raising questions in class about what these perplexing words could possibly mean. Surely they did not accurately describe reality. The remnants of the Holocaust were all around me — classmates with numbers tattooed on their arms, teachers who had lost entire families, friends who had experienced the displaced persons camps. Righteous people *had* been abandoned and their children left wanting.

My yeshiva rabbis made heroic efforts to explain this passage. Perhaps those who were abandoned were not really righteous in their souls. An insulting and denigrating rationalization! Surely some of the abandoned were truly righteous — at least more righteous than many who were not abandoned. How dare the commentators, I remember thinking, sit in smug collective judgment of all who were abandoned. Perhaps, the rabbis said, the passage refers to being abandoned by God in the hereafter and not by fallible fellow men on earth. That won't work either, I thought, since the obviously human author ("I was a child and then grew old") is describing what he has "seen," and one does not see the hereafter. Maybe the passage reflects the hope that the righteous will *no longer be* abandoned, my teachers suggested. Maybe, but that is not what it says. Other proffered explanations fell equally short.

To my mind, the best and simplest explanation is that the passage is wrong. It is pretty poetry but ugly philosophy. There is in fact no relationship between righteousness and good fortune, or unrighteousness and bad fortune. If there was ever any doubt about this sad reality — and I don't believe there ever was — all such doubt was permanently erased by the Holocaust.*

Indeed, the Holocaust, and the world's reaction to it, make it demonstrably clear not only that the observation is factually false, but also that it is morally unacceptable. The psalm implies, at the very least, that human beings are morally responsible for their misfortunes; had they been righteous, they would not have been slaughtered in the Holocaust, struck down by disease, or devastated by natural catastrophe. This is an obnoxious principle that gives rise to the kind of "naturalistic fallacy" underlying the doctrines of some fundamentalist religions, which declare disasters to be the fault of the victims. Some bigots even blame the Holocaust on the Jews.† A religious doctrine capable of such moral mischief must be unacceptable to Jews, especially after the Holocaust.

To be sure, there may be an obscure interpretation that would be entirely acceptable,‡ but even if that were to be so, I would still con-

---

* After writing this, I learned that some Orthodox Jews say the verse under their breath; Leonard Fein, "cannot . . . say the words." See Fein, *Where Are We?*, p. 41.

† In 1990 a leading Orthodox rabbi in Israel drew widespread criticism when he said that the Holocaust was God's punishment against the Jews for eating pork.

‡ The following is an ingenious interpretation: If an evil man becomes poor, the whole community knows his evil ways and will not give him charity. Therefore, he has to send his

clude that the homily is objectionable, since its obvious meaning — the one accepted by millions who daily recite it — is so fundamentally immoral. Like the daily blessing thanking the Lord "for not having made me a woman" — which has also been subjected to heroic contemporary efforts at rationalization — the homily about the righteous is dangerous if believed.

I am not proposing censorship. Let these anachronistic prayers remain in the prayerbooks, but as relics of a past age with different, and less acceptable, values. Let them serve as reminders of the fallibility of religious texts, and of the right — indeed the obligation — of every generation of religious adherents to reevaluate their scriptures. Let the homily about the righteous remind us of the tragic reality that justice does not always reward the just or punish the unjust, and let it serve as an inspiration to try to make day-to-day reality conform to religious theory (just as the prayer about women must remind us of continuing inequities against women and others in all societies).

We must continue to strive for justice in a world that is inherently nonjust. So long as dumb luck — both good and bad — plays so prominent a role in the rewards and punishments of human life, natural outcomes will never provide guidance for justice. So long as unrighteousness coupled with power continues to be rewarded within our legal and political systems, and righteousness coupled with weakness continues to be punished, human outcomes will never constitute an infallible criterion for justice.

The Jewish tradition is so rich in the diversity of its sacred texts that one can find an antidote to virtually any unacceptable statement. Perhaps the most powerful antidote to the homily about the righteous person is in the book of Job. The righteous Job suffered mightily, even though he eventually received new cattle, property, and children. Not only was he abandoned, he was actively punished ("tested" was the euphemism) and his children killed.

The Holocaust shattered the faith of many Jews in the natural Jewish justice of the quoted homily — in righteousness being rewarded here on earth. Even though many devout Jews walked into the chambers of murder declaring their faith in God — *"Ani maamin beemunah Shlaima"* ("I believe with full faith") — they had surely abandoned faith in earthly justice. Indeed, many died with another Jewish

---

children to search for food. But if a righteous person becomes poor, he is able to ask for food himself, and therefore the psalmist has never seen a righteous person abandoned *and* his children asking for food.

lament on their lips: *"Aili, Aili, Lama azavtani"* — "My God, my God, why has Thou abandoned me?" They knew that they and their children had been abandoned.

Nazi genocide also made us rethink many of the secular philosophies of justice. Legal positivism — the idea that legal justice is a function of existing law — suffered a severe blow by the example of Nazi justice, which had all the imprimatur of existing German law but lacked the characteristics of justice.[3]

The Holocaust engendered a cynicism over justice that may never be overcome. Many of the most righteous Jews and non-Jews suffered the worst fates. Many of the most unrighteous non-Jews, including leading Nazis and hands-on implementers of the "final solution," have lived out their lives surrounded by loving families and supportive friends. And some of the least righteous Jews, those who collaborated with the Nazis, managed to survive. (While I cannot find it in my heart to condemn Jews who collaborated in order to survive, surely they cannot be counted among the most righteous.)

Nor were these unjust outcomes merely a reflection of dumb luck. In many instances, the civilized world consciously *chose* to reward evil and punish virtue. The postwar immigration preferences given by some "moral" nations — such as Canada — to Nazi collaborators over Nazi victims is a striking example.[4] Another is the American decision to pardon many Nazi war criminals and return to them confiscated property they had derived from slave labor.

Every time I hear of a former Nazi — especially a genocidal criminal — living a long and rewarding life, I cannot help thinking of the righteous Jews and their children whom he helped to murder, while the world abandoned them in the name of pragmatism. I also think of heroes like Raoul Wallenberg, the Swedish diplomat who saved so many Hungarian Jews, and the abandonment he suffered at the hands of an unjust world.

Nor do I obtain much solace from any confidence that Nazi killers must be suffering pangs of internal guilt. Many are not. They still believe that what they did was right. Or they just don't think about it, even in dreams or nightmares. The world has encouraged that response by its silence and inaction.

Perhaps that is why President Ronald Reagan's obscene trip to the SS cemetery in Bitburg, Germany, in 1985 raised such strong emotions among so many Jews. The visit — especially when coupled with Reagan's perverse statement that the Nazi killers buried there "were

victims, just as surely as the victims in the concentration camps" —
was seen as the ultimate "pardon" of the SS for its genocidal crimes.
The press reported that former SS officers felt rehabilitated if not
vindicated: "Conversations with the [SS] veterans leave no doubt that
President Reagan's insistence on going to Bitburg . . . has made them
feel better about their role in history." Reagan, by the way, refused to
go to the Dachau concentration camp — where the SS killed Jewish
victims — because he was not interested in "reawakening the memories and so forth."[5]

I have to strive mightily not to become cynical about justice in the
face of such recurring injustice. I recall my conversation with a Holocaust survivor who had lost his entire family in the camps and had
himself been left for dead. After the war he came to America and
became a successful businessman. Now, near the end of his life, he
stood accused of tax evasion and faced imprisonment. While not trying to minimize his own guilt, he wondered how he could be expected
to accept a system of justice that punished his misdeeds by imprisonment, while allowing the killers of his family to live out their lives in
freedom.

I tried to explain that one could not compare Nazi injustice to
American justice, but he cut me off. "I'm talking about *American*
injustice." He told me how he had traced some Nazi criminals from his
region of Byelorussia to New Jersey, where they were living comfortable lives. He could not prove, of course, that any specific person had
murdered his family, but he told me that the Justice Department was
aware of the complicity of several of the people he had traced. "Maybe
they'll eventually deport one or two of them," he said cynically, "but
there are a lot of happy Nazis living good lives here in America." He
did not try to justify his own criminal actions on the basis of his
experiences, but he did say: "If those Nazi criminals saw me going to
prison for cheating the government out of a few thousand dollars while
they sat bouncing their grandchildren on their knees, they would be
laughing their Nazi heads off."

Others of my generation, such as Leonard Fein, take a somewhat
different view of Jewish reaction to the Holocaust, chastising Jews
"when we claim special indulgence" because of the Holocaust.[6] I am
a great admirer of Fein, but I do not understand why Jews should not
claim — indeed *demand* — special indulgence from a world that gave
them no indulgence at all. Why does Fein (and others who make this
argument) willingly grant — indeed demand that we all must

grant — special indulgence to other minorities because of the discrimination they have suffered, but deny to his own people that which is their due? The world owes Jews, and the Jewish state, which was built on the ashes of Auschwitz, a special understanding.* If we are a bit skeptical of assurances that the world or the United States will come to the aid of a mortally endangered Israel, we are right to be, even if it turns out that the world does help us *this* time. If Israel resolves security doubts in favor of its own people — even if it is wrong in a particular instance — the world should "indulge" the survivors of the Holocaust at least a generation of understandable fear, if not paranoia.

At bottom, Fein is wrong in even using the term "special indulgence." The world has never given — and does not today offer — any special indulgence to the Jewish people or the Jewish state. Nor is that what the Jews whom Fein chastises are seeking. What we demand — what *any* people has the right to demand — is that the world not indulge us *any less* than it does other groups. We have the right to insist that the world not apply a double standard of super-scrutiny and super-criticism to Jews. Our complaint is that the world, including many Jews, asks more of us — more sacrifice, more perfection, more morality — than it asks of others. We learned at Auschwitz that in an immoral world there is no virtue in holding ourselves to self-sacrificing standards of morality more suited to interaction with friends than enemies. The experience of the Holocaust should excuse us from complying with standards that no other people or nation has ever been expected to comply with.

So spare us, please, from the charge that we insist on "special indulgence." Understand, please, why we do not place our full trust in the kindness of strangers. And stop — in the name of basic decency and simple equality — demanding of us what no one demands of others.[7]

One does not have to believe that justice now exists in order to aspire to its improvement, if not perfection. The Bible commands, "Justice, justice shalt thou pursue," implying that it must be actively sought by human agencies, not passively expected from nature.

With this commandment in mind, I have become deeply, if frustratingly, involved in the belated efforts to bring Nazi war criminals

---

* Fein denies that Israel was built on the ashes of Auschwitz, but the reality is that the Holocaust persuaded the world — Jews as well as non-Jews — of the necessity for a Jewish state.

to justice. Justice requires not only that the innocent be acquitted, but also that the guilty be punished — especially when the guilt is as enormous as it is for perpetrators of the Holocaust.

I make no apologies as a committed civil libertarian for my efforts, and the efforts of other human rights activists, to bring every last surviving Nazi war criminal to justice, regardless of age or "rehabilitation." Both to prevent future Holocausts and to see justice done for past atrocities, it is essential that no Nazi war criminal live out his life in peace and obscurity. What we must apologize for is the tardiness of our efforts, a lateness that has allowed too many of history's most unforgivable criminals to live and die in the all-too-forgiving arms of family and friends.

Although I do not believe in collective *criminal* punishment, I do believe that the German (and Austrian) people — those who did not actively oppose Nazism — bear considerable *moral* responsibility for the Holocaust. Certainly every willing supporter of Nazism deserves some blame for its entirely predictable — indeed promised — genocidal outcome.

Just as the vast majority of German people expected to reap material benefits from Hitler's aggression, so too they should have reaped the bitter fruit of defeat. They should have suffered — as a *people* — after the Holocaust. Individuals who actively resisted should have been individually rewarded. But those who went along with Hitler's genocidal program, even passively so as to live the good life, should have been made to suffer in rough proportion to their complicity and culpability.

That is why the rebuilding of postwar Germany into one of the world's most affluent nations is a moral disgrace. A minimal appropriate response to the collective responsibility of the German people for the crimes of their leaders — whom they elected and enthusiastically supported and whose mass murders were carried out with the assistance and knowledge of so many citizens — should have been a generation of poverty, for most Germans,* coupled with rewards for those who opposed Nazism. Henry Morgenthau, Jr. — secretary of the treasury during World War II — wrote a book called *Germany Is Our Problem* (1945), in which he urged that postwar Germany be partitioned and transformed into an agrarian society. Morgenthau called for

* The Jewish instinct for justice, which impelled most of us to boycott German goods after the war — particularly goods manufactured by companies complicitous with Nazism — was right on the mark, though largely ineffective because of American subsidies.

the transfer of equipment and factories from Germany to the Allied nations as war reparations.

But instead of requiring the German people to live at subsistence level for twenty or thirty years, we immediately rewarded them with the Marshall Plan. We also pardoned convicted Nazi criminals who could help rebuild West Germany. We rewarded the evils of the past to confront the more "pressing" concerns of the future. The most pressing of these concerns — the Cold War against communism — certainly did not justify the rewards we heaped upon West Germany, Austria, and numerous individual Nazis whom we recruited in the name of our holy war against communism.* The ultimate reward — the reunification of the Germanies and the establishment of the most powerful nation in Europe less than a half century after the destruction of Nazism — did not even claim a pressing international need. It was simply the natural consequence of refusing to recognize the responsibility of the German nation for the incalculable evil it wrought.

In one respect, the success of postwar Germany marks the belated completion of Hitler's twin goals in starting World War II: the destruction of European Jewry, which he accomplished before his death; and the reemergence of Germany as the most powerful nation in Europe, which has now been accomplished with the aid of the United States and the other victorious survivors of World War II.

The sad reality is that the world's response to Nazi atrocities has been so inadequate that recurrence — probably in different form — is not beyond the realm of likelihood. I recently spoke to a group of German students studying at the Kennedy School as McCloy fellows (the program, as I mentioned earlier, is named, quite appropriately, for the former U.S. high commissioner to West Germany, who pardoned many Nazi criminals, returned confiscated slave-labor property to the Krupps, and helped rebuild Germany). I put the following question: "Would a calculating and amoral potential Nazi, knowing everything we now know about his rewards and punishments for joining or not joining the Nazi party back in the 1930s, be inclined to join or not to join?" Several of the German students agreed that the world's response to Nazism has been so inadequate that even today a calcu-

---

* West Germany certainly did not have to be rebuilt in order to compete with East Germany, Poland, or other countries under Communist domination, since the Soviet Union allowed these countries to languish in near-poverty. Nor did West Germany need to be rebuilt in order to prevent a recurrence of the militarism that followed the Treaty of Versailles, since an agrarian society cannot wage modern warfare.

lating potential Nazi would again choose to participate in the Holocaust on the basis of a simple cost-benefit analysis. Nothing could better demonstrate the failure of the world's response to the most awful crime ever inflicted on humankind.

It is important to recognize that American Jews — even those whose families left Europe before World War II — are themselves vicarious survivors of the Nazi Holocaust. We too were Hitler's intended victims. I was seven years old at the end of the war and would almost certainly have ended up in a crematorium along with my European cousins had Hitler won the war or had my grandparents not emigrated from Poland. We have nearly as much stake in bringing Nazi war criminals to justice as do literal survivors. The need to prevent recurrence is as compelling in me. Even the demand for justice and remembrance should be as real.

As part of my efforts to understand the injustice of the Holocaust and the world's immoral reaction to it, I have traveled to Poland twice. I first went in 1987, with my younger son, Jamin, who was then a Yale law student deeply concerned over issues of justice and injustice. My second trip was in mid-1990, with my older son, Elon, who is a Hollywood filmmaker and more interested in the psychology of vengeance. More about this second trip later.

The 1987 visit to this country, which can only be called a Jewish cemetery with no tombstone, was an emotional roller coaster for me and Jamin. But my dominant emotion throughout the entire visit was deepening anger, even fury, at the apparent refusal of large portions of the Polish people, their government, and many intellectuals to come to grips with the enormity of the genocidal crimes that took place in their homeland, before their very eyes, and often with their complicity and even encouragement.

To make the dimensions of the tragedy more comprehensible to American readers, some rough statistics may be helpful. The Jewish population of Poland on the eve of World War II was approximately 3.5 million (out of a total of 30 million). In the larger cities and towns, such as Warsaw, Kraków, Lódz, Kielce, and Bialystok, Jews constituted nearly one-third of the inhabitants. Although anti-Semitism had imposed limits on their political power, and the infamous *numerus clausus* (anti-Jewish quotas) had reduced their numbers at universities, Jews had become an important — some mistakenly thought, an inexpungible — part of Polish life. They had lived among their Catholic neighbors — some alongside, others in separate villages, or *shtetlach* — for nearly a thousand years. Their place in Polish life, in both numbers and influence, was roughly comparable to the place of Catholics in our country today.

Then in a few short years, beginning in September 1939 and ending in 1945, nearly every single Polish Jewish man, woman, and child was systematically murdered. This included half Jews, quarter Jews, converted Jews, baby Jews, atheist Jews, Catholic priests with a Jewish ancestor, even Jews who had long ago renounced their heritage. At first they were shot, but then the techniques were improved to include mobile gas vans and extermination camps with gas chambers and crematoria.

Nor was the killing in Poland restricted to Polish Jews. From all over Europe, some two million more Jewish men, women, and children were ingathered by train — from as far away as Norway, Corfu, and France. Even some American Jews, trapped in Europe during the fighting, were gassed in the giant Polish extermination camps at Auschwitz-Birkenau, Treblinka, Belzec, Chelmno, and Sobibór. The Nazi goal was not simply to get rid of Jews who were in the way or who were partisans or Communists, as it was with some other groups. It was to rid the world of every Jew — finally and systematically.

I went to Auschwitz-Birkenau — the site of the largest murder camp — expecting to be moved, perhaps to cry. But instead of my eyes tearing, my fists clenched.

Quite deliberately, Jamin and I decided not to go on an "American" or "Jewish" tour. We followed a group of Polish schoolchildren in order to find out what *they* are told about this museum and what it represents *to them*. Their teacher spoke some English and translated for us. It was a shocking and infuriating experience.

The children — indeed typical Eastern European visitors — are not told, as the Jewish visitor is, that nearly all of the three million people murdered in the various camps were Jews who were gassed solely because they were Jews.* The Polish visitor is told that the victims were Polish citizens: intellectuals, priests, soldiers, journalists, resistance members. He is shown the wall of death, where hundreds of political prisoners were shot, but not the remnants of the gas chambers where millions of Jews were murdered. Indeed, the Birkenau part of

---

* Historian David Wyman cites that figure in addition to the nearly 1.5 million Jews massacred in formal mobile killing actions. Most of the rest were murdered by mass shootings and the lethal conditions deliberately imposed on the ghettos or during the deportation transfers. David Wyman, *The Abandonment of the Jews* (New York: Pantheon, 1985), p. 5.

the complex is not even on the tour. It was to the Birkenau portion that the Jewish women, children, and men were taken to be gassed and burned. The tour only includes the Auschwitz camp where Polish prisoners — all of them adults — were kept, and where many perished.*

It is true, of course, that a considerable number of Polish adults were *individually* murdered for inexcusable reasons — their politics, their participation in the resistance, their religious activities as priests, their work as journalists, and so forth. But the Polish people, as such, was not marked for genocidal extermination as were the Jews and the Gypsies. (Approximately one-half million Gypsies were murdered by the Nazis.) It in no way diminishes the horrors inflicted on these Polish adults who were subjected to the camps to point out that there is an enormous difference between what the Nazis did to individual Polish adults and what they did to *all* Jews — babies and adults — whom they managed to ingather to the extermination camps. And that distinction is quite deliberately blurred for the Eastern European visitor to the Auschwitz Museum.

For example, in one room in the Polish pavilion — each country occupied by the Nazis has a pavilion — there are hundreds of pictures of the dead martyrs. My son and I gasped in shock as we passed the photographs and read the names under each of them: there was not a single Jewish name; every one was Polish. In the adjoining room, there is a display of photographs of babies and children gassed in the camps. Beneath their pictures there are no names, only numbers. The reason is apparent: to list their names would make it clear that Polish children were not murdered at Auschwitz-Birkenau; only Jewish (and Gypsy) babies and children were gassed as part of the Nazi genocide.

Each of the Eastern European national pavilions goes out of its way to downplay the uniquely Jewish nature of the Holocaust. None mentions the fact that entire Jewish populations were transported to Auschwitz-Birkenau from the far-flung corners of the Nazi empire for systematic genocide.

Not all the intended victims were Jews. But all the Jews were intended victims. That reality, made so eloquently by Nobel laureate Elie Wiesel, is lost on the typical visitor to Auschwitz.

Indeed, the opposite is sometimes conveyed quite explicitly. In the Hungarian pavilion, the following caveat appears in bold print: "The

---

* The latest figures suggest that the total number of Polish Catholics killed at Auschwitz was in the range of seventy-five thousand.

theme of this exhibition is not the fate of the Jewish people. What it wants to narrate is Hungarian history." At the entrance to the Czechoslovakian pavilion, there is a beautiful marble memorial to the victims of the extermination camps. The names of the camps are etched into marble: "Treblinka, Mauthausen, Oswiecim [Auschwitz], Bergen-Belsen, Dachau." Surrounding these names are hundreds of Christian crosses — but not a single star of David to honor the 150,000 Jewish victims from Czechoslovakia.*

The message to the Eastern European tourist, a message one hears and sees throughout Poland, is clear and deliberate: the Nazis randomly killed the occupied population until the Red Army defeated them and rescued the survivors. Because it omits the special nature of the "final solution" against the Jews, the message is false and pernicious. Nor has this message changed since the overthrow of communism, except for omitting the heroism of the Red Army.

The only instance at the Auschwitz Museum in which a Jew is singled out as a victim is at the cell of Father Maximilian Kolbe, the Franciscan priest who — we were told — had volunteered to die "in place of a Jew." This point, that Kolbe died in place of an intended Jewish victim, is repeatedly made by those who would try to persuade the world that many Polish Catholics risked their lives to rescue Jewish victims. An authoritative history of the church in modern Poland states categorically that "Father Kolbe voluntarily gave his life in place of a Jew at Auschwitz."[8] The *Boston Globe* reported on March 17, 1989, that

> Catholic leaders replied [to Jewish claims that Auschwitz was a place of agony for the Jewish people by pointing out] that many Christians died at Auschwitz, including thousands of Catholic priests who were targeted by the Nazis. The most notable was Reverend Maximilian Kolbe, who was canonized as a Saint in 1982 and is remembered especially for volunteering to take the place of a Polish Jew who had been scheduled for execution.

The *Christian Science Monitor* reported (October 5, 1984) that a requiem was written in Poland as a tribute to Kolbe, "who chose his own death in Auschwitz to save a condemned Jew." A rabbi recently told me about a moving interfaith service dedicated to Father Kolbe for having saved that Jew.

* This memorial was unchanged during my second trip in 1990, despite the change of government in Czechoslovakia.

The story that Father Kolbe gave up his life to save a condemned Jew is a beautiful one. I only wish it were true. Unfortunately, it is a total fabrication, circulated by those who would rewrite history. The Vatican itself recognizes that the man whom Father Kolbe saved was a fellow Catholic named Franciszek Gajowinczek, a Polish sergeant from the town of Brzeg. When Kolbe was canonized in 1982 — as the Saint of Auschwitz — Gajowinczek, a devoted Catholic from birth, was given a place of honor.

In his benediction, Pope John Paul II characterized Father Kolbe as "perhaps the brightest and most glittering figure to emerge from the darkness and degradation of the Nazi epoch." The pope continued: "He was a true Pole, and as a Polish patriot he was willing to give his life for that of a fellow countryman."[9] It speaks volumes that the Saint of Auschwitz was honored more greatly for his patriotism in saving a fellow Polish Catholic than were those Polish humanitarians who gave their lives to save the few Jews who survived.

The crowning irony of this telling story is not only that Kolbe never saved a single Jew, but also that he was a notorious anti-Semite who almost certainly would never have sacrificed his life for a condemned Jewish inmate. (In fact, it is unlikely that Kolbe ever even *met* a Jew at Auschwitz, since the Polish prisoners were kept entirely separate from the Jews.) Prior to the war, according to U.S. newspaper reports, Kolbe "edited a rabidly anti-Semitic Catholic newspaper," and railed against the "organized clique of fanatical Jews, who want to destroy the Church." He believed in the authenticity of *The Protocols of the Elders of Zion* and blamed the ills of Poland on "International Zionism." As a story in the *Washington Post* aptly summarized: "It is not unfair to say that [Kolbe] and others like him provided a hospitable environment for [the Holocaust]. By propagating anti-Semitism, they set the stage for the unimaginable horror that was to follow."[10]

The *Washington Post* story concluded that the Catholic Church, in sanctifying Kolbe, "meant only to honor the 'saintly' part of his life. Unfortunately, it may also have excused the bad. Sainthood," the *Post* continued, "connotes perfection — a life worthy of emulation. In an important area, Kolbe's life was not only unworthy of emulation but cries out . . . for condemnation. Instead, it was swept under the carpet. . . . Once again anti-Semitism has been viewed as insignificant."[11]

This, then, is the story of Jewish suffering told at the Polish pavilion at Auschwitz (and the other Eastern European pavilions as well).

It is all too typical of the false story taught in Polish schools, preached from Polish pulpits, and written about by Polish intellectuals.

To be sure, there is a Jewish pavilion at the Auschwitz Museum, but it is not a regular part of the tour. Only Jewish visitors, Americans, and other "special groups" are even told about the Jewish pavilion. It is the last pavilion — number 27 — and it is a dark, out-of-the-way house, with no guide. When I found it, the lights were off. The caretaker, who spoke no English, Hebrew, or Yiddish, seemed almost reluctant to open it up. Walking along with my son through the Jewish pavilion, I felt my fists unclench and my eyes tear. But my fists quickly clenched again as I realized that those who most need to see what happened to the Jews were not even aware of the pavilion and what it represents.

On a list of those gassed at Auschwitz-Birkenau, I found the names of two Dershowitzes (in the original spelling) and the name of one man with my mother's family name. The appearance of my name brought home the message that, but for the grace of God and the foresight of my grandparents, I and my entire family might have been eliminated. I imagined us in the extermination camps fully aware that no one would survive, and I wondered what I would have been thinking. I could read similar thoughts in Jamin's eyes.

As a token expression of his anger at what we saw, Jamin ripped down a rusty piece of barbed wire from the camp's original fence and put it in his pocket. He smuggled it all through Europe and was caught, ironically, by an airport border guard in Frankfurt. I tried to explain that the wire came from Poland and not from Germany. My son quipped to the German guard, "It was yours originally." Fortunately, he didn't seem to understand what Jamin was saying. The barbed wire now hangs in our home as a reminder of what human beings are capable of doing — and quickly forgetting.

Other Jews of my generation who have traveled to Auschwitz, including some of my Brooklyn group, have had a very different reaction to the experience. They have visited with Jewish or American tour groups and have been guided through the camps with appropriate messages of sorrow and forgiveness. They cried, recited the Kaddish prayer for the dead, and swore that it would not happen again. But they did not see what Jamin and I had seen: that it could very well happen again, precisely because the Polish and other European visitors to Auschwitz are never told that "it" — the genocide against the Jews — happened at all.

From Auschwitz, we drove through the area of southeastern Poland from which my family emigrated. On the way, we stopped at a small town where a fair was being held in the square. Kids were petting rabbits, teenagers were flirting, adults were buying produce. Only later did I learn that at that very square, the entire Jewish population of the town was gathered on July 28, 1942. This is how the ensuing evils are described in a history of the Holocaust by Martin Gilbert:

> All had to remove their shoes and, barefoot, were driven with rifle butts and whips into the market square. . . . The children were taken to a shed at the edge of the square and shot. Indescribable lamentations, sobbing and weeping filled the market, [an] eyewitness recalled. Old men and women were also shot, while the others were taken to the camps, from which none returned.[12]

In some cases, four generations of a family were murdered in each other's presence and the family seed obliterated forever, literally made extinct after thousands of years of Jewish family history. Now the village square is a place of joy, with no memorial to, or reminder of, the tragic events of July 28, 1942 — events that were repeated throughout wartime Poland and whose memory is obliterated throughout modern-day Poland.

In the next town, I saw two old synagogues in which the Jews were gathered and slaughtered. One is now an art gallery, the other a town archive with no records of the vibrant Jewish population that lived there for centuries. In the town my grandfather lived in, Przemyśl, which was once a center of Jewish learning, publishing, and commerce, I could not even find the old synagogue or the Jewish cemetery. The official Jewish guidebook of Poland — published by the government — does not list Przemyśl as among the cities or towns with surviving Jewish buildings, cemeteries, or archives, despite its long and distinguished Jewish past. Like so many other places in Poland, Przemyśl has obliterated or hidden from view all traces of its Jewish history.

As Jamin and I were sipping a cold drink on a street corner, I observed an eerie sight. The passersby all had characteristically Polish faces. Suddenly a man in his late forties turned the corner. He bore a striking resemblance to me. His face looked very Jewish. Impulsively,

I walked up to him and tried to communicate — in Yiddish, Hebrew, English. He did not understand and walked on. I could not help wondering whether he could possibly have been of Jewish birth, one of the Jewish babies abandoned by its doomed parents or given over to a non-Jewish family so that it might survive. Probably not, but the haunting possibility stayed with me for the remainder of the trip.

When the war finally ended and the Germans retreated in 1945, the few Jewish survivors emerged from their hiding places in the sewers, the forests, and the makeshift bunkers. Few families remained intact, but some remnants were determined to try to rebuild Polish Jewry. They came back to their homes, only to find them looted and occupied by locals, some of whom were angry at their return and disappointed that the Nazis had not completed their work. In the town of Kielce, on July 4, 1946, *a year after the Germans had withdrawn*, local Poles murdered more than forty Jewish survivors and wounded another sixty. When the Catholic Primate of Poland, Augustus Cardinal Hlond, was asked to condemn the mass murder, he stated that the Jews had brought it on themselves. Because some Jews had become Communists, the cardinal reasoned, it was understandable that Polish nationalists would kill all the Jews of Kielce, even the children.

Cardinal Hlond also refused a request by American Jewish leaders to condemn anti-Semitism, because "the facts do not justify such a proclamation from the Church," and because Poland's rising anti-Semitism was "to a great degree due to the Jews." The *New York Times* headline read: "Cardinal Puts Blame on Some Jews for Pogrom."[13] In light of this attitude expressed by the head of the Catholic Church in Poland, it should not be surprising that more than fifteen hundred Jewish survivors of Hitler's genocide were murdered *by Poles* in 1945 and 1946. There is, of course, no mention of this entirely Polish, post-Holocaust mass murder of Jews in the Auschwitz Museum or in Polish history books. Nor is there any mention of the Polish primate's bigoted response to it.

When I recently wrote a letter to the editor of the *New York Times* mentioning the pogrom at Kielce, an apologist for Poland responded that "the 1946 Kielce pogrom was carried out not by Polish nationalists, but by the Soviet controlled army . . . precisely to discredit the non-communist opposition."[14] This revisionist fiction has now become fashionable in post-Communist Poland. Anti-Communists now blame the Communists, while Communists still blame the anti-Communists.[15] Nobody blames indigenous elements of the Polish population, brought up for centuries on anti-Jewish sermons and folkways. To this day, no one has ever investigated the Kielce pogrom, beyond the hands-on perpetrators, despite the obvious complicity of at least some government and church officials.*

In light of this persistent strain of anti-Semitism in high places, it should not be surprising that in the 1950s and again in the 1960s, governmentally sponsored campaigns of anti-Semitism frightened the remaining Jewish population — except for a handful of assimilated intellectuals and a few people too old to leave — into emigrating to the United States or Israel. What the Nazi army failed to do — make Poland completely *Judenrein* (free of Jews) — the Poles themselves managed to complete. You would never know of the Polish complicity in this effort from a visit to the Auschwitz Museum.

To be sure, some Polish individuals risked their lives to protect their Jewish friends and neighbors during the Nazi occupation. But others actively participated in the Nazi genocide by themselves killing Jews or by disclosing their hiding places to the German soldiers. As of the time of my first trip, Polish authorities — in the government as well as the church — had made no serious effort to acknowledge or disavow the postwar campaigns of anti-Semitism that resulted in the final, and apparently welcome, exodus of Polish Jewry. Although there now seems to be some movement toward acknowledging past crimes and sins, it remains to be seen how serious and intensive this effort really is.

In light of this despicable history it was quite disappointing to learn that even some contemporary Polish intellectuals and human rights activists seem to understand so little about the lessons of the genocide in Poland. For example, one of Poland's most prominent human rights lawyers, Wladyslaw Sila-Nowicki, who has represented Cardinal Wyszynski, Lech Walesa, and the Solidarity movement, wrote an article recently seeking to justify the role played by the Polish people during the Holocaust. In it, he invokes many classic canards of crude

---

* In 1990, Lech Walesa wrote an open letter urging his fellow Poles to abandon the pretense that the Kielce murders were a Soviet provocation. The crimes were committed by Polish people, Walesa said, and there should be a plaque commemorating the tragedy. Walesa did not, however, suggest an investigation into who actually provoked the pogrom. Walesa's views on the "Jewish question" are complex and confusing. He berated Polish citizens who hide their Jewish backgrounds, thus stimulating a "Jew hunt" in the 1990 Polish election for "secret" Jews. Then he said that he raised the issue because Jews should be proud of their heritage. Ultimately, he apologized for provoking anti-Jewish feelings. He was elected president of Poland and took office in late December.

anti-Semitism: dual loyalty ("They had to love their community more than the host community"); excessive wealth ("Who held the largest capital in Poland, the Polish majority or the 10% Jewish minority?"); Jewish success ("It is only natural . . . that a community [the Poles] will defend itself [by imposing anti-Jewish quotas] against letting its intellectual elite become eclipsed by others, which was a particularly likely prospect in areas such as medicine or law").[16]

Most disturbing, however, is that this respected human rights lawyer tries to blame the Jews themselves for their slaughter. He claims that the Jewish "population as a whole" believed that "passiveness was their solution." This is how Sila-Nowicki remembers the Holocaust:

> For us, Poles, it was often an astounding spectacle to see several thousand Jews being led from a small town along a road several kilometers long, escorted by only a few guards (six, sometimes four) carrying ordinary rifles. . . . Nobody escaped, although escape was no problem. . . . Perhaps they were held back by a gregarious instinct of that community.[17]

In addition to blaming the victims for passiveness, Sila-Nowicki also attributes active culpability to Jews, alleging that the Jewish police in the ghetto were "incomparably more merciless and brutal toward their own people" than were the Polish police.[18]

The great tragedy is that there are few Jews left in Poland willing and able to answer these lies and to point out the anti-Semitic assumptions underlying Sila-Nowicki's entire thesis.

It falls upon outsiders, whose writings are unlikely to be read by Polish intellectuals, to correct the historical record by documenting the numerous instances of Jewish resistance, the refusal of Polish partisans to supply requested arms to Jewish partisans, and the frequent betrayal of Jewish fighters by Polish individuals, including partisans.

The Holocaust was not caused by any failure of Jewish "instinct." It could not be prevented largely because many of the citizens of Nazi-occupied lands cooperated with the genocidal program of the occupiers. An account of Polish attitudes toward Jews that is far more accurate than Sila-Nowicki's self-serving and anti-Semitic collection of half-truths is given in Claude Lanzmann's film *Shoah* (1985), which interviews many Polish witnesses to the Holocaust.

Poland is a nation where anti-Semitism lingers even in the absence of Jews. The memory of the dead, and the guilty defensiveness of those who were complicitous in their death, are enough to invoke it.

*   *   *   *

While in Poland on the trip with Jamin, in 1987, I met with the intellectual leaders of what was then the Solidarity underground. The meeting was arranged by the American chargé d'affaires, who warned us that our conversation was probably being bugged and that the participants would likely be followed. Adam Michnick, who had recently been released from prison, pleaded with us to convey his message of desperation to American political leaders. Bronislaw Geremeck was pessimistic that Solidarity could ever regain the influence it had achieved several years earlier. Other underground activists seemed despondent about the future. No one at that meeting could even hope that within a few short years, Solidarity would be in control of the Polish government, Michnick would be the editor of Poland's most influential newspaper, and Geremeck would be the leader of the Polish parliament.

Everything changed drastically between my two visits to Poland in 1987 and 1990 — everything except as it related to Jews. There were some small changes in Polish attitudes toward the Jews. Certainly, there were significant improvements in official government policy in regard to Israel. There were also improvements in official policy in regard to Jewish culture and religion. But the dominant force in the lives of most Polish citizens has never been the government, whether run by the Communists or by Solidarity. It has always been the Catholic church.

The Polish Catholic church is a unique institution, especially since the imposition of Communist rule following the end of World War II. Communism was never popular with the Polish people, but political opposition to communism was not tolerated. The Catholic church became, therefore, the only lawful institution openly opposing communism. The church was too deeply entrenched and influential in Polish life for the Communists to outlaw it. Attendance at church services became a political symbol for Polish nationalism and anticommunism. Intellectuals who practiced birth control and abortion joined with practicing Catholics at Mass to listen to anti-Communist sermons and to show solidarity against the common enemy.

Even the Solidarity labor movement was integrated into the Catholic church. Although several of its intellectual leaders, including Michnick and Geremeck, were Jewish by heritage, the popular leadership had close connections with the church. During my 1987 trip, I visited the "Solidarity church," where Father Jerzy Popieluszko, a Solidarity activist priest, was buried after being murdered in 1984 by security guards. It was the only place in Warsaw where Solidarity banners could fly unmolested in 1987.

The Catholic church in Poland is hierarchical. At its head stands the Primate of Poland, whose title is a quasi-political one accorded the archbishop of Warsaw and Gniezno. The Primate of Poland is regarded by many as the single most influential person in the country. Political leadership shifts, but the primate remains supreme.

The Primate of Poland since 1981 has been Jozef Cardinal Glemp. Without mincing words, I can only describe Glemp as an old-fashioned anti-Semite, as were at least his immediate predecessors Wyszynski and Hlond. My second visit to Poland was caused by Cardinal Glemp. I went there to sue him for defaming an American rabbi by falsely accusing the rabbi and several of his students of attempting to murder Polish nuns. It was a twentieth-century "blood libel" that grew out of the highly emotional dispute over a Carmelite convent established at the Auschwitz-Birkenau extermination camp.

The failure of the Polish government and the Polish church to educate its people about the history of the Holocaust helps to explain the international furor over the Carmelite convent established at Auschwitz in 1984. Were it not for the systematic efforts to "de-Judaize" — to borrow Elie Wiesel's apt word — the Holocaust, there probably would have been little complaint when a group of nuns moved into a building in which the Nazis had stored the poison gas used to murder more than a million Jews between 1942 and 1944 at the Auschwitz-Birkenau complex.

The nuns moved into the building in violation of a United Nations resolution declaring the Auschwitz complex to be an international historical site, not to be disturbed. Fund-raising literature for the convent suggested that the Auschwitz nuns were praying for the conversion of the Jews. This enraged many Jewish leaders around the world, who claimed that placing a Catholic convent at the site of the greatest tragedy in Jewish history was insensitive to the unique suffering experienced by the Jews. It was seen by many Jews as another manifestation of Polish efforts to de-Judaize the Holocaust.

In 1987, an agreement was reached between Jewish leaders and several cardinals, including the cardinal of Kraków, in whose jurisdiction the convent was located. The agreement provided for the erection of a Jewish-Christian dialogue center outside the gates of Auschwitz and the relocation of the convent to that center by February of 1989.

When the deadline passed without the convent's being relocated, several Jewish leaders again protested. Among them was Rabbi Avraham Weiss of Riverdale, New York. Along with six students, he engaged in a peaceful "pray-in" at the convent. They rang the bell at the outer fence, asked to be invited in to discuss the relocation of the convent, and were turned away. They then climbed over the fence, put on their prayer shawls, and began to pray. They were soon attacked by several bystanders, beaten, sprayed with water and urine, and carried away, amid shouts of "Heil Hitler" and "Rip off their skullcaps."

The first Polish news reports of this event placed the blame for the violence on Rabbi Weiss and the students. But within days, the Solidarity newspaper reported the event accurately, providing a minute-by-minute account of the events leading up to the violence, and placing the blame squarely on the shoulders of the Polish workers who had roughed up the rabbi and his students.

Several weeks later, Cardinal Glemp delivered a homily to 150,000 Polish faithful at Czestochowa, the site of the holiest shrine in Poland. With the new Solidarity prime minister at his side, Cardinal Glemp delivered an anti-Semitic tirade that would have made his predecessors proud. He accused the Jews of "plying [Polish] peasants with alcohol" and of "spreading communism," as well as of anti-Polish attitudes. He accused Jewish businessmen of having "neglected and despised the Poles." And he repeated the false account of Hitler's genocide that has become standard in postwar Poland, equating the genocide against all Jews with the selective killing of some Polish adults: "Jews, Poles and Gypsies were people consigned to extermination by the Nazis but by different strategies and on a different scale." He then went on to describe the Polish suffering, without further reference to the "scale" of Jewish devastation, except for his mandatory invocation of the "collaborators among the Jews." He did not, of course, mention the enormous number of collaborators among the Poles.[19]

Glemp proceeded to accuse the Jews of being an aloof nation who "speak to us from the position of the chosen people," and who control the "mass-media in many countries, which makes you so powerful" and which the Jews use to "stir up anti-Polish sentiments." Without Jews provoking anti-Polish feelings, the cardinal assured his audience, "there would also not be any anti-Semitism here."[20] In other words, the Jews are the cause of Polish anti-Semitism, which would surely stop if only they would stop picking on the Poles.

Finally, Cardinal Glemp got to the events at the Carmelite convent.

This is how he described them: "Recently a squad of seven Jews from New York launched attacks on the convent at Oświecim [Auschwitz]. In fact, it did not happen that the sisters were killed or the convent destroyed, because they were apprehended."[21]

Newsweek reported that Glemp's statement was "against all the evidence." And Albert Cardinal Decourtray of Lyon, France, denounced it as "pure nonsense," as did several other church leaders. But it was widely believed by an audience all too eager to place the blame on "Jews from New York," and to accept the fantasy that a rabbi would kill helpless nuns.[22]

As soon as Cardinal Glemp's outrageous comments were published on the front page of the *New York Times*, Rabbi Weiss — with whom I had worked on Soviet Jewry issues in the 1970s and on other Jewish concerns since — called me and asked me to represent him in a defamation action against the cardinal. "He slandered me, as well as the entire Jewish people — and he cannot be allowed to get away with doing that," the rabbi said with a mixture of sadness and anger. "The Polish people have to be told that the cardinal's statements are untrue," the rabbi continued. "Accusing me and the students of wanting to kill the nuns is a modern-day version of the blood libel."

Nor was the homily at Czestochowa merely an isolated outburst on Cardinal Glemp's part. It was a culmination of a lifelong history of anti-Semitism. Glemp had been a longtime supporter of Endetz'ya, the virulently anti-Semitic Polish nationalist party. He had denounced Solidarity for being infiltrated by "Trotskyites" and persons "devoid of Christian ethics" — well-recognized code words for "Jews" in modern Polish parlance. He had delivered homilies similar to the one in Czestochowa over the years in local churches. The only difference is that this time he had gotten caught. Because of the increased news coverage of events in Poland following the victory of the Solidarity government, a *New York Times* reporter was in Czestochowa when Glemp delivered his speech.

When I had traveled to Poland in 1987, I was advised by several informed sources, Jewish and Catholic, that Glemp was an old-fashioned anti-Semite who had a primitive hatred of Jews. I was told that the pope disliked Glemp, as did the archbishop of Kraków, Franciszek Cardinal Macharski. Glemp was a protégé of Stefan Cardinal Wyszynski, a notorious anti-Semite.

Though Glemp was not popular among church or Solidarity leaders, he did have a large following among local parish priests and nuns.

For example, the mother superior of the Carmelite convent at Auschwitz, Sister Teresa Magiera, parroted Glemp's bigotry in an interview she gave to a Polish American journalist. She asked: "Why do the Jews want special treatment in Auschwitz only for themselves? . . . Do they still consider themselves the chosen people?" She accused Israel of anti-Semitism for "mistreating the Arabs." As she put it: "Greater anti-Semites are hard to find" than the Israelis. Sister Teresa placed virtually the entire blame for communism and for the failure of the Polish economy on the Jews: "The entire Polish government consisted of 75% Polish Communist Jews, appointed by Joseph Stalin, with the specific intention to introduce atheism into Poland." She proceeded to list all "the Jews" who had run Poland after World War II. Several of those she listed were not even Jewish. Indeed, the entire enterprise of listing the Jews who were "prototype Bolsheviks" goes back to Hitler's days. It is still in vogue in contemporary Poland, as evidenced by Sister Teresa, Cardinal Glemp, and others.[23]

I thought long and hard before agreeing to bring the defamation suit. As a civil libertarian, I generally disfavor libel suits. If reporters and authors have to worry that their honest mistakes could bankrupt them, they may become more timid in their investigative disclosures.

As a law clerk, I had worked on the Supreme Court's seminal decision in *New York Times Co. v. Sullivan* (1964), in which the high court interpreted the First Amendment as imposing stringent limits on libel suits directed against "public figures." It required that the public figure prove the false statement was made with "malice": either actual knowledge that the statement was false, or reckless disregard of its truth.

I generally agree with the *Sullivan* decision and believe that defamation suits by public figures should be limited to deliberate lies.

Several times a year, defamed victims call me and ask me to sue on their behalf. Prior to Rabbi Weiss's call, I had always talked the defamed person out of suing.

But Rabbi Weiss persuaded me that his case was different. There could be no doubt that Cardinal Glemp had deliberately lied in accusing the "squad" of New York Jews of intending to kill the nuns. No one could be so stupid as to believe that a rabbi and several students had traveled to Auschwitz to murder defenseless nuns. Several Polish American leaders have told me that Glemp *is,* in fact, stupid. They told me this in explanation, not justification, of his absurd remark. Indeed, in Poland, a new verb has been coined to describe the making of a ridiculous and embarrassing statement: "to *Glemp*."[24] The objective chronology, moreover, clearly proved that Cardinal Glemp *knew* at the time he made his slanderous accusation that it was false. The Polish press had retracted its earlier story and had placed the blame for the violence squarely on the Polish workmen. Well before Glemp delivered his homily, the press had reported unequivocally that Rabbi Weiss and the students had engaged in a nonviolent "pray-in" and had no intention of harming the nuns.

But unless and until Cardinal Glemp himself admitted that he had misinformed his listeners — or a court so found — there was a serious risk that the news reports would be ignored by many of his followers. There is no real marketplace of ideas within the Polish church. Rabbi Weiss could not possibly respond to Cardinal Glemp's slander in a way that effectively reached the faithful who heard, and undoubtedly believed, what their cardinal had told them.

There was no danger that Glemp or his church could be bankrupted by a libel judgment against them. Indeed, Rabbi Weiss was not suing for monetary damages, but rather in order to establish the falsity of Glemp's charges.

I decided to take the case. It was about time an anti-Semitic priest was called to account for his bigotry. No one is above the law, not even a cardinal. A lawsuit was the only way to make Cardinal Glemp understand that his bigoted rhetoric was unacceptable in a civilized society.

I mapped out a series of legal actions. First, we would file suit against the cardinal right here in the United States. Even though he made the speech in Poland, his libel was published in American newspapers, and he knew, or should have known, that accusations of attempted murder by an American rabbi made before a very large audience would receive international media coverage.

We prepared a traditional defamation suit under American law. To be able to bring such a suit in an American court, we would have to serve Glemp personally with a complaint while he was in the United States.

Serendipitously, Glemp was planning his first trip to the United States at the time he delivered his homily at Czestochowa. He had been invited by Joseph Cardinal Bernardin to visit Polish American communities in Chicago, Milwaukee, Cleveland, and Boston. As soon as we learned of his proposed trip, we announced that we would serve him with a complaint when he landed in this country. We had two purposes in making this announcement. First, we hoped that the threat of a lawsuit would encourage him, and those who invited him, to cancel the visit. We knew how anxious he was to come to America, and we wanted him to have to pay a price for his anti-Semitic lies. We also wanted his hosts to understand that we would not remain silent in the face of his bigotry. Accordingly, on September 5, 1989, I wrote the following letter to Cardinal Glemp at his residence in Warsaw:

Dear Cardinal Glemp:

I am the attorney for Rabbi Avraham Weiss. You have maliciously defamed my client by stating:

"Recently a squad of seven Jews from New York launched attacks on the convent at Oświecim. In fact, it did not happen that the sisters were killed or the convent destroyed, because they were apprehended."

Your malicious defamation constitutes an actionable tort under state law in the United States. It also constitutes actionable conduct under Polish and Catholic Church law. My client has authorized me to take legal action against you for your malicious defamation in every available forum.

Accordingly, when you arrive in the United States, you will be served with a complaint and required to appear in court to answer his charges.

Please show this letter to your attorney and have him be in touch with me about accepting service of process. I know that you will not want to engage in any unseemly behavior, such as attempting to avoid being served. Accordingly, I will be happy to serve your attorney, if that is agreeable to you. If not, we will serve you in person as soon as you set foot in this country.

My client demands that you unilaterally issue a retraction of your deliberate false statements about him and about the Jewish religion. Failure to do so will aggravate the inexcusable damage you have already caused.

Sincerely,
Alan M. Dershowitz

Within a few days after receiving our letter, Cardinal Glemp postponed his visit "indefinitely." The *New York Times* put the following in a box on its first page:

The Polish press agency announced that Josef Cardinal Glemp, the Archbishop of Warsaw, had cancelled a tour of American cities. The

Cardinal has been threatened with a lawsuit by a New York rabbi in a heated dispute over a convent at the site of the Auschwitz death camp.

Its correspondent in Warsaw elaborated:

Spokesmen for Cardinal Glemp were unavailable today, but the decision to cancel the visit comes only several days after Jewish leaders in the United States announced that during the trip they would file suit against the Cardinal for defamation.[25]

The *Boston Globe* published my reaction to the cancellation:

Yesterday, Alan Dershowitz of Harvard Law School, who has been preparing to sue Cardinal Glemp in Polish and U.S. courts for defaming the Jewish people, called postponement of the trip "a great victory for decency, particularly for those leaders of the Catholic Church who have distanced themselves from Cardinal Glemp's anti-Semitism."

Dershowitz, who said he finished preparatory work on the suit yesterday morning, noted that "we've gotten a lot of support from Catholics throughout the country."[26]

It *was* a great victory for decency. It was also a victory for Jewish power. It sent a clear message to Cardinal Glemp and his ilk: Jews no longer take this kind of bigotry without fighting back. We don't just hide in our homes and pray that there will be no pogrom. We don't come hat in hand begging for justice. We invoke our rights as equals. We fight back as equals. And we get results.

But in addition to requiring Cardinal Glemp to pay a high price here in the United States, we also wanted him to pay a price in Poland. We wanted the Polish people to learn that their primate had lied to them.

I called a Polish Catholic lawyer friend, who was teaching at an American law school and asked his advice. He immediately agreed to help in the Polish lawsuit and to help me find a good lawyer in Poland. This was important for two reasons. First, I needed expert help on Polish law and procedure. Even more important, I wanted it to be understood that this was not a lawsuit between Jews and Poles, or Jews and Catholics. It was a conflict between decency and anti-Semitism. We wanted decent Polish Catholics on our side. Glemp would — and does — have the anti-Semites on his side.

My friend put me in touch with a leading Catholic civil rights lawyer in Poland who, after reviewing both the speech and the relevant law, assured me that it was an open-and-shut case under Polish law. "It was a libel, and under the law you must win." Confident of his legal ground, our lawyer made an appointment with Cardinal Glemp's legal representatives and conveyed his conclusions to them.

What they told him I do not know. But the next time we talked, he was shaking with fear. We were still right, he assured me, but he could not go forward with the case. His professional and personal life would be destroyed if he continued to serve as our lawyer. We asked him to recommend another Polish lawyer, but he assured us that after what he had been told — threatened with — there was not a single lawyer in Poland who would be willing to help us. Both he and his wife apologized profusely for their "cowardice" — that was their word — and hoped that I would understand the impossible position they were in. They did not want their professional and political futures destroyed by any involvement in a lawsuit, no matter how meritorious, against the primate of the church. This lawyer now holds an extremely high post in the Solidarity government, a post he would never have gotten had he remained involved in the case.

Despite this setback, we decided to proceed: we would file the lawsuit in Poland by ourselves. My Polish American friend and I worked together and turned out a complaint in Polish which formally charged Cardinal Glemp with defamation under Polish law. Unable to receive the professional assistance of a single lawyer in Poland — several expressed interest but were then "discouraged" from helping us — we sent my two associates to Czestochowa to file our suit. One of my associates, Jack Zaremski, is of Polish Jewish background, his father having emigrated from Warsaw before the war. The other, Joe Lipner, wears a Kippah, keeps kosher, and observes the Sabbath. The Polish courts hadn't seen anything like this for many years.

Joe and Jack successfully filed the suit in the Czestochowa district court, and unsuccessfully searched for a Polish lawyer. They made contact with a Polish senator with close personal and political ties to Cardinal Glemp. He told us that it would be in the cardinal's "best interest, as well as in the interest of fostering good relations between Jews and Catholics and Jews and Poles" for a retraction to be issued. By transatlantic calls, we ironed out a statement of retraction that would be acceptable to the parties involved in the suit.

But on the day the senator was to present the statement of retraction to Cardinal Glemp for signature, Henry Siegman and Robert Lifton, respectively the executive director and the president of the American

Jewish Congress, met with Glemp and, without mentioning the cardinal's own contribution, criticized *Rabbi Weiss* for "contributing to anti-Semitism in Poland." As a front-page story in the Solidarity newspaper reported, these two Jewish leaders "explained to Primate Glemp that Rabbi Weiss acted destructively and in an irresponsible manner." They never even corrected Glemp's implication that Weiss had come to kill the nuns. The leaders of the American Jewish Congress thus publicly accused *Jews* of contributing to anti-Semitism in Poland, without placing the blame squarely where it belonged — at the feet of Cardinal Glemp and other Polish anti-Semites. They also told the cardinal that Rabbi Weiss had no following among Jews and that *they* spoke for the Jewish community. The message conveyed was that the Jewish community did not want or need a retraction from Cardinal Glemp. It was enough that Cardinal Glemp would deign to meet with these Jewish leaders.

Immediately following these statements, the Polish senator informed us that Glemp would issue no retraction. He told us that the American Jewish Congress leaders had validated Cardinal Glemp's statements and that he now "stands by them as true." Glemp's secretary confirmed that as a direct result of the comments made by Siegman and Lifton, the cardinal "sticks to the words of the homily as true" and would not issue any "revised statement."

Even after learning of these facts, Robert Lifton found it difficult to believe "that the Primate of Catholic Poland was so concerned with the case brought by Mr. Dershowitz . . . that he was prepared to sign a retraction."[27] That skepticism speaks volumes about his perception of the second-class status of Jews in relation to the Catholic church — a perception that my generation of Jews refuses to accept.

The actions of Lifton and Siegman constitute a grave failure. The idea of Jewish leaders going to Poland and accusing other Jews of contributing to anti-Semitism without criticizing the actual source of the anti-Semitism is unacceptable. It is blaming the victims instead of the perpetrators. By seeming to validate the cardinal's anti-Semitic statements while invalidating Rabbi Weiss's attempt to obtain a retraction, these leaders set back efforts to build Jewish-Polish relations on a foundation of equality and mutual respect.

I do not believe that Lifton and Siegman spoke for the grass-roots Jewish community when they went hat in hand to Cardinal Glemp and told him what he wanted to hear. Such sycophantic behavior garners no respect, either for the leaders or for those whom they purport to represent. By conveying the impression that the Jewish people are again willing to forgive and forget anti-Semitic utterances — without even a semblance of remorse or apology — the American Jewish Congress leaders failed the people they claim to represent.

Fortunately, there are other Jewish leaders with a keener sense of history. Following Glemp's change of mind about a retraction, Seymour Reich, chairman of the Conference of Presidents of Major American Jewish Organizations, wrote to Polish and Catholic leaders, urging them to use their good offices to ask the cardinal to resume discussions with us. Reich criticized the American Jewish Congress leaders for not raising the issue directly with Glemp. "They lost an opportunity," he said.[28]

The Jewish people cannot afford any more lost opportunities to combat anti-Semitism. We need leadership that is willing to speak the truth to anti-Semites rather than apologize for the actions of other Jews who have the courage to speak out. Following this lost opportunity, the *Jerusalem Post,* in its lead editorial on July 9, 1990, condemned what it called "the Siegman Syndrome" — unelected and unrepresentative Jewish "leaders" who do considerable harm to the interests of the Jewish community by their repeated appeasement of anti-Semites and apologetic attitude about Jews who fight back.

Well, Rabbi Weiss continued to fight back. He asked me to travel to Czestochowa in the summer of 1990 to pursue his lawsuit following the American Jewish Congress fiasco. I went to the Czestochowa district court with my older son, Elon, and a translator. The chief judge of the court and the magistrate assigned to the case agreed to meet with us and hear my argument. It was a good thing we made the trip, since the judges had assumed that following the meeting between Glemp and the "rabbis" — that is how the judges referred to the American Jewish Congress leaders — we would not want to pursue the matter. I assured them that we did want to proceed.

They asked me to argue several technical legal points: whether a recent amnesty provision of Polish law applied to Cardinal Glemp's actions; whether a cardinal could be sued in a civil court; whether a foreign citizen could sue in a Polish court. I was prepared to address those concerns and did so for the better part of an hour. At the end, to my surprise, the judges both said they agreed with our position. The suit could be brought and Cardinal Glemp would have to answer.

The judges also seemed to agree that it was clear, as a matter of fact, that Rabbi Weiss had come to Auschwitz intending to conduct a peaceful sit-in and that it was false to accuse him of setting out to murder the nuns. The judges both said that they hoped Cardinal Glemp would decide to issue a retraction and thereby settle the suit. "That would make me very happy," said the chief judge. I told them that I, too, preferred a settlement, but that we would not withdraw our suit without a retraction.

After we left the courthouse, pressure was obviously placed on these judges. In a written decision delivered several weeks later, they completely changed their tune, ruling that there was no proof that Cardinal Glemp's remarks were directed against Rabbi Weiss. He could have been referring to *any* "squad of seven Jews from New York"! Apparently every newspaper, magazine, and television reporter throughout the world — all of whom reported that Glemp was referring to Weiss — misunderstood the primate's words. The decision was an embarrassment to the Polish legal system forced upon the vulnerable judges by powerful supporters of Glemp. We immediately appealed, and the case is now before a higher court. We are continuing to fight back.*

But fighting back against Polish anti-Semitism is not without cost. Of all the vicious mail I receive, nothing compares with that sent by some Polish Americans whenever I dare criticize anything Polish.

As soon as I filed the lawsuit against Cardinal Glemp, there was a well-organized outpouring of hate, orchestrated by the editor in chief of a Polish American newspaper called the *Post Eagle,* published in Clifton, New Jersey. The paper accused me of leading a "Jewish sinful and criminal rape of the Polish image" and it swore "revenge" against "the animal from Harvard." This was not the first such attack against me. After I wrote an article critical of the Auschwitz Museum, the editor wrote to the president of Harvard demanding that I be fired:

> This professor does not have the right to teach classes and must be removed from such a post because of his discriminatory feelings against our ethnic group.
>
> We are bringing this hate monger to the attention of our Polish

---

* On January 20, 1991, a pastoral letter was read in every Polish church. While condemning anti-Semitism as "contrary to the spirit of the Gospel," it also condemned as "untrue" the "concept of Polish anti-Semitism" and overt Polish complicity in the Holocaust. It did not mention Kielce or other instances of Polish murder of Jews. It bore the hallmarks of compromise between the ecumenical forces represented by Cardinal Macharski of Kraków and the anti-Semitic forces represented by Cardinal Glemp.

organizations, clubs and other opinion makers, so that they too can let you know how we feel about such hatred against our ethnic group.[29]

When I made inquiry into who the editor, Chester Grabowski, was, I was not surprised to learn that he was a notorious anti-Semite and that his rag was the *Der Stürmer* of the Polish American community. He writes a weekly column that attacks rabbis, Zionists, and other Jews as "animals" and "vermin." Here's a typical example:

THE DAY OF RECKONING IS COMING, and then these animals will be answerable for their crimes against Poland and her people. Unfortunately, the just and righteous Jews will also suffer for the lies and distortions of their brethren. . . .

There are animals within the Jewish community, here in the U.S.A., who deliberately etched numbers on their wrists to benefit from the reparation funds.[30]

In an article on the trial in Israel of John Demjanjuk, who was convicted of being "Ivan the Terrible" of Treblinka, Grabowski urged Polish Catholics never to "forget and forgive them for deciding to kill our God, and their God, which they refused to recognize."[31]

The *Bergen Record,* a distinguished New Jersey daily, did an investigative report on Grabowski entitled "The Gospel According to St. Chester: A History of Hate," which described his writings as "vitriolic anti-Semitic diatribes." He publishes hate mail from the Ku Klux Klan, from unrepentant Nazis, and from Holocaust deniers. According to the Anti-Defamation League, the *Post Eagle* claims a circulation of sixteen thousand in forty states and five countries.[32]

After I announced my lawsuit against Cardinal Glemp, the anti-Semitic mail — and phone calls — began to arrive in torrents. This letter came from Boston:

Adolf, where are you when we need you.

This is all I have been hearing around the stores, the streets, everywhere since you have threatened the Polish cardinal with a lawsuit.

It seems Jews are disliked if not hated, everywhere by everybody. That isn't being anti-semetic [*sic*], that's a right guaranteed in our constitution.

Another defended the Polish people as the only ones who helped the Jews, but then expressed regret that "*Hitler made one mistake — that of not having more time to get rid of you Jew bastards.* No wonder the people of the world hate your people — plague on them! *Polish and proud of it!*"

A letter published in Grabowski's hate sheet tells his readers:

> It is well known that [S]olidarity is dominated by Jews. . . .
>
> Mr. Dershowitz, why is it that throughout the world, wherever Jews are found, there's anti-Semitism?
>
> Mr. Dershowitz, why did the Jews impose Communism on Russia, Poland and many other countries?
>
> Mr. Dershowitz, when are the Polish people and Poland going to see a Pole in Israel be made a Prime Minister of Israel?[33]

(Of course, virtually every Israeli prime minister — from David Ben-Gurion to Yitzhak Shamir — has been of Polish origin.)

In reading the *Post Eagle,* I discovered that despite its viciously anti-Semitic editorial policy, numerous congressmen, state legislators, and city officials advertised in its pages. They obviously did not support Grabowski's anti-Semitism, but merely used his publication to reach Polish voters. On November 28, 1989, I wrote the following letter to each public official whose ads had appeared in the *Post Eagle:*

> You were an advertiser in the last Christmas issue of the *Post Eagle.* When you submitted your ad, I'm sure you did not realize that it would appear alongside an ad from the Ku Klux Klan, wishing "all Polonia a merry *White* Christmas," and illustrating that racist wish with a drawing of Santa Claus wearing a Klan hood.
>
> The editorial policy of the *Post Eagle* is patently anti-Jewish, and deeply offensive to decent people of all religious backgrounds.
>
> Your ad supports Chester Grabowski's racism and anti-Semitism. . . .
>
> Now that you know of its negative message, I am confident that you will not want to support it with your advertising dollars. Please send those dollars to another Polish or Catholic newspaper of your choice, which reflects the greatness of the Polish and Catholic traditions.

All but one of the politicians stopped advertising in the *Post Eagle* after receiving my letter. This response was gratifying, because ads by public officials tend to legitimate a rag that should remain on the lunatic fringe of American political and media life.

One of the most stridently anti-Semitic diatribes generated by the Auschwitz controversy did not come in an anonymous envelope or a racist paper. It appeared in one hundred newspapers and was written by nationally syndicated columnist and former White House official Patrick Buchanan, who is not perceived as being on the lunatic fringe of American life.

In his column Buchanan invoked "Catholic rage" against the Jews. Instead of urging his readers to understand the pain that some Jewish survivors of Auschwitz must feel at Polish efforts to de-Judaize Hitler's final solution, Buchanan declared that "to orthodox Catholics, the demand that we be more 'sensitive' to Jewish concerns is becoming a joke." Then, in a tone reminiscent of an incitement to a nineteenth-century religious pogrom, he prophesied that "the slumbering giant of Catholicism may be about to awaken." Lest there be any doubt about the target of this giant's wrath, Buchanan pointed to "those who so evidently despise our Church" — namely "the Jews."[34]

Buchanan went on to warn the Jews not to count on the bridge-building efforts of American cardinals, such as John Cardinal O'Connor and Bernard Cardinal Law, who had supported moving the convent. He characterized their conciliatory statements, obviously blessed by the Vatican, as "the clucking appeasement of the Catholic cardinalate." He warned these princes of reconciliation to "step aside" and make room for "bishops and priests ready to assume the role of defender of the faith."[35]

I wrote a column responding to Buchanan's diatribe. I pointed out that Buchanan probably had in mind for the role of "defender of the faith" excommunicated archbishop Marcel Lefebre and other right-wing French priests who helped to hide unrepentant Nazi war criminal Paul Touvier in various monasteries until he was recently arrested to face trial for mass murder.[36]

I reminded my readers that Buchanan himself had stopped just short of hiding Nazi war criminals. He had come to the defense of such genocidal killers as Klaus Barbie, Karl Linnas, and the SS killers buried at Bitburg. Buchanan had even expressed doubts about whether Jews were gassed at Treblinka. His "evidence" was the following vignette: "In 1988, 97 kids, trapped 400 feet underground in a Washington, D.C., tunnel while two locomotives spewed diesel exhaust into the car, emerged unharmed after 45 minutes."[37] I challenged Buchanan to test his hypothesis by locking himself in an airtight chamber in which diesel exhaust is pumped.*

---

* An article in the *New Republic* points out that "much of the material on which Buchanan bases his columns [about the Holocaust] is sent to him by pro-Nazi, anti-Semitic cranks." Asked where he got the information about Treblinka, he reportedly said, "Somebody sent it to me." The article concludes that Holocaust deniers know "they can expect a hearing from Buchanan." Jacob Weisberg, "The Heresies of Pat Buchanan," *New Republic,* October 22, 1990, p. 22.

Buchanan's support for Nazi war criminals and for the abolition of the government office that investigates them, led former Justice Department official Alan Ryan to comment that "great numbers of people are asking themselves: Why is Pat Buchanan so in love with Nazi war criminals?"[38]

Buchanan's apparent lovefest with Nazi criminals certainly cannot be explained by any sustained commitment to the rights of accused defendants. In every other context he supports the rights of victims and rails against defense attorneys. Nor can it be rationalized by his objection to the use of KGB evidence, since several of the cases — notably Klaus Barbie's — relied on no Soviet evidence or assistance.

The most plausible answer to the question of why Buchanan seems to be more sensitive to Nazi killers than to Jewish victims was provided by Buchanan himself when he acknowledged to the *New York Times* that he had "frequently been accused of anti-Semitism."[39] Well, the shoe fits.

Patrick Buchanan is, of course, not the only writer in America to express anti-Jewish views. But he is the most widely read and listened to since Father Coughlin in the 1930s. He is also the only overtly anti-Jewish figure to serve in high federal office — as director of communications in the Reagan White House. In the fall of 1990, *New York Times* columnist Abe Rosenthal accused Buchanan of anti-Semitism — an accusation I had been making for half a dozen years. The Rosenthal column generated considerable controversy within the media and tarnished Buchanan's image. Nonetheless, he remains a spokesman for right-wing causes and a potential presidential candidate.[40]

When writers as widely read and lionized as Patrick Buchanan begin to express doubts about the Holocaust, it becomes clear that our failure to bring Nazi perpetrators to justice sends the dangerous message that if the hands-on perpetrators of the Holocaust are not guilty enough to be punished, maybe there was no crime serious enough to warrant punishment.

But to insist that perpetrators be punished requires that there be individualized proof of guilt. It would be tragic if, in the interest of punishing the guilty, we would allow innocents to be punished as well. There has generally been little doubt about the factual guilt of Nazi criminals such as Klaus Barbie, Adolf Eichmann, and Joseph Goebbels. The case of John Demjanjuk has been different, since he has categorically denied all involvement in the Holocaust. John Demjanjuk is the Ukrainian-born autoworker from Cleveland, Ohio, who was sentenced to death in 1988 by an Israeli court after being convicted of being Ivan the Terrible of Treblinka, a death camp in Poland where some 870,000 Jews perished.

My informal connection with the Demjanjuk case began before the trial, when my brother, who practices law in New York, and I both received telephone calls from the Demjanjuk defense committee asking us to join his legal team in Israel. It was one of those calls I literally have nightmares about. But because the request was to appear as a lawyer in a foreign court — and because it seemed clear that they had picked us because we were Jewish — I had little difficulty turning down the request. I told them, however, that if no member of the Israeli bar was willing to represent Demjanjuk, they should renew the request. Several Israeli lawyers agreed to represent Demjanjuk and an international legal team was quickly assembled.

One of Demjanjuk's prime defenders in the United States was — surprise! — Patrick Buchanan, who lobbied privately on Demjanjuk's behalf and publicly declared him to be "the victim of an American Dreyfus case."[41] The comparison outraged me, especially since I believe that if Buchanan had been alive at the time of the Dreyfus trial, he would have joined with those conservative French Catholics who led the anti-Semitic campaign against the framed Jewish officer.

In the Demjanjuk case, Buchanan could not pretend — as he tried in other Nazi cases — that "these people don't have a voice." Defense committees were established in Cleveland, Chicago, Toronto, and other cities with significant Ukrainian populations. The vice president of the major committee, Peter Jacyk, warned that Jews would pay for the conviction of Demjanjuk as they paid for the "crucifixion of Jesus Christ."[42]

Nor could Buchanan argue that all the evidence against Demjanjuk had been supplied by the Soviet Union. The prosecution's case, which began in the United States in 1986 with the denaturalization of the retired Cleveland autoworker, was based on three kinds of evidence. The first, and most direct, was the eyewitness identification of several Treblinka survivors and one former SS man who had worked alongside Ivan. Demjanjuk was first identified by survivors who had been shown — independently of one another — an array of photographs in an effort to identify another Treblinka guard. Each identified the guard and then pointed to the photograph of Demjanjuk and said that he was

Ivan the Terrible, a notorious sadist who had participated in the execution of Jews. Others corroborated the identification.

The second kind of evidence was an identification card with the name and photograph of Ivan Demjanjuk. Since the card placed him in an SS camp that trained guards for duty at the death camps and showed him wearing an SS uniform, the defense was forced to claim that the damning card was a forgery. The card had been turned over to the prosecution by the Soviet Union, thus giving rise to complaints from members of the Ukrainian community that it was part of a KGB plot to frame the Ukrainian. But scientific evidence established its authenticity and proved that the man in the photo was Demjanjuk.

The third kind of evidence came from the actions of the accused himself. He had had a tattoo removed from his left arm, from the exact location in which the SS placed blood group tattoos that could have identified Demjanjuk as a concentration camp guard. For many years, while fighting extradition to Israel, he had given conflicting and admittedly false alibis, varying the places he claimed he was and the roles he claimed he played during the Holocaust. And during his pretrial interrogation, he inadvertently disclosed information that could have been known only to someone who had been in the area of Treblinka, where he denied he had ever been. His own series of perjurious alibis coupled with this information "almost amounted to a confession," said the court later.

Though the totality of the evidence seemed entirely convincing — it certainly would have convinced the likes of Buchanan in an ordinary criminal context, where he always sides with the prosecution — the shrill voices of Demjanjuk's defenders created doubts in the minds of some Americans and Canadians. I decided to go to Israel to see for myself. For several days near the close of the trial, I attended the court sessions, after which I interviewed several of the participants. On April 18, 1988, I was in court for the delivery of the verdict.[43]

The courtroom was filled with Holocaust survivors who had lost parents, children, and spouses at the hand of Ivan and his fellow butchers. There were also Ukrainian friends and relatives of John Demjanjuk.

The three judges entered, one a bearded man wearing a religious yarmulke, another a woman of about fifty, the third a somewhat older justice of the supreme court, who would preside. Since there is no jury in Israel (or in most western democracies), the court was the finder of fact. After a thorough review of all the evidence — a review that consumed hundreds of pages and took nearly an entire day to summarize — the court found that Demjanjuk was guilty "beyond all doubt."

The care reflected by the court's judgment led even Demjanjuk's erstwhile lawyer, who had represented him during his five-year extradition proceeding in America, to declare the trial fair. On the basis of the evidence presented, no unbiased court or jury anywhere would have come to a different verdict.

A week later, the court reconvened to impose the sentence. I again attended the proceedings. The argument began on a technical note, and Demjanjuk looked bored, alternating wide yawns with inappropriate smiles. Whenever the prosecutor referred to the facts of the case — to unspeakable crimes such as cutting off women's breasts, bashing in the heads of babies, and torturing trembling women on their way to the gas chambers — Demjanjuk shook his head, muttering the words, "Not me," and making the sign of the cross with bold, defiant strikes.

Though I was interested in the legal arguments, I couldn't keep my eyes off the prisoner. I had been in the presence of many murderers, even some convicted mass murderers, but I had never been so close to so cruel and brutal a human being. Those who say you can see evil in a person's face or eyes have never been in the presence of John Demjanjuk. There was nothing special about his appearance. His evil was not in his persona but rather in his deeds.

I kept looking at Demjanjuk for another reason. I imagined him as *my* killer. At the time he was murdering babies, I was five years old. My family came from a part of Poland that was within the jurisdiction of his extermination camps. But for the grace of God, and the foresight of my grandparents who had left Poland well before the Holocaust, I could have been one of the thousands of nameless and faceless babies he grabbed out of the hands of screaming mothers and shoved into gas chambers. I imagined him laughing with sadistic joy as he killed entire families, ending their seed forever, after taunting and torturing them gratuitously.

I sat there wondering why I hoped his life would be spared. Certainly if any human being deserved the death penalty it was Demjanjuk. But I knew that if the court were to order his execution, that fact would entirely change the dynamics of the case. Opponents of capital punishment from around the world, of which I am one, would turn their energies to saving this miserable man's life. A sentence of life imprisonment, on the other hand, would relegate Demjanjuk to the obscurity of his cell.

The audience of survivors and survivors' children waited for the court to return its verdict. The mood was tense as the judge began to speak. He announced that the sentence was to be death, noting that there was no mitigating the awful crimes of Ivan the Terrible.

There were sobs of relief from the audience. One woman simply started to read off the names of family members murdered at Treblinka. Others sang religious songs. Demjanjuk's son John, Jr., spoke to the press. "This verdict will shame Israel, the United States, and the six million murdered Jews," he said with no shame. "I would characterize the three judges to be the criminals," he added, unable to recognize the difference between doers of justice and perverters of justice.

I left the courtroom saddened by the sentence, for I knew that the death of one man, even one as terrible as Ivan, would not soothe the memory of the murders of the millions.

My prediction, unfortunately, turned out to be true. No sooner was the sentence pronounced than protests arose throughout the world. Among the most damning was one written by Lord Denning of Great Britain, perhaps the most prominent living judge in the Anglo-American world. This is some of what he said in the *London Telegraph:*

> First, against what law had he offended? Not against the law of Israel. The offenses were committed in the years 1942–1943 before the State of Israel existed or had any laws of its own. It was not founded until 1948. Nor were the offenses committed against the laws of Germany or Poland. They were committed in the concentration camp of Treblinka and were done by the orders of those in authority in those states.
>
> In my opinion it was contrary to international law for the State of Israel to arrange with the United States for the deportation of Demjanjuk to Israel to stand trial there. . . . The accused protested his innocence throughout.
>
> The atmosphere at the trial can be seen by the report that there was "clapping, cheering and dancing" by the packed "audience" when he was sentenced to death. When I have sentenced [prisoners] to death there was a hushed calm and solemn silence.[44]

Despite my opposition to the death penalty, I felt impelled to respond to Lord Denning's errors with the following letter, published in the *Telegraph:*

I was pained to read Lord Denning's letter of April 28, 1988, regarding Israel's trial and conviction of John Demjanjuk. I was in attendance at the verdict and sentencing, and I am sorry to have to report that Lord Denning is simply wrong on his facts as well as his law.

He claims that Demjanjuk's crimes were not "offenses committed against the laws of . . . Poland," because they were done pursuant to "orders of those in authority. . . ." First, the evidence in the Demjanjuk case is to the contrary: "Ivan the Terrible" exceeded the orders of his SS superiors and gratuitously tortured, murdered and committed sexual offenses. Second, it has been a long time since any civilized nation accepted "superior orders" as a defense to the kind of unspeakable atrocities of which Demjanjuk was convicted.

Denning accuses Israel of having "arrange[d] with the United States for the deportation of Demjanjuk to Israel. . . ." That is not what happened. The United States commenced the investigation and Demjanjuk was extradited, not deported, pursuant to both U.S. and Israeli law.

Most regrettably, Lord Denning is simply unaware of the evidence. In fact, the evidence against Demjanjuk was overwhelming and would have more than satisfied the standards of proof of any civilized nation, including his own.

I assure Lord Denning that he and his fellow British judges [have] sentenced defendants to death on considerably less convincing evidence than was presented against Demjanjuk.

As for the "cheering" by the "audience," I was there when the sentence was read. The mood was solemn as the judge delivered the sentence of death. The only sounds were the muffled sobs of several survivors. It was only *after* the judges left the courtroom that a small number of people joined together in songs [and] prayers. . . . There were few cheers and many tears. Denning's sanctimonious comparisons with his own death sentences trivializes the Holocaust. "Hushed calm" is easier to achieve when a pathetic murderer is sentenced to die for a single crime than when a man responsible for the torture and genocide of thousands is finally brought to judgment. It is a credit to the Israeli judiciary that it rendered so thorough a judgment and performed so professional a job in the context of such barbarous crimes against so many victims. I recommend that Lord Denning read the 400-page judgment of the court before smugly rushing to his own injudicious judgment of others.[45]

Shortly after Lord Denning wrote his letter complaining that Israel could not prosecute Nazi criminals because their crimes were committed "before the State of Israel existed," he joined a majority of the House of Lords in defeating legislation approved by the House of Commons which would have empowered the British government — which did then exist — to prosecute Nazi criminals who live in Great Britain.[46]

I will continue to argue against the imposition of the death penalty, as I did even in the Adolf Eichmann case. (Putting aside the abstract issue of capital punishment, imagine the potential usefulness of an imprisoned Eichmann in identifying and helping to locate other Nazi criminals who lived out their lives undisturbed.)

Israel's highest court has yet to issue a decision on Demjanjuk's appeal. But it is clear that to the extent that justice is a fair process, John Demjanjuk has received justice. To the extent that justice is an accurate result, Demjanjuk has almost certainly received justice. To the extent that justice is a proportionate punishment, Demjanjuk has received justice, except in the eyes of those who are morally opposed to the death penalty for anyone, no matter how heinous the crime. Surely by the standards of justice generally employed by Patrick Buchanan and other Demjanjuk supporters, Demjanjuk has received more than basic justice. On balance, the Israeli legal system deserves high grades for doing justice to one who denied even the most minimal semblance of it to his thousands of victims.

But more always seems to be demanded of the Jewish nation and of the Jewish people than of others. Jews, unlike other groups, are expected to be in the forefront of defending the rights of their sworn enemies. This issue came to an ugly head in 1977 when a group of American Nazis sought a permit to march through Skokie, Illinois, the hometown of numerous Jewish survivors of the Holocaust.

Virtually every time I speak before a Jewish group, I am asked, "Where do you stand on the Skokie issue?" It is as if Skokie has become a kind of litmus test of a Jewish civil libertarian's commitment to Jewish values. I believe it is a false litmus test. I do not believe there is a real conflict between a strong commitment to Jewish values and an equally strong commitment to freedom of speech. Indeed, it is my belief that those who — for entirely understandable historical and psychological reasons — tried to stop the Nazis from marching through Skokie were *dis*serving Jewish values.

The tragedy is that the Nazis, though they eventually abandoned their planned march, won Skokie. They received millions of dollars of free publicity for their despicable cause precisely because some Jewish leaders tried to censor them. Had their pathetic march been ignored by the Jewish community, despite its deliberately provocative nature, the story would have been a one-day local incident about how a tiny group of racist ne'er-do-wells had tried to provoke Holocaust survivors but had failed.

Instead the story became an international event that persisted for years, culminating in a widely viewed TV movie starring Danny Kaye. It pitted the American Civil Liberties Union and other civil libertarians, both Jewish and non-Jewish, against elements of the organized Jewish community. It resulted in vast publicity for the Nazi party, including talk show appearances on programs that had never previously allowed them air time.

A similarly disastrous result was achieved in Canada in 1985, when Jewish pressure led to criminal prosecutions against two despicable Holocaust deniers with Nazi affiliations. Prior to the commencement of the criminal prosecutions, the pamphlets and speeches of these neo-Nazis were limited in their impact. But the trials brought all the professional Holocaust deniers out from under their rocks.

The case grew out of a pamphlet published by a self-proclaimed Nazi named Ernst Zundel, claiming that the Holocaust never happened. Invoking the name of his "hero" Adolf Hitler, Zundel — a German-born anti-Semite who became a resident of Canada in 1958 — described his "Aryan" mission as destroying "the monstrous lie that is the Holocaust."[47]

The First Amendment approach to such despicable speech is to allow it to sink or swim in the marketplace of ideas. The very fact that such notorious lies are permitted to be uttered understandably upsets many, especially those who personally experienced the devastation of the Nazi Holocaust. For them, the Zundel diatribe was a direct attack on one of the central experiences of their lives. It is difficult to expect people who witnessed their parents, children, or spouses being selected for gassing to debate whether the Holocaust is a fact of history, as every reputable historian confirms, or a "Jewish hoax," as these crackpots assert.

Accordingly, a group of Holocaust survivors persuaded the Canadian authorities to pursue criminal charges against Zundel for "wilfully publishing news that he knows is false and that causes or is likely to cause injury or mischief to a public interest."[48]

Inevitably, criminal charges of this kind result in the Holocaust itself being put on trial. And so, in 1985, a Canadian courtroom became the platform for a legal "debate" that should never have taken place — a debate about an incontrovertible historical fact. The prosecution summoned numerous survivors who provided graphic firsthand accounts of the Nazi death camps. As one man who spent two years at Auschwitz put it: "I saw 1,765,000 people walk into the space before my eyes, knowing that space is absolutely closed with no road out. And nobody came out, except as smoke. Would you suggest" — he pointedly asked Zundel's lawyer — "that they are still there?"[49]

Zundel's lawyer, who himself had expressed doubts about the Holocaust, called the survivor witnesses "liars" and argued with them about their memories. He also introduced witnesses of his own, a parade of kooks from around the world who claimed to have evidence that the Holocaust never happened. Among them was a Swedish propagandist — himself convicted of fomenting racial hatred in his native country — who swore that Auschwitz was a recreational facility equipped with sauna, dance hall, and swimming pool for the enjoyment of its guests.

Not surprisingly, the jury ruled unanimously against Zundel, and the judge sentenced him to prison for fifteen months.* But the admirer of Nazis claimed victory nonetheless: "It cost me $40,000 in lost work — but I got a million dollars' worth of publicity for my cause. It was well worth it."[50]

I think I understand how deeply offensive it must be to a Holocaust survivor to have to watch Nazis march through his neighborhood or to listen to Holocaust deniers lie about the most horrible experience in modern history. But the courtroom is no place to put ideas — no matter how false or hateful — on trial. I am reminded of a meeting I once attended to discuss whether major Jewish organizations should support the legal claims of a California man who was suing a "revi-

---

* Zundel's conviction was reversed by the Canadian appellate court and a new trial was ordered. The defendant emerged as a victim, if not hero, in the eyes of many Canadians. In his second trial, Zundel was once again convicted, and sentenced to nine months in prison. On appeal, his principal argument is that the trial judge had erred in ordering the jury to regard the Holocaust as a historical fact.

sionist" organization that had offered a reward to anyone who could prove that the Holocaust had occurred. A number of prominent Jewish lawyers were present, and the debate went back and forth. Also in attendance was Elie Wiesel, who sat quietly through the debate. Finally someone asked his views. He softly replied: "Do not put my existence on trial. We know what happened. We do not need judges or juries to prove what the Nazis did to us. If a judge or jury were — heaven forbid — to disbelieve us, would that change anything that actually happened? Let us leave it to our memories, our historians, our artists — and their conscience."

But just because Nazi bigots have a right to preach their garbage does not mean that decent people should lend legitimacy to the *content* of their pernicious lies. If I were asked to defend the right of a Holocaust denier to express his perverse views, I would agree to defend his right, but I would insist on exercising my own right to call his views anti-Semitic and false. Nor would I encourage anyone to read or listen to such garbage. To the contrary, I would urge everyone to reject it outright in the marketplace of ideas, to refuse to patronize that disease-infested part of the market.

I mention how I, as an opponent of censorship, would handle the issue of Holocaust denial, in order to contrast this with the disgraceful manner in which Professor Noam Chomsky took up the cause of a notorious neo-Nazi Holocaust denier named Robert Faurisson.

In the 1970s Faurisson, who was an obscure lecturer on French literature at the University of Lyon, began to dabble in Holocaust denial. He wrote a book — and gave talks — in which he mocked Holocaust victims and survivors as perpetrators of a hoax. The Holocaust, according to Faurisson, "never took place." The "Hitler gas chambers" never existed. "The Jews" bear "responsibility" for World War II. Hitler acted reasonably and in self-defense when he rounded up the Jews and put them in "labor camps," not death camps. The "massive lie" about genocide was a deliberate concoction begun by "American Zionists" — in context he obviously means Jews. The principal beneficiary of this hoax is "Israel," which has encouraged this "enormous political and financial fraud." The principal victims of this "fraud" have been "the German people" and the "Palestinian people." Faurisson also called the diary of Anne Frank a "forgery."[51]

Not surprisingly, as soon as Faurisson's crackpot tome was published, it was seized upon by Jew-haters throughout the world. In the United States, the notorious Liberty Lobby — which distributes *The*

Protocols of the Elders of Zion and other anti-Semitic best-sellers — translated the most hateful portions of the work and distributed them widely within its network. His videotaped speeches were distributed for use at neo-Nazi gatherings.

I sent for one such video and watched in horror as Faurisson smiled when describing the "alleged victims" of the "nonexistent" gas chambers. His neo-Nazi audience laughed as he mocked the testimony of survivor eyewitnesses.

Following the publication of Faurisson's book, the lecturer received threats from irate survivors. The University of Lyon, claiming that it could not guarantee his safety, suspended him for a semester. This decision, understandable as it may have been considering the fact that Lyon suffered greatly during the Nazi occupation, was improper and foolish. A teacher has the right to be protected for espousing even idiotic views.

Professor Noam Chomsky, of the Massachusetts Institute of Technology, a well-known linguist and anti-Zionist zealot, was asked to join in protesting Faurisson's suspension. I am sure that he welcomed the opportunity, because Faurisson's writings and speeches are stridently anti-Zionist as well as anti-Semitic. Indeed, Professor Chomsky has himself made statements about Zionist exploitation of the tragedy of World War II that are not, in my view, so different from some of those of Faurisson.

Chomsky immediately sprang to Faurisson's defense, not only on the issue of free speech, but on the merits of his "scholarship" and of his "character." Chomsky signed a petition that characterized Faurisson's falsifications of history as "findings" and said that they were based on "extensive historical research."[52]

Had Chomsky bothered to check on Faurisson's "historical research," he would have found it to be faked. For example, Faurisson relies on an entry, dated October 18, 1942, from the diary of SS doctor Johann-Paul Kremer written during the three months he spent at Auschwitz in 1942. An eminent scholar checked Faurisson's use of the entry, and demonstrated that Faurisson's "research" was entirely phony. The diary entry read: "This Sunday morning in cold and humid weather I was present at the 11th special action (Dutch). Atrocious scenes with three women who begged us to let them live."[53]

Faurisson concludes that this passage proves: (1) that a "special action" was nothing more than the sorting out by doctors of the sick from the healthy during a typhus epidemic; (2) that the "atrocious scenes" were "executions of persons who had been *condemned to death,* executions for which the doctor was obliged to be present"; (3) that "among the condemned were three women who had come in a convoy from Holland [who] *were shot*"; (4) that there were no gas chambers, since the women were shot and not gassed (emphasis added).[54]

A French scholar named George Wellers analyzed this diary entry and the surrounding documentation for *Le Monde.* He did *actual* historical research, checking the Auschwitz archives for the date of the diary entry, a simple matter. He found that 1,710 Dutch Jews arrived at Auschwitz on October 18, 1942. Of these, 1,594 were sent immediately to the gas chambers. The remaining 116 people, all women, were brought into the camp; the three women who were the subject of the Kremer diary must have been among them. The three women were, in fact, shot — as Faurisson concludes. But that fact appears nowhere in Kremer's diary. How then did Faurisson learn it? Professor Wellers was able to find the answer with some simple research. He checked Dr. Kremer's testimony at a Polish war crimes trial. This is what Kremer said at the trial: "Three Dutch women did not want to go *into the gas chamber* and begged to have their lives spared. They were young women, *in good health,* but in spite of that their prayer was not granted and the SS who were participating in the action shot them on the spot" (emphasis added).[55]

Faurisson, who said he had researched the trial, knew that his own source, Dr. Kremer, had testified that the gas chambers did exist. Yet he deliberately omitted that crucial item from his book, while including the fact that the women were shot. Faurisson also knew that the three women were "in good health." Yet he led his readers to believe that Dr. Kremer had said they were selected on medical grounds during an epidemic. Finally, Faurisson states that those who were shot had been "condemned to death." Yet he knew they were shot by the SS for refusing to enter the gas chambers.

That is not "extensive historical research." It is not research at all. It is the fraudulent manufacturing of false antihistory. It is the kind of deception for which professors are rightly fired: not because their views are controversial, but because they are violating the most basic canons of historical scholarship. It is typical of Faurisson in particular, and of Holocaust denial "research" in general. Yet Chomsky was prepared to lend his academic legitimacy to Faurisson's "extensive historical research."

Chomsky went even further. After signing the petition, he wrote an essay that he allowed to be used as a foreword to Faurisson's next book, about his career as a Holocaust denier! In this book, Faurisson again calls the gas chambers a lie and repeats his claims about the hoax of the Holocaust. Chomsky, in his foreword, feigns ignorance of Faurisson's work — "I do not know his work very well" — but concludes that Faurisson's arguments are not anti-Semitic, and that Faurisson himself is neither an anti-Semite nor a Nazi, but rather "a sort of relatively apolitical liberal."[56]

A few years later, after it became unmistakably clear that Faurisson was consciously lending his name to all sorts of anti-Semitic and neo-Nazi groups, Chomsky repeated his character reference:

> I see no anti-Semitic implications in denial of the existence of gas chambers, or even denial of the Holocaust. Nor would there be anti-Semitic implications, per se, in the claim that the Holocaust (whether one believes it took place or not) is being exploited, viciously so, by apologists for Israeli repression and violence. I see no hint of anti-Semitic implications in Faurisson's work. . . .[57]

I came across this unbelievably stupid statement at about the time that a puff piece appeared in the *Boston Globe* praising Chomsky as a defender of the underdog. I wrote the following letter to the editor:

> While some may regard Chomsky as an eminent linguist, he does not understand the most obvious meaning of words in context. To fail to see any "hint of anti-Semitic implications" in Faurisson's collective condemnation of the Jewish people as liars is to be either a fool or a knave. Failure to recognize the anti-Semitic implications of Holocaust denial is like saying there would be no racist implications in a claim that Blacks enjoyed slavery, or no sexist implications in a statement that women want to be raped. The Holocaust is the central historical event of modern Jewish history. Efforts to deny or minimize it are the current tools of the anti-semite and neo-Nazi. Not surprising, both Faurisson and Chomsky are frequently quoted with approval by those hatemongers.
>
> Chomsky's actions in defending the *substance* of Faurisson's bigoted remarks against valid charges of anti-Semitism — as distinguished from defending Faurisson's *right* to publish such pernicious drivel — disqualify Chomsky from being considered an honorable defender of the "underdog." The victims of the Holocaust, not its defenders or deniers, are the underdogs.[58]

Chomsky responded by arguing that Faurisson was an anti-Zionist rather than an anti-Semite, because he denounced "Zionist lies." He charged that "Dershowitz's easy translation from 'Zionist' to 'Jewish' is illegitimate," and that "in fact, it is a standard gambit of anti-Semites."[59] Chomsky failed to acknowledge that characterizing a lie as "Zionist," when one means "Jew" is also the standard gambit of modern-day anti-Semites.

Following this exchange, I challenged Chomsky to a public debate on the issue of whether it is anti-Semitic or anti-Jewish to deny the Holocaust. This was his answer: "It is so obvious that there is no point in debating it because *nobody* believes there is an anti-Semitic connotation to the denial of the Holocaust" (emphasis added).[60] That answer, which suggests what kind of perverse world Chomsky lives in, speaks for itself.

One is left to speculate about Chomsky's motives — political and psychological — for becoming so embroiled in the substantive defense of a neo-Nazi Holocaust denier.

The civil liberties–free speech rationale does not work for Chomsky: civil libertarians who defend the free speech of neo-Nazis do not get into bed with them by legitimating their "findings" as having been based on "extensive historical research," and by defending them — on the merits — against well-documented charges of anti-Semitism. Moreover, providing a foreword for a book is *joining* with the author and publisher in an effort to sell the book. It is intended not merely to leave the marketplace of ideas open. It is intended to influence that marketplace substantively in favor of the author's ideas.

Nor does Chomsky have very compelling credentials as a neutral defender of free speech and academic freedom. He picks and chooses among speakers whose rights he defends, depending on how closely their views coincide with his leftist and anti-Zionist politics. For example, when Henry Kissinger was nominated for a faculty position at Columbia University, Chomsky told three hundred people at a campus rally that the only department Kissinger should be appointed to was "the Department of Death or of Lies and Deception," and he called Kissinger's essays "a parody of the academic style."[61] I guess Chomsky is more willing to criticize Kissinger's writing than Faurisson's "research." Nor has Chomsky been as vocal in defense of other right-wing American academics whose freedoms were threatened by their support for the Vietnam War as he was in support of Faurisson.

In the end, Paul L. Berman, writing in the *Village Voice,* got it exactly right:

> Chomsky's view of anti-Semitism is positively wild. His definition is so narrow, neither the *Protocols of the Elders of Zion* nor the no-Holocaust delusion fit into it. . . . I am afraid that his present remarks on anti-Semitism and Zionist lies disqualify him from ever being taken seriously on matters pertaining to Jews.[62]

The Chomsky-Faurisson episode illustrates some important issues discussed throughout this book. Chomsky's bizarre definition of anti-Semitism — a definition that excludes denial of the Holocaust and the claim that it is a Zionist hoax — reminds us how anti-Zionism often provides a cover for anti-Semitism. When Faurisson says that the Holocaust is a hoax perpetrated by "Zionists," he means "Jews." Many non-Zionist Jews, in America and elsewhere, have been involved in Holocaust education and memorialization. Faurisson and Chomsky defend any accusation leveled against the Jewish people as long as the accuser uses the right code word: "Zionists."

Another important issue illustrated by the Chomsky-Faurisson episode is that the only difference between efforts to de-Judaize the Holocaust, such as those engaged in by some Polish authorities, and efforts to deny the Holocaust outright is one of degree. The Faurisson crowd does not, after all, deny that many Jews died during World War II. They simply deny that the Jews suffered any *special,* or *different,* fate from the Poles, the Ukrainians, the Russians, and other people. The common claim of both the de-Judaizers and the Holocaust deniers is that there was no attempted genocide of the Jewish people as such. De-Judaizing the Holocaust leads inexorably to denying that it ever took place. That is why concerned Jews become so incensed over efforts to "universalize" the murders committed by Hitler's Nazis during the war.

The difference between what happened to every *other* group and what happened to the Jews (and Gypsies) can be summarized in two words: "children" and "ingathering." Only Jewish (and Gypsy) *children* — infants, toddlers, preschoolers, elementary school children — were systematically murdered. I can never lose that image. Every time I attend a gathering of Jewish children — at a family event, at a Bar Mitzvah, at Simchath Torah — I imagine SS guards lining up these children for the gas chambers. During the Demjanjuk trial, I kept thinking of the crying babies he threw against the rocks and into the ovens. That is what was so special about the Jews — the babies. That is why the children's memorial at Yad Vashem in Israel is so evocative. In every other group, only the adults were killed, as if that were not bad enough. The difference is that the Nazis wanted to destroy the Jewish *seed,* the Jewish *gene,* the Jewish *people.* Genetic extinction was the goal. It was necessary, therefore, to kill every human being — regardless of age — who was capable of producing future Jews.

The second word, "ingathering," makes the point as powerfully. Only the Jews were gathered from all over the Nazi-controlled world for systematic genocide. With other peoples, only those adults who were *in the way,* were disposed of — again, as if that were not bad enough. But Hitler's plan was to hunt down and murder every Jew anywhere within his control, in order to destroy the seed, the gene, the people. That is why even fractional Jews (half-Jews, quarter-Jews), converted Jews, and others who carried the Jewish gene were marked for inclusion in the genocide.

This difference is best captured by the tragic story of Anne Frank, the German-born Jewish girl whose entire family was hunted down in Amsterdam and shipped hundreds of miles away to death camps, where — except for the father, who miraculously survived — they died. There were no Anne Franks among the non-Jewish Polish casualties. There were no entire families hunted down and murdered solely because they were Polish (or Belgian, or Hungarian, or Ukrainian). There was no attempt to destroy the seed of the Polish people. The "Sophies" who had to choose which of their children would live and which would die were Jewish, William Styron's *Sophie's Choice* notwithstanding.*

There was no ingathering of any other people from around the world for systematic extinction. Perhaps that is why Holocaust deniers like Robert Faurisson try so hard to "prove" that Anne Frank's diary is a forgery. Her story exemplifies the uniqueness of the Jewish Holocaust: the killing of more than one million children, the ingathering of millions of Jews from throughout the Nazi-controlled world for systematic extinction.

The world must remember (in some places, must learn for the first

---

* Discussing the title character of Styron's novel, Elie Wiesel wrote in the *New York Times:* "While in Auschwitz, has she even run into Jewish prisoners? It seems to me that she has been put there so as to illustrate something that 'universalists' have been claiming all along, namely that 'others' have also witnessed agony in Auschwitz." "Does the Holocaust Lie Beyond the Reach of Art?," *New York Times,* April 17, 1983, Section 2, p. 1.

time) that Jews were not killed "along with" Poles, Ukrainians, Russians, and others. It was *not* just a matter of degree or scale, as Cardinal Glemp and others have lied.*

My generation of Jews, and thinking non-Jews, understands this difference. My friends from Brooklyn and I, who never discussed the Holocaust when we were growing up, talk about it all the time now. But recent efforts to de-Judaize or even deny the Holocaust are directed at future generations — at the verdict of history over time. Soon there will be no survivors or perpetrators left. The next generation will read about it in books, see some gruesome but ambiguous films, and hear distant stories. It is essential that the *true* story be preserved, that everyone understand that Jews were not simply another group that experienced some casualties in the course of a terrible war. If the world forgets or denies that Jews — just because they were Jews — were singled out for total genocide, it will make it easier for such a terrible thing to happen again.

* Even the Polish pastoral letter of January 20, 1991, emphasizes the "fact" that "the Poles as a nation were one of the first victims of *the same* criminal racist ideology of Hitler's racism" (emphasis added). No mention is made of the enormous differences discussed above.

Visiting Synagogues Around the World

Exploring the Different Meanings of Jewishness

THE HOLOCAUST caused many Jews to question the theological basis of Judaism, while at the same time strengthening their identity as Jews. Whether "God died at Auschwitz," as some believe, or humankind was "desanctified" there, as others believe, few can doubt that the Holocaust altered the relationship between the Jewish God and his "chosen people." What, after all, had we been "chosen" for? The Holocaust has caused many survivors — and all Jews are survivors — to rethink the very nature and definition of Judaism.

The definition of Jewishness applied by Hitler during the Holocaust, based as it was on "racial" and "genetic" factors, was obviously a definition imposed from without, by enemies of the Jews. Its purpose was destructive, indeed lethal, rather than positive. No one today, except for bigots, would take this definition seriously, since it included people who had explicitly chosen other religions and had experienced no connection to Judaism for several generations.* But thinking about the Holocaust makes every Jew consider his or her own definition of Jewishness.

For Orthodox Jews — those who follow the Halakah, the road defined by immutable religious rules that go back centuries — the issue is a relatively simple one: a Jew is any person born of a Jewish mother or who has converted to Judaism pursuant to the rigorous procedures

* Israel's Law of Return, which is discussed in greater detail in Chapter VII, was enacted in reaction to Hitler's definition. The Law of Return extends its protection broadly to non-Jews who, because they are related to Jews, might require sanctuary from discrimination of the kind inflicted by Hitler.

of the Halakah. This definition, which is generally accepted by Conservative Jews as well but rejected by Reform Jews, lies at the root of the "who is a Jew" controversy that is continuously being confronted in Israel.

In an age of mass immigration to Israel from the Soviet Union, where intermarriage has been the rule rather than the exception for the past several generations, the Orthodox definition is becoming problematic in Israel. Even in the United States, where intermarriage is a growing reality, there are movements afoot proposing that Judaism should become inclusive rather than exclusive. Rabbi Alexander M. Schindler, president of the Reform Union of American Hebrew Congregations, defended the Reform movement's decision to include children of a Jewish father and a non-Jewish mother as Jews: "I felt it was in keeping with our fundamental Reform principle of making no distinction between the rights of men and women in religious life. . . . [I am also concerned over] the tens of thousands of children who have Jewish fathers and non-Jewish mothers."[1]

Many Jews, both within the Reform movement and outside it, are wondering whether it is good for Judaism to exclude the children of Jewish fathers who are born to non-Jewish mothers. These critics of the Orthodox rules want to make it easier for children of mixed marriages to remain Jewish. The next generation will, in my view, provide the testing ground, and perhaps the battleground, for these conflicting visions of Judaism and Jewishness.

But apart from the purely religious definition, there is the existential meaning of Jewishness. Can a person who regards himself or herself as "Jewish" be a good Jew without regard to the religious — particularly the ritualistic — aspects of Judaism? Does Zionism provide an alternative, or supplementary, mode of Jewishness? Can a nonobservant, non-Zionist person remain Jewish if he or she believes in and practices the "ethics" of Judaism? If so, what are these ethics? Do they change from generation to generation? Is there an unalterable "essence" or "core" of Judaism? How will coming generations of Jews pose these, and related, questions? And how will they answer them?

The great Jewish philosopher Maimonides in the twelfth century set out thirteen "immutable" principles of theological Judaism, which include God's unity, perfection, and eternality. Though many Jews do not necessarily believe in every aspect of Maimonidean Jewish theology, there can be little doubt that monotheism — the belief in one God — is one of its central tenets. The declaration of Jewish faith has

Ringel family portrait, 1919. Alan Dershowitz's maternal grandparents, with their children (Dershowitz's mother is at center).

Dershowitz at one year old, with his father and mother, 1939.

Dershowitz family portrait, 1939. (Alan in mother's arms at upper right, his father in hat at upper left, Great-grandmother Leah seated in front, grandfather in second row holding cigar.)

Above: Six of the Borough Park boys among graduates of Yeshiva Etz Chaim, 1951. (Seated on ground: Hal Jacobs, fifth from left; Zol Eisenstadt, fourth from right. Seated on bench: Bernie Beck, third from left. In row behind Beck: Dershowitz, sixth from left; Murray Altman, seventh from left; Josh Weisberger, far right.)
Left: Dershowitz with parents and grandmothers at college graduation, 1959.

Dershowitz family photo before Yom Kippur with Justice Arthur Goldberg (head of table) and Dorothy Goldberg (at his left), 1967.

Interviewing Golda Meir for the PBS television show "The Advocates," May 1970.

Dershowitz in front of his office door, which is filled with anti-Semitic mail, 1990.

Alan Dershowitz debates William F. Buckley, Jr., at Harvard University, spring 1980.

Dershowitz and the Reverend Jesse Jackson, 1984.

Teaching class at Harvard Law School, 1982.

A relaxed moment with Natan Sharansky at Maven's Kosher Court, Cambridge, Massachusetts, 1988.

Micki Keno

Steve Hansen

Elsa Dorfman

Dershowitz preparing to serve papers in the Cardinal Glemp lawsuit, Czestochowa, Poland, 1990.

Arguing the appeal of hotelier Leona Helmsley in state court, New York City, 1990.

Discussing anti-Semitism
with Mikhail Gorbachev,
Moscow, 1990.

Alan Dershowitz in front
of the gates at Terezin concentration camp, Czecho-
slovakia, 1990.

In Egypt with wife,
Carolyn Cohen.

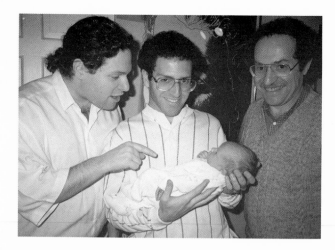

Elon Dershowitz (left) and
Jamin Dershowitz with
their father and his baby
daughter, Ella Kaille
Cohen Dershowitz, 1990.

Alan Dershowitz playing
basketball with son Elon
in backyard, 1983.

Fiftieth birthday party with Borough Park friends on Martha's Vineyard, 1988. (Left to right: Barry Zimmerman, Josh Weisberger, Alan Dershowitz, Zol Eisenstadt, Carl Meshenberg, Bernie Beck, Murray Altman.)

On the set with Ron Silver, the actor who portrayed him in the film *Reversal of Fortune*, 1990.

always been the *Shma Yisrael:* "Hear O Israel, the Lord our God, the Lord is One."

Jews take pride in having given monotheism to the world as a great advance over the worship of many deities. But even as a kid studying in yeshiva, I questioned the theological underpinnings of Judaism. I never understood why monotheism is seen as somehow "better" or "more advanced" or "more believable" than polytheism. If there can be one God, why can't there be many? Indeed, in some respects monotheism is a regression and an invitation to conflict. If there is only one true God, then all people must worship Him. There is no room for religious heterogeneity or pluralism. Religious imperialism becomes justifiable in the face of this one Truth. At best, monotheists may tolerate other religions, in the way we tolerate other people's honest mistakes or wrongheaded political views, without accepting them as full-fledged equals.

For example, the suffering experienced by Jews at the hands of Christians over the past two millennia grows primarily out of the conflict over whether Jesus was the true Messiah. Jewish rejection of that religious declaration of faith means, to Christians, that Jews are not true believers. And Christian acceptance of Jesus, to Jews, means that Christians have accepted a false messiah. Would it not have been (and still be) better if Jesus were seen as the *Christian* Messiah, but not as the *Jewish* Messiah? Why must we both have *one* true Messiah, or one God?

Monotheism may be an advance in the atheist's view — in the sense that it can be seen as part of a progression from many gods, to few gods, to one god, and eventually to no god. But to religious people, it should be neutral — in the sense that it should not matter that other religious people believe in a different god or gods. One God is — arguably though not inherently — a more abstract concept than many gods. But why is abstraction a particular virtue in religion?*

---

* The progression from one God to an "unknowable force" and then to "nature" has, in fact, been part of the history of religion. In the colonial United States, for example, religious skeptics called themselves deists. Today the same set of beliefs, disbeliefs, and uncertainties is called — more candidly — agnosticism, universalism, humanism, ethical culturism, or other fancy-sounding names. (Atheism is different: it is an abiding faith — a certainty or truth — indistinguishable, it seems to me, from religion. Indeed, if religions can be divided into orthodox, conservative, or reform; or fundamentalist, moderate, or liberal; so too can atheism. I know some atheists who would make Jerry Falwell seem like a doubting Thomas, by their unshakable certainty in their faith in no god. They remind me of Woody Allen's quip about the atheist couple — one who had been a Jew, the other who had been a Catholic — who had a fight over which religion *not* to bring their child up in.)

I remember discussing this issue with my own children, while we were watching a particularly phantasmological episode of "Star Trek." We had already seen Captain Kirk beam up Mr. Spock from a distant planet, and Bones McCoy cure a crew member with his ray machine. But then the scene shifted to a planet that bore a striking resemblance to Al Capone's Chicago. Suddenly my son Elon, who was then about ten, blurted out, "*That* couldn't really have happened."

I responded, "What do you mean, *that* couldn't really have happened? *None* of this could really have happened. It's all futuristic fantasy." Elon understood that, of course, but he had a point. "I know that, Dad, but at least the rest of it is logical — if you accept the basic futuristic premise. But that last episode wasn't even logical under the premise." (Not surprisingly, Elon has grown up to become a filmmaker in Hollywood.)

If one accepts the premise of monotheism — indeed of any theism — it is certainly not illogical to conclude that there may be more than one god. Even monotheistic religions flirt with the idea of more than one supernatural force, whether it be the Devil, or the Son of God, or divine prophets. It has always seemed to me something of a semantic tour de force to insist that Judaism, Christianity, and Islam are monotheistic religions and then to attribute divine powers to an assortment of other major figures in the religious pantheon.

I saw the "Star Trek" episode as an opportunity to turn the discussion to religion. More particularly, we began a dialogue — which continues to this day — about whether theology is essential to Jewishness, or whether a sense of historical and emotional connection is enough. I've always been a skeptic about every aspect of life. I never remember believing — in the sense of accepting on faith and without question or doubt — anything of significance. The same has been true of my children. My favorite T-shirt, bought for me by my kids, shows a teacher telling his students: "Question Authority . . . But raise your hand first!" Yet despite my skepticism about theology, I feel a close tie to my religious heritage.

Even my parents, who certainly practiced and almost certainly believed on faith, always encouraged questions, even when they did not approve of our tentative answers. Ours has always been a family where you score more points for the insight reflected in the question than for the persuasiveness of the answer. We not only wear the T-shirt that declares "Question Authority," we live by those words. (But we rarely raise our hands.)

One of the most embarrassing — and proudest moments — of my life as a father occurred during Yom Kippur services at the Harvard Hillel when my younger son, Jamin, was thirteen and a half. (I brought up my two sons, after a divorce, from the time they were twelve and ten.) Every year during the service, Rabbi Ben Zion Gold, the Hillel spiritual leader — opened the floor up to questions from the congregants. The hall was always packed with hundreds of students, professors, and people from the community. After a few general questions and answers about the prayer book, Jamin raised his hand and was called on. "Rabbi," he asked, "is it not true that under the Jewish religion, when a boy turns thirteen, he becomes responsible for his own religious observance?" Rabbi Gold answered, "Yes, Jamie, you learned your Bar Mitzvah lessons very well." "Then why," Jamin continued, with a gloating quality of one-upmanship in his voice, "does my father have the right to *make me* go to services if I don't want to?"

There was a murmur from the crowd, as people whispered to each other, "That's Dershowitz's kid." My other son, Elon, kept saying, "C'mon Dad, admit it, you're proud of him. You wish you'd have had the guts to pull that on your father."

I was both embarrassed and proud, but I never would have pulled that on my father for two reasons. First, my father would have been more embarrassed and less proud of me in the context of the community in which I grew up. Second, despite my skepticism about beliefs, I enjoyed going to services as a youngster. In the Borough Park community, it was an important part of our social and cultural life. It was simply unthinkable not to go to services every Shabbes and every holiday. If you weren't there you were sick at home, or away for the holiday attending services elsewhere.

Our community in Cambridge was very different. It was far more difficult to draw an acceptable line between beliefs and actions. If you could not justify your actions by references to your beliefs, you were a hypocrite. Religious practice was personal, not communal. There was no reason to practice unless it grew out of a set of religious principles. But in Cambridge, the concept of religious principle was more inclusive than in Borough Park. It extended to the kinds of nontheological beliefs that I felt.

I remember seeing a cartoon in a Jewish publication showing a father pulling his son into the synagogue. The caption read: "Atheist, shmatheist, that's no reason not to go to shul and *daven* [pray]." That kind of argument would not work with my children's generation.

Like the father in the cartoon, I wanted my sons to go to the synagogue, at least occasionally, and to participate in the other holiday rituals. But I knew that they didn't enjoy it the way I did. They certainly did not go out of any commanding theological belief. Nor were they attracted, as I now was, by a sense of tradition or nostalgia.

Part of the reason they went had to do with Jewish survival and ethnic solidarity. My sons and I have made visits to synagogues all around the world that were abandoned by all but a few remnants of the prior population. These visits have had a powerful impact on our sense of the need for continuity. A synagogue tells a great deal about the situation of the Jewish community in a particular city or country, since religion and politics have never been completely separate where Jews are concerned.

Before the advent of *glasnost* and *perestroika,* Soviet Jews, on the Sabbath and Jewish holidays, would mass outside the synagogues in Moscow, Leningrad, and other cities with large Jewish populations. They would meet there — the only place they could legally congregate — to discuss emigration, Jewish culture, and the condition of prisoners of conscience. Very few, mostly old, Jews attended the KGB-controlled services inside the synagogues. The KGB was outside as well as inside, occasionally dispersing crowds and making certain that Arkapova Street in Moscow, and comparable streets in other cities, did not become comfortable meeting grounds for refuseniks and dissidents. Now more Jews enter the synagogues to pray, and the KGB is no longer in evidence in the streets, even though Jews sometimes need protection from Pamyat thugs who gather outside the synagogue to taunt them.

In Kraków only the dead are in evidence around the principal synagogue. Significantly, the Kraków synagogue is located in the middle of a graveyard. This symbolizes the situation of Jews throughout Poland. There are millions of them, but they are almost all in graves, mostly unmarked, some marked, others desecrated.

In Riga, the small synagogue is lodged tightly between two other buildings, serving as a support for their walls. That is why this synagogue, alone among the more than forty that thrived in prewar Riga, survived Hitler's occupation. It could not be blown up, as the others were, without endangering the valuable Latvian buildings. The Jews of Riga look to their shul as a symbol. As one survivor told me: "Like our shul, the Jewish community of Riga is permitted to survive, because we provide a degree of support for the Latvian community, especially in its struggle against Russian domination."

In Prague, the major Jewish synagogue — built in the thirteenth century and still in operation — is an important tourist attraction for all visitors to that beautiful city. Prague, today proud of its Jews and their contribution to Czech culture, has had its dark side. For example, during the Hussite revolts of the fourteenth century, pogroms were frequent, and the Jews were expelled from the crown cities of Moravia, an exile that lasted into the nineteenth century. Now the Jewish quarter is among the best-preserved and most beautiful parts of the old city.

In Bucharest, the synagogue is located in the middle of a neighborhood that was demolished by Romania's late dictator Nicolae Ceausescu in anticipation of a major urban renewal project that awaits completion. It lies uncomfortably between Ceausescu's tyrannical world of the past and his successors' uncertain world of the future. Its longtime rabbi, Moshe Rosen, also sits uncomfortably between these two worlds, having supported Ceausescu in order to protect his vulnerable community and now supporting the current government for much the same reason.

In Budapest, the magnificent structure housing the major synagogue and Jewish communal buildings is austere and churchlike. Its dramatic cantor — whose tapes and compact disks are for sale in the lobby — could be mistaken for the baritone lead in a Mozart requiem. Despite the assimilation of much of the Jewish community in this cosmopolitan city before World War II, its Jewish citizens suffered greatly not only at the hand of Eichmann but also from the actions of Hungarian fascists, who continued to murder Jews even while the Germans were retreating from the city in the closing months of the war.

In Italy, France, and Spain there are metal detectors in the entryways to the synagogues. Once when I was leaving for a visit to Paris, my mother pleaded with me to stay away from dangerous places. I thought she meant Place Pigalle. But she quickly told me it was the synagogues — which had recently been bombed by terrorists — that she had in mind.

Outside the Cairo synagogue, dozens of men typically await the beginning of services. But all of them are Egyptian security guards, assigned to protect the synagogue and its worshipers. Until recently a PLO office occupied the building across the way. And since the large,

massive synagogue structure on Adley Street is the single most significant and accessible Jewish presence in Cairo, the authorities are
obviously concerned lest it become a target of terrorist activities.

A trip by my family to an American synagogue on a Jewish holiday
is as much a political statement as a religious one — a demonstration
that the Nazis failed. When I go to synagogue, I often feel that I am
complying with the theologian Emil Fackenheim's 614th commandment: "The authentic Jew of today is forbidden to hand Hitler yet
another, posthumous victory."[2] I do not comply with all of the original 613 mitzvoth — the biblical commandments — but Fackenheim's addendum resonates powerfully with me and my family.

On Rosh Hashanah every year, my family goes back to Borough
Park. We love to walk over to the large Hasidic shul that houses the
Bubover movement. Whenever I see the thousands of Hasidic men,
women, and children in their European garb, the thought reoccurs
that this is the way it must have been in Eastern Europe before Hitler.
Hitler and the Third Reich are dead, and Judaism — even in its most
primitive form, so despised by the Nazis — lives on, in spite of so
great a loss.

I'm reminded of a story Herman Wouk told me when we were in
Israel together in 1988 as visiting scholars living at Mishkanot Sha-
nanim, the Jerusalem academic and art residence. Wouk, an Orthodox
Jew, had been working in Kraków on the TV version of his book *War
and Remembrance*. One morning, after he had put on his *tallis* and *tefillin*
and prayed — something he did every day — he had wandered into a
small Jewish museum in the old Kasimirov section of Kraków. He saw
a pair of *tefillin*. It was exhibited under a glass covering and carried the
following description: "These are *tefillin* which used to be worn by
Jews while they prayed." Herman told me how it struck him with
especial power precisely because he had just finished praying with his
tefillin. I responded that the story had even greater impact on me
because I was one of those Jews who *used* to wear *tefillin* when I prayed
every day.

I was — am — one of those Jews, as are my children, who are
making the museum case statement become true. If anything could
drive me back to *tefillin*, it would not be religious conviction; it would
be a political desire to fight those who want to see Judaism and Jews
relegated to interesting museum exhibits and poignant memorials.

Judaism has survived these millennia for a complex series of reasons,
political and cultural, as well as religious. My Judaism, and that of my

generation and friends, is certainly as much political as it is religious. The question I often ponder — and I pondered it throughout my visits to synagogues — is whether there is a place for this kind of political Judaism. If Judaism, at its core, is a religion, how can one be a political Jew?

For my generation of Jews, political Judaism is not only possible, it may well be the most logical prototype. The Jewish events that shaped my generation were political, not religious. The Holocaust was not about religion; it was about ethnicity (Hitler called it race). It mattered not a whit what the victims believed. It mattered only what they — and their forebears — were. Their status as Jews was immutable.*

Anti-Semitism throughout history has, of course, been a major factor both in driving some Jews from Judaism and in keeping other Jews within the Jewish people. I have already quoted the very secular Soviet literary figure Ilya Ehrenburg, who proclaimed after the Holocaust that "so long as there is a single anti-Semite in the world, I shall declare with pride that I am a Jew." Theodor Herzl, the nonreligious founder of modern political Zionism, acknowledged that "the same way anti-Semitism drives cowardly Jews toward Christianity, anti-Semitism strongly brought out my Jewishness." And Albert Einstein made a similar point: "Perhaps even more than on its own tradition, the Jewish group has thrived on oppression and on the antagonism it has forever met in the world. Here undoubtedly lies one of the main reasons for its continued existence through so many thousands of years."[3]

The establishment of a Jewish state by secular Jews on the ashes of Auschwitz gave a more affirmative and concrete expression to political Judaism. If early Zionists such as Theodor Herzl, Chaim Weizmann, David Ben-Gurion, and the atheist kibbutzniks could define a political Judaism for themselves, surely our generation can also define one.

But generational definitions are exactly that. They do not endure beyond the memory of the events that nurtured them. My children's generation and my students' generation have been shaped by different events. Instead of the Holocaust, there were the war crime trials of old, stupid men who stood charged with being sadistic cogs in a machine

---

* The number of Jews murdered by the Nazis depends, of course, on the definition of "Jew." Six million is the most inclusive number, reflecting those whom Hitler killed because he regarded them as Jews. The number would be only slightly less if the Halakic definition were used; at that time there was less intermarriage than at present.

not of their making. Instead of a beleaguered nation turning swamps into orchards, ingathering poor Jews from Arab countries, and fighting against superior Arab armies, there was a powerful Israel undertaking preemptive military operations, expelling Arab troublemakers, and engaging — along with most other nations — in trade with South Africa.

If there is no core of immutable *religious* beliefs that my children and I share in common, how can I expect them to share my *political* Judaism, when our political memories have so little in common? This is the challenge of Judaism without Halakah, or with "selective" Halakah. This is the challenge many in my generation try to face, while others hope for the best. This is the issue my old friends from Brooklyn discuss more than any other when we gather for our periodic nostalgia retreats. We know that *our* generation understands the tragic history out of which Israel and current Judaism developed. But we know that our children's generation has experienced something very different, and we worry about the basis for their Judaism. If their generation, which never experienced an external threat to the very survival of Judaism, does not appreciate the need for its perpetuation, how can we persuade them not to intermarry and — if they are males — end the Jewish lineage of their families, at least according to Jewish Halakah? What is it about *their* experiences that will persuade them that Judaism should survive internal threats, as it survived external ones?

Not only have I endlessly discussed these intractable dilemmas within the privacy of my circle of Brooklyn friends, I have publicly debated them with prominent proponents of particularistic visions of Judaism.

In every age there have been false prophets who claim to know the one true path to Jewish righteousness. They present Judaism as a single-dimensional approach to life (and death) and condemn all deviators from their way. Since Judaism is a messianic religion with a tradition of prophecy, these false prophets have always had their ardent followers.

Contemporary Jewish life has its share of soothsayers. Among them have been the likes of Rabbi Meir Kahane, founder of the Jewish Defense League, who saw the true Jewish way as bellicose fundamentalism. Until he was assassinated in New York City in November 1990, Kahane threatened Jewish nonbelievers with doom and devastation unless they followed him into literal battle. On the other extreme are the likes of Professor Noam Chomsky, prophet of the extreme Jewish left. He, too, threatens that unless we all join his neo-Marxist revolution and follow him lockstep toward his third world vision of Jewish socialism, we will be trampled underfoot by the march of history. Closer to the Jewish center, but on its secular right wing, are the Jewish neoconservatives, such as Norman Podhoretz, editor of the influential Jewish monthly *Commentary,* who preaches the gospel of American conservatism and threatens that unless American Jews come to realize that their "home" is in the Republican party, along with other conservative Americans who have "made it," we will not be serving our own economic and political interests.

I have debated Kahane, Chomsky, and Podhoretz at public meetings and have taken issue with their road maps. I find them all too particularistic. Each uses — or misuses — selected Jewish sources to lend support to his secular goals. None of them has much to say to my children, my students, my friends, and others who do not already share his values and programs. They trivialize the richness and diversity of Judaism by seeking to shoe-horn thousands of years of experience — reflecting virtually every political perspective — into the narrow path they seek to travel.

The great danger posed by these single-dimension prophets is that defining Judaism or Jewish values in a particularistic fashion may chase away many good Jews who do not agree with their particular myopic vision.

My debates with Meir Kahane are a story in themselves. For years no prominent Jew — certainly no members of the Jewish establishment — would debate Kahane or share a platform with him. Because of his ultraright views and advocacy of violence to rid Israel of Arabs, the major Jewish organizations had imposed a virtual shroud of censorship around him. The Hillel Houses (named after the prominent first-century Jewish scholar) had banned him from appearing on college campuses under their auspices. This, of course, did not stop Kahane. He would simply show up on the doorstep of the local Hillel House and make his speech there. The resulting news story — usually a combination of his complaint about censorship and his substantive message — was widely covered primarily because of the efforts to ban him.

I had long opposed these attempts at censorship. While condemning Kahane's ideas on their merits, I defended his right to state them. I was particularly appalled at the double standard applied by some

Jewish organizations and leaders to Kahane's freedom of expression. While defending the rights of racist bigots like Louis Farrakhan and Vanessa Redgrave to spew forth their venom, these embarrassed Jews drew the line at Kahane, because — as one of them put it to me — "he's one of our own, and we don't want to parade our dirty laundry in public." My grandmother would have called him a *shanda fur de goyim*.

But Kahane was not "one of our own," as if that should really make any difference when it comes to freedom of speech and censorship. Kahane was no part of anything I stand for or identify with. That is true even though we shared a common personal background. Our grandparents knew each other in Williamsburg. We both attended Yeshiva University High School, and indeed were both captains of the debate team, although our years there did not overlap. My mother tells me that our family may be partly responsible for Meir Kahane's very existence, since my grandfather sold Meir Kahane's parents the ring with which they were married.

I had gotten to know Kahane in 1973, when I represented a member of the Jewish Defense League (JDL) in the Sol Hurok and Columbia Artists bombing case. A bomb exploding in Hurok's Manhattan office had caused the tragic death of an accountant there, a young Jewish woman named Iris Kones.[4]

During the course of this case, I occasionally ate lunch with Meir Kahane at Shmulka Bernstein's delicatessen, where he would harangue me about the importance of Jewish armed self-defense: "Every Jew a .22," was not only his slogan, it became a reality for his small band of terrorists, which nearly succeeded in its efforts during the early 1970s to assassinate high-level Soviet diplomats, including the ambassadors to Washington and the United Nations.

I came away from these meetings with an appreciation for Kahane's shrewdness and contempt for his promiscuous use of violence.

For several years following the JDL murder case — which we won — Kahane would call me whenever his free speech rights were abridged. I decided that I would not impose a double standard on the rights of a Jewish racist (he preferred the term "religionist," since he believed that Jews were "superior" regardless of their race) as distinguished from other bigots. Whatever rights any racist, sexist, or other -ist would be entitled to, Kahane and his audiences should have as well.

In 1984, Rabbi Weiss, of Riverdale, New York, called to tell me that Meir Kahane was challenging me to a "great debate" over the "fundamental Jewish issues of the age." I thought about it, and decided to accept.

My acceptance sparked a "great debate" of its own within the Jewish community. I received telephone calls and letters from several Jewish leaders urging me to cancel. I was lending "legitimacy" to Kahane by debating him. Two local Riverdale rabbis ordered members of their congregations to boycott the debate, because — as one of the rabbis put it — "Kahane is a pervert, demagogue, and inciter to murder and terrorism."[5] Even my mother urged me to back out, but her reason was different: she was concerned for my safety, since there had been death threats directed against the participants.

The debate went forward as scheduled on November 10, 1984, on a cold, rainswept night. Security was in evidence both inside and outside the synagogue as twelve hundred people from throughout the metropolitan area lined up to get one of the eight hundred seats. People sat in the aisles and listened through the windows as the event began.

The encounter was widely covered by the press. One journalist speculated about the meaning of the heavy security — two dozen policemen, double frisking, undercover detectives, and private guards — in the context of a debate between two Jews.[6]

The *New York Times* reported:

> They attended the same Yeshiva high school in Brooklyn and grew up conversant with the sacred Jewish texts, but the lives of Meir Kahane and Alan Dershowitz have taken radically different courses.
>
> Rabbi Kahane, the founder of the Jewish Defense League, was elected in July to the Israeli Parliament on a platform calling for the expulsion of all Arabs from the country.
>
> Mr. Dershowitz, a professor of law at Harvard University, has defended Jewish activists in the Soviet Union and has worked to build bridges between Jews and non-Jews in the United States and Israel.
>
> . . . The encounter was marked by fiery exchanges, Biblical quotations and exhortations to the audience.[7]

The debate itself was surprisingly substantive. My opening statement focused on why I was the first Jewish public figure willing to debate Kahane — why I had rejected the counsel of my associates:

"I am debating Rabbi Meir Kahane," I said, "because too few blacks debated and responded to Reverend Jesse Jackson and Louis

Farrakhan.* I am debating Rabbi Kahane because virtually no Arabs are willing to debate Yasir Arafat. I think it is imperative that the world understand not only that the vast majority of Jews repudiate Rabbi Kahane's views but also *why* we repudiate those views."

Rabbi Kahane did not appreciate my defense of his right to speak: "The greatest of tragedies is [that] there are those who would grant me the right to speak because they would also grant the right of speech to Yasir Arafat. That is the greatest tragedy — that Jews are unable to understand the difference between a Farrakhan and an Arafat on one hand, and Rabbi Meir Kahane on the other hand."

Kahane began the substantive debate with a question:

"Assuming that the Arabs become saints — and they sit down democratically, and they reproduce saints — I don't want to live under a majority of Arab saints. So the question that I ask of people who are upset at the things that I say, is: What is your answer to the voting question? Do the Arabs have a right to become a majority, democratically, peacefully, in the state of Israel?"

I tried to answer in a manner consistent with both my Jewish and democratic values.

"Rabbi Kahane would throw up his hands and say there is no room for democracy, there is nothing Jewish about democracy. I beg to differ. The vast majority of Jews in this world support both Zionism and democracy. The false dichotomy that Rabbi Kahane is seeking to impose on us is not correct, and the ultimate implications of his dangerous view are that once the Arabs are expelled from Israel, then Jews who do not fit Rabbi Kahane's particularistic definition of his kind of Jew will also be expelled."

I further challenged Meir Kahane with this question: "The vast majority of Jews in Israel today are not Orthodox Jews, and yet Israel is a Jewish state. What would you do under your principles to the vast majority of Jews who dispute your approach?"

"Obviously," Rabbi Kahane answered, "it would be better to teach people. But the Torah mandates coercion."

He went on: "Certainly, at this moment, the possibilities of creating such a Jewish state, that is a real Jewish state, as opposed to Israel today which is a state where Jews live, seems remote. But our ultimate aim must be to create a Torah state.

"If Israel will not be a Torah state, then God forbid, the Almighty

* I was referring, of course, to Jackson's insensitive references to Jews during the 1984 presidential campaign and to Farrakhan's crass anti-Semitism.

will bring down upon us the punishment that he warned about in a Bible that is as applicable in 1984 as it was in the year 84."

I argued that Zionism and indeed Judaism are options that enhance choice, rather than obligations that compel adherence. "Rabbi Kahane," I went on, "sees Zionism as a principle of compulsion, of separatism, of exclusion. There is no way of debating or arguing with someone who thinks all that is right is on his side and he speaks in the name of God. Until God speaks to us in much clearer ways, we, as human beings, will have to resolve these disputes among ourselves."

The debate ended with a question that mentioned our similar backgrounds and then asked about the different roads we took. "Today you personify different views within the Jewish spectrum. What motivated you, and who motivated you most to travel the paths you did?"

I answered by talking about my family and the Jewish values they transmitted to me. "I grew up in a household where my father, of blessed memory, always talked about defending the underdog, always talked about standing up for those who were least able to stand up for themselves. He always drew from the deepest Jewish values. My grandparents before him, my mother who is here tonight, have always seen much more clearly and with much greater Jewish vision than Rabbi Kahane.

"The great challenge is to try to be a good American and a good Jew. And I will never allow Rabbi Kahane to define my Jewishness for me any more than I will allow Ronald Reagan to define my Americanism for me.

"In the end, the values for which we, as a people, have struggled for thousands and thousands of years will not be solved overnight by a false prophet. You will solve them, the people of Israel will solve them."

Rabbi Kahane got the final word:

"I say to you Judaism is not for you to pick and to choose and to decide, that is not Judaism. That's Dershowitzism.

"My opponent is a product of America, a smattering of Jewishness. I tell you, I appeal to you — time is running out for your living here in America — go home, go home to Israel.

"Be good Jews, be observant Jews, accept the yoke of heaven, the religious way."[8]

I cannot — and surely my children cannot — be "Kahane Jews." In our debates — we had a total of three — he espoused a single-dimensional view of Judaism that is simply unacceptable to us on moral grounds. Unless I follow his way, I am not a true Jew. I may be, in his words, a "Harvard Jew," or a "liberal Jew," or an "assimilated Jew," or a "delicatessen Jew," or a "Hellenized Jew," but my Jewishness is "racial," not religious — an accident of birth, not a matter of principled commitment. To Kahane, and to some of my own less vociferous relatives, there was but *one* Jewish road. It is mapped out in detail by the Halakah, literally "the way" — in the singular — of Judaism.

But even the Halakah has divergent paths. From the earliest days, there were the very different schools of Bet Hillel and Bet Shammai, representing — in oversimplified terms — a somewhat more liberal or open approach versus a somewhat more conservative or closed approach to religious doctrine, interpretation, and practice. Later, there was the breach between Hasidim and Misnagdim, representing — again in oversimplified terms — a somewhat less pedantic and more existential approach to Judaism versus a more academic and intellectual approach. Then, of course, there were regional differences, represented by the Ashkenazim, Sephardim, and other variants. Now, of course, we have ultraorthodox, modern Orthodox, Conservative, Reform, Reconstructionist, and variations on each of these themes. Even within the Israeli Orthodox, there is a peace movement committed to returning land for peace on Halakic grounds — as well as the Kahane movement, which not only believes that giving up land is religiously prohibited, but that the Halakah requires the expulsion of Israeli Arabs from all of Israel.

When I debated Kahane, he would come with but one book — the Torah. The Torah, with its authoritative commentaries, contained all the answers to every possible question.

In some respects, Kahane reminded me of the rejected Supreme Court nominee Robert Bork, who likewise seemed to believe that every constitutional answer to our contemporary problems could be found in the cryptic words of an eighteenth-century document written by white Protestant landowning males.

A legend related in the Talmud casts an interesting light on the contemporary American debate over the original intent of the framers of our Constitution. Rabbi Eliezer was engaged in a dispute with other sages about an arcane point of law. Eliezer was certain that his interpretation was the correct one and he "brought forward every imaginable argument, but they did not accept them." Finally, in desperation, he invoked the original intent of the author of the Torah. Eliezer implored, "If the Halakah" — the authoritative meaning of the law — "agrees with me, let it prove from heaven." Whereupon a heavenly voice cried out to the others: "Why do ye dispute with Rabbi Eliezer, seeing that . . . the Halakah agrees with him?" (Pretty authoritative evidence of the original intent!) But another of the rabbis, Joshua, rose up and rebuked God for interfering. "Thou hast long since written the Torah, and we pay no attention to a Heavenly Voice." The message was clear: God's children were telling their Father that "it is *our* job, as the rabbis, to bring meaning to the Torah that you gave us. You gave us a document to interpret, *and* a methodology for interpreting it. Now leave us to do our job." God agreed, laughing with joy. "My children have defeated me in argument."[9]

I recounted this legend when I participated in a debate over constitutional construction, a debate involving several federal judges, including Chief Justice William Rehnquist. I reminded the judges that no single person, divine or otherwise, drafted the American Constitution or its Bill of Rights or its post–Civil War amendments (which together comprise our current Constitution). Our contemporary rabbis in robes cannot call for a heavenly — or even an earthly — voice to confirm the correctness of their interpretations of such phrases as due process, equal protection, freedom of speech, or cruel and unusual punishment. But I wondered if Jefferson, Madison, Hamilton, and our other farsighted framers would not respond to a contemporary Eliezer's call for authoritative interpretation by declining to interfere and by saying: "It is a constitution you must expound. We wrote its phrases long ago in a different era. Do not pay undue attention to those who would invoke voices from the grave or the heavens."

In religion, of course, one may not totally ignore the sacred texts, any more than a judge could totally ignore the Constitution or a relevant statute. But the words of ancient, authoritative writings are always open to interpretation. And interpretation is rarely neutral; it is often value laden. It is the role of every society to infuse old writings with new meanings appropriate to the times. And it must therefore be acknowledged that no single interpretation excludes others, just as no single set of values excludes others. As Rabbi Mordecai Kaplan, one of the great Jewish thinkers of the twentieth century, used to say: "Jews are not in the antique business." "Just because something is old," he added, "that does not make it 'authentic.'" He acknowledged that "the past has a vote," but insisted that it does not have a "veto."[10]

Traditional Jewish writings and experiences are a very important source of my morality — perhaps among the most important sources, both consciously and unconsciously. But they are not, and cannot be, the sole source. Living in a diverse and heterogeneous world, I must be eclectic. I must pick from among the best moral perspectives, and choose the ones that most closely suit my needs and express my values. No group has a monopoly on morality. Indeed, what we have come to call Jewish morality is, of course, an amalgam of traditions from many sources. Original Judaism reflected the cultures and beliefs of neighboring Egypt and other societies.

Our sages were not oblivious to, or immune from, the competing and complementary moralities around them. Maimonides both taught and learned from his Arab neighbors. The great religious sages of Eastern Europe understood western philosophy and even Christianity and could not help but be influenced by their contemporary world. Jewish music, Jewish food, Jewish garb, Jewish synagogue architecture, Jewish languages (Yiddish, Ladino), have all been influenced by the world in which they developed. It would be remarkable if Jewish theology and philosophy were not similarly affected.

We live in a world of diverse values. Because our world has shrunk to the size of a television set, we are bombarded with many competing moralities and philosophies. Perhaps the Hasidim — or at least the sects that do not permit their adherents to watch TV, read newspapers, attend secular schools, or interact with outsiders — do not experience this clash of ideologies. But the rest of us, and especially our children, most assuredly do.

It follows, therefore, that we have values that come from outside Judaism. They may enter our consciousness through the lens of our Judaism, but they become part of a world view that incorporates everything around us. We have views on racism, on sexism, on the environment, on disarmament, on sexuality, on abortion, on drugs, on justice, on capital punishment, on freedom of speech, on nuclear energy, and on the array of other contemporary issues that matter.

We must not demand of our children — as Kahane demanded of us — that they *choose between* their own contemporary moral values and those of traditional Judaism. Kahane told us that we cannot believe both in democracy and in Judaism. I do, and most of my Jewish friends do. If we were to have to make a choice between Kahane's Judaism and American democracy, most of us would accept American democracy — precisely because it would allow us to incorporate and express our Judaism. Thank God, we don't have to make any such choice. We adapt our Judaism to our democracy and our democracy to our Judaism. Both Judaism and democracy are sufficiently pluralistic to permit such a marriage, and each is enriched by the influence of the other.

Similarly, if we demand of our children that they choose between our Judaism (however defined) and their values, we are making it far too difficult for them to live with Judaism. My children, friends, and students will simply never accept Kahane's violent and exclusionist approach to life — even if a heavenly voice were to tell them that he was the true prophet.*

Nor can my children, friends, or students accept the prophets of the left, who would willingly sacrifice Jewish values and the Jewish state to some Marxist view of the world. The most popular false prophet of the left — at least on college campuses — has been Noam Chomsky, whom I have debated on several occasions.

My first debate with Chomsky was in 1973, several weeks after the Yom Kippur War, in which Arab states unsuccessfully tried to drive Israeli forces from territories captured six years earlier in the Six-Day War. It was in a large Boston church, before a largely "peace" audience, and was sponsored by the American Friends Service Committee. Chomsky's proposal at that time was consistent with the PLO party line. He wanted to abolish the state of Israel, as it then existed, and to substitute a "secular, binational state." His secular, binational state was to be based on the model of binational "brotherhood" that then prevailed in Lebanon. Chomsky repeatedly pointed to Lebanon, where Christians and Muslims "lived side by side," sharing power in peace and harmony.[11]

This is what I said about Chomsky's hare-brained scheme in our 1973 debate: "Putting aside the motivations behind such a proposal when it is made by the Palestinian organizations, why do not considerations of self-determination and community control favor two separate states: one Jewish and one Arab? Isn't it better for people of common background to control their own life, culture, and destiny (if they so choose), than to bring together in an artificial way people who have shown no ability to live united in peace. I confess to not

---

* My last contact with Rabbi Kahane came just before his murder. He called, asking me to represent him in negotiations with Brandeis University, which was refusing to allow him to address a student group unless he paid for extensive security. I got Brandeis to withdraw the condition, and Kahane spoke uneventfully. A few days later, he was dead.

understanding the logic of the proposal, even assuming its good will."

The remainder of this first debate was over whether the values of the "peace movement" favored the Israeli or Arab position. Since I had represented many members of the peace movement during the Vietnam era, I believed that we shared similar values. I emphasized our shared preference for peace over property and our shared opposition to using force to regain land.

"I am not — as some of you are — a pacifist; I believe that killing to save life is sometimes appropriate; I also believe that on rare occasions armed violence to secure liberty is also appropriate. But I can never — under any circumstances — justify killing to secure property, even when that property is one's birthplace, one's homeland. . . . That, I would have thought, would be an absolute tenet of the peace movement and of the Quaker religion. And that is why I have so much difficulty understanding how so many of you see much virtue in the Palestinian position, which espouses the use of violence to retake land."

I then came to my counterproposal to Chomsky's demand for a single binational state based on the model of Lebanon. "Israel should declare, in principle, its willingness to give up the captured territories in return for a firm assurance of lasting peace. By doing so, it would make clear what I think the vast majority of Israelis believe: it has no interest in retaining the territories for any reason other than protection from attack."

Chomsky rejected my proposal out of hand. He characterized it as a mere return to the "colonialist status quo." Only the dismantling of the colonialist Jewish state would satisfy the PLO, and only the creation of a secular, binational Palestine in "all of Palestine" would satisfy Chomsky. This was the "Jewish way," Chomsky claimed, citing some Jewish anti-Zionists. And this was the wave of the anticolonialist future, Chomsky assured his audience, citing his European neo-Marxist gurus.

A dozen years later we met once again, this time at Harvard Medical School. The second debate was far more personal and acrimonious. Much of it focused on his credibility. He initially denied having advocated a Lebanon-style binational state for Israel, only to have to back down upon being confronted with the evidence. He also tried to dispute the fact that he had authorized an essay he had written in defense of Robert Faurisson to be used as the foreword to Faurisson's book about Holocaust denial, but again had to back down. He took the position that before Faurisson had written his book, he — Chomsky — had no interest in "revisionist" literature. When confronted by a distinguished professor who recalled discussing revisionist literature with him well before the Faurisson book, Chomsky first berated the professor for disclosing a private conversation and then he shoved him contemptuously.

Noam Chomsky continues to be a popular speaker at universities. His anti-American, anti-Israel, antiwestern, and somewhat paranoid world view will always have a kind of superficial hold on college sophomores. But the attraction rarely extends into the junior year.

By the senior year, and certainly by graduate or professional school, most students seem more attracted to the neoconservatism of Norman Podhoretz and his crowd. The popularity of the neoconservative view seems to grow with age and financial success. If voting patterns are any evidence, however, Jews seem to vote more in accord with their traditional moral principles in support of the downtrodden than with the financial principles of supporting "number one." Thus, although Jews constitute the intellectual leadership of the neoconservative movement, the "neocons" have had little impact, thus far, in moving Jewish grass-roots voters from the liberal to the conservative column. Indeed the predominant shift among Jews from the Democratic to the Republican party has occurred among the ultraorthodox, who do not read such secular magazines as *Commentary*. But the influence of the neocons is growing, in at least two ways. First, as Jews become wealthier and more established, some look for rationales to vote their pocketbooks, and the neocons provide such a rationale. And second, because the neocons have a perceived influence way out of proportion to their actual influence, the entire Jewish community is often "blamed" for what this vocal minority espouses.

In 1987, I was invited to debate Norman Podhoretz on the issue of whether liberalism or conservatism is better for the Jews.[12] The setting was the Central Synagogue in New York, which was so full to overflowing that the rabbi opened the event by saying he thought it must be the Yom Kippur evening service. Podhoretz began with a powerful attack on the left and defense of the right.

"While the tendency on the left has been toward greater unfriendliness towards Jews in the past fifteen or so years, the tendency on the right has been in the opposite direction. . . . We find a strong pro-

Israel sentiment [and] a strong anti-quota sentiment. The tendency on the left has been in the opposite direction. I therefore say that whether or not Jews feel comfortable in the right, there seems to me very little question that Jews no longer have a home on the left."

I began on a somewhat lighter note by recalling 1951, "when Bobby Thomson got up to bat against the Brooklyn Dodgers and hit that ill-fated home run, and all of us in the family looked so sad, and my grandmother turned to us and said, 'Well, was it good or bad for the Jews?' And the answer was, it was good for the Jews. Not Bobby Thomson's home run, which turned a lot of the Brooklyn Faithful into skeptics on the eve of Yom Kippur, but the realization that in America the Jews did not have to evaluate every single event by reference to their own survival. What was good for America was generally good for the American Jews."

I then proceeded to relate the story to the current situation of American Jews.

"Our own destiny is not tied into the success of any particular party or narrow philosophy, any more than it was to the Dodgers or the Giants. It is tied into the success of a system. Indeed it would be a terrible mistake for American Jews to cast their lot, even if anybody was capable of casting our lot for us, with any party or any philosophy. We should not become identified as a people with any extremes, or even with any particular doctrine. . . .

"Hillel, of course, said, 'If I am not for myself, who will be for me?' Conservatives tend to remember that part of what Hillel said. But you should also remember the second part: 'If I am for myself alone, what am I?' The challenge to the American community, as we approach these changing times, is to neglect neither side of that delicate balance. To give up neither self-protection, nor compassion for others less fortunate than we, as we change from a community of have-nots to a community of haves — at least for now."

After these general introductions, we proceeded to a discussion of specific issues.

I challenged the following statement about AIDS in a Podhoretz column: "Curious, that in an age of ubiquitous pornography and blunt speech, it should be hard to say in plain English that *AIDS is almost entirely a disease caught by men who bugger or are buggered by dozens or even hundreds of other men every year*" (emphasis added). I argued that "When Norman Podhoretz writes that, he does not speak for me, he does not speak for the Jewish community. When the Nazis went after gays in

Nazi Germany — the rights of gays were inexorably intermeshed with the interests of Jews. Discrimination against gays today is discrimination against Jews tomorrow."

Podhoretz responded in anger: "The sentence that Alan Dershowitz quoted from my column on AIDs, which he ridiculed by his tone, was factually correct, and I defy him or anyone else to challenge the truth of that statement. My position on gay rights has to do with my fear of the rise and spread of tendencies in this society and in this culture which undermine in a very drastic way the possibility of maintaining the family as the key institution of our society, and of raising our children and our grandchildren in a context which makes it possible for them to live and take their place in the natural chain of the generations."

I did not find his response satisfactory. "There is no room for debate about use of the kind of language that Norman Podhoretz used. . . . That is not language one should use against an oppressed minority in this country. That is a buzzword, that is a bad word. Norman Podhoretz did not write this as a Jew, but many gay men and gay women read this as if he were writing this as a Jew."

I argued against the right wing's being able to co-opt the term "family values," insisting that there is nothing in the liberal agenda that is opposed to the family. I pointed out that much of that agenda — aid to dependent children, medicare, family planning, and affordable housing — is designed to protect families from the ravages of poverty, illness, and homelessness. I had chosen a traditional family life, I explained, but "I am here to defend the right of others to choose differently from the way I choose, because today, if you give Norman Podhoretz the right to tell you that you have no choice but to accept his concept of family values, tomorrow it will be the Reverend Falwell and the Reverend Robertson* [who] tell you what your choices are. Today, Norman Podhoretz will tell us not to read pornography. Tomorrow, the Reverend Falwell will tell us not to read Norman Podhoretz."

During the question period, Podhoretz was asked whether he stood by his statement that he didn't feel strongly about prayer in the public schools. His answer: "I am not particularly passionate about prayer in the schools. One of the reasons is that I remember where I came from,

---

* The Reverend Jerry Falwell, fundamentalist Baptist clergyman and founder of the Moral Majority (now the Liberty Foundation); the Reverend Pat Robertson, TV evangelist and 1988 presidential candidate.

namely, a Brooklyn public school in which every single day we went to the assembly and we sang, 'Holy, holy, holy, Lord God Almighty, Christ [*sic*] in Three Persons, Blessed Trinity.' Most of the Jewish kids in that school came from Yiddish-speaking Orthodox homes, and it was only when I was about thirty years old that I actually realized what it was I had spent my childhood chanting in school. With that experience behind me it's very difficult for me to feel one way or the other about prayer in the schools. But I will make this one point about prayer in the schools. I consider it a screen issue for something very much deeper. And that is the debate that is going on in this country about whether there's anything we can or should do about the flood of pornography, easy promiscuity, teenage pregnancy, and all of the social pathologies that go with it. This is a very, very serious question, perhaps the most serious that faces us."

Not surprisingly, I was appalled at Podhoretz's minimization of the significance of the movement toward prayer in the public schools and his claim that opposition to it is a cover for "pornography" and other evils.

"This issue of prayer in the public schools today," I said, "is not what it was in the 1920s. . . . Today it is part of a conscious two-step process to Christianize America. It is part of a program to get Anne Frank out of the schools, to get creationism into the schools, to get the Bible to become the fundamental vehicle of American literary and political life. It is a screen. But it is not a screen for . . . pornography. It is a screen for the next step of saying religion is to be preferred over nonreligion. And if religion is to be preferred we have to decide which religion. . . .

"We will be inevitably thrust into second-class status if we accept the first step of prayer in the school, and the second step the religionization, and the third step the Christianization of America."

In my closing remarks, I condemned the anti-Zionism and anti-Semitism of the left and challenged Podhoretz to "unequivocally condemn those elements of the right which are anti-Jewish," such as Pat Buchanan. I urged him to "use the same energy against bigots of the right that I will consistently use against [bigots] on the left. And I will continue the fight to oppose them at every turn, because I believe there is still a mainstream liberalism in this America. I am convinced that if we maintain our positions, and maintain our traditions of doing justice in the broadest sense of that term, we will continue in the great tradition of . . . defending ourselves, but also defending the down-trodden."

Podhoretz declined my invitation to condemn the anti-Semitism of the right. Instead, he ended with a renewed attack on the left:

"I submit to you that Alan Dershowitz, while a noble fellow and while taking many positions with which I agree, and while I also wish him the very best of luck in fighting his fight on the left, evaded [my] points. He said he was against these developments on the left, and he meant to fight them as long as he has energy and breath. Good, good luck to him. I think he's going to lose. I think he has already lost. But I admire people who wish to fight in lost causes. . . .

"Not only is the left bad for the Jews, I believe the left is bad for social justice, for moral values, for the security of western civilization, for the future of democratic institutions in this country, and on the face of the earth. I now consider it a community dedicated to bad and immoral values; I consider this as an American.

"Speaking strictly as a Jew, now, I would say that it is virtually suicidal for Jews to go on pretending to themselves that their security rests in a permanent and steady alliance with the liberal community and its characteristic spokesmen and institutions."

The great danger of Podhoretz's approach — of the approach of all the false prophets of particularism — is that if a listener rejects the politics, nothing remains of the Jewish message. If liberalism is the *constant* in the life of a given Jewish listener — as it is for many — then Podhoretz and Kahane's bottom-line message is that such individuals cannot be good Jews and should give up all efforts at integrating their religious and secular philosophies. If conservatism is the constant, then Chomsky's message is essentially the same: they cannot be both good Jews and committed conservatives.

My conception of Jewishness is broad enough to encompass the entire spectrum of politics, even the parts with which I fundamentally disagree. I acknowledge that one can be a good Jew and also agree with the politics of those who disagree with me. Unless the Kahanes, Chomskys, and Podhoretzes begin to understand and acknowledge that their adversaries can also be good Jews, they will chase far too many Jews from any identification with their religion and tradition.

Specifically, if my students or children come to believe that a good Jew cannot support gay rights, black rights, environmental rights, women's rights, and other secular causes, then many will stop being good Jews, rather than give up their support of these important causes. The same is true of other controversial political views espoused by the prophets of particularism. We must recognize that the Jewish way is not a singular road, but rather an almost endless series of interconnecting paths with a common origin and an uncertain and unknowable destination — or destinations.

My own view is that American Jews will never be — and should never be — corralled, domesticated, and turned over to one extreme or the other, or even to one establishment or another. Jews will always be — and should always be — eclectic and independent, at least on most issues. We know an enemy when we see one, but our enemies do not all come from one side or the other.

Jews tend to thrive in open, pluralistic, moderate, nonnationalistic, secular societies. That does not mean that every Jew will advocate such societies. No group has always known what is best for it, and what may be best for a group as a whole may not be best for each of its members or subgroups.

This is especially true as we experience the transition of many American Jews from an immigrant underclass to part of the majority overclass that now participates in the perceived "repression" of others. We now see ourselves as the victims of crime who need protection — even the death penalty — from the "thems" who now invoke the Bill of Rights. We forget that when the Bill of Rights is compromised for anyone, the precedent is there to be used against everyone. When I speak of the Constitution, I am often reminded by critics that "a conservative is a liberal who has been mugged." But I remind the critic that a civil libertarian is a conservative who has been indicted or audited or subjected to a drug test. I tell the audience about a tragic case I have been involved in against the Des Moines police. They arrested a first-year law student for being in the wrong section of the library. When they found out he was Jewish, they taunted him, beat him, and decided to teach him a lesson. He was taken to the hospital in handcuffs by two policemen. After they spent several minutes alone in a room, gunshots were heard. The law student had been fatally shot. The police claimed that the slight young man — who had never touched a gun in his life — had tried to grab for one of the policemen's guns. Preposterous as this tale sounds, it was accepted by a Des Moines jury. We, too, are the victims of police abuse and jury bigotry in some parts of the country.

We want our borders secured against an influx of immigrants from Mexico and Asia seeking a better life for themselves and their children. (The Russian-Jewish comedian Yakov Smirnov tells of the strange feeling that overcame him the moment he took his oath of citizenship at the Statue of Liberty: "The feeling that we must do something to keep these damn immigrants out of our country.")

We want to be sure that our children do not lose their (our?) hard-earned places at the Ivy League universities to the special preferences given to minorities.

We don't mind a little religion in public life — as long as it is "the Judeo-Christian" brand of mainstream American religion.

We realize that unionism and welfarism once played an important role in assuring a fair share of the pie for the worker, but now "they're overdoing it," and welfare recipients — even single mothers — should certainly be made to work. After all, *we* made it without help from the government.

These are all oversimplifications of complex and ever-changing issues, but they signal a clear shift in the perspective and status of many within the Jewish community.

This shifting perspective threatens to divide Jews generationally, socioeconomically, politically, and in other ways. The great challenge confronting our next generation of Jewish leaders is to define a new common core of Jewish values capable of embracing a diversifying array of Jewish attitudes and conditions. The challenges of assimilation, intermarriage, growing fundamentalism and secularism, increasing sensitivity toward the rights of Jewish women and Jewish gays — all these are on the agenda of the coming century of Jewish life in America.

But these issues are all in the "luxury" category, at least when compared to the necessity of Jewish physical survival. The question I am asked most often about the future of the Jewish people — by audiences, students, family, and friends — is still "Can it happen again?" The "it," of course, is an unarticulated reference to the unspeakable — the Holocaust. When I was growing up, the Holocaust itself was not mentioned and the name Hitler was always followed by the Hebrew words *yemach shemo* — may his name be obliterated — as if eradicating an evil name from history could somehow cause the evil to disappear from our memory.

Neither the name Hitler nor his evil has disappeared from our memory, and that is why "it" will probably never happen again, at least in the same manifestation. But there are other terrible evils to be feared and prevented. Indeed, the most dangerous evils are those we cannot anticipate or even imagine, as our grandparents could not have imagined the destruction of European Jewry.

The most serious threats to the physical survival of Jews are today directed against Israel, where more than three million Jews make their home. Israel, which has become the secular religion for millions of other Jews around the world, presents both the greatest hope and the most profound challenge to the future of the Jewish community.

Israel

An American Jewish
Civil Libertarian Goes to Israel

IF MODERN Zionism has become for many Jews a new and more affirmative raison d'être for their Judaism — for some a political or secular form of Judaism — then it is still "not easy to be a Jew" (a translation of an old Yiddish expression: *Shver zol zayn a yid*). Particularly for the Zionist who has not returned to Zion, but who has chosen instead to practice his or her Zionism a safe distance away from the embattled state of Israel, there are many tensions and conflicts. This was not as evident in the early days of the Jewish state, when Israeli policies did not receive the kind of critical scrutiny that has now become commonplace.

For Jews like me, to whom Israel represents Jewry's positive response to centuries of anti-Semitism in general and to Hitler's attempted genocide in particular, these tensions and conflicts are emotionally wrenching.

Israel has been our answer to the second-class (at best) status imposed upon Jews throughout most of the world for millennia. Israel has been our answer to the world's — including our own country's — inexcusable decision to close its doors to millions of Jews who might have escaped the gas chambers if there had been a country that welcomed them. Israel has been our answer to Jewish powerlessness — our inability to defend ourselves against Crusades, pogroms, and the Holocaust — and our reliance on the generosity of others who did have power (but who all too often refused to use it on our behalf). Israel has been our answer to those who say that Jews cannot govern themselves but must always be a minority in other people's land. Israel has been our answer to those who claim that Jews will not work the land and will always exploit those who do. Israel has been our answer to the false charge that Jews are different from other peoples and can never achieve "normalcy."

Most of the tensions and conflicts over Israel result, in fact, from Israel's having proved this final charge to be false. Over the past forty-plus years, Israel has shown that Jews are not that different from other people and that Jews have achieved a modicum of "normalcy." And normalcy means having the usual attributes — both good and bad — of other peoples and nations. Yet more seems to be demanded of Jews — both by Jews and by the rest of the world.

It is impossible to understand why Israel receives the attention — most particularly the criticism — it does receive without recognizing that Israel is the "Jew" among the nations. One of the tiniest nations of the world, Israel receives disproportionate attention, hatred, and envy, in much the same way that the world's tiny population of Jews receives disproportionate attention, hatred, and envy. As Pulitzer Prize–winning journalist Thomas L. Friedman recently put it:

> Quite simply, the West has a fascination and preoccupation with the story of Israel, a curiosity about it, an attraction and even an aversion to it that is out of all proportion to the nation's size. And equally, Israel has an uncanny ability to inject itself into the news like no other country of four million people. [1]

Israel is treated by the nations of the world as the Jews have been treated by the people of the world. Much of the unjustified international criticism — such as the UN General Assembly's resolution equating Zionism with racism — is simply a manifestation of international anti-Semitism. Other criticism reflects the higher standards to which Jews are often held, both as individuals and as a nation. Some — but only a small amount — of the super-scrutiny results from the unfortunate reality that Israel's neighboring enemies include oil-rich and strategically located nations.

One of the most perplexing issues facing *galut* Zionists — Jews who generally support Israel but have not chosen to make their lives there — is how to respond when the Israeli government takes actions that conflict with the world's — and our own — higher expectations of a Jewish state.

Throughout my years as a civil libertarian and advocate of liberal causes, I have often been accused of inconsistency, hypocrisy, or worse because of my support for Israel. Though I have been critical of specific Israeli policies and practices — indeed, far more critical than any Arab academic has been of the PLO — I have been accused by the likes of Noam Chomsky, William Kunstler, and Andrew Cockburn (a radical anti-Zionist who writes for the *Nation*) of being an Israeli "hack," "strict party liner," "tool," and apologist. Other critics have charged me with being "blinded" into hypocrisy by a pro-Israel bias, or of "being a liberal who takes a somewhat more conservative line when it comes to Israel," or of being a "clear-eyed civil libertarian [who] can get a bit foggy when it comes to Israel." And some have argued that I apply one standard of criticism to everyone else, on the one hand, and another standard to Israel, on the other.

None of these criticisms is true, as I will demonstrate in detail. I apply precisely the same standard to Israel as to other industrialized western nations. But I refuse to bend over backward to single out Israel — or other things Jewish — for super-scrutiny. I refuse to gloat, as so many in academia and the media seem to, over Israel's short-comings. I cannot take I-told-you-so pleasure in Israel's failures. I will not be defensive about Israel or about my Jewishness. I refuse to use criticism of Israel as a litmus test of my patriotism, my commitment to civil liberties, or my willingness to melt into the American main-stream.

What is significant about these false accusations is that they con-tinue to be leveled in the face of an unambiguous public record that disproves them. The assumption persists that no principled civil lib-ertarian and liberal could possibly support Israel. "We understand why the liberal politicians kowtow to the Israeli lobby," I have been told. "They have to get reelected. But you," I am admonished, "have no excuse."

They are right. I would have no excuse for applying a double standard to Israel and other countries. But I need no excuse, because I simply don't do it. If anything, I occasionally have to stop myself from following the crowd and demanding of Israel what has never been demanded of others. I find myself, from time to time, having to prove that I am still entitled to my liberal and civil liberties credentials in spite of my support for Israel. Israel deserves the support of liberals and civil libertarians — not for each and every one of its actions over its forty-plus-year existence as a nation, but because, in general, it has acted more in accord with principles of civil liberties and liberalism than almost any other country, and certainly more than any country faced with comparable external and internal threats to its survival.

Critics of Israel who generally take no interest in human rights or civil liberties — right-wing columnists such as Rowland Evans and Robert Novak, Georgie Anne Geyer, Joseph Sobran, and Patrick Buchanan come immediately to mind — have some explaining to do as to why they single out Israel for special condemnation. The same, of course, is true of nations with abominable records on human rights who lecture and hector Israel on its lack of perfection in these areas.

Even many Israelis I know often forget the big picture, in their rush to condemn particular policies (especially when implemented by the party to which they are opposed).

The case for Israel can and should be made not by compromising principles of justice, egalitarianism, civil liberties, and liberalism, but rather by reference to those lofty principles. I do not shrink from making that case, even though it requires an occasional criticism of specific Israeli practices — any more than I shrink away from making the case for America with full awareness and acknowledgment of our imperfections in practice.

When my friends and I were growing up in our Orthodox *shtetl* in Brooklyn, the problem of Israeli actions conflicting with personal philosophy arose almost exclusively in the context of religion: the secular state of Israel was just not religious enough for us.

Our families and teachers did not take the extremist view, associated with organizations such as Neturai Karte, that the establishment of a Jewish state before the arrival of the Messiah was a misguided heresy. We were too practical for that. There were tens of thousands of displaced persons, survivors of the Holocaust, who had nowhere to go. Whatever one's religious views — and we debated these endlessly — the Holocaust had made Israel a practical necessity. But that didn't mean it had to be so secular!

As long as the issues remained on that level, the conflict between our Zionism and our criticism did not create any dilemma. Nobody except the Jews gave a damn about our little internal disputes! It was a fight within the family.

Everything changed after the Six-Day War of 1967, when Israel's status seemed transformed from underdog to victorious warrior. Now everyone in the world seems to give a damn — and have an opinion — about what Israel does, how American Jews judge Israeli actions, and what we say, or don't say, about Israel. This is understandable, within limits, since the issues now do involve others, primarily Palestinians both inside and outside Israel. The disputes are no longer within the family.

The stakes for Israel are also far higher than they were when we used to criticize it as kids. Every current criticism of Israel — whether made by Israelis, American Jews, or others — is used by its enemies as part of an explicit international campaign to delegitimate Israel. The notorious "Zionism is a form of racism" resolution is the most striking example. Nor is it over, as the repeated efforts to withdraw Israel's credentials in the UN General Assembly attest, and the constant comparisons between Israel and South Africa — which *has* been delegitimized by the world community.

I have been actively struggling with this dilemma since 1967. Before that time, I saw — and still see — no conflict between my Zionism and my moral principles. Israel was almost entirely in the right. The Israeli-Arab conflict was as simple a clash between good and evil as existed in our imperfect world. It is important to recall the pre-1967 situation in order to give context to the post-1967 criticisms.

The Jews had earned their right to a homeland. They had settled and worked mostly barren areas of the British mandate of Palestine, which they had bought — with the help of contributions from our blue-and-white Jewish National Fund boxes — largely from absentee landlords. They built hospitals, schools, and kibbutzim, and established the infrastructure of a state. They quite literally turned swampland into orchards and made the desert bloom. More important, because of the actions of the entire world toward Jews — their second-class status and the barriers to their immigration — it had become clear that the Jews needed a state.

They were prepared to compromise their biblical and historic claims and to accept a fraction of Palestine as theirs. But after the United Nations' 1947 decision to dissolve the British mandate and partition Palestine into two states, one for Jews and one for Arabs, the Arabs refused to agree to Jewish sovereignty over an inch of Palestine, even over land on which no Arab lived. Only three years after the close of the Holocaust, Arab leaders, many of whom supported Hitler's genocide, were calling for a war of extermination against the Jews — a "momentous massacre which will be spoken of like the Mongolian massacres and the Crusades." The grand mufti of Jerusalem, who had spent the war years in Berlin with Hitler, expressed "greatest joy and deepest gratification" for the Nazi accomplishments and declared a "holy war" whose goal was to "murder the Jews! Murder them all!"[2]

The 1948 war was entirely the fault of the Arab states (with a little encouragement from the British), which were determined to abort the new nation of Israel before its birth. Israel endured, with much loss of life, including many who had survived Hitler's ovens. When a truce was finally declared, Jordan was left in control of the Jewish quarter of Jerusalem — which had been continuously populated by Orthodox Jews for centuries — and destroyed the Jewish holy places, including historically significant synagogues and yeshivas. Graves and artifacts were desecrated. Jews were denied access to the Western Wall, long a place for prayer and lamentation. (It was not destroyed because it is a retaining wall for the Temple Mount, on which one of Islam's holiest mosques was built).

Little protest was heard from the international community — or from the religious world. Israel and the Jewish people accepted the loss of the Jewish quarter and went on with the business of building a state. The Arabs kept fighting, diplomatically and terroristically.*

According to the Arabs, all of Israel was occupied territory. There was no room for compromise. As the king of Saudi Arabia put it in 1954: "The Arab nations should sacrifice up to 10 million of their 50 million people, if necessary to wipe out Israel. . . . Israel to the Arab world is like a cancer to the human body, and the only way of remedy is to uproot it, just like a cancer." In 1959, President Gamal Abdel Nasser of Egypt announced "on behalf of the United Arab Republic people, that this time we will exterminate Israel." Nasser repeated that pledge just nine days before the start of the Six-Day War in 1967. Four days later, President Aref of Iraq declared: "The existence of Israel is an error which must be rectified. This is our opportunity to wipe out the ignominy which has been with us since 1948. Our goal is clear — to wipe Israel off the map."[3]

The big issue between 1948 and 1967 was the Arab "refugees" who had left Israel and moved to areas under the control of Arabs. There was great controversy, both within Israel and outside, over whether

---

* Remember, this was before there was any occupation or annexation of the West Bank, the Gaza Strip, or East Jerusalem. At least before any occupation by Jews! All of this "Palestinian" land had, of course, been occupied by Jordan and Egypt, but with no protest from the international community.

these Arab refugees had been pushed out by Israel or had left on the instructions of Arab leaders with the promise of a glorious return. There is obviously some truth to both positions. Certainly, many Arabs were frightened away by Israeli soldiers; some obviously left after hearing of civilian "massacres." (Whether these accounts were true, false, exaggerated, or covered up is not as relevant as whether they were believed by the Arabs who left.)

As a civil libertarian and human rights activist, I was never much moved by the claims of these refugees. Political solutions often require the movement of people, and such movement is not always voluntary. Making Arab families move — intact — from one Arab village or town to another may constitute a human rights violation. But in the whole spectrum of human rights issues — especially taking into account the events in Europe during the 1940s — it is a fifth-rate issue analogous in many respects to some massive urban renewal or other projects that require large-scale movement of people. For example, the building of the Aswan High Dam in Egypt necessitated the relocation of 100,000 Arabs and the destruction of numerous Arab villages.[4] There were certainly numerous precedents following both world wars, as well as other recent dislocating events of history — including the establishment of new states. There were so many refugee groups throughout the postwar world, and in so much worse condition, that it is difficult to understand why this particular dislocation assumed such international proportions.

For example, following the end of World War II, approximately fifteen million ethnic Germans were forcibly expelled from their homes in Poland, Czechoslovakia, Hungary, Romania, Yugoslavia, and other Central and Eastern European areas where their families had lived for centuries. Two million died during this forced expulsion. Czechoslovakia alone expelled nearly three million Sudeten Germans, turning them into displaced persons. The United States, Great Britain, and the international community in general approved these expulsions, as necessary to secure a more lasting peace. The presence of "disloyal minorities," or so-called fifth columns, had helped to destabilize Europe on the eve of World War II. It would be a source of increased stability if "population transfers" could produce a new Europe where Germans lived only in the two Germanies and other nations had populations that reflected their own ethnic and linguistic backgrounds. President Franklin Roosevelt's assistant Harry Hopkins memorialized his boss's view that although transfer of ethnic Germans "is a hard procedure, it is the only way to maintain peace." And Viscount Cran-borne said in the British House of Lords:

> The humanitarian case must be considered in relation to the causes of war. It can fairly be said, I think, that the suffering caused by a week's war would be more than the suffering caused by the efficient resettlement of these populations whose present situation is liable to endanger future peace.[5]

The ethnic German populations of these European countries had included individual traitors, saboteurs, and fifth columnists. But they had also included significant numbers of simple farmers, factory workers, and apolitical people who just happened to speak German and live in German enclaves. But since "their people" had started the war and then lost, it was deemed appropriate for entire ethnic German communities to bear the burden of relocation in order to reduce the likelihood of future wars. On the scale of human rights violations, forced transfer of minority ethnic populations in order to enhance the stability of the region did not weigh heavily in the postwar era.[6]

Comparable transfers of populations, though far less systematic, were occurring in the Middle East at about the same time. Hundreds of thousands of Sephardic Jews, who had lived in Arab and Islamic countries for centuries, were officially encouraged to emigrate. Some wanted to go. Others were frightened into leaving by the prospect of an Islamic holy war directed against them, or by the danger that they might be held hostage (as the remnants of Syrian Jews have been).

Similarly, many Arab residents of the new Jewish nation of Israel were encouraged to emigrate to Islamic countries by a combination of factors, including fear, a desire to live under Islamic rule, and political considerations.*

The exchange of populations in the Middle East served some of the same goals as the far more extensive, lethal, and systematic one that was taking place in Europe. It would remove potential fifth columns, stabilize the region, and enhance the prospects for peace.

But the Arab leaders did not want peace. They used the refugee

---

* In assessing the morality of these transfers, it must also be recalled that many Palestinian leaders supported Hitler during World War II. They also actively and successfully opposed opening the doors of Palestine to Jewish immigration during the Holocaust. They were not — as is sometimes claimed — entirely innocent bystanders to the Holocaust. They bear some moral responsibility.

issue to encourage continuing belligerency. It became an excuse for not making peace — for not accepting the reality that the ancient land of Israel-Palestine could be populated by two peoples and divided into two nations. It should be recalled that between 1948 and 1967, Israel posed no barrier to the establishment of a Palestinian state on the West Bank and in Gaza. There was no Palestinian state because the Arab leaders did not want a Palestinian state alongside a Jewish state. Their collective goal was the total destruction of the Jewish state. The Palestinian refugees would better serve that goal if they were kept in camps as a homeless people than if they were allowed to move out of the camps and establish their own state.

I believed then, and I believe now, that those who singled out the "plight" of the Arab refugees were more interested in singling out those who had allegedly caused the problem — namely the Jews — than they were in helping those who were its victims. Elevating the Arab refugee problem above the far more compelling problem of other groups was a form of indirect international anti-Semitism, acceptable in a world too close to the Holocaust to legitimate direct anti-Jewish bigotry.*

Any fair assessment of the Arab refugee problem made it clear that at bottom it wasn't primarily a human rights issue. The human rights aspect of the dislocation could easily have been solved by the Arab states, with the assistance of the United Nations. Several Arab states were, and still are, desperately in need of population. Had these states been willing to settle the Arab refugees — as Israel settled the Jewish refugees from Arab countries — the human rights aspect of the problem would have disappeared. The refugees would no longer be stateless. They would be citizens of an Arab nation, with all the "rights" that such citizenship entails. But a determined and coordinated effort was made to stop — actively prevent — Arab refugees from being settled in other states. They were brought in as stateless workers but denied citizenship or permanent residence. The decision was made to keep many of the refugees in horrible camps, precisely to encourage

---

* A *New York Times* story of August 12, 1990, described the plight of "fifteen million men, women and children" who have been "internationally recognized as refugees." Following World War II, the number was between thirty-three and forty-three million, and at the time the Palestinian refugee problem began — with 600,000 to 750,000 refugees — the number throughout the world was between sixteen and eighteen million. Many of the current group are refugees from Islamic nations. Yet the world knows little of their situation. Only the Palestinian refugees have received widespread international support. It is fair to ask why.

festering resentments and to show the world that nothing short of a
return of all the refugees and their children to tiny Israel would solve
the problem.

The hypocrisy of refusing to allow Palestinian refugees to become
citizens of other Arab countries was demonstrated by the claims of
Pan-Arabism. Arab leaders like Nasser were loudly proclaiming that
the Arab people were in reality one nation. (As recently as September
1, 1990, George Habash, the head of the Popular Front for the Liberation of Palestine, explained his support for Iraq's invasion of Kuwait
on "Pan-Arab" grounds.) To the extent that the Arab nation is one —
in theory or in practice — the force of the claim that all Palestinian
refugees must return to their homes in Israel is considerably diminished (as is the argument for the necessity of a particularistic Palestinian state).

If the Arab refugees had been settled in Arab states, the end result
would have been a transfer of populations of the kind common when
new political entities are constructed: Jewish refugees from Arab countries were settled in the Jewish state; while Arab refugees from the
Jewish state would have been settled in Arab nations. Not perfect, but
not so terrible, in terms of human rights.

Alternatively, the refugees could have been given — or could have
taken — the West Bank from Jordan and established their own state,
as contemplated by the UN Resolution Partitioning Mandatory Palestine. There would still have been claims to the abandoned land and
structures. But real estate disputes are easier to settle than human
rights disputes, and they deserve a far lower status on the hierarchy of
international concern.

The real reason the Arab leaders refused to settle the refugees was
entirely political and religious. These leaders didn't care whether particular Arab families lived in Umm el Fahm (which is in Israel) or in
Anin (which was a few kilometers away on the West Bank). They
wanted to *use* the refugee issue — and to use the ill-fed and ill-housed
refugees themselves — to destroy the Jewish state. They would never
have been satisfied even if Israel took back every single Arab refugee
who had been chased out in 1948 — unless there were large enough
numbers to turn the Jewish state into an Arab state. Arab leaders who
were willing to "sacrifice up to 10 million" of their people to "wipe
out Israel," would certainly not shrink from maintaining several hundred thousand Palestinians in miserable camps to help achieve the
same goal.

All of this is not to diminish the suffering of the Palestinian people between 1948 and 1967, but it is to emphasize how much of that suffering was deliberately engineered by the leaders of those Arab nations that were determined not to settle the Palestinian issue in a manner that permitted the continued existence of the Jewish state.

The refugee issue, with its festering resentments, was hypocrisy run amok. Americans who sided with the Arabs and against Israel before the 1967 war because of the refugees fell into several categories: those with a vested financial (or other) stake in remaining on the good side of the Arabs, such as the petroleum industry; church organizations, like the American Friends Service Committee, with influence in the Arab but not the Jewish world; political amoralists, like certain State Department officials, who believed that American strategic interests favored Arab rule, regardless of the moral rights or wrongs; anti-Zionists, both Jewish and non-Jewish; and anti-Semites.*

As a moralist who believed that rights and wrongs were everything, I was not in conflict. I didn't even feel it necessary to address the arguments of the anti-Israel lobby. I worried about their influence, just as I worried about the influence of any irrational anti-Semites or other do-badders. The arguments were tactical, not moral. One does not debate morality with immoralists.

But the fact that so many influential individuals, government officials, and nations generally sided with the Arabs, despite their relatively weak moral claims and their inexcusable use of terrorism to secure those claims, made it doubtful that the Israeli-Arab dispute would ever be considered on its merits by the world community. When the moral arguments favored Israel, these perennial anti-Israelis argued for ignoring the moral issues and focusing on the pragmatics of Arab power and wealth. When some moral arguments began to favor the Arabs, these same hypocrites suddenly became neomoralists.

Legitimating Palestinian terrorism as an acceptable response to the plight of the refugees — as much of the world has done — demonstrates the double standard toward Jews and the Jewish nation. People with the highest claims on the conscience of the world have not generally resorted to random terrorism. For example, the victims of

---

* I recently came across an article in my college newspaper, dated October 24, 1958, which shows how little of the anti-Israel rhetoric has changed. The headline reads: "Arab Charges Jews Employ Hitler Tactics on Refugees." The article related how an Arab spokesman had complained about the "unfair division of land, especially when it was against the will of the rightful owners." This was, of course, before the Six-Day War; the West Bank, Gaza, the Golan Heights, and East Jerusalem were all under Arab control.

Hitler's Holocaust and Pol Pot's genocide in Cambodia did not randomly kill civilians. Nor was it weakness alone that caused these — and other — moral sufferers to forbear from easy recourse to random violence. It was a refusal to lower themselves to the immoral means used by their oppressors.

In contrast, Palestinian terrorism began *before* the Israeli occupation of the West Bank and Gaza Strip. The grievance of the pre-1967 Arab terrorists was primarily over disputed land. Even after the occupation, the grievance was over statehood, not life or liberty. This is not to denigrate the claim of Palestinians — or stateless people such as the Kurds, Armenians, Tatars, or numerous others — to political nationhood. It is to demonstrate that on a scale of moral claims, that of the Palestinians ranks comparatively low. Nor does it rank particularly high in terms of the need to focus attention. Disproportionate world attention, as measured by support from the United Nations and individual countries, has been paid to the Palestinians, as compared to other stateless and aggrieved people.

Yet despite the relative weakness of their moral claims, various Palestinian groups — beginning with Yasir Arafat's Fatah and the PLO — have resorted to the most vicious forms of terrorism against innocent civilians, including children.

The world may have to deal with terrorists in order to save lives. But the moral scandal is that in addition to simply dealing with these terrorists, much of the world has *honored* them. The standing ovation accorded Yasir Arafat — the architect of international terrorism — by many UN representatives in Geneva in 1988 will live in infamy. The willingness of world statesmen — including the pope and other moral leaders — to treat Arafat as a person deserving of tribute is beyond moral comprehension.

In response, it is often argued that Israeli prime ministers Menachem Begin and Yitzhak Shamir had also been terrorists, during the years of the British mandate. That is a false analogy. The nature of the Begin-Shamir terrorism — unjustified as it was in my view — was very different from Arafat's. It was directed primarily at British and Arab military targets, not at families traveling on civilian airlines. Neither Begin nor Shamir was rewarded for his terrorism; indeed, they paid a heavy price, being relegated to minority status within the Israeli political system for decades. And even today, they do not receive standing ovations at the United Nations.

*   *   *

Despite the hypocritical opposition to Israel by some influential officials, grass-roots support for the beleaguered Jewish nation was widespread in America and throughout the western world. Much of this changed following Israel's victory over the united Arab armies in 1967. Israel captured the Sinai from Egypt, the Golan Heights from Syria, and the West Bank (including East Jerusalem and the Old City) from Jordan. The Six-Day War was plainly a defensive one from Israel's perspective. Although Israel struck the first military blow with its preemptive strike against the Egyptian air force, there can be little doubt that Egypt had started the war by its closure of the Strait of Tiran to Israeli shipping; the closing of an international waterway is recognized as an act of war, justifying a military response. Israel had clearly warned that the closing of the strait would be so taken.

Moreover, President Nasser of Egypt had publicly declared that a state of war existed between Egypt and Israel and that he would select the appropriate moment to unleash his formidable military machine — and those of his Syrian, Jordanian, and other Arab allies — in order to "drive the Jews into the sea." International law recognizes that no nation need wait until it is placed on the defensive by a military invasion before it strikes back. A preemptive strike designed to prevent an imminent invasion is universally regarded as proper and lawful. For example, if the United States had obtained reliable intelligence information, on December 1, 1941, about an imminent invasion of Pearl Harbor, no one would have disputed its legal — and moral — right to destroy the Japanese air force before it could reach Hawaii.

The capture of the West Bank was even more defensive in nature than the capture of the Sinai. Israel did not immediately move its troops into the West Bank, even though Jordan, as required by the terms of its military alliance with Egypt, had opened hostilities in and around Jerusalem and was inflicting heavy Jewish casualties there. Instead, the Israeli government sent an unambiguous message to the Jordanian government, assuring it that the Israeli army would make no move into the West Bank or even the Jewish quarter of the Old City *if* the Jordanians would cease fighting. But Jordan persisted in its aggression, and the Israeli army responded by capturing the West Bank and establishing its military border at the Jordan River.

The story of the Golan is somewhat different. As anyone who has been atop the heights realizes, whoever controls the steep high ground controls the valleys and lake below. And beneath the Golan Heights sits the heartland of Israel, with its numerous agricultural kibbutzim. While the Golan Heights were controlled by Syrians, the children of the kibbutzim had to live — literally — in underground bunkers. Nightly rocket shellings from atop the heights took a recurrent toll. Every such firing was, of course, an act of war, justifying invasion of the area from which the rockets were launched. During the Six-Day War, the Israeli army finally captured the Golan Heights, with enormous Israeli casualties.

The Sinai has since been returned to Egypt, so that problem is now history. The Golan Heights are still in Israeli hands; the area is largely unpopulated and its strategic importance far outweighs the inconvenience to its small native population. In any event, it was the Syrians who originally turned the heights into a military zone — in effect a battleship — and no nation would ever be expected to return such an area to an enemy who would surely continue to use it as a launching pad for rocket attacks against a vulnerable civilian population. Indeed, there is no historical precedent for any victorious nation ever returning a piece of land as strategically situated as the Golan Heights to an aggressor nation that still considers itself in a state of war. There is little pressure on Israel, therefore, to return the Golan Heights to Syria outside the context of an overall peace settlement.

Nor is it realistic to expect Israel to return the Jewish quarter of Old Jerusalem. That rebuilt section of the walled city was inhabited by Orthodox Jews from the time of the destruction of the Second Temple until the Jordanians captured it in 1948, expelled the Jews, and destroyed Jewish buildings dating back several centuries. If ever there was a justified recapture and reoccupation, it has been the reclaiming of the Rova Yehudi — the Jewish quarter of Jerusalem.

The justification for continuing Israeli control of the remaining three quarters of the Old City — the Armenian, Christian, and Muslim quarters — is somewhat different. When the Jordanians controlled the Old City, it was entirely closed to Jews and others who were unwelcome by the authorities. The world stood by silently, without objection. Under Israeli control, Jerusalem is open to all (at least to all who are free to visit Israel). The small number of Armenian and Christian residents who live in the Old City do not seem to be complaining about Israeli control of their quarters, so long as their religious rights — and control over their holy places — are respected. Occasionally, Israeli authorities do something insensitive, such as encouraging the presence of armed Orthodox Israeli settlers in a neglected complex owned by the Greek Orthodox church in the Christian quarter of Jerusalem.

The Muslim quarter, as well as heavily populated East Jerusalem, raises issues that are far more complex. Virtually all Israelis agree with the mayor of Jerusalem that the city should never again be divided and that it should remain under Israeli control as the capital of Israel. But this does not necessarily mean, nor should it, that the Arab residents of East Jerusalem should not exercise substantial control over their day-to-day political and economic life. They should, consistent with some degree of unification of Jerusalem. There are many ideas afloat as to how this can be achieved as part of an overall peace settlement. But in the meantime, Israel has formally annexed all of Jerusalem and offered full Israeli citizenship to its inhabitants. Few Arabs have accepted the offer. Nearly all retain their Jordanian citizenship and regard themselves as occupied by a foreign power.* The offer of citizenship does, however, place Jerusalem on a different footing from the remainder of the West Bank and the Gaza Strip.

The population centers of the West Bank — primarily the cities of Hebron, Nablus, and Ramallah — as well as the heavily populated Gaza Strip present the most difficult civil liberties and human rights concerns. The residents of these areas have not been offered Israeli citizenship, and they do not have civil or political rights comparable to Israeli citizens — either Jewish or Arab.†

Although the economic, educational, health, and liberty situations of most West Bank and Gaza Arabs improved when Israel replaced Jordan and Egypt as the occupying power, it should come as no surprise that this nearly quarter-century Israeli occupation has engendered bitter resentment among many Arabs. Tensions have been exacerbated by the construction of Jewish settlements in close proximity to — and sometimes in place of — Arab villages. This resentment has undoubtedly been exploited by Arab nationalists and fundamentalists, as well as by the PLO.

Experience demonstrates that people resent it more when their rights are denied by outsiders — whether defined religiously, racially,

* The situation on the Golan Heights is somewhat similar. Most of the Druze residents of the Golan Heights have refused Israeli citizenship, and maintain allegiance to Syria.
† Though Israeli Jews and Arabs have the same political and civil rights in theory if they are Israeli citizens, the reality is quite different. Israeli Arabs do not, for the most part, serve in the army (and thus are denied various veteran's benefits); they are not eligible to purchase or use land owned by the Jewish National Fund; and they do not qualify for some loans and aid disbursed by their state through the Jewish Agency. None of this is justified, in my view.

ethnically, or nationally — than by insiders. Put more cynically, people should be entitled to be repressed by tyrants of their own race, religion, nationality, and ethnicity. The world, too, reacts rather more critically when the source of repression is outsiders. Experience also demonstrates that the world seems to have a considerably lower threshold of tolerance when it is Israeli Jews who are perceived as being the deniers of rights than when it is any other group.

Why this is so is open to speculation. *That* this is so seems beyond dispute. Part of the reason is a transparent extension of anti-Semitism from Jews to the Jewish state. This is most apparent when extreme right-wing anti-Semites — such as the Liberty Lobby, the *Post Eagle,* or Patrick Buchanan — take up the cause of the PLO, an organization whose left-wing anti-Americanism they should despise. But they hate the Jews, and thus the Jewish state, even more.

Israel, as a Jewish nation, absorbs much of the world's lingering anti-Jewish feelings, feelings that are easier for many to express as anti-Zionism than as anti-Semitism. Another part of the reason it is a target of so much hatred relates to the fact that Israel is a surrogate for sublimated hatred really directed against others. Israel, as the United States' most loyal ally in the Mideast, is the focal point of anti-Americanism. Israel, as an industrialized and developing country in a largely undeveloped part of the world, represents many of the third world's grievances at being left out of the benefits of industrialization.

These attitudes have been manifested in many discriminatory actions against Israel, primarily in the United Nations. Despite decades of Arab terrorism against civilian targets, the condemnation has been one-sidedly directed against Israel. (The 1990 condemnation of Iraq by the Security Council for its naked aggression against Kuwait was the first time in recent memory that the United Nations had condemned Arab aggression. Even in this new age of international cooperation between the United States and the Soviet Union, it is questionable whether an international consensus could have been reached if Iraq had attacked Israel, as it eventually did after the Gulf War began.) Former Israeli foreign minister Abba Eban — a critic of current Israeli policies — once said: "If Algeria introduced a resolution declaring that the Earth was flat and that Israel had flattened it, it would pass by a vote of 164 to 13 with 26 abstentions." Indeed, at a 1980 UN-sponsored conference on the rights of women, a resolution condemning sexism failed (because so many third world nations practice such blatant sexism), but a resolution condemning Zionism as an affront to women prevailed with the usual majority. Although the United States generally votes against absurdly one-sided denunciations of Israel, it often joins in UN condemnations when it regards them as warranted. As an American human rights advocate — committed to a single standard of judgment in human rights compliance — I have consistently opposed American participation in these orgies of condemnation.

My argument against America's voting to condemn Israel in the United Nations relies on an analogy to racist courts in the 1950s. I ask my friends in government to imagine themselves as an honorable judge in an all-white court system, say in Mississippi, during the height of racism. The court is obliged to deal with repeated clashes between a group of black civil rights workers and white Ku Klux Klan members. Every time the KKK attacks the blacks, they are acquitted by the jury, though the judge views the evidence as sufficient for conviction. Eventually, some blacks from the civil rights group — out of frustration, revenge, or an overprotective view of self-defense — attack the KKK men. They are convicted, with several of the votes cast by jurors with ties to the KKK. What the blacks did was a crime, in the view of the honorable judge, and conviction is warranted.

Yet, if he imposes the prison sentence that a totally impartial view of justice would demand, he believes, injustice will in fact result, because of the double standard being applied to white versus black defendants. In this scenario, there would be a compelling case for the judge to refuse to impose prison terms on the blacks who, in other contexts, would deserve to go to jail.

This scenario is comparable to the current status of UN votes regarding Israel. It is virtually impossible to get the United Nations to condemn any Arab terrorist group or state for any attack on Israel or on Jewish institutions. Yet there is an eagerness to condemn Israel, whether Israel is right or wrong. The United States votes to condemn Arab terrorism, and it also votes to condemn Israel, but only when it thinks Israel is in the wrong. *It operates on a single standard in an organization that operates on a double standard.* Without the United States' single-standard votes, the organization's double standard would fail. Should the United States allow itself to be used to perpetuate such an outrageous — even racist — double standard at the United Nations? I believe that the case against America's voting to condemn Israel *at the United Nations* — even when Israel deserves condemnation by American standards — is quite compelling.

But what about Israel's friends — the American government, American Jews, and others — criticizing Israel in other forums when the Israeli government violates basic standards of human rights? This is an issue being widely debated among my generation of Jews and among my friends from Brooklyn.

In my view, an American Jew should feel more comfortable criticizing *methods* employed by the occupying power than criticizing geopolitical decisions regarding the security of Israel. Those of us who have long expressed outrage at the use of excessive force throughout the world should not remain silent in the face of comparably excessive force employed by Israeli soldiers. The criticism of Israel should reflect, as it should with respect to any other government, an understanding of the situation faced by those employing the force, as well as the less lethal alternatives that may or may not be available to them.

For example, when Israeli soldiers were given plastic or rubber bullets as an alternative to lead bullets and instructed to use them more freely than they ordinarily use the more lethal lead bullets, there was an immediate outcry. Lost in the political response to this change of tactics was the realization that there has long been a debate within law enforcement and civil liberties circles over the fact that reducing the *lethality* of weapons tends to increase the *incidence* of their use. Many civil libertarians, fully aware of the fact that law enforcement personnel will be less constrained in employing less lethal weapons, favor their introduction precisely because they are less lethal. Some take the opposite view, arguing from the analogy to nuclear weapons: the more lethal the weapon the better, since lethal weapons are actually employed less frequently. Every experienced law enforcement official realizes, of course, that there is no such thing as an absolutely nonlethal weapon; all effective weapons carry some risk of death for some potential targets.

The point is that when Israel is criticized, much of the criticism seems to be without a context, comparative or otherwise.

Another contextual reality that is often ignored in criticizing Israel's response to rock throwing and all forms of violent protest is that one of the most important goals of the violence is precisely to provoke overreactions by the Israelis. And overreaction by a democracy confronted with violence is quite easy to provoke, as demonstrated by British overreaction in Northern Ireland, Canadian overreaction to the Front de Libération du Québec in the early 1970s, or American overreaction at Kent State University. Israeli overreaction, especially as televised in a relatively free and open society, plays into the hands of the protestors; it is part of their script.

The last thing that many Arab provocateurs and their supporters *really* want is Israeli compliance with the highest standards of civil liberties in responding to the violence. That would mute the impact of their grievance. Consider, for example, an incident I observed while on a visit to Israel in 1988. There had been a confrontation between a group of Israeli children on a hike in the West Bank and some local Arabs. It had been started by Arab stone throwing and ended with a bullet from the rifle of an Israeli guard accidentally killing a Jewish girl. Americans were told by distinguished journalists that the Israeli military response was lawless. For instance, Anthony Lewis of the *New York Times* reported that following the accidental shooting, the Israeli army deported six Arabs without any due process: "As always in these cases, there were no charges, no trial, just a quick dumping of the men into Lebanon."[7] Other newspapers carried similar reports.

These accounts were simply inaccurate. In fact, there was an appeal from the deportation order. The six men were represented by excellent lawyers, including members of the Association for Civil Rights in Israel. The hearing was going extremely well for the accused, and it looked as if they were going to win. At that point, the accused all decided to withdraw their appeals. Their lawyers advised them that they had a good chance of winning, but the accused apparently did not want to blunt the political impact of their deportations by having them rescinded by the Israeli authorities. Only after the withdrawal of the appeal were they flown into Lebanon. I saw this and confirmed it with my own eyes and ears. The American press simply misreported the story by claiming that the deported Palestinians received no legal process. There was no correction printed even after I provided documentation to the contrary.

The world's reaction to civilian deaths, particularly among women and children, also ignores the obvious fact that the number of such deaths is largely, though not entirely, within the control of those who decide whether to send women and children into vulnerable situations. As one West Bank leader candidly acknowledged to an American television reporter who asked him whether the deaths of so many youngsters were really worth the struggle: "It would cost us millions of dollars to receive this kind of publicity on European and American television." The Intifada practice of deliberately sending women and children into dangerous confrontations is a logical extension of the well-documented PLO policy of placing women and children in terrorist staging camps, so that Israel cannot bomb terrorists without running the risk of causing "civilian" casualties.

Another example of valid criticism expressed in an invalid (i.e., knee-jerk) manner relates to free speech and censorship. There is both more censorship *and* more free speech for Arabs in the occupied territories than in many democratic nations. Japan, Sweden, Costa Rica — as well as many small, homogeneous towns throughout America — have less *actual* dissent than that which exists today within the occupied territories. Despite the existence of formal military censorship of a kind that would not and should not be tolerated in the freest of democracies, and despite the unjustified administrative detention of some of the most outspoken anti-Israel critics, considerable freedom of expression *against* Israel is permitted throughout the occupied territories. Arabs within the territories find they are freer to condemn Israel than to criticize the PLO or to support Israel. Virulent condemnation of Israel may result in the temporary shutdown of a newspaper or the temporary detention of a political leader, but dissent from the PLO line may result in what George Bernard Shaw called the ultimate form of censorship, namely assassination. For example, in response to the mayor of Bethlehem's proposal of a cease-fire in the Intifada, Yasir Arafat threatened: "Whoever thinks of stopping the Intifada before it achieves its goals, I will give him ten bullets in his chest."[8] To adapt an old joke about the Soviet Union to the occupied territories: Arabs in Hebron have the same freedom as Jews in Tel Aviv — they both can criticize Israel and praise the PLO.

Indeed, it is fair to say that the freest press in the entire Arab world is the all-too-censored Palestinian press in the West Bank. It is also fair to say that if elections were to be held on the West Bank, they would be the freest elections in Arab history. And it is beyond dispute that the most independent judiciary to which Arabs have access anywhere in the Middle East is the Israeli court system. None of this is to say that the press, elections, or the judiciary in the occupied territories are free enough for my tastes. But it surely is better than anything currently available in the Arab world.

There are several possible standards against which Israeli conduct in the occupied territories can reasonably be judged. First, as generally accepted under international law, there is the standard of human rights practiced by the previous government. No one can deny that Israel is according the occupied population far more legal protection and far greater human rights than did the preexisting governments. There was total censorship and tyranny under Jordanian, Syrian, and Egyptian rule.

A second, and related, standard would be to compare the rights available to the occupied populations with those available to nonoccupied citizens of other Arab and Islamic states in the region. Again, Israel does considerably better by comparison. The governments of neighboring states such as Iraq, Syria, and Saudi Arabia offer their residents almost no human rights. Invariably, they stand at the most repressive end of any objective ranking of human rights violators. Egypt and Jordan do a bit better, but the average Arab in the territories occupied by Israel has at least as much freedom as the average citizen of Egypt and Jordan, and in some respects far more.[9]

A third basis for comparison would be how other nations in the world today treat their citizens or citizens in areas they occupy, and how the community of nations responds to such treatment. The short answer is that several handfuls of democracies afford their citizens greater rights than those granted by Israel to the population it occupies. The vast majority of nations treat their citizens no better or worse. Occupying powers throughout history have brutally suppressed those under their control, especially when active resistance, such as that reflected in the Intifada, has continued. The usual response to violent uprisings has been capital punishment carried out on a large scale.

Finally, there is the standard of human rights applied by Israel to Israeli citizens. It is that very high standard — among the highest in the civilized world — that the Israeli occupying authorities fail to comply with in their treatment of the occupied population. The Israeli citizenry, both Arab and Jewish, has far greater rights to free expression, political assembly, judicial review, and other fundamental safeguards than does the occupied population. But then again the Israeli citizenry has far greater rights than the citizenry of the vast majority of nations in the world today. Never before in history has an occupying power been expected to extend to those it occupies all of the rights enjoyed by its *own* citizens. It is in the nature of an occupation that many of the rights exercised by citizens will not be available to the occupied population. That was certainly true when the United States occupied Germany and Japan following World War II. Those occupations did not last almost a quarter century, as the Israeli occupation has. But the German and Japanese occupations ended in the context not only of a peace treaty but of real peace. No Arab state, except Egypt, has offered Israel either a peace treaty or real peace.

The Israeli occupation must end quickly, both for the good of the occupied Palestinians and for the good of the occupying Israelis. But it must end in the context of an overall peace, not simply a temporary resolution of a dispute between Israel and its occupied population. Saddam Hussein's use of Scud missiles, and his threats to use chemical weapons against Israeli civilians, underlines the need for a buffer zone between armed Arab nations and Israel's population centers. For Israel to surrender that buffer zone to an enemy sworn to its destruction would not serve the interests of peace. Tragically, the occupation, perhaps with increased local autonomy, will almost certainly continue until there is a comprehensive peace between Israel and its neighbors to the east and north. Until the occupation ends, Israel will be harshly judged by the world community for responding to the Intifada in about the same way the United States, England, Canada, and France have responded — and would today respond — to comparable threats to their security.

As a Jew and a supporter of Israel, I feel comfortable urging Israel to comply with the highest standards of civil liberties: it would be both good for human rights and good for Israel. It would also help put an end to the violence, overreaction, and death, which would then cease to serve their intended political and public relations purposes.

Any reasonable criticism of Israeli methods — from excessive force, to excessive censorship, to excessive detention — is permissible in my view, so long as it is contextual and comparative. One does not have to be a citizen of a state to level that kind of criticism. Indeed, international human rights organizations, such as Amnesty International, do that all the time. But a far different issue is raised by outside criticism of the geopolitical options selected by the government of Israel, though sometimes the line between human rights issues and geopolitical ones is more a matter of emphasis than of substance.

Palestinians have learned the political value of invoking human rights rhetoric. Indeed, former U.S. State Department official Alan Keyes has argued that by changing the terms of the Mideast debate from a political issue between Israel and the Arab states into a human rights complaint by occupied Palestinians, the PLO has won an undeserved political and diplomatic advantage. Palestinian political organizations now present themselves as "human rights" organizations, and the media fall for it.

In 1989, former president Jimmy Carter awarded Al Haq the Carter-Menil Award for its work as a Palestinian human rights organization. Anthony Lewis always refers to Al Haq as "a Palestinian human rights organization." Lewis criticizes Jews who write to him and argue that Palestinians are not really "working for human rights."

But, in fact, there are no Palestinian *human* rights organizations. There are Palestinian *Palestinian* rights organizations, whose sole purpose is to maximize the rights and goals of *Palestinians*. There is nothing wrong with a group's promoting its own parochial interests, but no such self-serving group should be entitled to pretend that it is a *human* rights organization. Human rights means the universal rights of *all* human beings. And I have no knowledge of any Palestinian groups working on behalf of oppressed Jews in Syria, stateless Kurds in Iraq, or Jewish victims of PLO terrorism. To the contrary, some have urged the Soviet Union to end emigration of Soviet Jews, for fear that Soviet Jews will come to Israel and be settled in the occupied territories. There are, on the other hand, genuine Jewish human rights organizations, which do work for the rights of Palestinians, and against the practices of their own governments and people. I do not recall Lewis, or others who call Al Haq a human rights organization, ever referring to the Anti-Defamation League as a human rights organization, even though the ADL's mandate is far broader than Al Haq's. Until Palestinian "human rights" groups broaden their concerns beyond self-serving advocacy of their own rights and interest, they do not deserve the noble title of human rights organizations.

The same can be said of many nations and groups that oppose only *particular* violations of human rights. Black South African activist Nelson Mandela created considerable controversy in 1990 when he declared Muammar Qaddafi, Fidel Castro, and Yasir Arafat to be great supporters of human rights. When pressed, he explained that he regards anyone who supports his struggle against apartheid as an advocate of human rights, regardless of how repressive they may be to their own citizens or others. This is simply a misuse of the term "human rights."

One of the important reasons for the success of organizations like Amnesty International and the American Civil Liberties Union is precisely that when they are at their best they do *not* criticize geopolitical options, even ones as indefensible as the Soviet invasion of Afghanistan, the British attack on Argentina, or the American "rescue mission" in Grenada. They stick to human rights and civil liberties violations. Indeed, on those few occasions when such organizations have blurred the lines between civil liberties and politics, they have suffered loss of credibility.

That is not to say that an American Jew has no right to disagree with Israeli geopolitical policy. I think — though I am not certain — that Israel is making a mistake in continuing to occupy heavily populated Arab areas on the West Bank and in Gaza. But the decision to exchange lawfully captured territory (even heavily populated territory) for the promise of peace (even if such a promise were forthcoming) is so complex, so fraught with risk, so unprecedented in world history, so involved with domestic political considerations and consequences, that I, for one, am reluctant to participate in the cacophonous chorus of know-it-all criticism that is currently directed at Israel for its inaction. I am also wary of criticizing Israel for failing to take risks, since my life and the lives of my children are not immediately placed on the line by Israeli geopolitical decisions that relate directly to its survival as a Jewish state.

Jews are among the most publicly self-critical people on the face of the earth. The amount and intensity of public debate, dissent, and division within the Jewish community over aspects of Israeli policy is not replicated within most other groups. Indeed, nothing comparable to the degree of public criticism has ever been tolerated within the United States during any war, except perhaps Vietnam — and even during the Vietnam War, we had Kent State, the Spock trial, vindictive drafting of war dissenters, and an atmosphere of political suppression. There is certainly no comparable degree of dissent within the Arab world, partly because it would simply not be tolerated, but also because virtually all public criticism is directed at the Jewish state, the Jewish community in America, and the worldwide "Zionist conspiracy." There are, to be sure, deep divisions within the Arab world, but they tend not to be reflected in public debate, dialogue, and discourse — though there is surely some of that among academics and intellectuals who live a safe distance from the battlefields. Rather, Arab divisions tend to be reflected in assassination, internecine warfare, and massacres.

Criticism of Israel by American Jews enjoys a special status in the media. This special status cannot be ignored by those who would exercise their right to public criticism. A vignette from my own experience will illustrate this phenomenon at work. I devote a considerable portion of my professional life to criticizing human rights violations throughout the world. I have signed petitions against South African apartheid, Soviet repression, the Greek colonels, the Chilean military, the Argentinian "disappearances," the Marcos exploitations, the excesses of the shah and the ayatollahs, to mention just a few. For the most part, these petitions are either not covered in the media or are relegated to a back page. But in 1979, I joined several other "prominent Jewish figures" in criticizing the Israeli decision to build a religious settlement, called Elon Moreh, on confiscated Arab land within the West Bank. I felt comfortable taking this position, because the decision to build Elon Moreh on confiscated Arab land was expressly *not* based on security needs. Indeed, that was precisely why we criticized it. A decision to create nonstrategic Jewish settlements on Arab lands for *religious reasons* is wrong, in my view, and a proper subject for public criticism.

Suddenly the world was listening to me! The story of our petition appeared prominently on page three of the *New York Times* and was featured in other media. Why? Was the Israeli violation of Arab property rights all that egregious as compared to other ongoing human rights violations throughout the world? Certainly not. In a comparative context, Elon Moreh was a sixth-rate human rights violation. Was our petition so brilliantly written? Not at all; it was rather ponderous and inelegant. Was the list of names so impressive as to justify this sort of coverage? No; it consisted primarily of academics and writers like me who had lent their names to numerous other petitions and causes without receiving comparable attention.

The only reason this petition received the kind of attention it did was because it was signed by prominent *Jewish* figures in the United States voicing criticism of an aspect of Israeli policy. Our *Jewishness* became the megaphone through which the sound of our critical voices became magnified. Our Jewishness also became a certification for the accuracy and validity of our criticism: "See, even Jews agree that . . ."

On the Sabbath following the story about our petition, my mother's rabbi in Brooklyn launched a full-fledged attack on the "Jewish traitors" who had dared to publicly protest Israeli policy. It was a mortifying experience for my mother and a disturbing one for me. But it did not persuade me to withhold all public criticism. Indeed, the public *praise* I received for "having the guts" to criticize Israel had a more profound — and distinctly negative — impact upon me than the rabbinic castigation from the pulpit of my old synagogue. Too many people seemed too pleased with the public spectacle of Jewish criticism of Israel.

My discomfort over my role as public critic of Israel was enhanced several months later when the Israeli supreme court ruled that the taking of Arab land for the religious settlement of Elon Moreh was illegal. This decision brought home to me the realization that there exist *within Israel* the institutions necessary to resolve conflicts between governmental overreaching and human rights. These conflicts are not always resolved in favor of the human rights claimants. The Israeli supreme court does not always come to the right decision, from a civil libertarian perspective. (Nor, of course, does our judiciary.) But the Israeli system works well institutionally, and that is an important consideration in the decision whether or not to engage in external public criticism.

The one decision that I have made since the Elon Moreh case is that I will no longer criticize Israel *as a Jew*. I will not sign exclusively Jewish petitions against Israeli policies. I will continue — hopefully on a principled basis — to criticize specific civil liberties and human rights violations as an individual, as a lawyer, as a civil libertarian, even as a supporter of Israel. But I will no longer criticize as a Jew. This may seem naive and formalistic, since as an individual I am always publicly identified *as a Jew*. But the distinction is important to me.

Its importance has been illustrated during the recent, ongoing Intifada. Numerous Jews with no history of prior identification with Israel or other Jewish causes suddenly decided to speak out against Israel *as Jews*. Most of these people — some of them my own colleagues — would have been furious if they had been asked to protest the Vietnam War or other protest-worthy activities *as Jews*. (Some have even expressed anger when solicited to give to Jewish charities as Jews.) Why, then, were they willing to join a uniquely Jewish protest — indeed, in some instances to identify themselves publicly as Jews for the first time — over Israeli policies? I asked some of them that question. Their answer was appalling. The Israeli actions in the West Bank were *embarrassing* them *as Jews*. They would never have used the Yiddish term *shanda fur de goyim,* but they were making precisely the same point my grandmother's generation used to live by. I was shocked to hear it from members of my generation, some even of a younger generation. By joining the Jewish protests against Israel, these later-day "guests" were seeking to distance themselves *as Jews* from the perceived excesses of the Jewish state. They wanted their "hosts" — the "real" Americans — to understand that *they* were the good Jews, not like the ones in Israel who were doing those embarrassing things. They were identifying themselves as Jews specifically in order to *disassociate* themselves from other Jews. It was as if they were publicly declaring to their non-Jewish colleagues: "Don't blame us for what you are seeing other Jews do on television. They are Israelis. We are American Jews. We have no responsibility for them. We are not part of *them*. We are part of *you*. We are the good guys. We are good guests in your home."

Many of these who joined these protests of embarrassment and disassociation do not follow events in the Middle East, had certainly never visited Israel or the West Bank, and had no intention of ever doing so.

Since the Elon Moreh travesty, I have had long discussions with my Brooklyn friends, and others of my generation, about the criteria we should employ in deciding whether and when to criticize Israel. Some of my friends take the position that it is wrong to join a one-sided chorus of hypocritical criticism. Some say that the hypocrisy of the rest of the world should not cause us to become hypocrites ourselves. We should, this argument goes, ignore the rest of the world and criticize Israel — as well as other countries — whenever it does anything deserving of criticism. I have been trying to work this issue through for myself over the past several years, and have come to an intermediate position.

I now rarely criticize Israeli policy without going to Israel to see for myself. As part of this constructive process of criticism I have been to Israel numerous times, both before the Elon Moreh episode and even more frequently since. I have visited prisons, detention camps, courtrooms, the Ministry of Justice, the occupied territories, the borders, military installations, Arab and Druze homes, schools, coffeehouses. I have attended Peace Now demonstrations, Kahane rallies, Arab student protest meetings, and political speeches by the major candidates. I have met with Israeli prime ministers and with supporters of the Intifada.

To illustrate the kind of contextual, comparative, and constructive criticism that I believe is appropriate for an American Jew, I will tell several brief stories based on some of these trips (I have already discussed the Demjanjuk case in Chapter V).

In 1970, I went to Israel under a Ford Foundation grant to study the Israeli practice of "administrative detention" of alleged terrorists.

I reviewed more than a dozen cases, several in great detail, and then prepared a report on my findings in which I stated the following conclusion:

> My investigation led me to conclude that virtually all of those detained had, in fact, been involved in terrorist activities; that the vast majority could not be tried under Israeli law; and that a considerable number would probably engage in future terrorism if released. Some of the detainees were not bomb throwers themselves; they were recruiters, money raisers, and . . . commanders. Not one of them was a mere politician, or a writer without connection to terrorist activities.[10]

Notwithstanding this conclusion, I wrote that

> on balance, I favor repeal of the Emergency Defense Regulations. If Israel feels that it cannot live with the normal rules of evidence in cases of suspected terrorists, then the Knesset should enact special rules of evidence for a narrowly circumscribed category of cases during carefully defined periods of emergency. All other safeguards should be provided, as in ordinary cases. In the last analysis, such a system might result in the release of some who are now detained. It is in the nature of any judicial system that in order to prevent confinement of the innocent, it must sometimes release the guilty. And those released might engage in acts of terrorism. But risks to safety have always been the price a society must pay for its liberty. Israel knows that well. By detaining only two dozen of its 300,000 Arab citizens, Israel today is taking considerable risks.* Indeed, I know of no country — including our own — that has ever exposed its wartime population to so much risk in the interest of civil liberties.[11]

In support of my concluding sentence, I reviewed American responses during our wars, including the suspension of habeas corpus and civilian trials, the detention of more than one hundred thousand Americans of Japanese descent, the declaration of martial law, and the virtual abrogation of the First Amendment. I made these comparisons not to justify Israeli actions, but to provide a context for American criticism.

In 1978, another law professor and I traveled to Israel at the behest of a group of human rights lawyers to look into allegations of torture

---

* The number has, of course, risen dramatically during the Intifada, as has my criticism of the practice.

being raised by supporters of an Arab American named Sami Esmail, who was being tried in Israel for receiving terrorist training in Libya by the Popular Front for the Liberation of Palestine. We spoke to Mr. Esmail, his lawyers, and the Israeli authorities. We carefully investigated each of the allegations and came to the conclusion that the evidence contradicted most of them. Rather than being held incommunicado, as he had claimed, Esmail had been visited by his brother and several American consular officials both before and after he confessed to his crimes. There was no evidence of sleep deprivation or physical torture. Indeed, the American consul general "found it hard to believe from his appearance that he had not slept. He was surprisingly alert. His eyes were clear, there was no redness in them, no bags under his eyes, puffiness, or anything like that."[12]

We were, however, critical of Israel for not excluding Esmail's confession from the evidence at his trial. In an op-ed piece published by the *New York Times,* we said:

> As civil libertarians who have long been concerned about safeguards surrounding the interrogation and confession process, we wish that the court had nevertheless ruled the confession inadmissible. In our view, a confession should be excluded whenever the accused is not given access to a lawyer before confessing, as required in the United States by the Miranda rule.[13]

We tried to place our criticism in a comparative context:

> We do not mean to suggest that abuses have never occurred in Israel. Among those people in any country who choose police work, there is a given percentage who are inclined to brutality. The test of a society is not whether violations of human rights occasionally occur, but how they are dealt with by the authorities. In Israel, policemen have been removed from office and imprisoned for mistreating prisoners. Unhappily, there are cities even in the United States today that do not have as good a record.[14]

The prosecution of Sami Esmail by Israel in 1978 became an issue in an American courtroom in 1989. A Palestinian named Mahmoud Abed Atta was accused by the Israeli government of machine-gunning a civilian bus en route from Tel Aviv to Jerusalem, killing its driver and wounding several passengers. Atta was arrested in the United States and Israel requested his extradition. He resisted on the ground that in Israel he would be tortured and beaten, just as Sami Esmail claimed he had been. Sami Esmail, who had been released by Israel after serving a short prison term, was Atta's star witness. I was called as an expert witness by the U.S. government, which supported Israel's extradition request.

Atta's lawyer was my old friend Ramsey Clark, a former attorney general of the United States and a lawyer with whom I had worked on several cases and causes. Representing the United States was a former student of mine named Jack Semmelman. The trial judge was Jack Weinstein, one of the most highly regarded judges in the country.

I was asked whether torture was used against suspected terrorists in Israel. This was my answer, as recorded in the trial transcript:[15]

> All of my sources of information have categorically denied that actual torture has been used in the sense of direct use of physical force to elicit the confession. But threats and fear of torture are used, often subtly conveyed and communicated to obtain the confession.

I was then asked to explain "why an inmate would claim that he had been tortured if that's not so." I replied:

> Well, particularly that is true among inmates who belong to organizations such as the PLO or PFLP or Abu Nidal. . . . Those organizations forbid on punishment of death members of the organization to cooperate with the Israeli authorities. Therefore, it is absolutely essential when a member of such an organization has cooperated that that person be able to publicly state . . . that he had no choice but that he was physically tortured into confession.
>
>   . . . [B]oth sides have reasons for wanting it to be believed that interrogated persons are tortured; the Israeli security services want it to be believed there is torture, so that their psychological strategem of obtaining confessions and statements without torture would be effective, and the interrogatees want it to be believed they have been physically tortured into confessing so they can maintain credibility with their organizations.

Finally, I was asked for my opinion as to whether Atta would be tortured if he were sent back to Israel for trial. My opinion was unequivocal:

> The cases that fit that profile [are] where there are ongoing terrorist activities that this person would know about, where the information that he has is current and where the person is faceless and nameless.

Here you have a situation where this man has been basically out of
contact with any activities for a period of years.

. . . When you couple that with the fact that this is a highly visible
case, a case where certain representations were made by the State Department, I would be very surprised if Israel even subjected him to the
kind of very tough interrogation described in the Landau Commission
report.*

I was also questioned about "how the Israeli prisons compare with
prisons elsewhere in the world." On the basis of my rather extensive
visits to prisons — my children know that the two places we are most
likely to visit on any foreign trip are the synagogue and the jail — I
testified that although the Israeli prisons did not compare favorably
with Scandinavian prisons, they were as good or better than prisons in
most other parts of the world.

Several weeks after my testimony, Judge Weinstein issued his opinion. The judge, relying on my testimony, concluded that the evidence
presented at the extradition hearing showed it was unlikely that Atta
would be tortured. Judge Weinstein also found that Israeli prison
conditions had been shown to compare favorably with those of most
prisons in this country and the western world. Atta was ordered extradited to Israel for trial.[16]

In 1988, I spent a month in Israel lecturing and teaching on civil
liberties. I was publicly critical of Israeli overreactions to the Intifada
and of the denial of counsel to a large number of administrative
detainees from the West Bank and Gaza Strip. I also wrote an article
criticizing certain actions of the Israeli security service in employing
means of pressure, including physical pressure, to obtain information
from terrorist suspects. A commission had decided not to prosecute
these security agents on the grounds that their actions fell within the
legal defense of "necessity." I thought the commission was wrong, and
stated in my article:

The necessity defense is by its very nature an *emergency* measure, it is not
suited to situations which recur over long periods of time. This is
especially so when the claimant to the benefits of the defense is a state
agency (or its members).

A state agency faced with systemic problems over a long period of

* The Landau Commission was established by the government of Israel in 1987 to investigate
charges that the Israeli security services had engaged in physical pressure and then lied about
what they had done.

time has options available to it other than civil disobedience — other than the deliberate decision to violate the law repeatedly.[17]

I was cautious in second-guessing the actions of a security service responsible for protecting vulnerable civilians against terrorism:

> I lack the information necessary to reach any definitive assessment of whether the [Israeli security service] should be allowed to employ physical pressure in the interrogation of some suspected terrorists under some circumstances. (I am personally convinced that there are some circumstances — at least in theory — under which extraordinary means, including physical pressure, may properly be authorized; I am also convinced that these circumstances are present far less frequently than law enforcement personnel would claim.) My criticism is limited solely to the dangers inherent in using — misusing in my view — the open-ended "necessity" defense to justify . . . the conduct of the [security service].[18]

I am not suggesting that the criteria for public criticism indicated by these accounts are the only valid ones. I am suggesting that before an American Jew publicly joins the chorus of often unprincipled and selective world criticism, he or she should at least think through the implications of the action and make a knowing, principled decision. A theory of criticism — whether right or wrong — is surely preferable to the kind of emotional dirty-laundry washing and *shanda fur de goyim* defensiveness that has characterized far too much of the public Jewish criticism of Israel to date.

One of the most contentious issues that arises frequently today is whether Israel's Law of Return — which makes Jews eligible for virtually automatic citizenship — is "racist" or inconsistent with principles of equality.* These criticisms may reflect more general tensions

---

* I am not speaking now of the more particularized division within the Jewish community over the definition of who is a Jew. Although that largely symbolic issue arises in the context of the Law of Return, it actually has little practical importance under it, since any close relative of a Jew — whether that relative is Jewish or not — qualifies for citizenship under the Law of Return. The relevant text of the law states: "The rights of a Jew under this law, and the rights of an Oleh under any other enactment, are also vested in a child and a grandchild of a Jew, the spouse of a Jew, the spouse of a child of a Jew, and the spouse of a grandchild of a Jew, except for a person who has been a Jew and has voluntarily changed his religion. . . . It shall be immaterial whether or not a Jew by whose right, a right under subsection A, is claimed is still alive and whether or not he has immigrated to Israel." The Law of Return, 5710-1950, §4A (as amended).

between some third world leaders and Jews over the very existence of Israel as a Jewish state.

Over the past several years, various African American and black African leaders — ranging from Jesse Jackson to Nelson Mandela — have criticized the very theory of Zionism, pointing especially to the Law of Return. I have been quick to respond to these charges, arguing that a world that closed its doors to Jews who sought escape from Hitler's ovens lacks the moral standing to complain about Israel's giving preference to Jews. It is particularly outrageous to hear those who demand affirmative action and special preferences for blacks because of past discrimination demanding that Israel not give special immigration preference to Jews because of past discrimination by the world.

During the 1984 presidential nomination campaign, for example, I engaged in a public debate with the Reverend Jesse Jackson which touched on these concerns.[19] It took place in Framingham, Massachusetts, shortly after Jackson had made the infamous comment in which he called New York City "Hymietown," but before he acknowledged and apologized for it. In the course of the debate, I posed the following question to the then presidential candidate: "Reverend Jackson, what advice would you give to an idealistic young black voter who asked you whether he should vote for an articulate and passionate white candidate with whose views he generally agrees on a large number of domestic and international issues — but who seems insensitive to black concerns about South Africa, who has used antiblack racial epithets, who has said that he has heard enough about the black slavery experience, and who has called black self-determination the 'poison weed' of black aspirations?" Each of these pointed references was, of course, my oversimplified attempt to draw parallels with Jackson's insensitivity toward Israel, his use of the term "Hymie," his statement about having heard enough about the Holocaust, and his characterization of Zionism as "Judaism poison weed."

The Reverend Mr. Jackson paused for a considerable amount of time before answering. Finally he said: "I would tell that young idealistic black voter that he should watch that white candidate closely and listen to his words carefully in order to determine whether the candidate learned from his mistakes and whether he has grown from the experience. I would urge him to keep an open mind and to give the candidate an opportunity to earn his vote in the future."

As soon as the debate was over, Jackson reached over to me and told me he thought that was the hardest question he had been asked and that it had really made him think. He invited me to spend the remainder of the day with him so that we could "begin a dialogue about these issues."

I agreed, and we drove around together for the entire afternoon and evening of campaigning. Jackson knew that I did not support his candidacy, but he was anxious to assure me that he was a candidate who could learn from his mistakes and grow from his experience. Perhaps he was hoping to earn my support for his 1988 or 1992 race. We talked at length about Israel, the Law of Return, affirmative action, the Holocaust, the civil rights movement, black-Jewish tensions, South Africa, and the Soviet Union.

After several hours of back and forth, Jackson made a remarkable statement. "Alan, you're one of the first Jews I have met who has a strong commitment both to racial justice and to Zionism. Most other Jews I know who are really committed to racial equality and progressive causes are anti-Zionist or at least skeptical about the Israeli cause. And most other Jews I know who are passionately committed to Zionism and Israel seem unconcerned with black issues. You are the exception."

I looked at Jackson in bewilderment. Suddenly, a sense of understanding came over me and I responded: "Reverend Jackson, some people think you are an anti-Semite. I now understand that such a characterization misses the point. You are simply ignorant about the Jewish community. You just don't know what we are about. You don't understand our complexity. And therefore you tend to stereotype, in much the same way that many whites — including Jews — who don't know the black community tend to stereotype your people." I told him how wrong he was, how many Jews there were like me, who strongly believed both in progressive causes and in the cause of Israel.

I reminded Jackson that the most prominent political supporters of the civil rights agenda, Jewish and non-Jewish, were strong advocates of Israel. Indeed, one of Israel's strongest supporters was Martin Luther King, Jr., who was not afraid to attack American foreign policy or American allies, as evidenced by his stance on the war in Vietnam. King was proud of his support for Israel and his condemnation of "irrational" anti-Israeli positions of the new left. Ten months after the Israeli occupation of the West Bank and just ten days before his death, King summarized his views on Israeli security:

Peace for Israel means security, and we must stand with all our might to protect its right to exist, its territorial integrity and the right to use whatever sea lanes it needs. Israel is one of the great outposts of democracy in the world, and a marvelous example of what can be done, how desert land can be transformed into an oasis of brotherhood and democracy. Peace for Israel means security and that security must be a reality.[20]

I also reminded Jackson that Jewish public figures, ranging from Arthur Goldberg to Howard Metzenbaum to Jacob Javits to Abraham Ribicoff to Elizabeth Holtzman to Robert Abrams to Barney Frank, were leaders in *both* the struggle for civil rights and the cause of Israeli security. Among non-Jewish supporters of Israel have been such civil rights activists as Hubert Humphrey, George Meany, Edward Kennedy, Walter Mondale, Alan Cranston, and Bayard Rustin. Even in South Africa, some of the leading white opponents of apartheid, such as Helen Sussman and Sydney Kentridge, have been long-term supporters of Israel.

I told Jackson that his exposure to Jews had obviously been limited to those radical extremists who had bought into his third world anti-Israel rhetoric. He countered that my examples were all of supporters of the old Israel, the Israel that was on the defensive against Arab attack. He told me that his interest in the Middle East had matured after Israel had become an occupier of Arab land and a trading partner with South Africa.* He assured me that his perception — that progressive Jews do not support Israel — was true of the generation of Jews who had reached political maturity after 1967.

I knew he was wrong. But he had certainly discerned a dangerous trend. Support for Israel, both by Jews and non-Jews, was increasing most dramatically among members of the political right (other than the lunatic extreme right, which continued to be anti-Semitic and anti-Israel) and decreasing most dramatically among members of the political left (including the lunatic extreme left, which was virulently anti-Israel and — though it disclaimed it — increasingly anti-Jewish).

The post-1967 generation lacked a memory of Israel's post-

---

* South Africa's major commercial trading partners include the United States, Great Britain, France, Germany, Japan, and the Soviet Union. Israel represents less than one percent of Pretoria's total trade. Saudi Arabia, Oman, Bahrain, the United Arab Emirates, and Kuwait have been the principal suppliers of oil to the South African military. Since 1970, South Africa has imported over ten billion dollars' worth of oil from these countries.

Holocaust roots and the constant unprovoked attacks that Arab neighbors had launched upon Israel from the point of its birth. That group
also lacked any memory of the racist, genocidal threats delivered
against Israel's very existence prior to the 1967 war, and of the opportunities for Palestinian self-determination wasted by Arab leaders
in their fervor to rid the area of any Jewish sovereignty. My conversations with Jesse Jackson reminded me how important it is to continue to make the liberal, progressive case for Israel, and not to leave
Israel's support in the hands of right-wing militarists and fundamentalists.

Another critical issue posed for American Jews who support Israel, and
related to the Law of Return, is the charge of "dual loyalty." The Law
of Return is relevant here, because many who allege dual loyalty do so
on the pretense that American Jews are all potential citizens of Israel.
(This preposterous argument was recently taken to its illogical extreme when a federal prosecutor tried to get a judge to deny bail to an
American Jew on the ground that he was "a citizen of Israel.") The
accusation of dual loyalty is neither new nor limited exclusively to
Israel.

    For as long as Jews have lived as a minority in "other people's"
lands, they have been accused of dual loyalty. Before the state of Israel
was established, the charge took the form of loyalty to the Jewish
people before loyalty to the host nation. Such charges led to discrimination, and worse, in Poland, France, England, Russia, Germany,
and throughout the Arab world.

    Indeed, the first recorded charges of dual loyalty date back to the
story of Esther. (Even earlier adumbrations are found in the story of
Joseph in Egypt and of the Jews enslaved under the pharaohs.) The
young Jewish queen of Persia and her uncle Mordecai conspired to save
the Jewish people from their planned slaughter at the hands of the
Persian prime minister Haman. In successfully redirecting the killings
from their intended targets — the Jews — onto Haman and his family, were Esther and Mordecai placing their loyalty to their co-
religionists above their loyalty to their prime minister and their host
country?

    Of course not! They were acting both out of entirely commendable
self-interest and out of principle. It would have been morally wrong to
allow the innocent Jewish population of Persia to be murdered simply
because the prime minister hated Jews. Mordecai and Esther were

entitled to believe that killing the Jews was not in the best interest of Persia, which in fact turned out to be the case.

Similarly those German Jews who opposed Hitler's anti-Semitism were not guilty of placing their loyalty to co-religionists over loyalty to Germany. It was Hitler who placed his loyalty to a destructive ideology above loyalty to the German people and nation. Those who opposed Hitler, both Jews and non-Jews, were the true German patriots. They were true not only to the best of German tradition and values, but also to universal principles of justice.

Nonetheless, charges of dual loyalty have persisted throughout history and throughout the world. So long as Jews were viewed as unassimilated (and even in Germany, where many were thoroughly assimilated) there was the canard that they owed their primary allegiance to some Jewish cause, whether it be Zionism, socialism, capitalism, Yiddishism, or Hasidism, or to some mythical conspiracy such as the so-called elders of Zion.

With the establishment of Israel in 1948, the charge of dual loyalty became more focused and more widespread. I now hear it within the highest circles in the United States — in politics, the media, academia, and industry. It has become a staple of talk shows and an important component of both anti-Jewish and anti-Israel propaganda.

This charge must be confronted directly, honestly, and without defensiveness. The truth is that most Jewish Americans — indeed, most Jews throughout the world — do support Israel. We support Israel financially, politically, and emotionally. We support Israel because that is the correct moral position to take in the world today. If that were not so, Jewish support for Israel would be significantly reduced. Indeed, as Israel has begun to lose the moral high ground in regard to certain specific policies — for example, its overreactions to the Intifada — it has lost support among American Jews. It is fair to say, although it is rarely said in the media, that Jewish Americans are more sensitive to the moral justifications for Israeli actions than are other ethnic Americans to the moral justifications for actions taken by countries and groups that they support.

Jewish Americans do not have a dual loyalty to America and Israel. Most have a single loyalty to principles of morality and democracy, principles which generally underlie both American and Israeli policies. We are among the first to criticize deviations from principle by *any* country, including America and Israel.

Like most Catholics, Protestants, Muslims, and other Americans, most Jews derive their morality from an unconscious combination of experiences, doctrine, affinity, and other sources. It is in the nature of a diverse and heterogeneous society like our own that individuals have multiple loyalties: to political party, to family, to religion, to race, to ethnic or national origin, to region, to friends, to college, to gender.

These multiple loyalties help shape each individual's choice on specific issues relating to the American agenda. What is good for America, a vibrant democracy, is not a static concept determined by any particular group of Americans. It is a dynamic and fluid composite of the multiple input of all Americans. No single group or person is empowered to determine what is best for America — not General Motors, not Oliver North, not the Daughters of the American Revolution, not Jesse Jackson, not a single branch of our government. The decision is made — after full input from all Americans — by a combination of legislative, executive, and judicial processes.

No one should charge a religious Catholic with having dual loyalty if he or she turns to the Vatican for guidance as to how America should address the abortion or AIDS issues. No one should accuse a black American of dual loyalty if he or she concludes that it is good for America to oppose South African apartheid. No one should criticize an Irish American for urging this country to support Irish aspirations in Northern Ireland. And no one should accuse a Muslim American of dual loyalty for urging that the United States defend Saudi Arabia against Iraqi aggression. In a pluralistic and heterogeneous society like ours, each group — indeed each individual — should have input into deciding what is good and bad for America. American Jews should continue — without embarrassment or fear of false charges of dual loyalty — to argue that American support for Israel is good for America.

I am often asked who I would support if America ever went to war with Israel. My first response is usually to cite the old story of the early cabinet meeting in which Prime Minister Ben-Gurion asked for suggestions on how Israel could avoid bankruptcy. The treasury minister urged that Israel follow the Japanese-German example by declaring war on the United States, losing, and then being rebuilt in splendor. Ben-Gurion replied: "But with our *shlimazl* [bad luck] we might win! Then what would we do?"

My second answer, though more serious, can also be illustrated by an old quip, this one from Galicia: "When a Jew eats a chicken and it's not Shabbes, then either the Jew or the chicken must be sick." If

America and Israel ever went to war against each other, one of them would have to be very sick indeed. The America I know and love could never be at war with the Israel I know and love. If there ever was — God forbid — a war, one of these countries would have to have changed dramatically. And if that happened, I would support the *right* side, the *just* side, the *moral* side, as I would expect other Americans, of all faiths, to do.

America's current support for Israel *is* good for America because it rests not only on sound strategic considerations, but because it is right morally and historically. If American Jews do not feel comfortable making these arguments *as loyal Americans,* no one else will make them for us.

The security of Israel is not assured. Israel is the only nation in the world whose very existence is threatened by enemies, external and internal, supported by a majority of the United Nations. It is the only nation in the world whose national movement, Zionism, has been declared "a form of racism" by the United Nations. It is the only nation in the world threatened by a genocidal war, the purpose of which is not military victory alone, but extermination.

The genocide of Israel's Jewish population — a population roughly the size of the Polish Jewish population at the beginning of World War II — is not an unrealistic nightmare. Nothing today prevents it other than Israel's military superiority over the combined Arab armies and terrorist organizations.* If the Arab armies and terrorists were capable of defeating Israel, destroying its Jewish population, and "reclaiming" *all* of current-day Israel, there can be little doubt that they would try to do so. Indeed, if any Arab leader were militarily capable of destroying Israel but refrained from doing so, he would be replaced by one who would at least try.

The recent exponential growth of Islamic fundamentalism increases the likelihood that an Arab military victory over Israel might be apocalyptic, if not genocidal. Although there are some moderate voices within the Palestinian and Arab movements, these voices are listened to only because Israel is too strong today to be defeated totally. Were Israel to become militarily weak, Arab militancy would increase. Arab moderation seems to grow in direct proportion to Israeli strength —

---

* My mother once asked me — while I was unsuccessfully trying to get her to compromise on one of her religious demands on me — what the difference is between a terrorist and a Jewish mother. Then, without pausing to give me a chance to answer, she answered the question herself: "With a terrorist, you can sometimes negotiate."

that is, to Arab inability to achieve the radical goals apparently desired by the vast majority of Arabs. Israeli military strength is thus a stimulus toward Arab moderation. Israeli weakness would be a stimulus toward increased Arab radicalism and militarism.

There is a point, of course, beyond which this would not continue to be true. Were Israel to grow more intransigent in the face of developing Arab moderation, that too might strengthen the hands of the radicals. A delicate balance must be struck, therefore, by those elected officials to whom the Israeli populace has entrusted its future. Israel must remain as strong — relative to the Arab military — as is feasible. But at the same time, it should not act solely on the basis of that military superiority. It should be strong enough militarily to permit it to take political risks for peace which do not endanger its basic security. But the world must never forget that a single Israeli strategic blunder may mean not only a military defeat, but a genocidal slaughter that the world would not be able, even if willing, to stop.

Every Israeli decision must be judged against this terrible reality. Too few of Israel's critics seem to understand the Jewish determination to avoid another Holocaust, this one in Israel. Too few understand why Israel cannot and should not trust its survival to nations that stood idly by while millions of innocent Jews were destroyed. Too many nations seem willing to have Israel take risks for an uncertain regional peace that they themselves are unwilling to take for a more important world peace.

None of this necessarily means that every Israeli decision is correct or immune from valid criticism. It does mean, however, that criticism of Israel's unwillingness to trust others to guarantee its security must take into account the history of the world's attitude toward Jewish suffering.

The future of Israel remains uncertain in the face of the continuing ultimate Arab goal of politicide if not genocide. Israel's determination to survive, coupled with its understandable distrust of the world's response to Jewish tragedy, may well have driven Israel into the nuclear age. And who could blame it, especially in light of the Iraqi threat in the summer of 1990 to annihilate half of Israel by gas and chemicals? Certainly not the nations that stood by as Germany annihilated nearly half the world's Jews by gas, guns, and chemicals. Certainly not the nations that ignored Jewish pleas for the Allies to bomb Auschwitz or to supply the Warsaw Ghetto residents with pistols and rifles so that they could try to protect their children — and the future of Judaism.

I wish Israel did not need defensive weapons of mass destruction or the region's most powerful defense forces. I wish the world had not driven the Jewish state into allocating its limited resources away from its universities and toward its military. But survival must come first, and Israel's military strength is the key to its survival. Anyone who believes that survival can be assured by moral superiority alone must remember the Warsaw Ghetto and the Treblinka gas chambers.

Indeed, it took the Iraqi rocket attacks on Tel Aviv — coupled with the threat of chemical and gas warfare — to bring home to the world the tragic reality that the Jewish population of Israel remains in danger of another Holocaust. Though Israel was not at the time directly involved in the Gulf War, Saddam Hussein perceptively understood that millions of Arabs and Muslims would cheer him if he managed to kill innocent Jewish women, children, and men. Can anyone doubt that there would be widespread enthusiasm among the Arab and Islamic masses for a populist leader who swore to make the Middle East *Judenrein,* or at least free of the Jewish state? Can anyone doubt that this would be true even if Israel had done everything demanded of it by the United Nations, the Peace Now movement, and the American left? The sad truth is that nothing Israel does — short of committing political suicide — would completely eliminate the widespread (how widespread is impossible to gauge in nondemocratic entities) Arab and Islamic support for the destruction of the Jewish state. That does not mean that Israel should refuse to do what is right. But it should have no illusions that doing what is right will alone assure peace and security. Israel will not survive by superior morality in the absence of superior strength. Because it is the Jewish nation — and the Jew among nations — it will need *both* a high degree of morality and an invincible military capacity.

In the Soviet Union

Are We Our
Brothers' and Sisters' Keepers?

SINCE THE HOLOCAUST, when an impotent American Jewish community stood by helplessly, world Jewry has paid keen attention to the situation of Jews in especially vulnerable situations, such as the Jews of the Soviet Union, Syria, Argentina, and Ethiopia. The international efforts to rescue Soviet refuseniks — those Jews who wanted to leave because of anti-Semitism but were denied the right to emigrate — have become a model of human rights activism. I was privileged to play a legal role from the beginning.[1] The culmination of my efforts — and those with whom I worked — came with the release from a Soviet prison of the world's most famous Jewish refusenik, Natan Sharansky, in February 1986.

As I watched on television and saw his animated body bouncing across Berlin's Glienicke Bridge, his smiling face, I began to cry. I knew that Sharansky — whom I had been representing since his arrest in 1977 — had emerged intact from his nine-year ordeal in the Gulag.

I had grown very close to Anatoly Shcharansky, as he was first called when I became his lawyer, over the years of his imprisonment, despite the fact we had never actually met. From the day of his arrest, Shcharansky had been held in seclusion. His wife, Avital, had not been permitted to speak to him. His lawyers, Irwin Cotler of Canada and I, were refused repeated requests to meet with him. Our legal correspondence never reached him. Nonetheless, I monitored his every move — from prison, to camp, to hospital, to solitary confinement. I knew what he was being given, and not given, to eat. I followed his medical condition (he had headaches, vision problems, and chest pains) and arranged for American doctors to diagnose him on the basis of our incomplete information.

Occasional visits from his mother provided the most reliable updates. These were supplemented by sketchy accounts from former prisoners who had seen him or exchanged a few words — or in several instances nonverbal communications — with him. His heavily censored letters also provided some clues to his situation. Finally, there were the official reports, conveyed to me through our State Department and nongovernmental agencies. On one occasion, a former student who had become a high-ranking legal official of an Eastern European country, was used to transmit information about Natan's health.

Over the nine years of Natan's confinement, his spokesperson to the world was his wife, Avital. She traveled the globe focusing the world's attention on his precarious situation. It was she and Natan's mother, Ida Milgrim, who had asked me and Irwin Cotler to serve as Natan's lawyers. We met with Avital in Israel, in New York, in Washington, in Madrid, in London, in Paris, and in Cambridge. She was the heart and soul of the collective effort to save Natan — an effort joined by millions of Jews and non-Jews throughout the world.

But it didn't start that way. The story of the beginning of our efforts to help Natan has never been told, and indeed could not be told until after his release. But it must be told now, despite some painful revelations, because it conveys an important and misunderstood point about the sometimes uneasy relationship between the state of Israel and the Jewish people, between Medinat Yisrael and Klal Yisrael.* The underlying point goes beyond the Shcharansky case and Soviet Jewry. It goes to the essence of the role of the Jewish people as distinguished from the Jewish state, and assumes particular significance for American Jews today.

When Shcharansky was first arrested, on charges of espionage, Irwin Cotler and I traveled to Israel to interview recent Soviet émigrés who had relevant information. Irwin is Canada's leading human rights lawyer, and one of its most distinguished constitutional lawyers and professors. We have been working together on human rights causes for almost twenty years, and we often teach courses and appear on panels together. We are so alike in perspective on Jewish legal concerns that I am often called "the United States' Irwin Cotler," and he is described

---

* Medinat Yisrael is the nation of Israel in the political sense, while Klal Yisrael is the people, or congregation, of Israel in the religious, ethnic, and historic sense.

as "Canada's Alan Dershowitz." I don't know about Irwin, but I am flattered by the comparison.

It was Irwin's idea to debrief every witness the KGB had interviewed about Shcharansky's alleged "spying." In this way, we would know what "evidence" they had against our client and could try to counter it.

My attempt to reenter the Soviet Union — I had been there representing Prisoners of Zion* back in 1974 — to interview witnesses was turned down, but Irwin managed to get to Moscow and speak to several refuseniks who had been interviewed by the KGB. I interviewed the American émigrés as well as *Los Angeles Times* journalist Robert Toth, who had been detained and questioned by the KGB about his contacts with Shcharansky.

Cotler and I both went to Israel intending to meet with the Soviet émigrés who now lived there. I had done that before, when I represented — along with Professor Telford Taylor, who had been the American chief prosecutor at Nuremberg — the original Prisoners of Zion, including the seven Jews and two non-Jews who had tried to escape from the Soviet Union by commandeering a small airplane. The plot had failed and the perpetrators were sentenced to long prison terms. We had met with Soviet officials in Moscow and filed briefs on their behalf, after interviewing numerous witnesses in Israel and elsewhere. The interviews in Israel had proved helpful in securing the early release of several of these prisoners.

The Israeli authorities had been cooperative in our efforts to interview witnesses for the series of cases, and we fully expected comparable cooperation in Shcharansky's case.

But the cooperation was not forthcoming. Indeed, the Israelis in charge of Soviet Jewry matters advised us in the strongest terms to "drop the Shcharansky case." When we asked why, we were told that "Anatoly Shcharansky is not a Prisoner of Zion, he is not one of ours." They told us that Shcharansky was a human rights activist closely allied with the prominent scientist and dissident Andrei Sakharov. We reminded them that Sakharov and his Jewish wife, Yelena Bonner, had stood outside the courtroom during the Shcharansky trial and had joined in the singing of the Israeli national anthem. It was Sakharov

---

* Prisoners of Zion — a phrase used by the Israeli government — included all who had been sentenced for seeking to emigrate to Israel or for practicing or teaching Jewish culture or religion. Several non-Jews who had worked together with Jews were also given this designation.

who tried to console Natan's mother when she heard the barbaric sentence of thirteen years at hard labor and burst into tears. When the KGB separated Sakharov from the grieving woman, it was Sakharov who risked his own arrest when he shouted at the KGB, "You are not people. Hear me, a member of the Soviet Academy of Science, you are fascists."

The Israelis remained unmoved. "We have our concerns, and the Sakharov group has its concerns. We do not condemn Sakharov, Shcharansky or the Helsinki Monitors." (The Helsinki Monitors were a group of Soviet citizens — dissidents, refuseniks, and others — who monitored Soviet compliance with the human rights provisions of the 1975 Helsinki Accords.) "Indeed, we know that they are courageous advocates of human rights. But that is not our concern as the government of Israel. Our concern is exclusively with Jews who want to emigrate to Israel and who are being prevented from doing so, or punished for their Zionism." He explained further that this was the implicit "understanding" between the governments of Israel and the Soviet Union under which Israel would concern itself only with refuseniks and Prisoners of Zion.

The Israeli officials told us that Shcharansky, by joining the Helsinki Monitors, who helped other groups as well as Jews, and by aligning himself with Sakharov's attempts to change Soviet society, had disqualified himself from inclusion in the categories of refusenik or Prisoner of Zion. The Israeli government could have nothing to do with the defense of a human rights case like Shcharansky's.

Our attempts to argue that Shcharansky was *both* a Prisoner of Zion and a human rights activist fell on deaf ears. The Israelis were fully aware that Shcharansky had become a human rights activist only after his application to join his wife in Israel had been turned down. They knew he was a refusenik and an ardent Zionist, a man who had learned Hebrew and who wanted nothing more than to join Avital in Jerusalem. But his broader human rights activities had disqualified him from Israel's protection.

We asked if they would help us discreetly, without any public attribution, but one of the officials quickly responded, "There are no secrets where the Soviet Union is concerned," implying that among the thousands of Soviet émigrés in Israel, there were surely some KGB spies.

Unless we dropped the Shcharansky case, we were told, we could not expect any cooperation from the Israeli government on any Soviet

Jewry matters. The Israeli government could deal only with lawyers who limited themselves to cases within the sphere of Israeli concerns.

Our first reaction was shock. How dare the Israeli government dictate to us whom we should represent? Didn't a Soviet Jew in deep trouble have the right to be represented by Jewish lawyers? Why should a Zionist's compliance with Hillel's second admonition — "If I am for myself alone, what am I?" — disqualify him from Israel's protection? On a more personal level, both Irwin and I identified with Shcharansky's universalism in human rights. Though we were both committed Jews who put Jewish issues at the top of our human rights agenda, we did not shy away from other human rights causes. We had been involved on behalf of dissidents from many parts of the world, including our own countries, South Africa, China, Romania, Poland, Cuba, Chile, Iran, and Israel. We wondered how *we* would be regarded by Israel if we got into trouble for our defense of Jewish and non-Jewish human rights.

But when we began to think about the Israeli position, we recognized the deeper problem. We, as *galut* Jews — Jews who were not part of the political nation of Israel — sometimes had different agendas. The state of Israel had to protect the interests of its own *citizens* first. Their interests included Israel's future relations with the Soviet superpower. Their interests also included increased immigration to Israel.

The state of Israel had apparently made a considered decision that it could best serve its national interests by limiting its involvement to a narrow category of Soviet Jews. That decision may have been right or wrong* — tactically and morally — but it was at least understandable, and within Israel's discretion as a sovereign democracy.

But decisions made by the state of Israel could not bind us —

---

* Some American Jews have difficulty believing that Israel can do wrong. The story that best illustrates this blind trust is the one about the New York couple making their United Jewish Appeal "mission" to Israel. They were taken to a Tel Aviv nightclub, where they enjoyed the singers and dancers. Then the comedian came on and started telling jokes in Hebrew. Their Israeli guide was concerned, because the New York couple knew no Hebrew. But they laughed uproariously at every punch line, along with the Israeli audience. Their guide was puzzled: "I thought you didn't understand our language. How do you know the Israeli comedian is funny?" The American woman answered: "We don't understand him, but we trust him."

But the record is clear that Israel has blundered on many occasions. One recent mistake was trying to prevent the publication of a "kill and tell" book in the United States by a former member of the Mossad. Had the Israelis consulted any experienced American constitutional lawyer, they would have been told that by bringing the suit, they assured that the book would become a best-seller, and that they would lose in court.

legally or morally — as Jews, as members of Klal Yisrael, the larger congregation of Israel. As private citizens of other countries, we could undertake certain actions on behalf of endangered Jews that the state of Israel would be unwise to try. We, of course, understood our limitations. Private citizens do not carry anywhere near the influence that states do; but neither do they have some of the constraints.

In this instance, we would not abandon a fellow Jew and human rights activist just because he had done what we hoped we would have had the courage to do if faced with what he faced: namely broaden his concerns beyond those of his own co-religionists.

Cotler and I decided to politely inform the Israeli officials that we would continue our efforts on behalf of Shcharansky either with or without their assistance. Reluctantly, they told us we would have to be denied access to the considerable files kept by the Israeli agency in charge of Soviet Jewry. The separation was cordial. We were thanked for our past help and wished good luck on our future efforts.

A few years after our "confrontation," the Israeli government sponsored a general conference on Soviet Jewry and invited American lawyers who had been active in the cause. When the list of invitees was published, we both received numerous phone calls and letters noting our conspicuous omission. I wrote to the chairman of the conference, and he responded with a curt note that said: "Either you march lockstep with us, or you do not march with us at all."[2] We continued to march to the pace of a slightly different drummer, though the underlying *nigun* — melody — was the same.

The major Soviet Jewry organization in the United States, the National Conference on Soviet Jewry, took a similar attitude toward Shcharansky. One leader of that organization tried to persuade me that Shcharansky was actually a spy and we should keep hands off his case.

But American Jews always create redundant organizations, which often turn out not to be redundant. That proved true of the Soviet Jewry organizations. The grass-roots groups — which are more independent of the major Jewish organizations and of Israel — began to take up the Shcharansky case. Eventually, even Israel could not resist the grass-roots pressure, and Shcharansky was officially declared a Prisoner of Zion.*

* Nor was the National Conference on Soviet Jewry the only organization that refused to take the Shcharansky case. I wrote to the National Lawyers Guild, a leftist lawyers' organization, and requested them to seek observer status at the Shcharansky trial in 1978. They turned me down flat, on the basis of the following convoluted reasoning:

When Shcharansky was finally released and flown to Israel, he was greeted as a national hero. Among the people who met him at Ben-Gurion Airport was at least one Israeli official who had been most insistent on ignoring his case and keeping us out of it.

Throughout Natan's confinement, we pursued a multiple strategy: legal, political, public relations, and diplomatic. We filed numerous briefs, affidavits, and arguments, fully cognizant of the reality that legal advocacy alone could never do more than provide a hook on which the Kremlin might hang a result achieved by other means.

Shortly after Shcharansky was arrested, I went to the White House to try to persuade President Carter to issue a statement expressly denying the Soviet charge that Shcharansky had been a CIA operative. Despite pressure from the CIA to continue the American policy of never affirming or denying anyone's alleged association with the agency, President Carter did issue the following statement:

> I have inquired deeply within the State Department and within the CIA, as to whether or not Mr. Shcharansky has ever had any known relationship in a subversive way, or otherwise, with the CIA. The answer is "no." We have double-checked this, and I have been hesitant to make that public announcement, but now I am completely convinced.[3]

Shortly after this statement was made, the Soviets stopped referring to that charge.

At the time of his trial, I cabled a brief to the court, which was excerpted in *Newsweek* magazine. And I worked with Cotler on a massive appellate brief, which Cotler filed in the Soviet Union.

During the years of Shcharansky's confinement, Cotler and I ap-

---

"The problem," they told me, "is that we do not approach matters such as this purely from a human rights perspective. We regard it as well from the standpoint of the importance of focusing attention on human rights violations in a particular country. With respect to the U.S.S.R., we have not had discussion or come to any decision about the appropriateness of focusing on human rights issues there."

They also suggested that Shcharansky's alleged involvement with "the C.I.A." — an absolute falsehood — bothered some of their members, and that other members "approve of the Soviet justice" system and would "not want to criticize it." The National Lawyers Guild did not have any similar reservations about sending observers to Israeli trials and roundly criticizing the Israeli legal system. This double standard by an organization claiming to be a supporter of human rights has caused it to suffer a considerable loss of credibility among both Jews and non-Jews.

peared on dozens of television programs and at hundreds of rallies, mock trials, and hearings on the case. We tried our best to keep Shcharansky's name and face in the forefront of the media. This, we were assured, was the best life insurance we could buy on his continued health and welfare. The Soviets were counting on what one Soviet official had called the "very short memory of the American people." That official assured me that "within a few months [of Shcharansky's trial] nobody will even remember his name. He will become just another faceless prisoner." We were determined to keep Shcharansky in the news.

On January 27, 1986, just shortly before his surprise release, I published the following syndicated column, one of many I had written about Shcharansky, entitled "Another Birthday in Prison":

Do you remember Anatoly Shcharansky? In 1978, his smiling face was on the cover of *Time* and *Newsweek* and his story was front-page news throughout the world. Today he is languishing in the Soviet Gulag, completing the ninth year of a 13-year prison sentence. . . .

As a *Newsweek* correspondent who knew Shcharansky in Moscow said, "His only crime was that he spoke the truth, and his worst crime was that he spoke it in English." The truth he spoke was about the Soviet Union's denial of the most basic human rights to Christians, Muslims, Jews, Ukrainians, Crimeans, ethnic Germans and even Russian Communists who deviate from the Party line.

Last week was Anatoly's 38th birthday. He spent it alone as he has his last 8 birthdays. His mother's recent efforts to visit have been rebuffed.

In the meantime Anatoly's wife Avital waits for her eventual reunion with her beloved husband whom she has neither seen nor spoken to in more than eight years. When he was sentenced back in 1978, her first reaction was: "In thirteen years I will no longer be able to bear children."

The only difference between the Soviet hostage takers and the Shiites who are holding Americans in Beirut is that the Soviets employ the facade of a legal system — with synthetic statutes and kangaroo courts — to justify the detention of their hostages.

All free people should continue speaking up for Anatoly Shcharansky — and for the millions of other political prisoners in the Soviet Union, South Africa, the Philippines, China, Iran, and throughout the world — until they are free to speak for themselves.

While this public advocacy was taking place, we were always trying
to work behind the scenes to arrange a prisoner exchange. At first,
there was reluctance on the part of those closest to Natan to have him
participate in any "spy swap," for fear that such a move might be
interpreted as an admission that he was indeed a spy. We finally
succeeded in persuading them it was better to have a free Natan, who
could tell the truth, than an imprisoned Natan, whose silence could
not answer Soviet lies.

After receiving the go-ahead for back-channel efforts, I met secretly
with a mysterious East German named Wolfgang Vogel. A few weeks
earlier, an East German professor had been arrested in Boston on
charges of spying against the United States. Vogel was in this country,
trying to get him an American lawyer. I told him I wouldn't take the
case because I was Anatoly Shcharansky's American lawyer. Vogel
looked at me as if I were naive. "Of course I know you are Shcharansky's lawyer. That's why I'm talking to you." His message, though
elliptical, was clear enough.

The reason I could not take the East German professor's case is that
I would have had a conflict of interest: as Shcharansky's lawyer, I
would want to see the East German professor convicted so that he
could become a chip in the bargain for Shcharansky. I did, however,
recommend a lawyer, who eventually worked out a deal for the East
German that did not include Shcharansky.

This meeting — and the events that followed — served as my introduction to the shadowy world of prisoner exchanges which finally
produced Natan's freedom in 1986. Many other people — prominent
among them Rabbi Ronnie Greenwald of Monsey, New York, who has
worked with Vogel over many years — played important roles in the
drama. But when Anatoly Shcharansky walked across the Glienicke
Bridge after nearly nine years in the Gulag, it was Wolfgang Vogel
who had brought him over. The final decisions leading to the eight-
person swap — one Soviet dissident and three western spies for four
eastern spies — were made deep inside the Kremlin and White House,
but the exchange would never have taken place if not for private
initiatives. A complex arrangement like the one that culminated at the
Glienicke Bridge requires a great many pieces to come together at
exactly the right time.

Vogel's brilliance is that he understands how to maximize the advantages of each of the participants. He can assess the currency value
of each prisoner to each international player and he tries to strike a fair

deal. And he knows who to deal with in each country, in both the private and public sectors.

One of the major sticking points on our side was the fact that Anatoly Shcharansky was not a spy. He was a human rights activist. The Soviets insisted on treating him as a spy, while the United States demanded that he be regarded as a dissident.

Vogel struck a symbolic compromise: he agreed to drive Shcharansky to the middle of the bridge first, in his golden Mercedes, so that Shcharansky would not walk along with the spies, thereby allowing each side to interpret the exchange as it chose. It was vintage Vogel.*

There are dangers, of course, inherent in any swap of dissidents for spies. The Soviet Union (or other countries) could become encouraged to arrest dissidents precisely in order to hold them as bargaining chips to exchange for their captured spies. But there are also dangers in insisting that our exchanges be limited to spy for spy. It is all too easy to frame a dissident on spy charges, as the KGB did to Shcharansky.

Obviously we have to draw the line somewhere. It would generally be wrong to exchange dissidents for terrorists. Terrorism is evil per se, and all civilized nations must do everything in their power to discourage it. But spying is only wrong when it is committed against one's own country. Every civilized nation has its own spies. Indeed, spying has been called the second oldest profession. And spy trading is as venerable as recorded history.

In the end, everyone gained from the Shcharansky and spy exchange. Since human rights is an important part of American foreign policy, and since our national honor had been challenged by Shcharansky's conviction following President Carter's public assurance that he was not an American spy, we won an important victory. The Soviets got their somewhat tarnished spies back. But the biggest winners were Natan and Avital, who were reunited after a decade of terrible separation.

My first in-person meeting with Natan was in New York shortly after the exchange. Although I had been invited to join in his welcome

---

* Playing the role of middleman in spy swaps is not without its risks. Following the overthrow of the East German Communist regime in 1989, Vogel was arrested on charges of "criminal blackmail" growing out of his representation of a notorious figure from the old East German regime. A few of us who had worked with him on prisoner exchanges offered to assist him in his time of trouble, but he extricated himself from his legal difficulties without the need for outside help. We were not surprised that this master of the prisoner swap could help himself. (Later, Vogel defended Erich Honecker — the deposed Communist head of state of East Germany.)

at Ben-Gurion Airport, my teaching schedule made that impossible. But I met with him during his first hours in New York. We threw our arms around each other and wept softly. He told me of the blessing he had made at the Western Wall when he first arrived in Israel: *"Baruch matir asirim"* — a blessing upon being freed from imprisonment. I was never certain that I would see him alive, since the rate of survival for a Soviet prisoner serving a long sentence at hard labor was not particularly high. But here he was, free, happy, relatively healthy, and grateful. It would be the first of many meetings between us, as we continued to work together for Soviet Jewry.

He, of course, knew far less about me than I knew about him. His isolation had kept him from learning of the efforts on his behalf, although some snippets of information had miraculously filtered through to him. He did not want to talk about the past. His concern was to keep the issue of Soviet Jewry in the forefront, despite the release of its most visible symbol. But the past was not yet behind him. I could see signs of his suffering in small gestures. For example, when we sat down for a meal, I noticed him unconsciously putting pats of butter into his mouth, as if to make up for the enormous nutritional deprivations he had suffered.

Despite these deprivations — fully recounted in Shcharansky's extraordinary memoir, *Fear No Evil* — Natan and Avital soon announced that their dream was about to come true: Avital was pregnant with their first child. Ten months after Natan crossed the Glienicke Bridge, Avital gave birth in Jerusalem to Rachel. In 1988, they had their second daughter, Hanna.

The first time I visited Natan, Avital, and Rachel in their Jerusalem home — Avital was then pregnant with Hanna — we reflected on how unlikely the scene we were experiencing had seemed just a few years earlier. We discussed the future of Soviet Jewry in the age of *glasnost, perestroika,* and Gorbachev. We knew that these changes were good for most Soviet citizens, but we were entitled to ask my grandmother's more particularistic question: Is it good or bad for the Jews?

The first signs were mixed. Mikhail Gorbachev was a pragmatist who understood that imprisoning dissidents and denying exit permits to the most active refuseniks was self-destructive. Dissent by any group becomes contagious. Accordingly, one of Gorbachev's first initiatives after becoming general secretary was to grease the squeakiest wheels, by granting exit visas to some of the most vocal Jewish activists. But most Soviet Jews remain highly skeptical about whether reforms can elevate Jews — especially committed Jews and Zionists — to first-class citizenship in the Soviet Union. There is no historical reason to believe that centuries of anti-Semitism under the czars, commissars, and Communists — with but a brief interlude during Lenin's time — will suddenly end because of a new pragmatic reform program.

Indeed, pragmatic considerations may point the other way. Anti-Semitism is very popular in many parts of the Soviet Union, and it would take enormous resources to suppress it. Moreover, the new freedom, if it is to be genuine, must include freedom to speak one's mind. And it is perhaps a sign of things to come that one of the first public demonstrations permitted under the new policy of freedom was an anti-Semitic rally held in Moscow by an ultranationalistic organization called Pamyat. That throwback to czarist anti-Semitism recently issued a "proclamation" that included the following:

> We call to all Soviet people: Mobilize all your forces for a fight against the threat of Zionism in our country! Stop the machinations of those who would sell their country for thirty pieces of silver!

> Zionism Has Now Launched
> An Undisguised Offensive
> Against
> The Patriot Front!

> Pamyat! Let the Russians cut the throats of each other and meanwhile the Zionists are plotting a takeover of Russia.
> Nazism was born out of Judaism!!!
> Nazism has jumped out of the Talmud: ". . . Kill the best of Gentiles!!!"[4]

They have also distributed even more provocative literature, such as the following leaflet:

> How long can we put up with dirty Jews, who have brazenly infiltrated our society, in particular into positions of privilege! Why have we allowed the filthy ones to make a Jewish mess out of our beautiful country?!

> Why do we, great, beautiful, wise Slavs see the Yids amongst us as a normal phenomenon?!

> Why do the Yid-cattle manage, by various means, to obtain Russian

surnames and under the section of "nationality" they write "Russian."
How can those dirty, stinking Jews hide and pass as heroic and proud
Russians?[5]

After a protest by Pamyat members on May 6, 1987, Moscow's
populist politician, Boris Yeltsin, now the president of the Russian
Republic, met with representatives of Pamyat for several hours. It was
the first time since the 1920s that protesters were received by an
official of such stature.

Several weeks after this highly publicized rally, I had the occasion
to speak to a Soviet lawyer. I mentioned the anti-Semitic rally. He
agreed that it was terrible and that anti-Semitism was a great evil, but
he asked me whether I would really want the KGB to censor this new
freedom.

I was reminded of a debate I had once had with a Soviet law
professor in Madrid on the subject of anti-Semitism. I produced a
series of anti-Semitic periodicals and cartoons published in the Soviet
Union and asked him how in the name of Lenin — who opposed
anti-Semitism — he could justify the dissemination of this racist garbage in his country. My opponent reached into his briefcase and pulled
out his own collection of anti-Semitic leaflets and cartoons published
in the United States. He showed them to me and asked which were
worse. I looked at the American stuff, and he was absolutely right.
Ours was much worse. It called for Jews to be gassed and burned. But
I turned to him, holding up an example of the Soviet published
garbage in one hand and the American published garbage in the other,
and put a question to him: "Look closely and tell me whether you
don't see a major difference which makes the Soviet material — even
though it is a bit milder — more dangerous."

He immediately understood what I was suggesting: in the lower
right-hand corner of the Soviet material was an official stamp of approval by Glavlit, the Soviet governmental censorship agency. There
was no stamp on the American material, other than "published by the
American Nazi Party." The Soviet anti-Semitism had been officially
approved by the government, while the American material had no
such governmental approval. It was simply the product of our constitutional policy against censorship. That was the distinction, and it was
a distinction of significance.

Despite *glasnost* and *perestroika,* few important policies are implemented in the Soviet Union without the approval of the Communist party and government apparatus. It is too early to tell whether the Soviet anti-Zionist — really anti-Semitic — publishing mill will close down or at least slow down. But at this writing, anti-Jewish books and pamphlets are still available, though they now emanate more from the "private" than the public sector. It is understandable why many Jews persist in their efforts to emigrate to Israel and elsewhere. Even during the early weeks of the Persian Gulf crisis — with Iraqi threats of chemical devastation of Israel — Soviet Jews continued to immigrate to Israel in record numbers. As the *New York Times* reported on September 3, 1990: "Through the month, many Soviet Jews interviewed in Israel and in the Soviet Union said they were more concerned about the growing anti-Semitism at home than the prospect of conflict in Israel." When I asked a Soviet refusenik why he was willing to risk exposure to gas in Israel, he answered: "In Israel, the government will protect us. Here the government encourages those who would attack us."

A story told to me by Ida Nudel, a longtime refusenik, when I met with her in Moscow back in 1974, illustrates why many Jews see no future in the Soviet Union. Her story was about the time they announced there would be a trainload of fresh oranges coming to Moscow from the Ukraine; anyone interested should come to the train station. Thousands came and waited all through the freezing night for the rare delicacy. At dawn, the commissar announced that there would only be a truckload, not a trainload, and so there were not enough oranges for Jews. The Jews complained but were sent home. The others waited all night at the truck depot. At dawn, another bulletin: It's just a carload of oranges, not a truckload; only members of the Communist party can wait, nonmembers go home. Again, a long wait followed by a terse announcement: No carload, just a single crate of oranges; only members of the Central Committee could get one. Again a wait and a message: It was all a mistake, there are no oranges at all. At this point, one frustrated member of the Central Committee turned to another and bitterly declared: "See, the Jews always get the advantages; they were the first to be sent home."

"The Jews," Ida Nudel told me, "are blamed for everything." Even in the current context of reform in the Soviet Union and throughout Eastern Europe, there is finger-pointing at "the Jews" and "the Zionists." Old scapegoats are hard to let go of. Indeed, *New York Times* columnist William Safire recently repeated a "new" joke they are now telling in Moscow. It was the old joke, only meat was now the scarce commodity rather than oranges. The Jews remained the same.

Natan Shcharansky has become the spokesperson for the current generation of Soviet Jews, and I continue to speak to him regularly about changing conditions. In 1986, I received a frantic phone call from Natan. Did I know about the American Bar Association's decision to officially recognize the Association of Soviet Lawyers and to enter into a formal agreement with them?

I did not know about the ABA's decision, but I certainly knew a great deal about the Association of Soviet Lawyers. It was the legal front for the Soviet system of repression. It did the KGB's bidding and dirty work. For example, it saw to it that the few lawyers who indicated any willingness to defend dissidents or refuseniks were expelled from their local bar associations. It provided "acceptable" lawyers who would insist that their clients must plead guilty to any and all charges. Among its more despicable activities was its joint sponsorship of the so-called White Book, an anti-Zionist and anti-Semitic diatribe widely circulated both inside and outside the Soviet Union. At the time of the ABA agreement, there had been no change for the better in the Association of Soviet Lawyers. It still reflected the worst of Soviet oppression.* Soviet refuseniks, Prisoners of Zion, and dissidents were unanimous in their disdain for the organization — as were decent non-Jewish Soviet lawyers and academics.

These who had experienced Soviet repression wanted the world to know that the Association of Soviet Lawyers contained no real lawyers and that Soviet justice was still largely an oxymoron. Natan reminded me of the joke the dissidents used to tell about the time the Czechoslovakian Communist party had asked the Kremlin for permission to create a Ministry of the Navy. The Kremlin scoffed on the ground that Czechoslovakia, which was landlocked, did not even have a navy. The Czechs responded, "But the Soviet Union has a Ministry of Justice!"

Natan asked me, as his lawyer, to work against the American Bar Association's agreement with the Association of Soviet Lawyers. It would undo years of effort by the Soviet refuseniks to persuade the world that "the ASL works *against* justice, not for it." "At the very least," he said, "we should get something in exchange for giving the Soviets what they have been trying unsuccessfully to obtain for years —

---

* As of September 1990, the Association of Soviet Lawyers was still a governmentally sponsored organization with no real independence.

international legitimacy for their legal system." Natan told me that there were a few courageous and independent Soviet lawyers and that these lawyers were trying to establish an independent bar association that would not be controlled by the government or the party. If the American Bar Association decided to recognize *only* the KGB-controlled Association of Soviet Lawyers, this important recognition would make it far more difficult for the independent lawyers to achieve any status within the Soviet Union.

I called the National Conference on Soviet Jewry, but its leadership had already decided, without consultation with refuseniks, to *support* the ABA proposal. The other major Soviet Jewry organizations, after consulting their members and clients, had determined to try to defeat the initiative, or at least to condition it on some improvement in Soviet justice, such as opening political trials to American observers. The Jewish community — whose grass-roots members were lopsidedly against the ABA proposal — would present a divided front to the American Bar Association.

The ABA granted me permission to address the annual convention, and I spoke against the one-sided agreement, likening it to an agreement with the "official" Apartheid Bar Association of South Africa. But our divided front gave the ABA a justification for going forward and the agreement was signed.

During the first year of the agreement, little progress was made on legal rights in the Soviet Union. We urged the ABA to reconsider. But Morris Abram, chairman of the National Conference on Soviet Jewry, urged renewal in a *New York Times* op-ed article, arguing that "without contact, we can have no hope of influence on Soviet conduct." I responded to the Abram arguments in a letter to the editor which drew a distinction "between *talking* to one's enemy and according it the *recognition* and legitimacy it wants but does not deserve." I urged us to "treat the Association of Soviet Lawyers and the PLO alike: talk to both, but recognize neither, until they show that they deserve such legitimation or [until] we have got something in return."[6]

As more time passed without any progress, even Abram seemed to admit he had been wrong. We debated the issue in 1987, and I complained: "There should have been wider consultation in advance among the Jewish organizations. We would have been much more effective if we had had our fights earlier and in private and if we had come to the ABA with a united front."

Abram acknowledged that he was "becoming very disenchanted

with the way that the Americans are handling" the exchange, and he predicted that Soviet Jewry was "not going to be freed by a sudden change of heart and change of direction of the Soviet state."[7]

At the time of our debate, no one could have imagined the change of direction that the Soviet Union would experience, largely without outside pressure in so short a period of time. These changes have brought about some improvements in the official status of Soviet Jews and a dramatic increase in emigration. But ironically, there has been little noticeable improvement in the Soviet legal system and none at all in the Association of Soviet Lawyers. Perhaps there are subtle changes for the better that will take time to surface, but they will not be attributable to the ABA, which refused — at least until very recently — to use its considerable leverage to press effectively for legal reform.

For example, when Nicholas Daniloff, the American journalist, was arrested in Moscow in 1986, many of us pressed the ABA to demand that he be given access to an American lawyer. But nothing was done. Eventually an exchange was arranged, under which Daniloff was freed from his Soviet jail and a Soviet spy, named Gennadi Zakharov, was freed from an American jail. When Daniloff returned to the United States, he came to see me about his case. He was as upset with the American Bar Association's recognition of the Association of Soviet Lawyers as were the Soviet dissidents and refuseniks. The one-way nature of the bridge was evident to him, especially in light of the refusal of the ABA to flex its muscles even when an American citizen was being held on trumped-up charges.

A few years after Nick's release, we ended up at a dinner together. The guest of honor was William Webster, the director of the CIA and former head of the FBI. Nick and I were talking to Webster when a photographer snapped our picture. Nick smiled and said, "Now they have it." We asked what he meant, and he responded: "Imagine what the KGB could do with that photograph. They would backdate it and use it as proof that I really was a CIA agent." I turned to Nick and reminded him that his hair had gotten a bit grayer since his arrest and that the KGB would have a hard time backdating the photo. He laughed and said, "Touching up photos is one of their specialties." Webster added, "But I wasn't even with the CIA at the time of Nick's arrest." Nick responded, "Sure you were. The KGB will say that the FBI job was just a cover."

I am reminded of this vignette whenever I consider the use of Soviet evidence in Nazi war criminal cases. Since the KGB has had absolutely no scruples about faking evidence, it is always possible for them to fool the experts. It is important, therefore, to insist — even in cases involving despicable Nazis — that every bit of Soviet evidence be independently corroborated. This was done by the Israeli court in the Demjanjuk case, and it has been done by American courts in the various deportation and extradition cases. Our experience in the Shcharansky case, and others like it, requires that we remain skeptical of all Soviet evidence. But skepticism about one source of evidence does not translate into criticism of the noble enterprise of bringing Nazi war criminals to justice.

There was yet another connection between the Shcharansky case and the Demjanjuk case. While I was in Israel attending the Demjanjuk trial, Natan was visiting Israeli prisons. In the course of his visit, a heavy man with a large, bald head called out to Natan in Ukrainian. The man was John Demjanjuk. It was a déjà vu experience for Natan, because he had been in Soviet prison with many Ukrainians convicted of Nazi war crimes. Demjanjuk called Natan his "brother" and claimed that they had much in common, since both were "victims" of KGB evidence. Natan said he would look into Demjanjuk's case, but asked him whether he didn't agree that he was fortunate to be in an Israeli prison and in the Israeli legal system rather than in the Soviet Gulag. Demjanjuk agreed.

After he returned from his visit to the prisons, Natan called me and asked me to brief him on the evidence in the Demjanjuk case. I did so in detail, assuring him that the non-Soviet evidence proved overwhelmingly that Demjanjuk was indeed the murderous and sadistic prison guard that he denied having been.

The recent dramatic changes within the Soviet Union in particular and Eastern and Central Europe in general caught the Jewish community, along with the rest of the world, by surprise. Both the opportunities and the risks for Jewish communities in the Soviet Union and its neighboring countries have increased. I have followed these changes with great interest, first from media reports and international telephone calls, and then from within these countries.

I traveled to the Soviet Union in May of 1990 because of threats directed against the Jewish community of Leningrad by Pamyat. In September of 1990 I went to Riga and Moscow as part of an American legal delegation to a conference on legal and economic cooperation between our countries.

My older son, Elon, and I arrived in Leningrad on the day that Pamyat swore would be the beginning of the new final solution for the "Jewish Problem" in Russia. A Slavic version of *Kristallnacht* was threatened. First the Jews must be "punished" for their sins and crimes against Russian Christians. Then they must be chased out of Mother Russia so that it may be "purified" of their alien influence.

Pamyat pledged to fulfill the nineteenth-century czarist prophecy: one third of the Jews killed; one third assimilated; and one third banished. Hitler and Stalin had already accomplished the first of these goals. Three-quarters of a century of communism had achieved the second. But despite the Soviet emigration movement of the 1970s and 1980s, there were still more than a million Jews in the Soviet Union, most of them in Russia proper.

Now some of them would be beaten and killed, so that the others would leave. Even assimilation was no solution to the racial purists of Pamyat. Like Hitler, they believed there was no such thing as an assimilated Jew. Jewishness was a racial characteristic that did not go away or blend in. The only solution was genocide or mass exodus. Some of Pamyat favored the former, others the latter. One prominent leader argued that the Jews should first be punished for their "collective guilt" and then expelled. It was more a tactical than an ideological debate.

It was impossible to ignore the May 5 threat. I was shown a newly published Pamyat edition of the infamous *Protocols of the Elders of Zion,* with a new introduction by one of Pamyat's "intellectual" leaders.* (Pamyat, unlike the Ku Klux Klan, is not just an organization of low-life ne'er-do-wells. It includes some prominent writers, teachers, and professionals.) I was also shown leaflets and articles that could have been lifted whole from *Der Stürmer.* There were also some crudely published freelance brochures, printed by individual fanatics within Pamyat, that explicitly called for the mass murder of Jews.

Jewish leaders feared that even if Pamyat was bluffing, individual fanatics, inspired by the call for blood, would attack Jews. And there was only one place that Jews congregated, at Leningrad's only synagogue. There are no Jewish neighborhoods, restaurants, or clubs in Leningrad. Nor are Jews easily identifiable on sight. If you want to find Jews together in Leningrad — whether your motives are good or bad — you must go to the synagogue.

* In January 1991 it was announced that the Soviet defense ministry's official journal was planning to publish the *Protocols.*

That's why Elon and I decided to spend May 5, 1990, in Leningrad at the synagogue. We hoped that there would be no pogrom. But we were determined that if Pamyat thugs were going to attack Jews in Leningrad that day, they would have to attack American Jews along with Russian Jews. They would not have the luxury of limiting their attack to politically vulnerable Russian Jews. They would have to pay the much higher political price that went along with attacking Americans who were exercising their human rights of association and religious exercise. We publicized our visit to the synagogue, in the hope that it would discourage a Pamyat attack. And we urged other Americans to make it clear that they would be in the synagogue, along with their brothers and sisters. With modern communication and transportation, Jews at risk anywhere in the world should never again have to face those risks alone, without the support and presence of fellow Jews from America or other countries where Jews cannot be attacked with impunity.

We arrived at the synagogue at ten in the morning. Although there were only a few handfuls of Jews there to pray, they had divided themselves into two congregations, or minyans. One group was meeting in the large choral synagogue. The service was conducted by a cantor with a beautiful baritone voice. We were told that he was an opera singer during the week. The other minyan was in a much smaller adjoining synagogue. Its service was conducted in the Hasidic tradition, with no cantor and more group participation. In seeing that this small community boasted two distinct congregations, I was reminded of the old joke about the Jewish Robinson Crusoe who was finally rescued after nearly ten years on a desert island. His rescuers observed that he had built two synagogues, and asked why. He responded, pointing to the first, "This one I pray in." Then he pointed to the second one and said, "That one I used to pray in, but I quit because I got into a fight over its policies."*

In Leningrad, the smaller minyan was formed after its congregants had gotten into a dispute over the policies of the larger minyan. But on the fifth of May, the two minyans were united by a common fear. It was decided by the leaders of the Jewish community that they would spend the entire Sabbath together. After praying separately, they all got together for a *kiddush*, a postprayer gathering started with a small

* There are varying punch lines to this classic story, each one making a slightly different point: "This one I pray in; that one I wouldn't go near." Or "That one I built in case I get into an argument with this one."

glass of wine and some honey cake. I was then introduced and asked
to speak about the political situation from an American perspective.

I began by quoting the traditional Hebrew prayer *"Hinay Ma Tov
uma naim, shevet achim gam yachad,"* which I translated loosely as "How
wonderful it is when brothers and sisters sit together both in joy and
in danger." On that day we were all experiencing a combination of joy
and danger. The joy was over the fact that we could be together in a
Russian synagogue without fear of official government reprisal. The
danger was that the very policies of *glasnost* that had freed us to pray
together had also given Pamyat the right to prey on us. It was the
paradox of democracy. With democracy, there comes the freedom to
express one's bigotry out in the open. Under totalitarianism, all
strongly held views — except those the party wanted to have openly
expressed — had to be repressed. These views, whether positive Judaism or negative anti-Semitism, had not gone away. They had merely
been held in check for many years. Now the top was off the pressure
cooker and these repressed views were boiling over.

I spoke about the fear we were all experiencing. It was early afternoon and nothing had happened. But there was still a long day ahead
of us. Shabbat in Leningrad does not end in May until about 10:30
P.M. And the synagogue would be in use until then.

As far as I know, no contingency plans had been made in the event
of an attack. No police or KGB were in view, as they had been when
it was their job to discourage synagogue attendance. No communication system had been put in place. When I learned this, I didn't know
whether to feel relieved or worried: relieved over the possibility that
the leaders did not regard the threat as sufficiently serious to warrant
precautions; or worried over the possibility that they had either neglected to take precautions, or — even worse — decided that precautions would do no good, since the authorities wouldn't care much if a
few Jews at prayer were roughed up and their synagogues desecrated.

The day continued uneventfully, to the obvious relief of the assembled Jews. Finally, when it looked as though the danger had passed,
we left, and my son dragged me to a rock concert. It was his revenge,
he said, for my making him sit through the cantor. I put tissue in my
ears and wrote this account, while my son, along with several thousand Russian kids, bounced up and down to the pounding amplifica-
tion of twenty local bands doing their best to outscream their American
counterparts.

As I looked out into the sea of Russian faces, I wondered how many of these kids harbored anti-Semitic attitudes. It would be hard to grow up as a Russian in Leningrad without having been influenced first by the anti-Zionist propaganda of the Communist party and now by the even cruder anti-Semitism of the ultranationalists. Indeed, the newly vocal anti-Semites were quite clever in co-opting the term "anti-Zionist." They simply broadened its vernacular usage to extend beyond hatred of Israel to hatred of all Jews. But it was still the "Zionists" who "brought communism to Russia." It was the Zionists who caused the Chernobyl disaster, the economic downturn, the closing of churches, and the "moral decay" of the Russian soul. It was the Zionists who got all the advantages — by being sent home first when there weren't enough oranges or meat.

I wondered, as I looked at these kids, whether our new friend Vladimir — a twelve-year refusenik who was trying to join his wife and daughter in Stamford, Connecticut — was correct when he told us emphatically, "There is simply no future for Jews in Russia. We were persecuted under the czars and under the commissars. Now we will be persecuted under the new order, because those in power realize that they must make their peace with nationalists, not with the Jews."

He explained that anti-Semitism is smart politics in Russia. It allows those in power to deflect blame from themselves and onto the perennial scapegoat. It encourages those seeking power to create broad-based populist coalitions, which naturally include anti-Semites and exclude Jews. "There are many more anti-Semites than there are Jews," he said, "and no one ever lost popularity for refusing to stand up for the Jews. In fact, you lose influence if you are perceived as a friend of the Jews. It is better politics to be a friend of the anti-Semites."

The only solution, Vladimir insisted, was for all Jews to emigrate. He did not understand the religious Jews who wanted to remain in Leningrad to continue the Jewish presence there. He admired their zealousness, but he believed their quest was hopeless. "Don Quixotes in *payess*," he called them, a reference to their ultraorthodox sidelocks. After our return from the Soviet Union, even *Pravda* acknowledged that anti-Semitism was growing rapidly in the Soviet Union and that "it affects the whole of Soviet society and its efforts at political, economic, and social reform."[8] (Also after our return, I made numerous calls on Vladimir's behalf and later learned, during our September visit to Moscow, that Vladimir had been granted an exit visa in early September and was on his way to Connecticut.)

From Leningrad, Elon and I traveled to Bucharest, Romania, where our hotel room overlooked the student demonstrations in University Square. There are hardly any Jews left in Romania, but there too a Jewish issue has emerged. I met with one of the leaders of the National Salvation Front, Professor Silviu Brucan. Brucan had stood up to Ceausescu and had been arrested by the dictator. Now, following Ceausescu's execution, Brucan was running for the legislature. One of his opponents, the vice president of the National Christian Peasants party, had been a member of the Nazi Iron Guard during World War II. His party "exposed" Brucan's Jewish ancestry, by plastering posters with stars of David superimposed on his quoted words. Brucan eventually had to resign his position as a member of his party's executive, in order to avoid hurting the party in the election. The former Nazi proudly retains his post as vice president of his party. In post-Ceausescu Romania, it is apparently better politics to have a Nazi background than a Jewish background.

From Bucharest we flew to Prague, where President Vaclav Havel has repeatedly condemned anti-Semitism. There is virtually no trace of anti-Semitism in the Czech portion of his country (where it was once rampant), but it remains widespread in Slovakia, where nationalistic parties praise Hitler for having established an "independent" Slovakian government during the Nazi occupation.

We then drove on to Poland, where the Solidarity labor movement had gained control over the government just a year earlier. In Poland, I learned that a prominent right-wing professor had recently expressed concern that "presently Jews are beginning to dominate in the Polish political establishment and in the editorial staffs of many newspapers," despite the reality that the average age of the few remaining Polish Jews is over seventy. Another right-winger raised the specter of the Auschwitz crematoria when he said that "each of us would happily roast one Michnick on a grill." Adam Michnick — an assimilated Jew — is a former dissident who went to prison for his courageous opposition to Communist party chief Wojciech Jaruzelski and had been a longtime adviser to Lech Walesa. I had met Michnick in 1987, when he was trying to gather support for Walesa's efforts on behalf of Solidarity. Now even Walesa has begun to attack Michnick and another long-term adviser with a Jewish background as "pluralists and intellectuals" — code words in Poland for Jews. Recently Walesa said that "sometimes it is Jews who create an anti-Semitic atmosphere in order to get into the limelight," but he denied that there is "any anti-Semitism here in Poland."[9] I guess that is a backhanded compliment to the remaining Jews of Poland: they haven't sought the lime-light recently.

One of the most striking aspects of the visit to the new Eastern Europe is how much the people seem to be preoccupied with Jews. Considering the fact that in Poland, Czechoslovakia, and Romania there remain fewer than twenty-five thousand Jews — out of a prewar population of nearly five million — it is remarkable that so much attention is paid to them. As one Soviet commentator recently observed, there is "only one issue: are you pro or anti Jew?"[10]

Nearly a half century after the Holocaust, how can this continuing obsession with the Jews be explained, especially in parts of the world where they were murdered into near extinction? Anti-Semitism also exists in the West, as evidenced by the desecration of cemeteries in France and elsewhere. The difference is that President François Mitterrand of France immediately condemned the desecrations. In Poland, Cardinal Glemp and Lech Walesa (who was elected president in December 1990) have remained worse than sinfully silent;* they have joined the chorus of complaints against "the Jews," as have leaders in Romania and Hungary. Even President Gorbachev had, at least until recently, limited his criticism to one vague comment against anti-Semitism "and all other isms." Only in Czechoslovakia has President Havel done the right thing.

It was President Gorbachev's failure to condemn anti-Semitism forcefully and publicly that stimulated my second trip to the Soviet Union in 1990. I accepted an invitation to deliver a paper to a large conference in Moscow on legal and economic cooperation between our two countries. I was asked to speak about the legal rights of criminal defendants, and I agreed to speak on that subject on condition that I also be permitted to deliver a paper on appropriate governmental responses to anti-Semitism. Permission was granted, and I delivered a talk to an audience of Soviet and American lawyers.

The conference took place during the week of Rosh Hashanah, and before I spoke my son Jamin — who accompanied me on this trip — and I met with Jewish refuseniks and activists in Moscow, all of whom told us that the single most important step that could be taken to protect the Jewish community would be for President Gorbachev to denounce anti-Semitism and the organizations that preach it. Such a

* The pastoral letter of January 20, 1991, took back with one hand virtually everything it gave with the other. See the footnote on page 160.

denunciation would make it clear, as it has not been up to now, that the Soviet and party leadership do not support the attitudes and actions of the private anti-Semites.

With this in mind, I extended the following invitation to President Gorbachev in my speech and in a published open letter:

> I invite President Gorbachev to join me at the Moscow Synagogue during the Rosh Hashanah services. I urge him to ascend the pulpit of that venerable old house of worship and use the occasion to condemn anti-Semitism in the most unequivocal of terms. Just as Pope Paul went to the Rome Synagogue to declare that he "deplores the hatred, persecutions and displays of anti-Semitism directed against the Jews at any time and by anyone," President Gorbachev should announce that anti-Semitism has no place in Soviet politics or Soviet life.
>
> Come to the synagogue, President Gorbachev, and condemn anti-Semitism, thereby demonstrating to your people that Soviet Jews are first-class Soviet citizens in the new world of *perestroika*.[11]

I knew, of course, that Gorbachev, who has never even attended a Russian Orthodox church service, was unlikely to go to a synagogue. But I thought that my invitation would put the issue of his condemning anti-Semitism on the table at the conference. After my talk, an American lawyer in the audience asked how many Soviet lawyers would be willing to sign a letter to Gorbachev urging him to condemn anti-Semitism. Most of the Soviet lawyers in the audience raised their hands. We immediately circulated a letter and obtained their signatures.

I then tried to get the conference organizers to allow me to ask the delegates either to vote a resolution urging President Gorbachev to denounce anti-Semitism or to let me announce that signatures were requested for a letter from a majority of the delegates. But the organizers were reluctant to do anything that might embarrass their hosts.

I had just about given up on getting our message to Gorbachev, when serendipity struck. President Gorbachev made an unscheduled appearance at the closing dinner of the conference, the night before we were leaving Moscow. Because I had a bad cold, I almost stayed back in my hotel room instead of going to what I thought would be a boring official dinner in the Kremlin Palace. But Jamin persuaded me to go. As we were sitting down to start our meal, president Gorbachev walked in and delivered a twenty-minute speech to the two thousand delegates on the need for economic and legal cooperation between our countries. When he finished, everyone expected him to leave as quickly and quietly as he had entered, because he was involved in ongoing controversy with the Supreme Soviet over economic reforms. But instead of leaving, Gorbachev sat down and began to eat. I noticed that no one at the dais was talking to him, and so, mustering up all the chutzpah of which I was capable, I got up from my table near the rear of the Palace Hall, walked up to Gorbachev, and asked if I could have a few minutes of his time. I fully expected to be stopped by security guards before I got near the president, but no guards were present.

President Gorbachev said he would be delighted to talk to me, and he extended his hand as I introduced myself. The American chairman of the conference — former secretary of state and attorney general William Rogers — appeared uncomfortable with my assertiveness, but Gorbachev seemed to welcome it. I told President Gorbachev that the Americans at the conference all favored increased cooperation, but that there was one thing he could say that would do more to enhance cooperation than any conference. He seemed intrigued and asked me what he could say that would have that effect.

I told him that he should issue a strong public condemnation of anti-Semitism and of organizations like Pamyat which preach it. He told me he thought that would be a good idea, and he promised me that he would make such a statement in the near future.

Gorbachev then added that there were problems of tensions between many of the ethnic groups that comprise the Soviet Union. I told him that I understood this, but that the problem of anti-Semitism was different because it had been governmentally sponsored for so many years. I told Mr. Gorbachev, on a personal note, that if not for czarist anti-Semitism, many of the American lawyers attending the conference might today be Soviet lawyers, for their grandparents might not have emigrated to America.

Gorbachev smiled and asked whether some of those lawyers would consider coming back to help rebuild the Soviet Union. I responded that it would be too late for him to get us back, but that he should not make the same mistake with the current generations of Jewish doctors, scientists, lawyers, and other productive Soviet citizens who wished to remain in the USSR and live lives of equality with Russians.

I said that I hoped it would be possible to end the tensions between the Soviet government and the American Jewish community by finally bringing down the curtain on anti-Semitism in the Soviet Union. Gorbachev agreed that this would be a good thing. He asked for my card. I gave it to him, and thanked him for speaking with me. As soon as I returned to the United States, I wrote President Gorbachev a letter reminding him of his promise and asking him to send me a copy of whatever statement he might make.

While I was in Moscow, Jewish activists talked to me about a complex and divisive issue regarding emigration of Soviet Jews. Before a recent change in U.S. policy, over 90 percent of Soviet émigrés came to the United States, rather than Israel. This was of great concern to the Israeli government, because Israel needs new immigrants, especially the kind of well-educated immigrants who leave the Soviet Union.

Accordingly, there was pressure from Israel for the United States to take steps to discourage Soviet émigrés from moving here. Many Israelis take the position that they must come to Israel as a matter of principle. Many American supporters of Soviet Jewry take the position that they should be free to go wherever they choose.

Once again this difference in perspective demonstrates that the state of Israel and the Jewish people may have conflicting interests on a given issue of mutual concern. In this case, most Jews — Israeli and non-Israeli — would probably prefer that most Soviet émigrés opt for Israel. The disagreement focuses on whether it is appropriate to employ any kind of governmental coercion to achieve that end. Every Soviet activist I have spoken to argues in favor of free choice for émigrés, though they hope that most will opt for Israel.

There is a middle-ground position that I believe is capable of narrowing the disagreement considerably. To understand this compromise, a bit of background is required.

The United States has a rule allowing "political refugees" to emigrate directly to the United States without waiting the long years that others, who are not refugees, have to wait. This rule makes sense, because political refugees — those escaping from repressive regimes — do not have the luxury of waiting for their turn. Émigrés from the Soviet Union to the United States had long been considered political refugees, though this has recently been changed. Émigrés from Israel to the United States have obviously not been deemed political refugees, because Israel is not a repressive society.

The net result of these rules has been that if a Soviet émigré goes to Israel *first,* he loses his status as a political refugee and may not reemigrate to the United States without going to the rear of a long line. If that same Soviet émigré came to the United States first and then changed his mind and decided to reemigrate to Israel, he could do so immediately under the Israeli Law of Return.

This meant that any calculating Soviet emigrant who was not absolutely certain of where he wanted to end up would pick the United States as his first stop. That decision enhanced his options, since he could always go to Israel later. The contrary decision, to go to Israel first, diminished his options, since he could not then change his mind and seek refugee status in the United States.

When this reality was coupled with the false negative image of Israel deliberately conveyed by Soviet authorities, it should not be surprising that so few Soviet émigrés went directly to Israel.

Now matters have gotten much worse. Although Gorbachev is allowing record numbers of Jews out of the Soviet Union, our government has stopped letting them into this country. In September of 1988, the State Department abandoned the long-standing presumption that Soviet Jews were refugees, thus making it harder for them to enter our country. In the fall of 1989, the State Department announced that a special route for Soviet Jews through Rome or Vienna would be closed. The number of Soviet Jews allowed into the United States has slowed to a trickle.

The reason for the change in U.S. policy was never clearly articulated. It may be that the United States was alarmed at the vast numbers of Jewish citizens emigrating from Russia and did not want to absorb them here. It may be that the United States expects or wishes to absorb refugees from other oppressive countries, in Central or South America or Eastern Asia. It could be a sign of goodwill to the Soviets in this age of *glasnost*. Finally, it is possible that the United States is joining forces with Israel so that Israel can get the stream of immigrants it desires.

Whatever the reason, it is wrong to deny Soviet Jews the status of political refugees for at least three reasons. First, there can be little doubt that as the result of a long history of anti-Semitic attacks and rhetoric — by the czars, the commissars, and now the nationalists — Jews are at risk in the Soviet Union today. They fit the criteria of political refugees.

Second, the fact that they have the option of immigration to Israel should not deny them the status of political refugees. The Law of Return is an *option,* not an obligation. Denying Soviet Jews the choice between America and Israel *compels* them to go to Israel. And no Jew should ever be compelled to go anywhere, just as they should never be excluded from anywhere. The memory of the Pale and the ghetto are still too fresh in the Jewish experience to allow others — even the U.S. government — to tell us where we *must* live and where we cannot live.

Finally, to distinguish between Jewish refugees and other refugees, on the ground that Jews can go to Israel, constitutes religious discrimination. It would also require that the United States enter into the controversy over who is a Jew! At the very least, our government would have to accept Israel's definition of who is a Jew (or the relative of a Jew) under the Israeli Law of Return in order to determine whether an applicant for refugee status has the option of going to Israel. Under Israeli law — Israel has no written constitution — it is permissible to ask "who is a Jew." Under our Constitution, however, that is not a permissible question for the government to ask.

The middle-ground position I support is one that both enhances choice and promises greater emigration to Israel. It would require the United States to change its law slightly, by allowing political refugees to retain that status for a year after leaving their repressive country. It would also require the United States to declare that until the level of anti-Semitism is reduced considerably in the Soviet Union, Soviet Jews will be deemed political refugees, as they should be. Thus, Soviet Jewish émigrés could freely start out in Israel, see how they liked it for a year, and *then* make their decision. This proposal would put pressure on Israel to improve the conditions of Soviet émigrés living in Israel. But at least, Israel would get a chance to convince Soviet émigrés to stay — a chance it received too rarely under the previous rules, which pressured most emigrants to opt for the United States.

Day-to-day life in Israel can be tough for the Russian immigrants. Because of the huge surge in Soviet immigration, more Jews immigrated to Israel in the first seven months of 1990 than in any year since 1951. In part because of this surge, Israel's unemployment rate was up to 10 percent. Housing prices rose, driven up by the huge numbers of Soviet Jews with government housing subsidies. Even with these subsidies, the housing shortage was growing serious and solutions were trapped in a morass of bureaucracy.

When I think of these Russian immigrants, I am reminded of my great-grandparents, who made the lonely voyage to a new life, and the frustration they must have experienced. But at least they were free. Freedom is a condition, an opportunity, not a guarantee. Even those few Soviet émigrés who have tried America or Israel and decided to return to the Soviet Union were exercising a freedom unavailable to most Soviet citizens. We must continue the struggle for the freedom of all Jews — indeed, all people — to be able to choose where they will live and how they will live. My conceptions of Zionism and of Judaism both entail choice and opportunity, not coercion and regimentation. The right to emigrate is among the most basic freedoms known to humankind. We cannot rest until it is available to all.

My work on behalf of Soviet Jewry has brought home to me the responsibility that American Jews — the most influential Jewish community outside Israel — have toward world Jewry. In many parts of the world, Jews are in deep trouble. Their condition in countries like Syria, Lebanon, Ethiopia, and parts of Eastern Europe is not much better than it was during prior centuries. In other parts of the world, they are tolerated as second-class citizens, with many rights but little power. In the United States, we have equal rights and considerable power. We can, and do, make a difference in the outcome of elections, both because of our electoral system — winner take all, electoral college, district representation — and because we vote and contribute in higher proportions to our numbers than do many other groups. We have learned Mark Twain's lesson well and have organized along American lines.

As American Jews, we have a moral responsibility to *use* our power in the interests of morality and human rights, and we must not exclude our own brothers and sisters throughout the world. We must work with our government and the government of Israel where possible, but we must work independently when that proves necessary, as we did in the Shcharansky case and in other areas of conflict.

Whenever I think of my responsibility as an American Jew, I recall the tragic meeting between Jan Karski and Justice Felix Frankfurter in 1943. Karski, a Polish Catholic who had recently graduated from the Lvov law school — was a member of the Polish underground who risked his life to tell the world of the Nazi horrors being inflicted on Polish Jewry. Karski volunteered to enter the Warsaw Ghetto disguised as a Jew so that he could recount his eyewitness observations to a skeptical world. He also agreed to be smuggled into the Jewish death camp at Belzec, dressed in an Estonian guard uniform. What he saw, heard, and smelled was beyond imagining. But he recorded every detail in his lawyer's memory: numbers, locations, methods. This is some of what he recorded at Belzec:

Alternately swinging and firing with their rifles, the policemen were forcing still more people into the two cars which were already over-full. The shots continued to ring out in the rear and the driven mob surged forward, exerting an irresistible pressure against those nearest the train. . . .

These were helpless since they had the weight of the entire advancing throng against them and responded only with howls of anguish to those who, clutching at their hair and clothes for support, trampling on necks, faces and shoulders, breaking bones and shouting with insensate fury, attempted to clamber over them. After the cars had already been filled beyond normal capacity, more than another score of human beings, men, women and children gained admittance in this fashion. Then the policemen slammed the doors across the hastily withdrawn limbs that still protruded and pushed the iron bars in place.*

All this while the entire camp had reverberated with a tremendous volume of sound in which the hideous groans and screams mingled weirdly with shots, curses, and bellowed commands.

The floors of the car had been covered with a thick, white powder. It was quicklime.

The moist flesh coming in contact with the lime is rapidly dehydrated and burned. The occupants of the cars would be literally burned to death before long, the flesh eaten from their bones. Secondly, the lime would prevent decomposing bodies from spreading disease.

It was twilight when the forty-six (I counted them) cars were packed. From one end to the other, the train, with its quivering cargo of flesh, seemed to throb, vibrate, rock, and jump as if bewitched. Inside the camp a few score dead bodies remained and a few in the final throes of death. German police men walked around at leisure with smoking guns, pumping bullets into anything, that by a moan or motion betrayed an excess of vitality. Soon, not a single one was left alive.[12]

After Karski completed his extraordinarily risky visits to the Jewish ghetto and death camp, he again risked his life and traveled secretly through occupied Europe to America to try to persuade our government to rescue Jews from the emerging Holocaust. The ambassador of the Polish government-in-exile arranged a meeting between Karski

---

* This eyewitness description contrasts greatly with the bigoted one given by Wladyslaw Sila-Nowicki, in which he says, "Escape was no problem." See Chapter V.

and Justice Frankfurter, who was one of President Roosevelt's most trusted intimates. The purpose of the meeting was to convince Frankfurter that the reports of genocide, which were filtering out of occupied Eastern Europe, were true and that he should communicate that truth to the president.

I recently met with Karski, who now teaches at Georgetown University, and he recalled his meeting with Frankfurter: "One does not forget such an encounter. Every word is emblazoned in my memory." Karski told Frankfurter precisely what he had seen with his own eyes. After Karski spoke uninterrupted for forty-five minutes, providing a detailed first-person account of the Warsaw Ghetto and the extermination camp at Belzec, Frankfurter stood up and began to pace back and forth. Karski recalled that "he seemed to be passing judgment on whether I was telling the truth." Karski had been warned that Frankfurter was "an extremely pompous man who demands respect, if not subservience." Karski waited as the justice paced. Then Frankfurter stopped and looked Karski straight in the eye and said: "A man like me talking to a man like you must be totally honest. So I am. So I say: I cannot believe you."

The Polish ambassador was flabbergasted: "Felix, how can you say such a thing? You know he is saying the truth. He was checked and rechecked in London and here. Felix, what are you saying?"

Frankfurter responded: "I did not say that he was lying. I said that I cannot believe him. There is a difference. My mind, my heart, they are made in such a way that I cannot conceive it."

Karski told me that to this day — nearly fifty years later — he does not understand Frankfurter's purported distinction. He suspects that, deep down, Frankfurter probably knew that he was hearing a truthful account of the horrors confronting Polish Jewry. Why, Karski asked rhetorically, would a Polish Catholic exaggerate what was happening to the Jews?

But Karski thinks that Frankfurter was afraid to acknowledge what he believed, because that would require him to convince others of the truth of Karski's unfathomable image of hell on earth. The justice and presidential adviser was concerned that others would not believe what he believed, thereby damaging his credibility on other issues and in other areas.

Frankfurter did not want to be regarded as one of those soft-hearted Jews who put Jewish lives before the American war effort. He did not want to endanger his valuable credibility with the president over an issue of Jewish sentimentality. And so he said nothing and did nothing, as millions of his brothers and sisters — and their children — were slaughtered.

David S. Wyman, in his monumental work, *The Abandonment of the Jews,* put it this way:

> Supreme Court Justice Felix Frankfurter had regular access to Roosevelt during the war, and he exercised a quiet but powerful influence in many sectors of the administration. Although he used his contacts to press numerous policies and plans, rescue [of the Jews] was not among them. [13]

Historian Jerold Auerbach is no kinder to Frankfurter:

> He concerned himself with affairs in India, Australia, and Vichy, France. Yet Frankfurter would not utilize his position and contacts, or his irrepressible energy, in the service of Jewish needs during the most desperate years of Jewish history. Among the varied causes that engaged his extrajudicial efforts, the rescue of Jews from the Holocaust was not among them. . . . [N]othing was more characteristic of American Jews [like Frankfurter and others near the center of power] than their acquiescence in Roosevelt's "abandonment of the Jews" of Europe. Proximity to power . . . all but silenced them to Jewish tragedy. [14]

The same can be said of most other Jewish political leaders and presidential intimates, such as Herbert Lehman, Samuel Rosenman, David Niles, and Bernard Baruch. Only Henry Morgenthau can be counted as a highly placed friend of European Jewry who was prepared to risk his credibility over a Jewish issue. This is a shameful record of inaction that must never be repeated.

No American Jew today wants his or her epitaph to read — as Felix Frankfurter's must always read in Jewish history — "He could have helped, but didn't. He could have believed, but wouldn't. He placed his own interests before those of his fellow Jews."

My generation of Jewish Americans lives with the dread that we may be the next generation's Felix Frankfurters — that we may be denying the reality of emerging threats to the security, and indeed survival, of large segments of Jewry in Israel and other parts of the world. Perhaps that is why we have been so aggressive on behalf of Soviet, Ethiopian, Syrian, and other endangered Jews. Perhaps that is why we are so unified in our support of Israeli security, while differing on other aspects of Mideast policy. We would rather err on the side of incautious action than cautious inaction. Felix Frankfurter preserved his reputation as a cautious Jewish leader who never cried wolf — even when the wolf was slaughtering his brothers and sisters. While my generation does not want to dilute the credibility of our cries for help, we sound the alarm when we see, or smell, the first evidence of smoke. We are prepared to shout "Fire" in a crowded theater if we believe there is a substantial possibility that the theater is, in fact, beginning to burn. We recognize the risks of being too thin-skinned, but we know the dangers of being too lethargic. As a people who came close to having no future, we guard our future as if it were the present.

In Marion Prison

The Pollard Case and the Crisis in American Jewish Leadership

In NOVEMBER 1985 the revelation that a Jewish American intelligence analyst named Jonathan Jay Pollard had been caught spying for Israel sent shock waves through the Jewish community in America. It was the ultimate *shanda fur de goyim*. The official Jewish response was an overreactive attempt to disassociate "loyal" American Jews from this one "disloyal traitor" who had betrayed not only America in general, but the Jews of America in particular. Spokespersons for the Jewish community attacked Pollard far more stridently than they had attacked non-Jews who had been caught spying for enemies, such as the Soviet Union. It was as if they could prove their own loyalty — and the loyalty of their constituents — by leading the lynch mob against their traitor. Some of the leaders seemed to be shouting "See, I'm a real patriot. I hate Jewish spies even more than you non-Jews do."

Grass-roots Jews reacted with mixed and complex emotions. Some were frightened. They remembered what had happened in other times and other places when Jews had been accused of spying, treason, or treachery against their host countries. They recalled the anti-Semitic reactions to the Dreyfus Affair and, much closer to home, to the Rosenberg atomic spy case. They remembered what had happened when a young Jew named Herschel Grynszpan assassinated a German embassy official in Paris, giving the Nazis an excuse to carry out the notorious *Kristallnacht* in 1938.

But some Jews were also understanding of, if not sympathetic with, a Jewish zealot who put Israel's survival — at least as he perceived it — before the bureaucratic niceties of the classification system. Israel was, after all, a trusted ally of the United States. The two nations exchanged the most delicate intelligence information. What was the big deal, some Jews thought, about giving Israel a bit more information than it was able to get through official channels? They remembered the early days of Israel's struggle for survival, when many Jewish soldiers, returning from combat in Europe, smuggled American weapons to the Zionist military organization Haganah in technical violation of our law. The government winked at such civil disobedience, as it apparently did at even more serious occasional violations, which helped Israel become a nuclear power.

The Pollard arrest, which was front-page news, generated a great debate, mostly *within* the Jewish community, about the nature of Zionism, dual loyalty, and the status of Jews in America. It has also provoked a continuing discussion about the Jewish leadership in this country, and whether it accurately reflects the attitudes and serves the interests of America's grass-roots Jews — both affiliated and unaffiliated.

It was against this background that I flew to an out-of-the way federal prison in Marion, Illinois, in 1988. Marion prison — the maxi-max of American prisons — is so secure that a staple embedded in the sole of my shoe set off the sensitive metal detector. A. M. Rosenthal of the *New York Times* described it, after a visit, as follows:

> Men are not sent to Marion for crimes committed in the outside, but for crimes committed in other prisons: escapes or assaults or murders of other prisoners or guards.
>
> The mission is not to rehabilitate but to secure and control the prisoners.
>
> Meals are delivered through the bars. . . . If inmates have to be moved anywhere they walk guarded and handcuffed through emptied corridors.[1]

The prisoner I was there to confer with was not a murderer or a rapist. He had assaulted no one while in prison. Indeed, the guard who took me through the labyrinth of bars and walls volunteered that he was the "easiest con I remember."

When I entered the triple-secured room — in the presence of a guard — I saw a small man, with a warm smile, glasses, and a receding hairline. What distinguished him most from the other inmates I had observed was the absence of a "prison build" or a "prison walk."

Most prisoners, even those in maximum security, try to work out and keep in shape. Whether for protection against predatory inmates or just because there is little else to do, muscle building is a way of life in prison. Most muscle-bound cons also affect a particular walk and posture, a confrontational strut calculated to display contempt and hide fear. My client, with his stooped shoulders and slouching posture, looked more like a college professor or an accountant than a dangerous convict.

My first glimpse of him revealed a scene incongruous to the prison setting. He was clumsily carrying an electric fan in one hand, while trying to balance a cup of coffee in the other. They were both for me. Marion, in southern Illinois, is both dry and hot, and was especially so during the summer when I visited, because of a drought.

As soon as he saw me enter the small room, Pollard came over and hugged me. His move took me by surprise since I am not a huggy-touchy-feely person, nor do I generally become friendly with my clients.

But Pollard's hug felt comfortable, perhaps because it was so genuine or because he seemed to need it so much. Our face-to-face meeting had been long in coming. Pollard's prosecutors had placed considerable barriers in its path. They did not want me to become one of Jonathan Pollard's lawyers. Pollard had seen an internal memorandum that characterized me as "a Jewish troublemaker." (I think they probably intended that as an insult; I would be happy to see it as an epitaph.) Until I entered the case, it had been handled discreetly and quietly. His previous lawyers had arranged a plea bargain under which the case would be disposed of in tidy fashion without the need for a messy trial. And a full-blown trial would have been messy indeed. The government would have had to declassify much of its secret evidence, and the defendant would have been free to put the government on trial for its duplicity in denying Israel intelligence information to which it was entitled under an executive agreement, and for its incredible sloppiness in maintaining secrets. It might have resulted in at least some of the charges being dropped, as in the case of Iran-contra figure Oliver North, or no criminal charges at all being brought, as in the case of diplomat Felix Bloch.

Indeed, it seems unlikely to me that Pollard would have been convicted of espionage had he exercised his constitutional right to remain silent, since the only real evidence against him would have to come from his Israeli "handlers," and Israel would never have allowed them to testify in open court subject to cross-examination. But his lawyers at that time apparently saw it differently and concluded that his best interest lay in arranging a plea bargain.

The "bargain" went something like this: The government avoided the need to conduct a trial; it was assured a conviction; it obtained full cooperation from the defendant in assessing the damages and fingering other culprits; it secured an agreement from the defendant not to disclose further classified information; and it obtained all rights to the defendant's publications growing out of the events surrounding the case.

In exchange for these valuable considerations, the defendant received a promise that at the time of sentencing the government would recommend that the court impose a sentence of "a substantial period of incarceration and a monetary fine"; this was understood to mean a sentence of less than life imprisonment. The government also agreed to enter into a plea-bargain agreement with his wife, Anne Henderson Pollard.

The maximum possible penalty for the crime of espionage is life imprisonment, a penalty rarely imposed even on those who spy for our enemies and never imposed on those who spy for our friends. Indeed, at the time, the average prison sentence imposed on a defendant convicted of spying for a U.S. ally, like Israel, was less than five years. But since there was always the theoretical possibility that a vindictive judge could impose life imprisonment, and since it was understood that "a substantial period of incarceration" meant something less than life, the government was actually giving something in exchange for what it got.

The other important consideration was the promise to make a plea bargain with Jonathan's wife, Anne. The expectation expressed by everyone — most significantly the defense lawyers who struck the deal — was that Anne would receive a suspended sentence. This was important, because Anne was quite sick with a medical condition that had become exacerbated by her stay in jail between the time of her arrest and her release on bail.

In the end, even these small considerations proved to be empty, since the judge rejected the government's formal recommendation — "a substantial period" — and accepted its real, if implicit, recommendation of life imprisonment for Jonathan. That sentence not only exceeded any prison term ever given for spying for an ally, it also was far greater than the average term given for spying for the Soviet Union and other enemies. Anne's expectations were also dashed when the judge imposed two concurrent five-year sentences on her for being an accessory after the fact.

The government also promised that it would tell the sentencing judge that the information provided by the defendant as part of his agreement to cooperate "is of considerable value to the Government's damage assessment analysis, its investigation of this criminal case, and the enforcement of the espionage laws."[2] That promise — essentially to tell the truth about the value of Jonathan's information — does not seem like something that should have had to be bargained for. But in the game called plea bargaining, everything — including the truth — is up for grabs. Even this minimal promise the government simply broke, in spirit and in letter.

After Pollard submitted to literally hundreds of hours of interrogation sessions and polygraph examinations conducted by the government, the prosecutors asserted that his cooperation "has been offered by defendant belatedly, and without remorse for the crime he has committed." In arguing against any leniency for Pollard on the ground that he had spied for Israel, the prosecutors told the judge that "a moderate sentence would not deter, and may even invite, similar unlawful conduct by others." They contended that if any leniency were shown "because the foreign nation involved is a U.S. ally, a potentially damaging signal would thereby be communicated to individuals, or foreign countries, contemplating espionage activities in the United States."[3]

This argument was widely perceived as intending to convey the message to the judge that since Israel is a popular American ally, with many American supporters, the punishment for spying for Israel must be at least as great as for spying for the Soviet Union. In a subsequent public debate with me about the Pollard case, the chief prosecutor expressed his personal view that spying for Israel may need to be punished even more severely than spying for the Soviet Union, because Israel has many friends in the United States, whereas the Soviet Union does not.

In March 1987, on the day of sentencing, the then secretary of defense Caspar Weinberger submitted to the court an affidavit in which he made the following statement under oath: "It is difficult for me, even in the so-called year of the spy, to conceive a greater harm to national security than that caused by [Pollard]." He argued that "only a period of incarceration commensurate with the enduring quality of the national defense information [Pollard] can yet impart, will provide a measure of protection against further damage to the national security."[4] It does not take any reading between the lines to understand that Weinberger was urging the maximum penalty of life imprisonment — the only penalty that would be "commensurate" with the greatest possible harm to our national security and that would allow the government to keep Pollard confined so long as the information he possessed had any "enduring quality."

When the Pollard story first broke, I was struck by the extreme defensiveness of Jewish public response. I recall watching Leon Weiseltier of the *New Republic* on "Nightline." He said: "I find absolutely nothing understandable about any sympathy for the Pollards. The man is an American traitor." He also said, "Even a perfunctory look at Mr. Pollard's own statements . . . shows him to have a rather twisted notion of what Jewish identity is, Israeli-Jewish identity is, American Jewish identity is. He represents nothing except his own delusions."[5]

Even after the judge imposed the maximum sentence of life imprisonment on Jonathan Pollard and an unprecedented five-year sentence on his wife, Anne, there was a resounding public silence from the Jewish community. I recall hearing the sentence and responding in shock. Pollard had, after all, cooperated; he had pleaded guilty; he had provided information only to a close ally with whom we shared — and were legally obliged to share — the most sensitive intelligence. I knew from my experience as a criminal lawyer that the Pollards had not received equal justice as measured by the sentences given to others who had engaged in similar conduct. What shocked me even more than the disproportionately harsh sentences was the deafening silence of a community that speaks out so loudly against injustices perpetrated on others.

I knew that many individual Jews, even individual Jewish leaders, felt outrage at the excessiveness of the sentence. But the Jewish community seemed frozen into silence by fear. The fear was real to those with whom I spoke. "They will think we are all potential spies for Israel," one leader worried. Another wondered whether the dual loyalty issue would be raised again, if not publicly, then at least in the minds of some government officials.

There was a great deal of speculation — including a considerable amount of armchair psychologizing — about the extreme statements made by Secretary of Defense Weinberger. He had told reporters that Pollard "deserved to be hanged."

Was Weinberger, whose father had been born Jewish, overreacting to espionage committed by a Jew for the Jewish state? Would he have been so vociferous if an Irish American had provided information to the Irish Republican Army, or if a black American had spied for the African National Congress? I doubt it, despite the fact that neither the IRA nor the ANC is a military ally of the United States.

A prominent lawyer who knows Weinberger quite well told me that he had no doubt that "if Weinberger did not feel burdened by his name and his grandfather's religion," he never would have taken the position he did in his affidavit. He explained that throughout his life, Weinberger "has leaned over backwards to show that there is absolutely nothing Jewish about him."

While this speculation was swirling about the publicly silent Jewish community, an important realization came over me. I was not at all frightened about charges of dual loyalty or Jewish lack of patriotism. It was simply not an issue for me, or — I suspected — for my generation of Jews. I discussed the Pollard case with my Brooklyn friends, especially with Carl, who works in areas requiring security clearance. My friends were all outraged by the sentences, and utterly unafraid of speaking out. The fear was emanating from Jews a generation older. As I thought about these generational differences, I decided to act.

I wrote an op-ed column for the *New York Times* which was critical of both the life sentence imposed on Pollard and the pervasive silence of the official Jewish community. This is part of what I wrote:

> Even discounting for the hyperbole, Secretary Weinberger's appraisal sounds irresponsibly overstated. It is easy "to conceive" of far greater harms to our national security. First of all, the information could have been sold to an enemy rather than an ally with whom we in fact share the most sensitive intelligence information. Second of all, the material given to Israel seems to have been primarily regional and tactical rather than global and strategic. According to press reports, the most dramatic information involved the coordinates and radar protections of the P.L.O. headquarters in Tunis. Other data related to Iraqi and Pakistani nuclear capabilities as well as other threats to Israeli security. Some of the items probably could have been obtained by Israel through proper channels, while others probably should have been shared with our most important military ally in the Mideast.

All countries spy on friends and foes alike. Certainly the U.S. spies on Israel through satellites, electronic eavesdropping and human sources. And Israel spies on us. The big news in the Pollard case is that the Israelis got caught.

This is certainly not to justify the crimes committed by the Pollards. But their crimes should be placed in a realistic perspective. Instead, there seems to be an overreaction by all concerned.

One reason for this overreaction is that everyone seems frightened to speak up on behalf of a convicted spy. This has been especially true of the Jewish leadership in America. The Pollards are Jewish. . . . The Pollards are also Zionists, who — out of a sense of misguided "racial imperative" (to quote Jonathan Pollard) — seem to place their commitment to Israeli survival over the laws of their own country. . . . American Jewish leaders, always sensitive to the canard of dual loyalty, are keeping a low profile in the Pollard matter. Many American Jews at the grass roots are outraged at what they perceive to be an overreaction to the Pollards' crimes and the unusually long sentence imposed on Jonathan Pollard.

Any American, regardless of his or her religion or ethnicity, has a right — indeed an obligation — to speak out in the face of a perceived injustice. As an American, and as a Jew, I hereby express my outrage at Jonathan Pollard's sentence of life imprisonment for the crime to which he pleaded guilty. I am confident that when passions cool and a sense of perspective returns many Americans will come to regard Jonathan Pollard's sentence as excessive.[6]

The response to my article was immediate and electric. I received hundreds of letters, phone calls, and personal messages. There were, of course, the usual hate letters. But this time, I also received a different kind of message: "Thank God you had the courage to speak out," as if it had taken special courage to say about the Pollard sentence what I had been saying about excessive sentences imposed on black and other minority criminals for nearly a quarter century.

The calls came as well — calls rather than letters, to avoid leaving a paper trail — from some of the silent Jewish leaders (and even from some government officials quietly dissatisfied with the excessiveness of the sentence). The calls from the Jewish leaders were the most interesting.

"It was important," one said, "for someone like you — who has a long record of concern about justice and equality in sentencing — to *legitimate* the feelings that many of us are experiencing. We, who are not experts in sentencing, can't be sure whether our anger over the sentence is ethnocentric — whether it grows out of feelings of *rachmones* for a fellow Jew — or whether it can be generalized. And unless it can be generalized, we have no right to express it. You have shown us that it *can* and *must* be generalized and that we have a *right* to be outraged."

A "right to be outraged"! Only a community supersensitive to the precariousness of its position in a society would think that way. This is not to say that thinking about the right to feel emotion is necessarily a bad thing. It does reflect a level of morality — a need to *be* right, not only to *feel* right — that is commendable. But it also reflects an excessive concern for what "they" will think.

What "they" — the gentiles, the establishment, our bosses, our non-Jewish friends, those who sit in collective judgment about our acceptability in "their" society — what they will think still dominates the public actions and expressions of our Jewish establishments. Perhaps that is why Jewish organizations have been so successful in this heterogeneous society of which Jews comprise barely 2.5 percent. However, this extraordinary organizational success has not come without a price.

In order to ascend the ladder of Jewish leadership, one has to be, if anything, acceptable to "them." One has to look acceptable, talk acceptably, think acceptably, and act acceptably. (Indeed, until quite recently, most Jewish leaders even seemed to have acceptable names — names such as Stephen Wise, Louis Marshall, Oscar Straus, Cyrus Adler, Julian Mack, Balfour Brickner, and Phillip Cowen, which didn't even sound Jewish. No -bergs, -steins, or -witzes to evoke the stereotypes.)*

---

* Lewis Weinstein, a great Boston lawyer and Jewish raconteur, wrote the following lyric for a show back in 1934:

> The Brotherhood has for its aim,
> A Rabbi with an Anglo-Saxon name,
> Whose application we'll have to decline,
> If his name ends in -vich, or -sky or -stein.
> In addition to being an Aryan,
> He must be a Parliamentarian,
> Who can table a motion and squelch hubbub,
> And who'll represent the Temple at the Rot'ry club.

> — Lewis Weinstein, *Masa: Odyssey of an American Jew*
>   (Boston: Quinlin Press, 1989), pp. 305–306.

The "rites of passage" to Jewish leadership have produced a certain type of Jewish spokesman (the gender specificity is deliberate). He is moderate in his politics, successful in his business or profession, exercises considerable restraint in criticizing the powers that be, is slow in seeing anti-Semitism in every slight, picks his targets thoughtfully, leans over backward to criticize Jewish bigotry, is careful to maintain credibility with "them," is calculated in his use of language, avoids making enemies (even of his and our enemies) unless they are outside the relevant "them," and — most important — takes few risks. As the first important American Jewish leader, Louis Marshall, characteristically put it: "The greatest wisdom consists in knowing when to remain silent."[7] (Generally, Jewish leaders are also very wealthy, as if the Jewish establishment sometimes forgets that Tevye the milkman in *Fiddler on the Roof* is mocking his townsfolk when he sings "If you're rich, they think you really know!")

Jewish organizations — such as the American Jewish Congress, the American Jewish Committee, the Anti-Defamation League of B'nai B'rith — work from the top down rather than the bottom up. They are not democratic in the sense that democratic leaders are supposed to discern and act on the attitudes and feelings of their grass-roots constituents. To the contrary, proper attitudes and feelings are supposed to be formed at the top after consultation among the elite and then transmitted down to the faithful. Obviously, grass-roots feelings are relevant to the elite — leaders can never be too far out of touch with their constituents — but they are only one of many considerations in constructing the "official" position of the community.

Jewish leadership in the *galut* — outside Israel — has always maintained an elitist position vis-à-vis the grass roots and the relevant "them," whether "they" were the Egyptians, the Babylonians, the Spanish, the English, the Arabs, the Polish, or even the Nazis. Indeed, the American Jewish Committee — the first major Jewish organization — was established expressly as a "committee" of "leading" Jews and not as a representative congress, precisely to avoid the appearance that it was a grass-roots political organization. Its president, Louis Marshall, ran the organization — indeed the entire Jewish community — with such elitist autocracy that it was said that "American Jewry was all but governed by 'Marshall law.' "[8] The influence of the masses relative to the elite has been a matter of degree, depending on the nature of the host community, the relative education of the masses, the dangers confronting the community at a particular time, and many other factors. The American Jewish community at the end of the twentieth century may be the most democratic in *galut* history on a relative scale, but it is far from democratic on any absolute scale.

The theory of cautious American Jewish leadership, of leadership concerned more about what "they" will think than what is right to do, was tested only once in our history. That test came during the Hitler period, and the theory, along with the leaders who practiced it, failed miserably. Felix Frankfurter was not alone in remaining silent about Hitler's atrocities. The other major Jewish American leaders — even those in official leadership roles — continued their cautious approach.

Rabbi Stephen S. Wise was the acknowledged leader among the Jewish rabbinate. And Joseph M. Proskauer, a former judge and prominent lawyer, was the most important lay leader, heading the American Jewish Committee. Neither was willing to confront the silent and apparently unconcerned Franklin D. Roosevelt about the ongoing Jewish tragedy in Europe. They feared that by raising this "Jewish issue" in the midst of a great "national" crisis, they might be pitting Jewish interests against American interests, thus raising the dreaded specter of dual loyalty.

Justice Louis Brandeis, who was generally quite assertive on Jewish issues, advised Wise that "it would make a bad impression on Roosevelt, in the midst of his overwhelming responsibilities . . . to trouble him with our, in a sense, lesser problems." Felix Frankfurter assented in this view. Even when Wise eventually received authoritative documentation of the Nazi plan to exterminate the Jews of Europe, he agreed to a State Department request not to publicize the information until it could be confirmed. By the time the information was confirmed and Jewish leaders spoke out, it was too late for most of the Jews of Europe.[9]

Wise realized that his cautious approach was risky. Early on in the Nazi crisis, he wondered "how much we have gained by walking warily, by being afraid to be ourselves, by constantly looking over our shoulders to see what impression we make on others."[10] Yet he continued to worry lest his advocacy of Jewish rescue make a bad impression on Roosevelt and the other "real" Americans, who, he assumed, would not care about the Jews of Europe.

Proskauer, of the American Jewish Committee, was worse. He refused even to join Jewish demonstrations against Nazism. "For Jews in America, *qua* Jews, to demand any kind of political action is a negation of the fundamentals of American liberty and equality," he argued, totally misunderstanding the pluralistic nature of American liberty and equality. As one historian aptly put it: "Proskauer asked Jews to accept the status of second-class citizens to earn approbation as first-class Americans."[11]

For that generation of American Jewish leaders, the paramount goal was to avoid conflict between their status as good Jews and as good Americans. They believed that the rescue of European Jews was good for the Jews, but they accepted our State Department's conclusion that it was not good for America — that it should not be an American priority. These Jewish leaders believed that it would be improper for them — as self-defined second-class citizens — to challenge the U.S. State Department and the U.S. president when it came to defining what was good for America. In failing to challenge American priorities, they displayed their misunderstanding of American democracy, which is a process by which all groups try to persuade the decision makers that what is good for them is good for America. Rescuing European Jews should have been an American priority, and American Jewish leaders should not have been embarrassed to fight for that priority, with every resource at their disposal.

Not only did Wise, Frankfurter, and the other Jews who did not want to make a "bad impression" on Roosevelt fail the Jewish people, they also failed President Roosevelt. History will never forgive Roosevelt his abandonment of the Jews. His otherwise outstanding record will always remain tarnished because of what he could have done but did not do. It would not have reflected "dual loyalty" for Roosevelt's Jewish advisers to have urged him to rescue the Jews of Europe. That course of action would have been good for the Jews, good for America, and good for president Roosevelt.

Elie Wiesel understands the concept of loyalty to country and president far more clearly than did Frankfurter, Proskauer, and Wise. When President Reagan was about to travel to Bitburg to honor the graves of Nazi storm troopers, Wiesel took advantage of a White House awards ceremony to urge his president not to go: "That place, Mr. President, is not your place. Your place is with the victims of the SS." Wiesel was not concerned that by "speaking truth to power," he would be making a "bad impression" on the president.[12] He told the president what the president did not want to hear, but the president respected Wiesel — and those for whom he spoke — for his honesty. The president also understood that Wiesel spoke out of loyalty to his country and to his president, as well as to his people. Wiesel tried, and failed, to convince the president that he would be making a terrible mistake — a mistake for America as well as for Jews — by going to Bitburg. A first-class American has a right and a duty to try to prevent his president from making a mistake.

Several years ago, Elie Wiesel flattered me by publicly stating that "if there had been a few people like Alan Dershowitz during the 1930's and 1940's, the history of European Jewry might have been different."[13] Generous as the assessment is, it is an obvious exaggeration. No private citizen alone could have changed the course of Nazism. But Wiesel's statement has made me ponder what I might have done, had I been a "Jewish leader" during the 1930s and 1940s.

When I travel to the places of the Holocaust — Auschwitz, Riga, Budapest, Bucharest, Frankfurt, Przemyśl, Kraków, Warsaw, Lódz — it is almost as if I am trying to travel backward in time. I have asked myself what draws me so often to these Jewish burial sites. On a recent visit to Poland, I finally understood: I *am* trying — on an unconscious level — to go back in time, so that I might be there when my people are being slaughtered. Although I fully realize, on an intellectual level, that I could have done nothing to help, I reach out for any possibility that I might have been able to save even a single Jewish life. It is a fantasy born of frustration, but to me it is very real.

Even with the benefit of hindsight, it is not easy to suggest a definite strategy that would have assured a higher American commitment to Jewish rescue. But silence was surely the worst approach. Efforts should have been made to bring over eyewitnesses — like Jan Karski and some of the Jews who managed to escape from the ghettos and camps — and have them tell their stories to the American public. A Jewish community so rich in communication skills could surely have done a better job of touching the American conscience. American Jews should have done for European Jews what they helped American blacks do only a decade later: make the moral case through dramatic acts of self-denial and civil disobedience. Jewish leaders were not afraid to go to jail for black civil rights. But they were afraid — not physically afraid, but afraid of what others might think — to go to jail, to chain themselves to the White House gate, and to scream to high heaven when the lives of fellow Jews were on the line. While Jewish leaders in Poland and throughout Europe were committing suicide in a futile effort to convey the depth of the Jewish tragedy, no American Jew in government — and there were many in high positions — *even resigned in protest* over American refusal to lift immigration barriers, to bomb the rail lines to Auschwitz, or to take other steps that might have saved Jewish lives. Jewish leaders insisted on maintaining their dignified silence, their caution, and their loyalty to a morally reprehensible American policy, for fear that to act otherwise would make a bad impression on their "hosts." They did not want to spend the reserve of capital — or goodwill — they had built up through generations of model citizenship. They failed to understand that this was the time to use that reserve, and indeed to borrow even beyond the limit of their credit. It was the ultimate proof that American Jewish leaders did not regard American Jews as first-class American citizens, entitled to demand action on behalf of their mortally endangered brothers and sisters.

In his monumental work *The Abandonment of the Jews,* historian David Wyman outlined twelve steps that could have been taken to rescue hundreds of thousands of Jews. Each of these steps was actually proposed during the Holocaust. Some were as simple as notifying the Jews of Europe of the fate that awaited them at Auschwitz and the other extermination camps. As one of the few Jews who escaped from Auschwitz, Rudolph Vrba, later put it: "Would anybody get me alive to Auschwitz if I had this information? Would thousands and thousands of able-bodied Jewish men send their children, wives and mothers to Auschwitz from all over Europe, if they knew?" It was central to the success of the Nazi genocidal plan that the victims be deceived into believing that they were being transported to work camps. Had the truth been communicated to them — by radio, leaflets, or even the specially trained Jewish agents who were eventually parachuted beyond enemy lines — many could have been saved.[14]

Another simple proposal was to open the door — even a bit — to Jewish immigration into the United States, Palestine, North Africa, the Virgin Islands, or any one of a number of locations where refugees could have been out of harm's way. But no one wanted the Jews, even Jewish children, in large numbers.

Other proposals were more complicated, such as bombing the rail lines to the camps and even the gas chambers themselves. John McCloy, then a presidential adviser, was instrumental in preventing any humanitarian bombing designed to save Jewish lives on the ground that all bombing decisions should be made on military grounds alone. He did, however, veto the bombing of an important industrial city in

Germany on the ground that it contained beautiful medieval architecture!

Other proposals that were never implemented included secret negotiations with Nazi allies such as Romania, Hungary, Bulgaria, and Slovakia in an effort to persuade them that it would be in their best interest — especially in the event of German defeat — for them to allow their Jews to escape.

Wyman concludes, after painstaking historical research, that "probably hundreds of thousands" of Jews could have been saved by these and other methods, had they been tried.[15]

But they were not tried, for two major reasons. First, there were many English and American officials who simply did not want large numbers of Jewish refugees to survive the war. They feared that hundreds of thousands of homeless Jews would complicate their postwar plans, would alienate Arabs in Palestine, and would increase pressure to permit Jews to immigrate into their countries. As one such official put it, if even a small number of Jews were rescued, this could "lead to an offer to unload an even greater number of Jews on our hands." This concern was echoed by Anthony Eden and other anti-Semites in high places.[16]

The other principal, and related, reason why proposals that could have saved Jews were not implemented is that American Jewish leaders just did not try hard enough to focus the attention of the world on the tragedy of the Holocaust. As Wyman sorrowfully reports: "American Jewish leaders [were unable] to break out of a business-as-usual pattern. Too few schedules were rearranged. Vocations were seldom sacrificed. Too few projects of lesser significance were put aside."[17]

Jan Karski had been warned of American Jewish indifference even before he left Europe. He was told that American Jewish leaders "won't be interested." "At 11 in the morning you will begin by telling them about the anguish of Jews in Poland, but by 1 o'clock they will ask you to halt the narrative so that they can have lunch." It was exactly how Felix Frankfurter and other American Jewish leaders — not all, but too many — reacted to Karski's report and to later confirmations of the scale of the Holocaust.[18]

I know that I and my generation of Jews would not have — and will never — go about business as usual while Jewish lives are at risk. We will scream, perhaps not to high heaven, but certainly to the highest human authorities. And we will not worry about making a poor "impression" on others, even on presidents, popes, and prime ministers. We have learned the deadly lesson of silence in the face of evil. Too many innocent, powerless people died because of the silence of too many culpable, powerful people, for the tactic of respectful silence ever to be tried again.

Following the tragedy of World War II, Jewish leadership became somewhat more assertive, learning from the chutzpah of the Israeli leadership, which almost never reflects an attitude of *shanda* in front of the non-Jewish world. But in recent years, there has been a tidal wave of criticism directed against the so-called Jewish leadership in America. Many of the nonelected leaders seem too anxious to please our "hosts," too willing to criticize Israel, too apologetic in their defense of Jews and Jewish values. Recently, there was a "revolt" within the American Jewish Congress, which claims to be the largest Jewish defense organization in the United States. (That characterization is grossly misleading, since you have to become a member of the organization to take advantage of its popular and money-saving package tours to Israel and other places of Jewish interest.) One of the chapters of the American Jewish Congress disbanded, issuing a statement that "we are tired of seeing those in the media who oppose Israel quoting our executive director, Henry Siegman. . . ." Siegman — who was appointed, not elected, to his influential job — has been a frequent Israel basher and apologist for leftist enemies of Israel and the Jews. He speaks for no significant segment of the American Jewish community. Yet he holds an office that makes him appear to speak with an important representative voice. A lead editorial in the *Jerusalem Post* recently criticized "deleterious" Jewish "leaders" who display "chutzpa" in "inverse relation" to their importance, and who have joined "the trendy bash Israel crowd." The *Post,* as I mentioned in Chapter V, named this phenomenon "the Siegman Syndrome."[19]

But the problem transcends Israel and indeed any specific issue. It reflects a continuing need by some American Jewish leaders to please their American hosts — to demonstrate that they are good Americans first. The best way to demonstrate this is to follow American trends. If it is trendy in America to bash Israel, they join in the bashing, regardless of how their constituents feel. If it is trendy in America to show uncritical support for Nelson Mandela, then they join this support, downplaying his pro-PLO and anti-Jewish statements. If it is trendy in America to react enthusiastically to the growing nationalism in Eastern Europe, then they join this euphoria, ignoring its potentially devastating impact on Jewish communities in that part of the world.

This defensive and apologetic *shanda fur de goyim* attitude is not reflected by all Jewish leaders, but it is typical of far too many, and it does help to explain the silence of Jewish leaders in the face of the grossly unfair sentence imposed on the Pollards.

I recall discussing the Pollard case with my Brooklyn friends at about the time that Marion Barry, the black mayor of Washington, D.C., was videotaped in a hotel room smoking crack. My friend Murray pointed out the difference between how the black and Jewish leadership responded to crime by "its own." Black leaders, even of mainstream organizations, immediately rallied around Barry, accusing the white establishment of selectively targeting him because of his race. To be sure, it was an overreaction and it damaged the credibility of some black leaders in the eyes of some whites. The important difference is that *they* didn't seem to care so much about what *we* thought. There was no concept of *shanda* in front of the white people.

Murray suggested that maybe we Jews could learn something about ethnic pride and solidarity in times of difficulty from our black fellow citizens. Some of my other Brooklyn friends disagreed, suggesting that the more cautious, universalist approach of the Jewish leadership increases our credibility. "We shouldn't go out on a limb for every two-bit Jewish pol who gets caught in a hotel room with his pants down," argued Carl. But he agreed, as did all my other Brooklyn friends, that the sentence imposed on Pollard was unjust by any standard and that the Jewish leadership should have spoken out on *that* one.

A comparison with the leadership of the American Cuban community may also be instructive. On July 17, 1990, the Bush administration freed a right-wing Cuban who — according to the *New York Times* — is believed by our government to be responsible for dozens of bombings aimed at the Castro regime, including the destruction of a Cuban passenger plane in which seventy-three innocent people were killed. The release of Orlando Bosch came after heavy lobbying by Americans of Cuban background who regard Bosch, said the *Times*, "as a patriot and have made his release a cherished cause." Despite the government's characterization of Bosch as a terrorist willing to "cause indiscriminate injury and death," the administration decided to release him because the Cuban American community, which is influential in South Florida's Republican politics, demanded the release.[20] They, too, did not seem concerned about any *shanda* in front of the Anglos. There is no possibility that our government will even consider releasing Jonathan Pollard, or reducing his sentence, without pressure from the organized Jewish community. Indeed, it is fair to say that the Jewish leadership seemed to *approve* Pollard's sentence at the time it was imposed.

This discernible difference between the cautious, elitist leadership of the Jewish community and the somewhat more expressive, populist leadership of other minorities may help to explain a racist phenomenon that has troubled many. There is, quite obviously, more than enough racism in every community. But the data seem to suggest that racism within the Jewish community is concentrated near the bottom of the socioeconomic scale and rarely is reflected in the leadership of the mainstream Jewish organization. In the black community, on the other hand, there seems to be more overt anti-Semitism near the top of the socioeconomic scale. As Charles Silberman puts it:

> Black anti-Semitism is not just a mirror image of Jewish racism. There is a lack of symmetry in the relationship between blacks and Jews that gives black anti-Semitism a distinctive and troublesome cast. Whereas Jewish leaders are considerably *less* racist (and considerably more sympathetic to black aspirations) than the rank and file, the opposite . . . is true of the black community.[21]

Silberman cites extensive data to support these troubling conclusions.

This phenomenon, to the extent that it may be true, reflects many factors, including the third world foreign policy of some black political leaders. But it also reflects the different hoops through which Jewish and black leaders must jump to attain their status within their own communities.

A Meir Kahane — or anyone expressing views similar to his — could never have achieved a position of leadership in the mainstream American Jewish community. Indeed, it is ironic that even a Menachem Begin or a Yitzhak Shamir — each of whom was elected prime minister of Israel — could never be elected to become head of the American Jewish Congress, American Jewish Committee, Anti-Defamation League, B'nai B'rith, or the United Jewish Appeal.

No one with views about blacks analogous to those of a Jesse Jackson about Jews would have a chance at leadership within the Jewish community. Some might point to former mayor Ed Koch of New York as a Jewish leader comparable to Jackson, but the analogy is flawed.

First, Koch was not a Jewish leader; he was an elected official who is Jewish. Koch would never be elected to head a major Jewish organization. Second, Koch is in no way comparable to Jackson in terms of racism. Koch's bluntness on racial issues stands out *only* in contrast to the statements of other Jewish leaders and elected officials. No one can find in Koch's long and controversial career in the public eye anything remotely comparable to Jackson's remarks about "Hymietown," about Zionism being a "poison weed," or about hearing too much concerning the Holocaust. Nor has Koch ever embraced anyone as overtly racist as Louis Farrakhan. Indeed, Koch repeatedly condemned Meir Kahane and other Jewish extremists and racists who were nowhere near as virulent as Farrakhan and other black anti-Semites whom Jackson has refused to disavow.*

The foregoing description of the dynamics (and statics) of Jewish leadership in America provides the contextual background against which the Jewish leadership's silence over the excessiveness of the Pollard sentence — even in the face of grass-roots concerns — can best be understood.

My op-ed articles on the subject — I subsequently wrote two besides the one cited earlier — lent a certain degree of legitimacy to the feelings of many grass-roots Jews about the unfairness of the sentence.[22] But the Jewish leadership was still concerned about becoming publicly involved on behalf of a self-confessed Jewish spy who had admitted that his loyalty to Israel had outweighed his loyalty to American law.

Pollard denied, of course, that he had placed the interests of Israel over those of his own country. His position was that he had given Israel *only* material that was necessary to its survival but that would not harm the United States — information to which Israel was both legally and morally entitled under the two intelligence exchange agreements executed between the United States and Israel. He pointed out that he had refrained from providing material to which he had access when disclosure, in his view, could harm the national interests of the United States.

* In Jackson's hometown of Chicago, Steve Cokely, an assistant to the mayor, declared that "the AIDS epidemic is a result of doctors, especially Jewish ones, who inject AIDS into blacks." He also stated that there was a Jewish conspiracy to rule the world and that Chicago Jewish merchants whose windows were broken on the anniversary of *Kristallnacht* had broken their own windows to gain sympathy. Jesse Jackson refused to condemn Cokely by name, and simply said that it was "time to consider the source and move on."

In retrospect, this perceived ability to distinguish between classified materials that could, or could not, harm American interests may appear naive. But there can be little doubt that this distinction was central to Pollard's state of mind when he gave the information to Israel.

But the press was not playing it that way. Pollard was painted in a number of different ways, each more unflattering than the other. At first, he was portrayed as a spy for hire who had stolen secrets for the money. When it was learned that he first provided secrets without even asking for money and that it was his Israeli handlers who insisted that he must be paid — what turned out to be insignificant sums in the spy market — the story changed somewhat. It became obvious that if Pollard had been motivated by money, even in the slightest degree, he could have sold secrets to enemies of the United States for exorbitant sums. Now he was portrayed as a confused zealot who had fantasized — even bragged — about spying for Israel years before his first delivery. There were allegations of mental instability, drugs, and alcohol. When these reports proved exaggerated to the point of falsity, yet another picture emerged, this time of an exceptionally talented intelligence officer who had become an exceptionally talented and valuable spy.

The Jonathan Jay Pollard whom I met that day in the Marion Federal Penitentiary did not fit into any of those rigid molds. At the time I first met him, he had already been in virtual solitary confinement for more than two and a half years, since his sudden arrest on November 21, 1985. He may, therefore, have been a somewhat different person from the one who, as early as June 1984, had approached the Israelis with classified information pertaining to Iraqi nuclear capabilities and agreed to provide further documents. He had been through a great deal since that time, from the excitement of providing classified documents about Syrian plans for chemical warfare on the Golan Heights, to the euphoria of seeing other information he provided turned into a successful pinpoint bombing operation against the PLO headquarters outside Tunis, to the nightmare of being caught, abandoned by Israel, pleading guilty, and being sentenced to life imprisonment without a word of public protest by the Jewish community.

Since those dark days in March of 1987 when Pollard and his wife were sentenced, momentum had begun to build slowly on Pollard's behalf in both Israel and the United States. There were still no public criticisms of the life sentence by the Israeli government or by the major American Jewish organizations. But the mood was changing perceptibly in Pollard's favor.

After my first op-ed article appeared in the New York Times, Pollard's father called me and asked whether I would be interested in joining the case as one of his son's lawyers. I was reluctant, because in my article I had expressed my belief that Pollard's actions were unjustifiable and that he deserved a reasonable prison term.

Dr. Morris Pollard, the defendant's father and a noted microbiologist at Notre Dame University, said that his son understood my perspective on his case and very much wanted me to represent him in an effort to get his sentence reduced. I agreed to speak to Jonathan over the phone. Jonathan and I spoke, in a monitored telephone conversation, about my views of his case, and he urged me to become his lawyer. I agreed.

More than a year after becoming Pollard's lawyer, I was finally given permission to visit him in prison, but only in the presence of a prison official who would monitor our conversation to assure that Jonathan did not disclose any classified information to me. This issue was clearly a pretext designed to hinder my ability to defend my client, since the same officials who required the presence of a monitor at our lawyer-client meeting had allowed Jonathan unmonitored meetings with a rabbi well known for his strident support of Israel, as well as with an Israeli journalist who owed no loyalty to the United States. I was furious at the Justice Department's deliberate erection of artificial and unnecessary barriers between me and my client, but it was imperative that I meet Jonathan. And so, without waiving any rights to challenge the conditions imposed, I traveled to Marion to meet my client face to face (to face — including the monitor).

The monitor's role was, of course, a total farce. He was a very nice man, an assistant warden of some kind who had no training in classified material. There was no way he could know whether the information we discussed had ever been classified, or if it had, whether it had become declassified. He simply sat there reading Time magazine while we talked about the case.

What we talked about primarily was Jonathan's feelings about his situation and his realistic goals for the future.

There was a great deal of agitation among the pro-Pollard groups for immediate action. These groups, to whom Pollard had become something of a hero rather than a victim of an excessive sentence, wanted Jonathan and Anne free *now*. Many of Pollard's most zealous supporters seemed to have no realistic sense of the possible. They were working hard for his release and they wanted to see results. I was coming under some pressure because I had not achieved anything dramatic since entering the case. My brother, who was representing Anne Henderson Pollard, had accomplished a great deal in working out an arrangement with the Justice Department under which Anne was transferred from Lexington prison in Kentucky to a hospital setting in Rochester, Minnesota, for an independent assessment of her medical condition and then to Danbury prison in Connecticut.

Jonathan assured me that he was more than satisfied with our approach and our timetable. He was most concerned about his wife's health and her prospects for release. He wanted all the energy to be devoted to her and nothing to be done in his case that could jeopardize her situation.

We talked about his feelings toward Israel. I didn't know what to expect from a man who had sacrificed his reputation, his family, his freedom, perhaps his life, for a beloved country, which then abandoned him — refusing him entry into its embassy when he was about to be arrested, refusing to bargain on his behalf after he was imprisoned, and, most painful, refusing to acknowledge the importance of his efforts on its behalf. (It is difficult to fault the Israelis for not having allowed Pollard into their embassy, since the American pressure to turn him over for trial would have been, in the end, impossible to resist.)

But Jonathan was unambiguous about his feelings toward Israel. They were pure love and dedication of the kind that survives rejection. He was "disappointed," of course, with certain statements attributed to some of his former contacts, handlers, and friends. But this was to be expected in the international game of life and death which only Israel, as a nation, had been subjected to during the past forty years. He had criticism, to be sure, of individual Israelis, much as he had of individual Americans. But he loved both countries, the one that had abandoned him and the one that imprisoned him. This was not the time for personal recrimination. It was the time for plans for the future.

Our plans for the future would include legal actions to vacate his guilty plea on the grounds that it was improperly coerced and that the plea bargain was broken by Secretary Weinberger's implicit demand for life imprisonment. Our plans would also include — in fact, would focus on — my brother's efforts to get Anne out of a prison setting and into a hospital where she could obtain the medical care she so desperately needed. We would continue to focus public attention on the disparity between the sentences imposed on the Pollards and the far more lenient sentences imposed on those who spied for the Soviet Union and other enemies of the United States. Finally, we would be alert to any possibilities for a political or diplomatic resolution of the problem, ranging from commutation of sentence to a "spy swap" of the kind that resulted in Natan Shcharansky's freedom.

As part of the campaign to maintain public interest in my imprisoned and virtually incommunicado client, I spoke all over the country about the injustice of the sentence. In the course of these speaking engagements I was repeatedly asked — often quietly and with an apparent sense of shame — why "so many Jews" were "getting in so much trouble." The reference to "so many" obviously included the recent spate of Wall Street cases, involving Ivan Boesky, Michael Milkin, and other prominent investment bankers with Jewish names and Jewish communal identification, as well as the large number of Jewish politicians, such as Stanley Friedman, Bess Meyerson, and Donald Manes, who had made headlines of late.*

I recall giving a speech in New York at an event sponsored by the Jewish Theological Seminary of America during the week the Boesky scandal broke. At the time, the seminary's library was named in honor of Ivan Boesky and his wife, and the concern over the *shanda* was palpable in the audience.

I explained that the recent visibility of Jews in the bad news was simply a natural phenomenon attributable in part to increasing Jewish opportunity. Most criminologists agree that crime, especially white-collar crime, is largely a function of opportunity, access, and situation. Fifty years ago, there were very few Jewish bank embezzlers because there were very few Jewish bank employees. Similarly, there were very few black embezzlers and very few female corporate criminals.

In earlier times, there were few Jewish "insiders" capable of trading on inside information; few Jews high enough in the intelligence community to become spies; and few prominent Jewish politicians in positions to make headlines for becoming corrupt. With the broadening of employment prospects comes the opportunity to do both

* A recent hate letter reads: "Milkin, Boesky, Levine . . . and throw in the 'Jewish Queen' Leona Helmsley would be . . . executed . . . in the old days [of] 1938–1940 in Germany. We have to send a message to the Jews to shape up or else!"

good and bad. It is fair to say that for every indicted Jewish businessman or financier there are hundreds of exemplary Jewish businessmen.
For every accused Jewish spy there are thousands of loyal Jewish Americans who support their government while working for the State Department or Defense Department. For every crooked Jewish politician
there are numerous honest Jewish public servants. We should do
more, of course, to instill living Jewish ethics into our educational
programs, where they might influence future business behavior.

This may touch on some raw nerves, because Jewish organizations
sometimes honor the wealthy without inquiring into the sources of
their wealth. We sometimes do not make the effort to see what is
plainly before our eyes. We are blinded by the facade of money, and
it is incumbent upon us to look beyond that facade. A criminal conviction does not change a person's morality. It only changes his legal
status. If we know things about people who are not yet convicted, we
cannot blind ourselves to those realities.

There are important lessons about corruption to be learned from the
recent news stories. They are of the good news–bad news variety. The
good news is that decades of effort have paid off. Jews are now in
positions of power and authority. The bad news is that Jews are just
like everyone else, and a certain small proportion of them will exploit
their power and become corrupt.

I recently recalled a conversation I once had with the great rabbi
Joseph Soloveicheck. We were sitting next to each other on a plane
traveling between New York and Boston, and the conversation turned
to Bernard Bergman, the prominent Jewish nursing home operator
who had been honored by many Jewish organizations and who was
then under indictment.[23] Rabbi Soloveicheck bemoaned the lack of
ethical teaching by many Jewish religious leaders. He focused his
criticism most directly at some Hasidic rabbis, who, he said, were in
unique position to instill high ethical values in their followers but had
neglected to do so.

This conversation came to mind when a federal judge, named I. Leo
Glasser, was imposing a sentence on a client of mine, who happened
to be a Hasidic Jew. The defendant had been convicted of burning
down unoccupied buildings for insurance and had been sentenced to
six years in prison. My brother and I had taken over the case on appeal
and had secured a reversal of his conviction. We had then arranged a
plea bargain under which he could be given no more than a six-month
sentence. We argued for a suspended sentence. The defendant had

received many letters from fellow Hasidim attesting to his fine character. The judge decided to suspend the sentence and allow him to perform community service. In imposing that sentence, Judge Glasser turned first to the large number of Hasidim who had come to court in support of their fellow Hasid and then made the following statement to the defendant:

> . . . There are many things which I am tempted, thoroughly tempted to say to you this morning, and through you, to the many people who are sitting out in this courtroom, some or maybe all of whom are authors of many letters which I have received. It will be with great difficulty . . . that I will refrain or attempt to refrain from saying the many things that I am tempted to say to you regarding your presence here which, I suppose, some persons might characterize as being a *chilul hashem* [a disgrace to the name of God]. I won't elaborate upon that.
>
> I wish that sometimes there would be more emphasis placed on substance rather than on form. Sometimes one wonders whether all the learning, all the studying that I have been reading about in all the letters that I received from deans of institutions of learning in Talmudic studies, that sometimes more emphasis is placed on form and not enough on substance.
>
> And I say to you as I [suspend your sentence] that you should regard yourself as being extremely fortunate. And I also say to you . . . that the words that you recite three times a day and the code and the laws that you study should be thought of in terms of what those words mean and what they are intended to move us to do in terms of the kind of life we lead.[24]

Judge Glasser's admonitions should be taught in every class on Jewish ethics. It sums up the proper relationship between the forms of Jewish observance and the obligations of those who observe, to live their lives in accordance with their prayers and learning.

As I write these words, Jonathan Pollard remains in prison. His wife, Anne, has been released after serving more than three years of her five-year sentence — the longest time spent in prison by any American for a comparable crime. The time in prison away from each other has taken an enormous toll, especially on their relationship. A divorce has resulted, as both Jonathan and Anne try to look to a more positive future.

In March of 1990, we filed a motion to vacate Jonathan Pollard's guilty plea and sentence.* In June of 1990, after I made a two-hour presentation to the Commission of Law and Social Action of the American Jewish Congress, that organization finally broke the silence of the organized Jewish community on the Pollard case. The American Jewish Congress issued the following statement:

> It has been brought to our notice that substantial allegations have been made that the fairness of the sentence imposed upon Jonathan Pollard and the manner in which the government has dealt with his case were affected by the fact that Pollard is Jewish and the nation he is charged with aiding is Israel.
>
> Because such allegations raise questions of concern to the American Jewish Congress, we support the call for full, open and fair hearings before appropriate tribunals on these issues.[25]

In announcing this change of position, the president of the American Jewish Congress remained as cautious as ever: "We're not saying Dershowitz has proved his case. But he presented enough material to say it's worth looking into."

And on July 4, the West Coast B'nai B'rith passed a statement that Pollard's treatment "was unduly harsh and excessive in that his sentence was unprecedented and far more severe than those historically meted out to most persons convicted of espionage."[26] Other organizations soon followed suit, and I predict that soon the organized Jewish community will begin to speak in one voice against the injustice of Pollard's sentence.

I will not give up until Jonathan is free. No American who pleaded guilty to spying for an ally has ever served as much time in prison as Jonathan has already served. Every day he languishes in prison constitutes a continuing injustice. It also constitutes an affront to American Jews and to Israel. I am convinced that if Pollard were a non-Jew who had spied for a non-Jewish country, he would not be in prison today.

In a recent discussion with my Brooklyn friends, the question was raised as to whether Jonathan Pollard's situation is a reflection of anti-Semitism. That is a complex and difficult question, permitting of no one-syllable answer. The government points to the fact that several of those who prosecuted the Pollards were Jewish as proof that anti-

---

* At the time of this writing, the trial judge's denial of this motion is on appeal.

Semitism has played no role in the case. That is an unconvincing and insulting argument, which itself smacks of not-so-subtle anti-Semitism. Governments have traditionally used "house Jews" to go after other Jews in cases raising the specter of possible anti-Semitism. Julius and Ethel Rosenberg were prosecuted by Jewish lawyers and sentenced to death by a Jewish judge. The murder prosecution of the Jewish Defense League for the death of Iris Kones was also conducted by Jewish lawyers before a Jewish judge. In the Soviet Union, the Soviet Anti-Zionist Committee was long headed by Samuel Zivs, a self-hating Jew who made a career of being among the most virulent anti-Semites in the Soviet Union. Asking Jews to prosecute fellow Jews as a test of their loyalty to country does not demonstrate the absence of any anti-Jewish elements in a case.

I do believe that Jonathan Pollard's Jewishness and the fact that he spied for the Jewish state are the most important factors explaining the otherwise inexplicable disparity between the sentences traditionally given those who spy for allies and the draconian sentences imposed on Jonathan and Anne Pollard. Though no single prosecutor or prison official may be an anti-Semite, or anti-Zionist, the net result of the discriminatory treatment received by the Pollards can fairly be characterized as anti-Jewish.

Shortly before his death, Justice Arthur Goldberg and I had a long series of conversations about the Pollard sentence and whether it was a product of anti-Jewish attitudes. Goldberg had written a letter to the *Jerusalem Post* critical of Pollard's actions. I called him to say that it was the sentence that was really unjust, and I provided statistics about other sentences for comparable crimes. Goldberg told me that he knew Aubrey Robinson, the sentencing judge, and that when he next spoke to him he would ask him why he had imposed so severe a sentence. A few weeks later, Goldberg called to tell me that he had discussed the sentence with Judge Robinson and that Robinson had told him that one of the reasons he had imposed the life sentence was that Pollard had provided Israel with information about American satellite monitoring of joint Israeli–South African missile tests. Goldberg told me that Judge Robinson — who is black — was infuriated by Pollard's link to the Israeli–South African connection and took that into consideration in sentencing him. "Robinson doesn't like Israel very much, though he's no anti-Semite, but this South Africa thing really got his dander up," Goldberg told me. I responded that this was the first I had ever heard of

Pollard's having provided Israel with any information about South Africa. He asked me to check and I did.

I told Pollard's local Washington lawyer about my conversation with Goldberg, and he made a special trip to Marion to discuss the issue with Pollard. Pollard told him that he never provided any information to Israel about South Africa. The Washington lawyer also asked the lawyers who had represented Pollard in his plea bargain, and they confirmed that there was nothing in the prosecution's papers accusing Pollard of providing any such information.

I related this to Goldberg, who was flabbergasted. He agreed with me that it seemed that someone in the government might have whispered false information into Judge Robinson's ear. Even more outrageous was that the nature of the false information, relating as it did to the Israeli–South African connection, seemed to have been calculated to pander to Judge Robinson's presumed hatred for nations that dealt with the apartheid government of South Africa. "If the government pandered to Robinson's anti-Zionism," Goldberg told me, "it was inexcusable." He promised me that he would seek an appointment with Attorney General Richard Thornburgh and would also try to have lunch with Judge Robinson. Three days after this last conversation — and before he could follow through on what he had promised — Justice Arthur Goldberg died in his sleep.

If Judge Robinson's excessive sentence against Pollard reflected an anti-Zionist bias, the response to Pollard's crime in some government offices was even worse. Since the Pollard case, Jews have been subjected to super-scrutiny by some intelligence agencies. Security clearances have been denied, agents in the Mideast have been reassigned elsewhere, questions have been raised about the "dual loyalty" of some American Jews.

The essence of anti-Semitism — of all bigotry — is overgeneralization. To generalize from Jonathan Pollard to "all" or "most" or even "some" Jews or Zionists is to engage in anti-Semitic stereotyping.

No Jew or Zionist should have to undergo, or should agree to submit to, any special loyalty test because of Pollard's crime. Many loyal Americans support the right of other foreign entities or organizations to exist. These entities range from the African National Congress, to the Irish Republican Army, to the Vatican, to the Chinese student movement, to various governments-in-exile. Some of these entities — unlike Israel — are not supported or recognized by the

U.S. government. Yet loyalty tests are not required of Americans who support the right of such entities to exist and thrive.

If the continued existence of Italy, France, or England were threatened by enemies sworn to destroy them, many loyal Americans of Italian, French, and English background would rally to their support. And no one would question their loyalty to America. If one American of English descent were to provide classified information to Great Britain, there would be no call for loyalty checks on all American government officials of English descent.

Jews should demand no less than to be treated like other loyal Americans. Jews should not be afraid to defend a co-religionist like Jonathan Pollard against discriminatory treatment. Jews should insist on a leadership that no longer reflects the frightened attitude of *shanda*. At this point in our history, we are entitled to a bold leadership, which insists that even the most guilty among us be treated with the equality that our laws require. By insisting that Jonathan Pollard be treated no worse than others who behaved similarly, we demonstrate our loyalty to America and to its principle of equal justice under law.

Jews in a "Christian America"

The Separation of Church and State

THE SEPARATION of church and state in America is the foundation on which the first-class legal status of American Jews rests. The wall of separation, along with our history as a nation of immigrants, is what makes America so different for Jews. The absence of a state-supported church, and the prohibition against religious tests for public office, guarantee that Jews will never merely be tolerated, as we were — and still are — in other "host" nations. There is no hierarchy of religions in America. All religions and nonreligions are deemed equal before the law. But what is guaranteed by law is not always implemented in practice.

This reality was brought home to me many years ago by my son Elon, when he was beginning the fifth grade. We were living in Palo Alto, California, at the time, and he was attending the local public elementary school. One day he came home asking: "Daddy, do we *have to* believe in God in America?" I explained to him that everyone is free to decide for himself. But I wondered where the question had come from. We had frequently discussed God and whether anyone could be certain of His existence, and Elon had even expressed some doubts about his own beliefs with the usual preteen questions: "How could God make a kid die?" he had asked after a neighborhood friend had died suddenly of an intestinal blockage.

But in our family one didn't *have to* believe in anything, so long as he obeyed certain rules. Elon told me that he was in assembly and the principal wrote the words of the Pledge of Allegiance on the blackboard and told everyone to recite it. When Elon read the words "under

God," he asked his teacher whether a person who didn't believe in God had to say those words. I asked Elon why that question had not come up in his school in Cambridge, where I knew he had recited the pledge. "I always thought the words were 'under *guard*,' " Elon said, because we were fighting a war in Vietnam and because that's the way "God" is pronounced in Massachusetts. Elon told me that his California teacher said that "everybody had to recite the whole pledge. That was the law. She then asked me whether I believed in God. I didn't know what to say, so I said it was none of her business. She told me to discuss it with my parents."

I asked Elon whether he felt uncomfortable about what had happened, and he said, "A little bit." I told him that as a kid, I used to enjoy reciting the pledge, though I also misunderstood its words. I thought the second word was "pledga" and the third was "legence." But we didn't have the words "under God" back then. Elon came back to his question: "Do I have to believe in God and do I have to say those words?" I assured him that he didn't have to believe or say anything. I took out a casebook on constitutional law and told him the story of the Jehovah's Witnesses and the wartime flag salute case that I had studied on my first day as a law student. A divided Supreme Court had ruled that public schools could not compel a religious objector to salute the flag. The majority had used ringing language that seemed to cover the pledge as well, especially with its added words "under God":

> If there is any fixed star in our constitutional constellation, it is that no official, high or petty, can . . . force citizens to confess by word or act their faith. . . . To believe that patriotism will not flourish if patriotic ceremonies are voluntary and spontaneous instead of a compulsory routine is to make an unflattering estimate of the appeal of our institutions to free minds."[1]

As I gave him the book, I remembered another famous Supreme Court decision by one of the strongest advocates of separation of church and state — the late justice William O. Douglas. In his opinion Justice Douglas declared: "We are a religious people whose institutions presuppose a Supreme Being."[2] I showed Elon this decision as well.

Now Elon was completely confused. What did "presuppose" mean? I told him it was a fudge word, intended to be ambiguous. We talked about the contradiction of a society that was at once religious and at the same time built a wall of separation between church and state.

Elon asked about "In God We Trust" on our coins. I told him that we also had salaried religious chaplains in Congress; that the Supreme Court opened its sessions with the invocation "God Save This Honorable Court"; that Christmas is a national holiday; that the Supreme Court had upheld state laws that require every store to be closed on Sunday, even if the owner celebrated his Sabbath on Saturday.

I told Elon that my father had once been arrested for keeping his small store open on Sunday. His defense was that he was obliged to keep the store closed on Saturday and he could not afford to close it two days each week. The judge asked my father if he attended synagogue on Saturday. When my father answered in the affirmative, Judge Barshay — who was himself an Orthodox Jew — fired back with a question: "So if you were in synagogue last Saturday, what was the Torah portion of the week?" Fortunately for my father, he answered the judge's "pop quiz" correctly. The judge let him off, but gave a steep fine to another store owner who tried the same defense but couldn't come up with the right answer to this wholly improper religious test. This, I explained to Elon, was the compromise nature of our society when it came to religion and God.

Elon wanted to know whether the God in the Pledge of Allegiance's "under God" was the same God we prayed to when we said the *Shma Yisrael*: "Hear O Israel, the Lord our God, the Lord is One." I copped out by telling him that this was a theological dispute. But Elon was adamant: "I don't want to say that the United States is under God if they mean someone else's God." I asked him what would be wrong with that, as long as we were free to pray to our God. Elon explained that if he were forced to say that this country is under the Christian God, not the Jewish God, then that would be admitting that "this is their country more than it is ours."

Elon had, in his own childlike way, articulated the concern that most Jewish Americans share about being treated as second-class citizens, who are merely tolerated rather than accepted as first-class citizens. I asked Elon if he would feel better if the God were "ours," but not the God of some other kids in the class. He said it wouldn't be fair in either case, and he told me that his class included some Chinese, Japanese, and Hispanic kids and he didn't know who their God was.

We discussed whether it was fair for a public school to get into these issues and to divide kids along religious — or nonreligious — lines. We agreed that a public school was not the proper place for religious differences to be played out.

Fortunately, the Palo Alto public school provided a relatively tolerant environment for dissent. My son returned to school and told his teacher that he didn't want to say "under God" during the pledge. The teacher told him to discuss it with his parents and get their approval. When he told the teacher of our discussion, he was assured that there would be no problem. Other than a few "weird glances," as he put it, from classmates and an occasional tease, Elon was none the worse for his small act of civil disobedience.

Susan Shapiro was not so fortunate. Just before Christmas several years ago, the seventeen-year-old high school senior refused to stand for the Pledge of Allegiance during her daily homeroom exercises. She told me later that her teacher had then embarrassed her in front of the students by comparing her actions to "spitting on the Star of David."

Susan was quite upset, particularly at the calls she had gotten the morning after the story appeared in the local press. "Dirty Jew bastards, too bad you weren't put in the ovens," said an anonymous caller. "Go back to Israel where you come from," another caller screamed at the Massachusetts native. Some calls contained specific threats to injure or kill Susan unless she stood up during the flag exercises. She eventually had to secure police protection and leave school for a while.

I agreed to help Susan vindicate her right to refuse to stand. Several proposals were then pending — including a constitutional amendment — to require "voluntary" prayer in the public schools. Similar proposals continue to be advanced on a regular basis. The assumption underlying these proposals is that prayer can indeed be voluntary — that there will be no pressures on anyone to join in the public prayer. The reaction to what Susan Shapiro did raises profoundly disturbing questions about that assumption.

Standing for the flag salute is also supposed to be voluntary — as a matter of law. But as a matter of fact, there are practical pressures to conform. It probably would be worse in the context of prayer. Well-intentioned teachers might ask students why they aren't joining their classmates: "Are you an atheist or a Communist?"*

---

* I recall my own experience when I was "sworn" into the bar. I decided to "affirm," rather than "swear" to God — as was my right. One of the judges on the panel asked me whether I was an atheist. I explained that it was precisely because I was religious, and my religion forbade swearing, that I was affirming. He seemed a lot more satisfied with that explanation than he would have been if I had said I was an atheist.

When the Polish government recently restored prayer in the public schools, some of the nation's Protestant minority complained that official school prayer — which would be

Most elementary and high school students hate to be singled out. Many will simply conform, even if it violates their own (or their family's) religious or conscientious beliefs. Will this be truly voluntary prayer? Or will it be prayer coerced, if not by law, then by official and unofficial pressure?

Many of Susan's detractors pointed to the fact that her homeroom teacher was a comparatively sensitive person with an excellent reputation for tolerance. That's precisely the point! If a sensitive teacher in heterogeneous Massachusetts can contribute to the kind of atmosphere of intimidation that Susan experienced, imagine what less sensitive teachers in more homogeneous regions of our nation might do to a student who didn't want to join in voluntary public school prayer.

Other critics pointed out that Susan hadn't been able to articulate persuasively the reasons underlying her decision. But constitutional rights are not reserved only for the sophisticated and articulate, nor are they limited to political or religious radicals. (Susan says she would have voted Republican, as her parents did.) Eventually we won the case: Susan was allowed to remain seated during the pledge and the teacher was required to inform the students that Susan was within her rights. Susan returned to school, but not without some bitter memories.

The issue raised in Susan's case was played out on the national level during the George Bush–Michael Dukakis presidential campaign in 1988. Candidate Bush made a political issue out of Governor Dukakis's veto of a mandatory Pledge of Allegiance law, even though his state's supreme court had rendered an advisory opinion that such a law would be unconstitutional.

A number of states experienced the divisiveness of introducing mandatory observances into the classroom during the early 1980s, when several state legislatures enacted laws requiring public school teachers to conduct "voluntary" prayer in the classrooms, and providing that the prayers would be rotated among the various religions. This is how it worked in one school. On the first day, the Catholics were given their turn and a student recited the Lord's Prayer. Several Protestants complained that he was reciting the "wrong" version. The next day, the teacher asked for a Protestant volunteer; several hands went up, and the teacher had to pick one. The third day, a Jewish kid was

Catholic — would make them second-class citizens. Consider what that makes the Jews of Poland.

picked, but another Jewish kid said that he didn't count because he was Reform. Two weeks into the experiment, a kid from the Unification church tried to volunteer, but the teacher said that the "Moonies" were not "'an acceptable" religion because they would use their time to proselytize others. All hell broke loose, and lawsuits were brought.

When the Massachusetts supreme judicial court ruled such a law unconstitutional, many teachers heaved a collective sigh of relief as they got back to *teaching* about religious wars, rather than trying to prevent them.

The school prayer experience demonstrates the reality that we have changed from a relatively homogeneous nation of white Protestants — all the Founding Fathers shared that background — into the most heterogeneous, religiously diverse society in the history of the world. (The religions of our original Native American populations were, of course, ignored, as were their political rights.) Our broad constitutional language, deliberately designed to adapt to unanticipated changes, must be read with this new reality in mind.

Jews often take pride in the cliché that we are a Judeo-Christian country. It is a false pride and it creates a false sense of security. The very concept "Judeo-Christian" is a seductively dangerous one, implying that Judaism is an incomplete religion and that the Judeo becomes complete only when it merges into the Christian. It is also not true demographically that we are a Judeo-Christian nation, if that phrase is intended to convey some numerical hierarchy. Jews constitute a tiny — and comparatively shrinking — percentage of our population.[3] We are not entitled, by our numbers, to be ranked up there with the Christians. Nor should we accept the second-class status that such ranking entails, even if second class is deemed preferable to third or fourth class.

It is true that the American legal system derives much of its content from the Old Testament, and in that respect it is Judeo-Christian (and also Muslim). When we were growing up, my friends and I would take great pride in discovering the Jewish sources of American laws, such as the privilege against self-incrimination,[4] the requirement of two witnesses for certain types of crime, and the very idea that punishment must be proportionate to the crime committed. But there are many other sources as well. Every society punishes murder, robbery, and rape. And every society praises honesty, charity, and virtue. It is when we get to the controversial and divisive specifics — abortion, homosexuality, euthanasia — that there is conflict between the Judeo-Christian sources (at least as they are interpreted by some) and current laws and constitutions (at least as they are interpreted by some). A law is neither presumptively valid or invalid just because it derives from the Judeo-Christian tradition. We should not read too much into the Judeo-Christian nature of our society, nor derive too much solace from the fact that we, as Jews, are included in it.

Jews must insist on being regarded as first-class citizens who are equal in every way to Christians and others. As a people, we have become accustomed to accepting toleration as the highest form of welcome. During previous "golden ages" of exile, Jews were tolerated in Spain, Poland, some Arab countries, and later England and France. But each of these host countries had an "official" church and only adherents to that established religion were first-class citizens. All others were, at best, tolerated. And mere toleration means, at best, second-class status.

We accepted second-class status and toleration because we had experienced much worse — even in countries as civilized as England (which expelled us), Spain (which converted, expelled, and executed us during the Inquisition), Russia (which moved us to the Pale of Settlement), Switzerland (which forbade us to own land), and France (which emancipated us legally but discriminated against us in practice). Until America we had never really experienced first-class acceptance, and even that has been of rather recent vintage. Notwithstanding George Washington's famous letter to the Jews of Newport, in which he assured them that mere "toleration" was no longer "spoken of" and that they were equal citizens, a number of states continued to treat Jews as second-class citizens — even prohibiting them from holding office and appearing as witnesses — through much of the nineteenth century.

Repeated efforts were made to constitutionalize the second-class status of Jews by amending the preamble to the United States Constitution, as well as state constitutions, so as to declare that we are a "Christian Nation." From the earliest days of ratification of the Constitution, complaints were voiced that "from the Constitution of the United States, it is impossible to ascertain what God we worship, or whether we own a God at all."[5]

Over the next half century, efforts intensified to amend the Constitution so that it would explicitly state that it was founded on the Christian religion. During the terrible days of the Civil War, momentum developed among mainstream Protestant leaders to reverse "the atheistic habit of separating politics from religion." Preachers argued that the fratricidal struggle was "God's punishment" against those who omitted Him from their constitution.[6]

The National Reform Association was established in 1863 to promote a so-called Christian Nation Amendment. Debates ensued over the precise language to be added. Proposals ranged from the general ("Almighty God") to the particular ("Jesus the Messiah, the Savior and Lord of all"). Finally, a compromise was reached which included both the general and the particular: "Recognizing Almighty God as the source of all authority and power in civil government, and acknowledging the Lord Jesus Christ as the Governor among the nations, His revealed will as the supreme Law of the land, in order to constitute a Christian government . . ."[7]

The president of the National Reform Association and the primary advocate of the Christian Nation Amendment, William Strong, later became a Supreme Court justice. Another "ardent lecturer" for the amendment was future justice David Brewer, as were several governors, senators, and congressmen. As precedent for its demand, the association pointed to President Abraham Lincoln's proclamation of a National Prayer Day during the Civil War, in which he asked all citizens to recognize "the sublime truth announced in the Holy Scriptures."[8]

American Jews organized against the amendment. "Are We Equals in This Land?" asked a headline in a leading Jewish publication.[9] It was a good question, and the answer was not as obvious then as it may seem now — as a matter of law or of fact.

By law, several states still excluded Jews from holding office. After Congress had invited a rabbi to open a session with prayer, a law was passed requiring all army chaplains to be ministers of "some Christian religion," and President Lincoln issued an order "in deference to the best sentiment of a Christian people" that Sunday was to be observed by all military commanders as the day of rest. This led the father of a Jewish Union soldier to write the president:

> I gave my consent to my son, who was yet a minor, that he should enlist. . . . I thought it was his duty, and I gave him my advice to fulfill his duty as a good citizen. At the same time I taught him to observe the Sabbath on Saturday, when it would not hinder him from fulfilling his duty in the army. Now I do not want that he shall be

dragged either to the stake or the church to observe the Sunday as a Sabbath.[10]

The Civil War, like most wars and other crises, provoked (or disclosed) widespread anti-Jewish attitudes on both sides of the Mason-Dixon line. The *Newburgh* (New York) *Journal* complained that "the descendants of that accursed race who crucified the Savior are always opposed to the best interests of the government in every land in which they roam. [The Jews] never enter our armies but for the purpose of depleting the pockets of soldiers." General Ulysses S. Grant picked up on this common theme when he singled out "Jewish merchants" as the worst war speculators, and instructed his officers to keep "Israelites" from traveling with his armies. The *Washington Chronicle* supported Grant's anti-Semitic order, arguing that Jews "have been notorious for [their illegitimate] modes of making money." It did not "believe that there will be found a dozen [soldiers] who will not approve of [Grant's order]." When Grant became president, he apologized to the Jewish community, but while the war continued, so did rampant anti-Semitism.[11]

The spirit of American egalitarianism eventually prevailed. Lincoln refused to support the Christian Nation Amendment, despite the wartime hysteria in its favor. Post–Civil War efforts similarly failed to win approval, vigorous lobbying notwithstanding. The Christian Nation Amendment remained a viable issue until 1945, when the National Reform Association finally dissolved. The most distinguished historian of this effort summarizes the Jewish contributions to religious pluralism in the United States as follows:

> The expansion of religious liberty was not an inevitable result of the [constitution]. . . . Religious liberty had to be fought for. . . . Not only were there discriminatory state laws to be eradicated, but federal practices had to be monitored constantly lest the Constitution be converted into a Christian document. Though few in number, unorganized, with their membership seduced by secularism, and against the advice of those who counseled silence or compromise, certain Jewish leaders insisted upon equality before the law. The Jewish presence in America and its vigilance were significant factors in broadening the definition of religious liberty.[12]

The only small victory achieved by the advocates of the Christian Nation Amendment was a phrase smuggled into an 1892 Supreme

Court decision by Justice David Brewer, who spent much of his life attacking non-Christians. The son of a Christian missionary to Turkey, Brewer became an informal Christian missionary in his own nation. He went around the country speaking against the evils of "Mormonism, Mohammadanism and heathenism." His biographer described him as "a missionary's son . . . until the end," a "dogmatic ultra conservative," an elitist and a segregationist. He was also a judicial activist who injected his personal and religious views into his court opinions.[13]

Brewer misused the vehicle of a conventional immigration case that happened to involve a Protestant minister to issue the dictum he had been preaching for decades: that "this is a Christian Nation." That dictum was utterly gratuitous to the decision in the case, as was his quotation from sources declaring that "mahomet" and "the Grand Lama" were "impostors."[14] Brewer's bigoted decision was a low point in American judicial pronouncements and is not cited by other courts in support of the false proposition that "this is a Christian nation." It is widely regarded as a judicial embarrassment — the personal opinion of a religious bigot in robes.

But in 1988, a "bunch of kooks" — as former senator Barry Goldwater characterized them — proposed the enactment of a resolution in Arizona declaring the United States to be "a Christian Nation . . . based on the absolute laws of the Bible."[15]

On May 19, 1988, the leader of the group wrote the following letter to Justice Sandra Day O'Connor:

> Republicans are making some interesting advances in this heavily controlled Democratic area. Some of us are proposing a resolution which acknowledges that the Supreme Court ruled in 1892 that this is a Christian Nation. It would be beneficial and interesting to have a letter from you.

This is how Justice O'Connor replied:

> You wrote me recently to inquire about any holdings of this Court to the effect that this is a Christian nation. There are statements to such effect in the following opinions: Church of the Holy Trinity vs. United States; Zorach vs. Clauson; McGowan vs. Maryland.[16]

Were Justice O'Connor a law student she would have received a D-minus for her answer. The last two cases contain no statements to the effect that this is a Christian nation. Their thrust is entirely to the contrary. If a lawyer practicing before the Supreme Court were as sloppy with his citations as Justice O'Connor was with hers, he would be properly rebuked. The first case is Justice Brewer's infamous immigration decision, decided in 1892, when the voting population of this country was composed almost exclusively of white Protestant males. From that time to the present, the nature of our nation has changed dramatically.

Modern Supreme Court decisions have recognized this change in our national character. Since 1892, the court has not referred to this nation as "Christian" or "Protestant." Indeed, the justices have gone out of their way to be inclusive. For example, when Justice William O. Douglas sustained a New York program permitting public school students to be released for an hour each week for religious instruction, he specifically gave as an example of religious accommodations "a Jewish student [asking] his teacher for permission to be excused for Yom Kippur."[17] Yet this was one of the decisions miscited by Justice O'Connor as containing statements to the effect that this is a Christian nation.*

When her letter was disclosed, Justice O'Connor issued a statement regretting that it has been "used in a political debate," and the Supreme Court media office said that O'Connor "had no idea" that the letter would be used politically. But the request to Justice O'Connor — stating that it would be "beneficial" to have a letter from her as part of a Republican proposal to enact a Christian Nation resolution — made it clear that she was being asked to write her letter specifically for use in a political campaign.

Justice O'Connor's letter was circulated as part of that campaign, and her miscitation of cases was relied on in a resolution enacted by the Arizona Republican party, which begins, "Whereas the Supreme Court of the United States has holdings to the effect that this is a Christian nation . . ."[18]

Justice O'Connor should be ashamed of herself for aiding and abetting religious bigotry. Fortunately, her judicial opinions do not reflect the bigotry of her political friends in Arizona. She has, for the most part, written opinions in support of the separation of church and state.

*   *   *

---

* In at least one case, a justice said — in passing — that "we are a Christian *people*." But he then quickly added in the same sentence that we are a people who accord "to one another the *equal right* of religious freedom" (emphasis added). *United States v. MacIntosh,* 283 U.S. 605, 625. Justices Holmes, Brandeis, Stone, and Hughes dissented. Justice O'Connor failed to mention this case.

Despite the important role played by Jews in preserving the separation of church and state in America, we are currently in danger of once again becoming a tolerated religion in a society in which Christianity is the "official" religion. The signs are all around us. When I meet with my Brooklyn friends, we often compare our perception of this issue. Some of the cynics among us argue that we are indeed second-class citizens and will always remain in that status, at best. They point to the fact that it is almost always better to be a white Anglo-Saxon Protestant when applying for any job. As Murray Altman once put it: "It is even better to have a Wasp name when you're applying for a job as rabbi in some congregations."

All of my friends have personally experienced the second-class status they feel. They have been passed over for jobs that were given to less qualified non-Jews. They have felt the sting of rejection in some social settings. They see the real America in which they live. They point to the fact that we have never had a Jewish president, vice president, speaker of the House, or chief justice. Again Murray: "I always knew that the first Jew who ran for president would be an Episcopalian," alluding to Barry Goldwater. "How many Jews anchor the national, or even local news?" Carl asks. "And look what happened when Hank Greenberg almost overtook Babe Ruth's home run record, and Ruth wasn't even a Wasp."

"This is a Christian country," Bernie says. And he ought to know, since his business is selling Christian religious items. "All you have to do is go to any downtown business area during Christmas and what do you see? Jewish businessmen busily hanging Christmas decorations in their store."

I get angry at my friends, and others of my generation, who seem resigned to accepting less than first-class status. "We are our own enemy," I argue. It's precisely because we are willing to accept discrimination in the selection of our presidential candidates, our anchorpersons, and other high-status positions, that it continues. We can't end it all alone. But we certainly can help perpetuate it by our acceptance of second-class status.

I argue that there is a real difference between what this country may be socially and demographically and what it is *legally* and *constitutionally*. Social and demographic conditions change, but the law and especially the Constitution tend to remain the same. It is crucial, I argue, that we fight the battle for first-class status on all fronts. We must insist on equal social treatment and refuse to accept the "reality" that a Jew — even a Jewish Jew — can never become president. After all, look at France, Great Britain, Italy, and even Austria, which have had Jewish prime ministers. But more important still is to preserve our status as first-class citizens under the law and under the Constitution.

Without first-class *legal* status, there is absolutely no possibility of achieving first-class social or political status. But if we preserve our first-class legal status, everything else is possible.

It is our legal status that is once again in danger. There can be no doubt that an explicit campaign is under way, by the Christian right, to establish Christianity as the official religion of America. This time the means is far more subtle than an explicit constitutional amendment. A two-step process is envisaged: the first step is to have the government "prefer" religion over nonreligion, without expressly preferring or establishing any particular religion. This is a seductive step, especially for religious people. After all, what's wrong with a little religion? No one has ever been hurt, former president Reagan assured us, by nondenominational prayer in school or at public gatherings.

There are practical benefits as well for religious Americans. The state can financially assist parochial schools, so long as money is offered to all such schools. After-school religious programs can be paid for by public funds. And other financial benefits — school lunches, textbooks, school buses — can be given to the struggling religious schools, which surely need them.

But if history is any guide, the first seductive step will inevitably push us toward the second step. Every society that officially prefers religion over nonreligion eventually selects one religion as the true or preferred or dominant one. A government that pays the religious piper tells him which requiem to play.

In recent years, the Supreme Court has repeatedly, though subtly, affirmed the dominant position of Christianity and the secondary status of Judaism. The Sunday closing law cases rejected the argument made by my father years earlier, that to require all stores to close on the Christian Sabbath discriminates against Jews and others who observe their Sabbath on a different day. The Court's 5–4 ruling in March 1984, in the first so-called crèche case, permitted the city of Pawtucket, Rhode Island, to construct and support a Christian nativity scene on public property so long as it was part of a "secular" celebration of Christmas.[19]

In other instances, state primaries held on the Jewish Sabbath or holidays have been approved, despite the reality that such scheduling effectively disenfranchises Orthodox and some Conservative Jews.* The argument implicitly relied on by the Court is that when the majority supports a religious observance — such as Christmas — it *becomes* a secular holiday. But when only a minority supports it, then it cannot be secular and must necessarily be religious. This backdoor method of "establishing" the majority religion by secularizing it is dangerous both to religion and to the Constitution.

The most disturbing manifestation of the emerging second-class status of Judaism in America was the "yarmulke" case, in which the same Supreme Court that permitted nativity scenes in public places ruled that an Orthodox Jewish rabbi, whose name was Goldman, did not have the right to wear an "unobtrusive" yarmulke while serving in the air force as a clinical psychologist. Justice William Rehnquist, writing for a 5–4 majority, agreed with the air force's argument that "standard uniforms encourage the subordination of personal preferences and identities in favor of the overall group mission."[20]

Perhaps the most troubling aspect of the yarmulke decision is that its author (and several other justices) generally sides with religion when the government is supporting it, such as city-sponsored nativity scenes at Christmas. Governmentally approved religious practices (which are almost always *majority* religious practices) are given preference over individual claims to religious liberty (which are generally *minority* religious practices). This is precisely the opposite of what our Founding Fathers seemed to have had in mind.

The effect of this Rehnquistian view of the Bill of Rights is to relegate minority religions, in this case Orthodox Judaism, to a second-class status. The armed forces go out of their way to accommodate their military needs to the religious obligations of the majority, for example, to attend Christmas services and other religious celebrations. But they refuse to accommodate the religious needs of a small minority, and are supported by the courts in a variety of contexts.

The most immediate impact of the yarmulke decision was to discourage Orthodox Jews from volunteering for the armed forces, thus reifying an old stereotype. I know how Rabbi Goldman must have felt, since my friends and I wore yarmulkes until our college years. In my

* Observant Jews were denied the right to go to the polls to vote against the most notoriously anti-Semitic senatorial candidate in recent history. The 1990 Louisiana preliminary election, in which "former" Nazi and Klansman David Duke ran, was held on a Saturday.

Orthodox Jewish neighborhood, a yarmulke was as natural an item of clothing as shoes or a shirt. We wore it everywhere: to school, at work, and even sometimes on the basketball court, held down by a bobby pin. (I recall one of my teammates once pulling an opponent's yarmulke off his head to prevent a fast break; it worked, because the religious law forbids a man from walking more than four paces without his head covered, and so the breaking ballplayer was stopped in his tracks. My teammate got a technical foul.) Occasionally we would be teased about our "beanies," but they would rarely come off, except when we slept or showered, as permitted by religious law, or when we left the safe confines of our neighborhood. My Yeshiva High School principal would occasionally conduct surprise yarmulke inspections, looking for the telltale creases of a pocketed skullcap. I will never forget the dispute among a group of my high school friends over whether to take off our yarmulkes when we attended a burlesque show in Union City, New Jersey. Most of us took ours off, but a couple of my friends kept theirs on. They became extremely self-conscious when some of the fans in the balcony started yelling, "Take it off, take it off."

My mother loves to tell the story of getting a midnight call from the nurse at a Catholic hospital. I had been taken to the hospital after being run over by a truck. I was three years old at the time. My parents had been with me during the day, had put me to bed, and had gone home. The nurse said that I was refusing to take my medicine and that I was screaming something about Miami, Florida. My mother was flabbergasted, since I had never even heard of Miami. She spoke to me on the phone and learned that they were trying to get me to take the medicine without giving me my yarmulke. In those days we called the yarmulke a yami, for short. I was screaming for "my yami," not Miami. I would simply not swallow anything, even medicine, without it. That was how important the yarmulke was to us when we were growing up.

No war was ever lost because a handful of soldiers wore yarmulkes. (Indeed, many soldiers in Israel's superb army wear yarmulkes even in combat.) But wars have been lost because of a nation's intolerance toward a minority religion. Imagine how different the outcome of World War II might have been if the father of the atomic bomb, Albert Einstein, and the Jews who worked on the Manhattan Project had not been made unwelcome by their native Germany.

In the 1943 Jehovah's Witnesses flag salute case,[21] Justice Robert

H. Jackson condemned "village tyrants" who "begin coercive elimination of dissent [and] soon find themselves exterminating dissenters."
He reminded us that "compulsory unification of opinion achieves only
the unanimity of the graveyard."*

These are strong words to quote in the context of what appears to
be a trivial case involving one Orthodox Jewish air force doctor. But
what Justice Rehnquist demanded of Dr. Goldman — surrender of his
religious principles in the name of conformity — may tomorrow be
demanded of Catholics, Muslims, Hindus, and other practitioners of
minority religions. And what is today limited to the military may
tomorrow be extended to schools, courtrooms, and other public places.

My father was once rudely ordered to remove his cap by a federal
judge, when he came to court to watch me argue. The judge quickly
apologized when he learned it was my father he was yelling at. But the
fact that he yelled at all shows how intolerant and ignorant a judge can
be of a minority religious practice, even in a city as Jewish as New
York.

Eventually, Congress enacted a law expressly permitting Jews in
the armed forces to wear yarmulkes, and to my knowledge there has
been no discernible weakening of our national security. But the Supreme Court's insensitive yarmulke decision still stands as the authoritative construction of the First Amendment's application to
such issues.

The lack of sensitivity for minority religions is played out every year
when schools ranging from kindergartens to graduate schools schedule
important events on Jewish (or other minority) holidays, thus requiring many students to choose between family and peers, between religion and success. My younger son Jamin, who was a star soccer player
in high school, had to choose between playing in the league champi-
onship or attending Kol Nidre services on the eve of Yom Kippur.
When he began college, he learned that registration was scheduled for
Rosh Hashanah. I called the Hillel rabbi at the University of Pennsylvania as well as some distinguished alumni, and the date was
changed, but only after I received a nasty call from the school's Jewish
provost — and house Jew — assuring me that *he* saw no problem with
the conflict, that I was being too "sensitive" and "pushy," but that he
was being overruled by the university's non-Jewish president.

---

* Even that is not always true, as evidenced by recent desecrations of Jewish graveyards.

A most extreme instance of this insensitivity recently occurred in California, where a black sociology professor deliberately scheduled a midterm examination on Yom Kippur, refused to schedule a makeup, and warned students who were contemplating missing the midterm that they would have to do a research paper that he would grade "by a stricter standard."

Imagine a white professor in a state university announcing to his class that he intended to grade "by a stricter standard" all black students who attended a memorial service for Martin Luther King. There would be an immediate and justified outcry from civil rights advocates throughout the country. Leading the chorus of criticism would be Dr. Harry Edwards, the Berkeley sociologist who has become the symbol for the demand for sensitivity toward, and equality for, black athletes.

Yet it was Professor Harry Edwards who scheduled the midterm in his introductory sociology class for October 9 — well before the middle of the term — the day of Yom Kippur, the holiest Jewish holiday of the year.

Professor Edwards knew exactly what he was doing, because a memorandum was circulated to the faculty specifying the date on which Yom Kippur fell and setting out the official Berkeley policy of avoiding conflicts between "the academic calendar and religious holy days." He also knew that in a class of five hundred students, there would be a considerable number of Jewish students who, like Naomi Snyder, had always observed Yom Kippur, but felt pressured by Edwards into "backing out of my own religion."[22]

When numerous students complained about Edwards's insensitivity, the professor gave an excuse that would have made a white Mississippi voting registrar proud during the 1950s: "It was the best time for an exam." He then added the following provocation: "That's how I'm going to operate. If the students don't like it, they can drop the class."[23]

This is unequal treatment based on religion.

It is also a violation of both federal and state law. A California statute guarantees state college students the right to take all tests "without penalty, at a time when that activity would not violate the student's religious creed," unless this would create "undue hardship."[24] Professor Edwards could easily have scheduled the exam on another day, or provided for a makeup examination to be graded by the same standards as the regularly scheduled test.

I urged the Anti-Defamation League to bring a lawsuit against Professor Edwards. Jewish students should not have to fight these battles by themselves, especially when the fight was begun by the professor. The ADL wrote to him, but no suit was filed. Jewish students continue to be second-class citizens in Professor Edwards's classes at Berkeley.

Another manifestation of Jewish second-class status is the growing trend toward introducing Christian religious principles into public life. This dangerous trend becomes most evident when religion becomes an issue in elections — as it has in several recent campaigns — and candidates wrap themselves in the cross as well as the flag. Former president Reagan did that so often during the 1984 campaign that his opponent, Walter Mondale, reminded him that the president of the United States — unlike the Queen of England — is not the "defender of the faith"; he is the "defender of the Constitution," which proscribes governmental establishment of religion.

There are, of course, some public officials who see nothing wrong with establishing religion. One current view holds that it would be perfectly all right for each state to establish its own religion, so long as the federal government did not establish a single official religion for all of America. A literal reading of the First Amendment may even support that view. The First Amendment says that *"Congress* shall make no law respecting an establishment of religion . . ." (emphasis added). It says nothing about the states. Most constitutional scholars agree that the enactment of the Fourteenth Amendment, which prohibits the states from denying any person the "equal protection of the laws," now prohibits any state from establishing a religion, but not everyone accepts that reading.

One federal judge, W. Brevard Hand of Alabama, recently ruled that each state may establish its own particular religion, just as it may pick its own state bird, flower, flag, and song. He added that "a member of a religious minority will have to develop a thicker skin if state establishment offends him."[25] The very concept of thick-skinned religious minorities is a manifestation of toleration, as distinguished from equality.

After Judge Hand rendered this harebrained decision, I wrote a column awarding him the "Ayatollah Khomeini award for attempting to divide a country along religious lines." I explored the implications of such a ruling in different parts of our country:

In Massachusetts, the struggle would be between Catholics and Protestants for official recognition. Where I grew up in Brooklyn, the religious warfare would be *among* the Jews: should Orthodox, Conservative, or Reform Judaism become the official religion or should it be a particular Hasidic sect? In Utah, Mormonism would win. In California, the various cults and fringe religions might unite and present a common front. Even if a state settled on Protestantism, there would be the question of *which* Protestant denomination would become the official one? The officially designated religion would then be empowered to have *its* prayers declared the official ones. *Its* churches, and only *its* churches would be paid for by public funds. Members of other "second-class" religions would simply have to develop thick skins in reaction to Judge Hand's thick-headed opinion.[26]

The Supreme Court reversed Judge Hand, characterizing his view as "remarkable" — a judicial euphemism for "ridiculous." But there were some in high places, including former attorney general Edwin Meese, who reportedly supported Hand's view of the establishment clause.

If the election season turns politicians toward religion, then the Christmas season tends to engender religious conflict — or more precisely to uncover the festering conflicts that lie dormant through most of the year. A recent headline in the *New York Times* mirrored captions from coast to coast: "The Season of Peace Brings New Battles on Nativity Scene." The sad story it told was how the issue of governmentally supported crèches was dividing communities along religious lines.[27]

The great tragedy is that this problem need never have reared its divisive head. Many cities and towns around the country had been dealing with the "crèche issue" reasonably, nondivisively, and in a spirit of compromise appropriate to a religiously diverse, heterogeneous society: public officials would sell the crèche to a private organization — a religious, business, or fraternal group — which would then become responsible for displaying it. That is precisely what the city of Pawtucket, Rhode Island, had done prior to the U.S. Supreme Court's decision in March of 1984. Nearly everyone — except a few zealots — seemed relatively satisfied with the compromise. The crèche would be displayed in its usual place during the Christmas season, but it would not be sponsored by the city. To be sure, the compromise was only symbolic, but the issue itself is largely symbolic.

Then the Supreme Court, in a bitter 5–4 decision, sowed the seeds of religious discontent by ruling that Pawtucket could buy back and sponsor the crèche. Nothing was "broke" in Pawtucket, but the Supreme Court insisted on "fixing" it, and in doing so the Court itself created disharmony.

Suddenly everything changed. The spirit of compromise turned into a contest over religious dominance. The court had ruled that a city could own and sponsor a crèche. Few bothered to ask whether their city *should* employ its resources — both fiscal and symbolic — in so divisive a manner.

The war had begun, the opening salvo having been fired by the very institution that is supposed to resolve such disputes — the Supreme Court.

Reducing Christmas tensions would go a long way toward narrowing a divide that has separated Jews from Christians for nearly two millennia. Christmas, the most joyous of holidays to Christians, has been among the most dreaded of days for Jews throughout history. In many parts of Europe it was a time for pogroms and beatings; Jews were to be punished for their refusal to acknowledge the divinity of Jesus. The very idea that the nativity scene — the Christian representation of the divine birth of Jesus — is not a *religious* symbol, as former chief justice Warren Burger declared for a divided Supreme Court, is not only wrong historically and religiously; it is an insult to the memory of the many Jews who were killed for not accepting the divine birth depicted in the "secular" nativity scene.

In light of this history, it is surprising that right-wing Christians who would introduce religion into public life as a first step toward the Christianization of America have garnered support from some unlikely bedfellows within the Jewish community. Some elements of the Jewish right — among them the Hasidic sect known as the Lubavitch Movement — welcome a tearing down of the wall of separation between church and state. These right-wing Jews favor crèches and menorahs on public property, prayer in the public schools, and tuition payment for yeshivas.

That view recently achieved a modicum of support from the Supreme Court in a 5–4 decision regarding Christmas and Chanukah celebrations in Pittsburgh, Pennsylvania. In the Pittsburgh case, the Catholic church had constructed a purely religious nativity scene in the center of the local courthouse, and the town fathers had placed a forty-five-foot Christmas tree in front of the city council building. Not to be outdone, the Lubavitch Movement placed an eighteen-foot Chanukah menorah alongside the Christmas tree. As expected, the American Civil Liberties Union challenged both the nativity scene and the menorah, but not the Christmas tree, which it regarded as part of the secular celebration of Christmas, the national holiday.

Justice Harry Blackmun ruled — in yet another 5–4 decision — that the Pittsburgh crèche was too religious and too isolated from any secular symbols to be deemed part of a secular celebration. He concluded therefore that in the setting in which it stood, it constituted an impermissible establishment of religion. Blackmun then turned to the Chanukah menorah, which stood "in the shadow of" the Christmas tree. After reviewing the history of Chanukah in some detail,* he concluded that it is both a religious and a secular holiday:

> Chanukkah, like Christmas, is a cultural event as well as a religious holiday. Indeed, the Chanukkah story always has had a political or national as well as a religious dimension: it tells of national heroism in addition to divine intervention. Just as some Americans celebrate Christmas without regard to its religious significance, some nonreligious American Jews celebrate Chanukkah as an expression of ethnic identity, and "as a cultural or national event, rather than as a specifically religious event."
>
> . . . The tradition of giving Chanukkah gelt [money] has taken on greater importance because of the temporal proximity of Chanukkah to Christmas. Indeed, some have suggested that the proximity of Christmas accounts for the social prominence of Chanukkah in this country. Whatever the reason, Chanukkah is observed by American Jews to an extent greater than its religious importance would indicate: in the hierarchy of Jewish holidays, Chanukkah ranks fairly low in religious significance. This socially heightened status of Chanukkah reflects its cultural or secular dimension.[28]

This secular characterization led Justice William Brennan — who was the Court's strongest separationist — to complain that Justice

---

* This review drew a somewhat insensitive objection from Justice Anthony Kennedy, who suggested that he would rather remain ignorant of the details of other people's faith, than sit "as a national theology board." Blackmun responded as follows: "Surely, Justice KENNEDY cannot mean that this Court must keep itself in ignorance of the symbol's conventional use and decide the constitutional question knowing only what it knew before the case was filed. This prescription of ignorance obviously would bias this Court according to the religious and cultural backgrounds of its Members. . . ." *County of Allegheny v. ACLU*, 109 S. Ct. 3086, 3112 n.60 (1989).

Blackmun's view of Chanukkah "has the effect of promoting a Christianized version of Judaism."[29]

Getting back to Justice Blackmun — who spoke for the majority — he ruled that in the context of the Christmas tree, the menorah was constitutionally permissible:

> If the city celebrates both Christmas and Chanukkah as secular holidays, then its conduct is beyond the reach of the Establishment Clause. Because government may celebrate Christmas as a secular holiday, it follows that government may also acknowledge Chanukkah as a secular holiday. Simply put, it would be a form of discrimination against Jews to allow Pittsburgh to celebrate Christmas as a cultural tradition while simultaneously disallowing the city's acknowledgement of Chanukkah as a contemporaneous cultural tradition.[30]

Note, however, the careful use of the word "may" in discussing the government's acknowledgment of Chanukah as the Jewish secular equivalent of the secularized Christmas. What if a city decided to recognize Christmas as a secular holiday but not Chanukkah? *Must* it avoid "discrimination"? And what about the secularized holidays of other religious groups? Must they too be celebrated in order to avoid discrimination? These complex and divisive issues were left open and are certain to recur as the season of "goodwill" itself recurs each December.

Despite the "victory" of the menorah, the view that a little bit of religion in government is okay as long as it includes ours "in the shadow" of Christianity is both shortsighted and selfish. It is shortsighted because it fails to foresee the second step toward Christianization. And it is selfish because those Hasidim who propose such steps do not have children who attend the public schools in which the prayers would be recited; nor do they hang around the town squares on which the crèches are exhibited. They attend the yeshivas whose tuition they would like to see the rest of us pay for.

Even some of my Brooklyn friends support government aid to the yeshivas their kids attend. They argue that since they are paying for their neighbors' children's public school education, why shouldn't their neighbors help pay for their children's yeshiva education? They also support the governmental display of the menorah — *if* there is already going to be a Christmas tree or crèche. I disagree with these conclusions, but I understand why my friends would reach them, even though they are not members of the Orthodox Jewish right wing.

Some on the Jewish religious right also join the Christian religious right in favoring restrictions on a woman's right to choose abortion, in opposing gay rights, in favoring the death penalty, and in demanding censorship of sexually explicit material. It is remarkable how some secular Jews who regard U.S. Senator Jesse Helms as a Neanderthal, regard the Lubavitcher rabbi — who shares Helms's right-wing views on virtually every social issue — as the epitome of wisdom. In many parts of the country, liberals who are appalled at denying a woman the right to choose abortion, who oppose censorship, and who fight against prayer in public schools, donate large sums of money to the Lubavitch Movement, which actively supports these views. I suspect that support for the Lubavitch Movement is more psychological than it is political, that it reflects nostalgia for, and guilt over abandoning, the "old" ways. It also seems to reflect a sense that the Lubavitch way is the "authentically" Jewish way, and that secular Jews are not authentic Jews. More important, it reflects the reality that the Lubavitch Movement works very hard at getting Jews to return to their roots. As long as the main impact of the Lubavitch Movement remains psychological, spiritual, and nostalgic, it will continue to be a positive force. But its right-wing agenda of breaking down the wall of separation between religion and government is dangerous to the status of Jews in America. It is bad for Jews, and it is bad for America.

There is a related development from the Jewish right — a development that parallels what is occurring on the Christian right — that is also dangerous to democracy. Some rabbis are now *forbidding* their followers to vote for particular political candidates whose views are inconsistent with their right-wing religious-political ideology. An election ad in the *Jewish Press* announced that several prominent rabbis met and "clearly stated that, according to the Torah, it is forbidden to vote for a radical/liberal like Congressman Stephen Solarz." Steve Solarz is the liberal congressman from my old neighborhood in Brooklyn, and a friend. He is very supportive of Jewish issues, but he has run afoul of some elements of the Jewish religious right because he supports the Equal Rights Amendment, a woman's right to choose abortion, and gay rights. The ad also pointed out that the "Gedolai Torah" — the giants of the Torah — demanded his defeat because he was against current policy in Central America, favored a tax increase, and did not support "preventive detention" of defendants before trial. How these issues were related to "Torah values" was never explained. The ad ended by proposing that the voter "ask your Rav [rabbi] —

find out the truth." It demanded that the voter abdicate his individual vote to the rabbis by asking what it regarded as a rhetorical question: "Do you agree that Gedolai Torah [the giants of the Torah] should be the one to speak out for Klal Yisrael [the Jewish people]?"[31]

The answer in a democracy should be a clear and resounding no! In a democracy, individuals must not abdicate their votes to anyone. They should vote — in private — by their own lights. They should listen to everyone and anyone. But the decision must be left to each individual. (Some Hasidic rabbis living in America have tried to extend their political influence to Israel, by paying for planeloads of Jews who live in America but hold dual citizenship in Israel to fly to Israel and vote in a block for a particular religious party.)

Orthodox Jews who get into bed politically with the Christian right make a big mistake, in my view. The goal of the Christian right is to convert Jews or, at the very least, to relegate them to second-class status in their Christian America. The Christian right, like most authoritarian groups, rejects *choice* as unnecessary in a world where there is only one true path. At the moment there may appear to be a comfortable fit between the Christian right and the Jewish right, but that appearance is belied by generations of history and by the ultimate goals of the contemporary Christian right.

A televised interview I conducted with the Reverend Pat Robertson in 1988, when he was a presidential candidate, aptly reveals both the seductive appeal of the Christian right to some Jews and the danger inherent in too uncritical an alliance.[32] I began by reading back to him one of his own statements: "Christians and Jewish people are the only ones qualified to have the reign." I asked him whether he could vote for a candidate who practiced Buddhism, Shintoism, Islam, or any of the numerous other non-Judeo-Christian religions in this great heterogeneous nation of ours.

His answer was unequivocal: "I never would do it, I never would do it because of the view they take of mankind. . . . Would you want a president who believed that women should commit suttee and jump on the funeral pyre of their husbands?"

I challenged him: "That sounds like the kind of bigotry that you have accused others of having against evangelical Christians." He replied: "You must understand what people believe. The Ayatollah Khomeini has launched a war in which one million people were killed." I interjected: "But he doesn't speak for all Islamic people. He doesn't speak for all Muslims. What if you had a Muslim who agreed with peace and agreed with being anti-Soviet, but who didn't believe in Jesus Christ, but who believed instead in Mohammed, would that disqualify him?" Robertson did not back down: "If you are a strong Muslim, you believe in Kismet; you believe that Allah has determined the destiny of all people. Therefore it is not necessary to alleviate the plight of the poor."

Robertson assumes that all members of a particular faith must necessarily believe in — and presumably act on — the most extreme tenets of that faith. I am certain that there are some Muslim extremists who hold similar biases toward all Christians and Jews. And there are enough extreme tenets and practices in every religion to allow critics to point to some which might seem incompatible with current values.

Indeed, a classic technique of both anti-Semitism and anti-Christianity has been to cull from the Old and New Testaments biblical prescriptions that when taken out of context seem bizarrely out of place in contemporary life. And it was the essence of the anti-Catholic campaign waged against John Kennedy to suggest that all Catholics owed a higher allegiance to Rome than to Washington. That bigoted campaign failed because most Americans insist on judging individuals on their own personal set of beliefs, rather than on the orthodox tenets of the church at which they worship or into which they were born.

Robertson acknowledges that for mainstream Christians and Jews, religious beliefs and practices tend to be individualistic. And he is prepared to vote for members of those faiths on the basis of their own views. But he apparently does not understand that similar variations exist among Americans of non-Judeo-Christian background. That is where his prejudice — literally prejudgment — lies.

We will be a far richer nation when we become mature and self-confident enough to elect as our president any qualified American, regardless of his or her religion or race. Our Constitution demands that "no religious test shall ever be required as a qualification to any office," and it provided that an "affirmation" may be taken instead of an "oath."*

Pat Robertson, who proclaims allegiance to the original intent of the framers, should comply with the spirit of the Constitution. Con-

* Indeed, recent presidents, including George Bush, have violated the express terms of the Constitution by adding four unauthorized words — "so help me God" — to the presidential oath of office prescribed by the Constitution.

ditioning one's willingness to vote for an American on the basis of his or her religious affiliation is simply not the American Way.

Nor am I persuaded by Robertson's elevation of Jews to a special status of tolerance. First, I'm not sure I believe him when he says he would vote for a Jewish presidential candidate. Robertson proclaimed, just a few years ago, that he wanted a president who would rescue the Supreme Court from non-Christian influences. Second, I strongly believe that anyone who holds such bigoted and stereotypical views of any religion — Islam, Buddhism, Shintoism — must hold similarly stereotypical views of Judaism. Those who turn against one religion today may well turn against Jews tomorrow.

This was demonstrated recently by a telling episode — in which Robertson played a role — that revealed how brittle the coalition between the Christian right and the Jewish right really is. The episode grew out of the 1988 motion picture version of Nikos Kazantzakis's award-winning novel *The Last Temptation of Christ.* Although the book's author was Greek Orthodox and the film's director, Martin Scorsese, is Roman Catholic, influential elements within the Christian right targeted the Jews as responsible for making the allegedly blasphemous film. The Reverend Jerry Falwell, Donald Wildmon, and R. L. Hymers, Jr., participated in this orgy of misdirected anti-Semitism. Focusing on the fact that some executives of Universal Films' parent company happened to be Jewish, Falwell warned that distribution of the film might generate anti-Semitism. Wildmon urged that pressure be brought on the "non-Christian" officials who run Universal. And Hymers excoriated "members of the Jewish community who either support or finance the film."[33]

When the ADL asked the Reverend Pat Robertson to condemn these manifestations of anti-Semitism, Robertson responded by saying that the best way to put an end to these charges would be for the ADL to "exercise [its] influence with Lew Wasserman and others at MCA [Universal's parent company] to eliminate this affront to Christianity before the trouble begins."[34] The Jewish community should not have to negotiate condemnations of anti-Semitism out of its "friends."

In 1990, Robertson issued a newsletter in which he emphasized that "all of the controlling principals" of the parent corporations that produced the film "are Jewish." Robertson warned — threatened? — that "if the Jewish community pressed for the removal of Christian symbols and customs in our society, sooner or later there would be a Christian backlash of major proportions."[35]

Robertson is constantly warning Jews not to provoke anti-Semitism by demanding equality, when they are but "a small embattled minority" that needs the support of Christians to survive.[36]

The reason Robertson's message cannot be ignored is that he is still a powerful force within the Christian right — despite his resounding defeat in his quest for the American presidency — and his message to the Jews is that we are indeed second-class citizens who have a right to be tolerated by the Christian majority but no right to demand equality in "Christian America."

Robertson argues that "this country was founded on Judeo-Christian principles" and that Christians and Jews — the only people "qualified" to govern America — are "partners" in the American enterprise.[37] But he insists that the Christian majority is the senior partner and that the Jewish minority retains its share of the partnership only if it does not alienate the Christian majority. This, of course, is simply another way of suggesting that we are tolerated guests in someone else's home. A guest does not have the right to demand that his host remove Christian religious symbols from his own home. But if all persons living in a home are of equal status, no one has the right to impose his religious symbols on the others. If Robertson is correct about the relative status of Christians and Jews in America, then the consequences he suggests flow naturally from his premise. We should return to our grandparents' attitude of *shanda fur de goyim,* a fear of alienating our Christian hosts.

Only if Robertson is wrong — only if we are equal partners in America, along with Christians, Buddhists, Shintoists, atheists, and others; only if there are no senior and junior partners in the American enterprise — are we entitled to demand equality in every aspect of American life. And equality means that no one group's religious symbols be given the imprimatur of government.

Some leaders of the religious right argue, in defending mandatory school prayers, that any child whose religion is offended by the content of the official prayer can simply walk out of the classroom. Why can't these leaders tell their followers simply to "walk out" of the movie theater if their religious sensibilities are offended? The answer is clear and frightening: deep down these religious leaders believe that as Christians they *belong* and don't have to leave any place, but that as Jews we don't belong, and can be asked to leave if we don't like what is going on in *their* schools, theaters, or country. As Judge Brevard Hand candidly put it: "A member of a religious minority will have to develop a thicker skin." This was said in the context of prayer in public schools. But the Christian right is unwilling to develop a "thicker skin" even when it comes to privately produced movies that no one is forcing them to watch. This view constitutes the essence of toleration as distinguished from equality.

And toleration means second-class citizenship as distinguished from first. That is why American Jews, and others concerned about preserving the separation of church and state, must fight against all entanglements between religion and government. That is why Norman Podhoretz does not speak for American Jews when he says he is "not particularly passionate about prayer in the schools" because a little bit of Christian prayer didn't hurt him as a student. What Podhoretz fails to understand is that in *his* school, back in *those* days, he *was* very much a second-class citizen, and he knew it. That is why neither he nor his parents ever dreamed of complaining about so obvious a violation of his constitutional rights. My mother, who was also forced to intone Catholic prayers as a public school student in Brooklyn, now resents that imposition greatly, though neither she nor her parents believed they had the right to complain at the time, because they viewed themselves as guests in someone else's home.*

Whenever the Christian right tries to impose its religious will — whether by censoring what it disapproves of or mandating what it approves of — it is sending a message of second-class status to all non-Christian Americans.

For example, the recent decision by local school officials in Hawkins County, Tennessee, to refuse to allow a stage production of *The Diary of Anne Frank* is a dangerous sign of the times.[38] Anne Frank's account of her final years, as a teenager during the Holocaust, is among the most poignant and uplifting literary works that a school-age person can experience. It is not a specifically Jewish play. Nor is it only about the Nazi occupation of Holland. It is universal in its appeal — a story about a family in crisis, about love, about growing up, and about hope.

The reason given by the Hawkins County school officials was fear that fundamentalist Christians would want equal time. Equal time for what? A *pro*-Holocaust play? Surely there is nothing in *The Diary*

* Mandatory Christian prayer in the public schools drove many Jews out of those "Christian" schools and into Jewish schools, thus depriving them of a more pluralistic experience. This phenomenon probably helps to explain why some right-wing Orthodox favor prayer in the public schools: they want to drive Jews out of the public schools and into Jewish yeshivas.

of Anne Frank that could reasonably offend a true Christian or indeed any decent human being. Opposition to staging the play can only reflect the basest kind of primitive bigotry. Surely our Constitution does not demand "equal time" for every crackpot who seeks to respond to decency with his or her own indecency.

The very concept of "equal time" is troubling. If a play is a religious exercise, it should not be presented at all in the public schools. It would be no answer to give other religions "equal time."

The Diary of Anne Frank is not a religious work, any more than *Moby Dick* or *Uncle Tom's Cabin* or *The Scarlet Letter.* The great diversity of our nation's population demands that all students be exposed to the experiences of our varied population. White Christian children should learn about the experiences of Jewish children during the Holocaust, of black children under slavery, of Japanese American children during the World War II detention, of Native American children during the period when we decimated them, and of other groups during times of crisis. Such learning should take place not in the name of "equal time" for all religions, but rather in the name of good education. No group of parents should have the right either to prevent other people's children from being educated or to require — as a quid pro quo — that they be equally exposed to the religious doctrines of Christian fundamentalism. It's bad enough that these parents may be denying their own children the educational tools necessary to cope with the diverse society into which they will be graduating. It is too much to give them a veto over the education of the rest of our children.

The future of Jewishness in America will best be assured in an atmosphere of governmental neutrality. If we do not want the government to tell us what we can and cannot do, then we must not ask the government to pay our way. The government did not support Jewish religious institutions when we, as a community, were relatively poor. Yet our institutions endured and even thrived. Now that we can afford to pay our own way, we should surely not be asking for handouts, especially since government handouts *always* come with strings attached. Some Jewish religious institutions will fall by the wayside as a result of governmental neutrality. But that is in the nature of a free society. If we want an institution to survive, we must — and we will — pay for it.

Every community makes choices about priorities. Yesterday, Jewish hospitals seemed essential. Today, there seems less need for these hospitals to remain under official Jewish auspices, since they serve the general community. Jewish charities are always rethinking priorities. That process will continue. But it is crucial that private Jewish fund-raising continue to support Jewish institutions, as well as other important causes.

Charity is a form of both self-giving and self-defense. The former is obvious, but the latter is important as well. By supporting our religious institutions, we protect them from governmental interference and control.

The United States is one of the very few countries in the history of the world that does not have a governmentally established religion, either in theory or in fact. Even Communist countries "established" atheism as the official doctrine. In Poland, until recently, there were two established "churches," each vying for supremacy: communism and Catholicism. It is no surprise, therefore, that the dissident movements in Poland have come, for the most part, from within, or had the imprimatur of, the Catholic church.

It is no accident that the true golden age of *galut* Jewishness — Jewishness outside Israel — has taken place in a nation without a state-supported church. We have had to fight unofficial anti-Jewishness here, and we will continue to have to fight those battles. Our legal status seems secure, at least for now, despite some recent judicial setbacks. We must do everything in our power to keep it that way, especially as our numbers dwindle in comparison to others. We must insist on being treated — and treating ourselves — as first-class citizens. The moment we accept a lesser status — the way Norman Podhoretz did when he accepted Christian prayers in his public school — we invite others to consider us less than first-class citizens.

It may sound awfully abstract to say that our best guarantee of continued power and success is governmental neutrality. It is more concrete to look at governmental largess as a sign of power and success. But in this instance the abstract is more realistic than the concrete — the long term is more important than the short term. Let us keep high the wall of separation in the United States, while insisting on our right to exercise our religious beliefs with neither entangling help nor disabling hindrance from our government. The future of Jews and Judaism in America may depend on a wall of separation between church and state erected by Protestants, for the protection of Protestants, more than two hundred years ago.

Epilogue
The Past and the Future

THE LARGE screened-in porch overlooked Menemsha Pond. In the distance, you could see the fishing boats unloading their catch. Visually, it was a scene out of Hogarth. But the sounds were somewhat discordant. From the porch came the familiar words and melody of the Shabbes kiddush. Eight men, all in their fiftieth year, joining in unison. Their wives stood beside them, waiting to say amen and sip their wine. I wondered whether the New England fishermen could hear us as we loudly chanted, *"Ki vanu vacharta, viosanu kidashta mikal ha'amim"* — "Because you chose us and sanctified us from among all the nations."

We sang only the Hebrew. That is one of the advantages of the Orthodox upbringing: because you never pray in English, there is less of a confrontation with the actual meaning of what you are singing. The Hebrew words, like the familiar lyrics of rock songs, rarely enter into your consciousness. Their very familiarity, and that of their accompanying melody, produces a warm glow — sometimes even a tear — of emotion and nostalgia.

Some of us would have been embarrassed to articulate these words in English — words that are suggestive of the "chosen people" concept of Judaism. Others of us might, perhaps, be more comfortable with the concept, understanding that it reflects the double-edged sword of responsibility and burden.

The eight middle-aged men chanting the kiddush in unison on Martha's Vineyard had grown up together in the Borough Park neighborhood of Brooklyn. In the 1950s we had begun spending New Year's

Eve together, out of necessity. When we were young teenagers, our parents didn't let us go out on dates, especially on New Year's Eve dates. So we arranged parties, usually at one of our homes, where we could dance to the tunes of "Your Hit Parade" while a watchful parent chaperoned at a discreet distance.

This tradition of spending New Year's Eve together has continued for nearly forty years now. I have spent virtually every New Year's Eve of my adult life in the company of my Borough Park friends. I have flown in from distant locations — Europe, the Caribbean, the West Coast — to make our annual party. During the year, we gather occasionally — at family weddings, Bar and Bat Mitzvahs, and, increasingly, at parents' funerals. But until recently, the focal point of our long friendship has been the yearly New Year's Eve get-together.

In the last few years, however, our gatherings have become more frequent and of longer duration. We were spending "nostalgia weekends" together, at the Concord Hotel in the Catskill Mountains or in Atlantic City.

Indeed, one such weekend became the subject of a *New York Times Magazine* "About Men" column. I described how the

guys played one-on-one basketball and horse (even those who hated hoop as kids). We told jokes so old you could give them numbers (itself one of the oldest jokes). And we wondered about why our lost adolescence exerted such magnetic attraction.

"Those were the worst days of my life," one of the guys — who used to talk with a high voice — confided. Suddenly, we were all contemplative. Our adolescence was miserable, we acknowledged. As the Musak played, "Love Is a Many-Splendored Thing," another related how he dreaded the slow dances because he would always become palpably tumescent (certainly not a phrase from our youth) while doing the fox trot. Another shocked us all by soberly confessing that he had become tumescent only once during his adolescence, but then he reassured us by bragging that "it started when I was 12 and I didn't stop until I was 21."

I recalled one of my most mortifying moments. It was prom time, and the girls (they really were girls, not young women, as the rest of the story will prove) had established a committee of three to which the boys had to apply for dates. I had my eye on a pretty blonde from an adjoining neighborhood (her distance, I hoped, might have kept her from learning of my questionable reputation among the local parents).

As I approached the committee and shyly uttered "Karen," all three arbiters laughed. "Don't you know," the cruelest admonished me, "that Karen is on the A list and you're on the C list? You can only pick from the C or D lists." It was a relief to learn there was a list lower than mine, but a shock to be confronted with my official ranking. I went to the prom alone and danced with my cousin, who was also on the C list. Perhaps there was a genetic flaw; we both had too many zits.

Those were miserable years, all right, the seven of us on the basketball court agreed. They were years of self-doubt, sexual guilt without sexual pleasure, fears and transitions. Before you were comfortably into one stage you were already entering another, more precarious, one. They popped up as if on schedule, like the beginning of the yo-yo, marbles or mumblety-peg seasons.

Why then do we insist on recapturing the most miserable period of our lives? Why does our collective recall fail us? Sometimes I think I'm being nostalgic about someone else's happy adolescence. . . .

As my buddies and I finished our shoot-out at the Concord and headed for a shvits in the steam room, we encountered our wives and told them about our game-cum-discussion. (Men — at least my friends and two sons — tend to talk to one another most openly when we're doing something together, rather than sitting across a table where our eyes can meet.) Our wives — most of whom had known us as adolescents — agreed that we had been pretty nerdy back then, but they prided themselves on having seen through the external faults that had relegated us to C lists. "You don't need to buy the 1950's in a store," one spouse quipped, "you guys are walking memorabilia." Another turned an old phrase: "I was able to take my husband out of the 50's, but I can't take the 50's out of him."[1]

This time we would be gathering together for an entire July week. My wife and I had invited the group — the men, their wives, and whatever children could make it — to our summer vacation spot on the Vineyard. This was a special occasion. It was our joint fiftieth birthday party. We would help each other through this midcentury passage.

We formed our group as adolescents. We were very close then, as if running in a pack. We remained close during college and through our early twenties. Then we grew somewhat distant, though we always maintained the annual New Year's get-together. But the twenty or so years between our mid-twenties to mid-forties were devoted more to raising our own families. Now, nearly all of our children are of college age or older. Most are out of the house. Our nests are empty, and so we have turned more to each other. We all have other friends in our own communities — perhaps in some ways even closer friends. The parents of our children's friends, our professional colleagues, the guys we play ball or drink with — all are important to us.

But in addition, we have our oldest friends, who play a special role in our lives. We speculated out loud about why the group had become so much more important to us as we turned fifty, and asked why it seemed more important to some of us during certain periods of our lives. In the end, we decided that in a world of continuous change, of new experiences, and of constant challenge, it was important to have a baseline. And this group — with its shared memories — served as that baseline.

Our wives — six of them were the original young sweethearts and two, including my own, were of somewhat more recent vintage — were of differing ages (though all within a decade of each other). We Borough Park boys were all the same age because we had first met in the same grade in elementary school.

Because of the similarity in our religious education and backgrounds, we had begun our lives with virtually identical levels of religious observance. We were all Orthodox, but on the liberal wing. We followed the letter of the law, but to the minimum degree required. For example, we did not turn on lights on Shabbes, but we did use preset electric timers to do our "work" for us.

The level of our religious observance was determined not by the holy books or the holy men, but rather by community mores. Religious decisions were made on the basis of conformity, not theology. Our community was always seeking to make religious observance as easy as would be compatible with compliance. Certain of the 613 mitzvoth — religious obligations — were simply ignored without explanation. Despite futile efforts by the rabbis to enforce compliance with all of them, and despite the equal theoretical importance of each, a certain practical hierarchy emerged over time. For example, wearing the yarmulke is not among the 613 obligations. But it has become so important a part of the religious tradition that it virtually defines the wearer as Orthodox.

On the other hand, the command not to wear any garment that mixes linen and wool — the technical term for the prohibited mixture is *shatnes* — is far more important. Theoretically, it ranks up there with the prohibition against mixing milk and meat and with the requirement to eat only kosher food. But in my Orthodox community, the *shatnes* laws were all but ignored. Even in Orthodox Borough Park, we — or the implicit opinion formers — picked and chose among the religious obligations we were going to observe.

I mention the similarity in the level of our religious observance as kids because of the relative differences now. Each of us is married to a Jewish woman. We are all strongly committed as Jews, and we all consider ourselves strong supporters of Israel. We all attend synagogue, but the degree of regularity ranges from daily, to weekly, to half a dozen times a year. Some of the group keep kosher, others maintain kosher homes but eat unkosher "out." Some do not keep kosher at all. Some ride on the Sabbath, while others do not. Some of our children attended — and still attend — Jewish religious school; others never did. (The beach on Martha's Vineyard has a nude section to which some of the couples went. This led one of the women who was packing lunches to divide us into groups: "Nude kosher over here! Nude unkosher over there! Clothed kosher . . .").

This week together — the first in our long friendship — was to be something of a test of our tolerance for each other's different levels of religious observance. Most of us were somewhat skeptical, and during the first few days rather tentative. We never expressly discussed our levels of observance, but they soon became clear, especially as Shabbes approached. Implicit rules developed without a word's being said. When we went out to eat, nobody ordered any unkosher items. This made good practical sense because we all love to exchange food — to taste each other's dishes. One unkosher dish would create problems. On Shabbes, those who drove went to the beach, while the others hung around the house or walked to town.

The degree of mutual tolerance reached its humorous apex on Sunday afternoon, when the son of the most kosher of the couples returned from a scuba dive with two live lobsters he had caught. His mother expressed a combination of parental pride in her son's accomplishment and religious concern lest he become a heathen. We all laughed as the young diver instructed the unkosher couples in the fine art of preparing the "abominations" for an afternoon snack. The kosher kids all gathered around in a mixture of awe and disgust as the others boiled, cracked, and devoured the beasts. One of the kosher kids declared: "This is all a plot by our parents to make sure we never want to eat lobster."

We talked a lot about our kids and what kind of Jews — and people — they are likely to become. Even the most Orthodox among us were worried — that understates it considerably — that their children would marry non-Jews or would abandon the faith. We wondered whether, short of taking the totalitarian approach of some ultraorthodox sects, there was any way of assuring that children would retain any particular level of Jewish observance or commitment. We asked ourselves whether we could instill in our children a sense of personal responsibility and individual religious choice while guaranteeing that they would exercise that responsibility and choice in a positively Jewish manner. We all agreed that there were no guarantees — just hopes nurtured by education and values.

Everyone in the group agreed that as we have gotten older, our friendship has become more important to each of us. Whatever competitive edge that may have existed when we were beginning our very different careers now seems gone. We never talk about money or compare our successes.

We have little in common in our careers or those of our wives. Most of us are liberal Democrats, but there are a couple of Republicans and at least one neoconservative.

Our conversation tends to focus on our common experiences: our past, our children, our changing bodies (bifocals was a major topic during our fiftieth birthday; we predicted that prostates would be high on the list for our sixtieth).

We know each other so well — especially our weaknesses and vulnerabilities — that it is impossible for anyone to get away with bullshit about anything. We have been through so many passages, stages, and crises together that we constitute, in effect, longitudinal cross-studies of each other. To me it's remarkable that our group goes back so far and has remained so close despite the fact that no one currently lives in Brooklyn or indeed in the same city as any other member of the group.

As I sat on the porch of the Martha's Vineyard house and wrote this chapter, I saw the fishing boats on Menemsha Pond, but the sounds of the Shabbes kiddush were gone. My friends had left and I was alone with the memories of a profoundly important week together. Maybe you can't go home, but you can bring a bit of home — even your earliest home — back into your life. My old friends do that for me.

*   *   *

The visit left me not only with poignant memories of my Orthodox youth but with complex thoughts about the future of Judaism and of my Jewishness. During our week together, I felt as Jewish as any of my friends. Indeed, among the group, I had come from the most observant background. Ironically, the one who had come from the least observant background was now the most Orthodox. As it was in our youth, the levels of observance are as much a function of local community mores as of theological belief. But now it was different, because each of us had relocated to his current community, with its different mores. Living in West Hempstead, New York, meant complying with a certain level of observance. Living in Cambridge, Massachusetts, meant something rather different.

As we discussed the differing nature of our Jewishness, I thought of the story I had told during my family centennial gathering about the congregation that couldn't make up its collective mind about whether to stand or sit during the recitation of the *Shma Yisrael*, and of my mother's addendum to the story: that at least they all recite the *Shma Yisrael*. Amid the often cacophonous diversity within Judaism about practices and levels of observance, there is, after all, a broad consensus about certain fundamentals. These fundamentals may not include the daily recitation of the *Shma* or any other concrete observances, but they are as real as any practices or prayers. Defining these fundamentals may be difficult, but we know them when we see and hear them. Most of them are unspoken assumptions of the kind my Borough Park friends and I share. They grew out of the common historical experiences of the Jewish people, both ancient and modern. They grew out of common values, though the means of achieving these values may be very much in dispute. They grew out of a common concern for the survival of Israel, for the rescue of Jewish communities in danger, for the survival of Judaism. These are our *Shmas*.

My friends understand my Jewishness — my commitment to Jewish political causes coupled with my selective attitude toward religious observance. In their nonjudgmental way, they support what I am doing, even though it is quite different from what some of them are doing. As one of my buddies put it, "You were always a rebel and a gadfly as a kid. Why should you change in middle age?" Well, I do find myself changing — at least a little — as I enter my fifties. My questions are the same, but some of the answers are different, at least in nuance.

The week with my boyhood friends on Martha's Vineyard reminded me of how quickly life passes. It was just yesterday that we were taunting our teachers in elementary school. And now, half a lifetime later, we are still full of chutzpah, but a bit less certain about our answers. I hope to retain some of those irreverent qualities of youth — some of the Brooklyn chutzpah — as I continue to confront the eternal questions inherent in being a Jewish American and an American Jew.

As I have thought about these questions and how my friends and I are continuing to struggle with them, I find myself pondering a Jewish future that has always defied prognostication. I began this book by pointing to the profound yet entirely unpredictable changes in the nature of Jewish life, death, and existence over the past century. In the spirit of chutzpah, I end it by offering some tentative predictions about the near future of the American Jewish condition. Not even a chutzpahnik would venture to prophesy our long-term future.

We will continue to live in that most uncomfortable of temporal zones, "the meantime." Jewish life in America will neither be as secure as we would like it, nor as insecure as it has historically been. Although we will continue to witness the external indica of primitive anti-Semitism — the swastika graffiti, the hate mail, and the verbal slurs — this will not reflect mainstream attitudes. Some mainstream figures, like Patrick Buchanan, will continue to be insensitive to Jewish concerns, but such insensitivity will diminish rather than enhance their general influence. Buchanan will remain influential *despite* his anti-Semitism, not *because* of it. Social and economic anti-Semitism will continue to abate, as Jews become more like other groups. Anti-Semitism will become less acceptable among black leaders as they learn — and as we help teach them — that insensitivity to Jewish concerns is fatal to electoral success in many parts of the country. Black politicians who are sensitive to Jewish concerns will continue to be elected with Jewish support, and black politicians who are anti-Semitic or who court anti-Semitic support will continue to be defeated with Jewish opposition.

The greatest challenges to the survival of the Jewish people will take place in Israel, as American support for the Jewish state vacillates. It will become more acceptable, politically, for American office seekers to be "evenhanded" on Israel. And American "evenhandedness," in the face of European and third world support for the PLO, can prove disastrous to Israeli security. The physical threat — as distinguished from the moral and media threats — to Israel will come not from the PLO, but from Arab states and from Islamic fundamentalism.

Anti-Zionism will replace anti-Semitism as the primary manifestation of anti-Jewish expression and feeling. We will also continue to experience the new strain of Judeopathy — the resentment against Jewish success, the gloating over our inability to achieve the perfection that we often demand of ourselves and that others demand of Jews and the Jewish nation. Anti-Zionism will be far more difficult to combat, especially since American Jews have so little influence on the growing conservatism of Israeli domestic and foreign politics. America, of course, is also growing more conservative in its domestic and foreign politics. Yet conservative Americans feel entirely comfortable berating embattled Israel for its unwillingness to take the kind of risks to its security that fortress America — surrounded by two oceans and without any powerful enemies — seems unwilling to take in the interest of world peace. Talk about chutzpah!

It is significant that Israel received its first recent increase in public support as a result of being attacked by Iraqi missiles *and not* immediately retaliating. The image of the Jewish state as *victim* is far more acceptable to many in the world than the image of the Jewish state as warrior, aggressively defending its population.* Support for Israel will diminish as it returns to its policy of aggressive retaliation and proactive defense. It is impossible to predict the long-term effects on the Middle East of the American-led coalition's decisive military victory over Iraq, except to say that it will likely further destabilize an already volatile situation.

Even the short-term consequences of America's victory are unclear. Surely the Gulf War should educate the world to the untrustworthiness of the PLO, which supported Saddam Hussein's attack on innocent civilians. It should also lend credence to Israeli claims that giving up the West Bank in the absence of an overall Arab-Israeli peace would endanger its security, since the long distance that Iraqi Scud missiles had to travel was one reason they could not be armed with chemical or biological warheads. On the other hand, America's destruction of the strongest Arab army will give it credibility in asking Israel to under-

---

* "Not since the Yom Kippur War nearly 18 years ago, in fact, has the world looked so warmly on [Israel], seeing it once again as a victim." Joel Brinkley, "Israel, Enduring Missiles, Expects a Political Victory," *New York Times,* January 27, 1991, Section 4, pp. 1–2.

Traditional anti-Semites, such as the Liberty Lobby, refused to believe that Israel was not directly involved in the Gulf War. The headline in the February 4, 1991, issue of the *Spotlight* read: "Israeli Planes Attack Iraq." It was reprinted in the February 13 *Post Eagle.*

take some risks in the interest of regional peace. The real unknown is whether American credibility with our Arab coalition partners will help persuade Saudi Arabia, Kuwait, and perhaps even Syria to join Egypt in recognizing Israel, as part of an overall resolution of the Arab-Israeli dispute. Another unknown is the future of King Hussein and his Hashemite rule over Jordan. If the Palestinian majority in Jordan were to turn that unrepresentative monarchy into a Palestinian state, the entire nature of the Israeli-Palestinian dispute would change from a conflict over Palestinian statehood into an argument over the occupation of land, including heavily populated areas. In the end, everyone's interest will be served if Israel's security can be assured without the need for it to control a hostile population of noncitizens.

One central reality remains unchanged by the outcome of the Gulf War: the hatred against Israel will persist among many Arabs, and Israel's physical security will continue to depend on its military capacity to defeat the combined armies of its enemies — a capacity that will continue to require material support from the United States.

In addition to increasing American prestige in the Middle East, the Gulf War also strengthened the influence of the United Nations, and especially the Security Council. But all it proved was that the United Nations is capable of being fair and effective in an intra-Arab and intra-Islamic dispute. There is no evidence that the UN is capable of being an honest broker in the Arab-Israeli dispute. Indeed, decades of experience are to the contrary. Yet there will be increased pressure on Israel to submit to resolution of disputes under the auspices of the United Nations. This will also increase the pressure on the United States to withhold its Security Council veto of anti-Israel resolutions.

American Jews will, in my view, remain united in the near future primarily as a result of continuing threats to the security of Israel. If "it" were ever to happen again, the most likely locus of a future Holocaust would be Israel. Indeed, if Israel's military power were ever to be diminished to the point that the combined armies of the Arab world could defeat it, I believe there *would* be another Holocaust. No Arab dictator who *could* defeat Israel and forbore from doing so would survive the continuing frenzy for jihad. And an Arab military victory over Israel — unlike the Israeli victories over the Arabs — would not result in a mere occupation or even detention of Israeli Jews. It would result in a mass slaughter, designed to rid Arab "holy" land of Jewish intruders.

Most Jews know this, though they rarely speak it openly. But then again, most Jews did not speak openly about the Holocaust before it happened, while it was happening, or for several years after it was over.

So long as anti-Zionism is rampant throughout the world and growing in America, Jews in this country will remain united against this newest form of anti-Jewishness. Our Jewishness will, over the near term, continue to be defined more by the negative mission we share — to combat anti-Zionism and to defend Israeli security — than by any positive consensus about the core of Judaism. And we will continue to see the cautious, elitist, wealthy — often out-of-touch — leadership that currently prevails in most Jewish organizations. We will also see the development of grass-roots Jewish organizations, more reflective of popular Jewish attitudes and more willing to act assertively in support of Jewish institutions.

We will continue to witness a sharp decline in support for Israel among college and university students. Even after the Gulf War, that decline is in evidence. For example, at Harvard Law School, some students within the Jewish Law Students Association have expressed concern that support for Israel is too controversial on campus to become part of the organization's agenda. These students are tomorrow's leaders, and unless this trend can be reversed, it bodes ill for the longer-term interests of Israel. Few among the current generation of students have felt the sting of anti-Semitism, and many regard anti-Zionism as an entirely acceptable political position.

If anti-Semitism and anti-Zionism were, in fact, to begin to disappear — an unlikely prospect, in my view — would American Jewry be able to define a more positive consensus? After all, among the core of common values in today's Jewish community has been opposition to anti-Semitism and anti-Zionism. The Anti-Defamation League was built on the struggle against such evils. Its very name is negative, though its work has been extremely positive. The other major Jewish organizations would also have greater difficulty arriving at a positive program for, or consensus among, its diverse constituencies, were it not for our common enemies.

Leonard Fein likes to remind us that the law protects against rape but not against seduction. We have survived — sometimes by the skin of our teeth — millennia of rape attempts against the Jewish body and soul by villains and monsters of every description. Efforts to convert us, assimilate us, and exterminate us by the sword have taken an enormous toll, but in the end they have failed. Now the dangers are

more subtle: willing seduction, voluntary assimilation, deliberate ab-
dication. We have learned — painfully and with difficulty — how to
fight others. Can we develop Jewish techniques for defending against
our own success?

Pogo once said: "We have seen the enemy and he is *us!*" As Jews,
we have not yet been given the luxury of seeing ourselves as the enemy.
There are still too many external enemies who challenge the very
physical survival of the Jewish people in Israel and throughout the
world. But as we become stronger in the face of our external enemies,
we must prepare to confront ourselves. As *Jewish* Americans, are we
prepared to demand the first-class status we have earned in America
and that we have helped others to move toward? As *American* Jews, are
we prepared to insist on being treated as first-class Jews, rather than
as exiles from our only true and normal home, Israel? The answer to
these questions is largely, if not entirely, in our own hands. One
conclusion is certain: unless we regard ourselves as first-class Americans and as first-class Jews, no one else will so regard us.

Notes

INTRODUCTION

1. Theodor Herzl, *The Jewish State: An Attempt at a Modern Solution of the Jewish Question* (New York: American Zionist Emergency Council, 1946), p. 75.
2. Shlomo Avineri, "Letter to an American Friend: Soured Promise," *Jerusalem Post*, March 10, 1987, p. 10.
3. The concept of *shanda fur de goyim* is not a uniquely Orthodox one. The founder of the American Reform movement, Rabbi Isaac Mayer Wise, wanted to purge Jewish ritual of "whatever makes us ridiculous before the world." Jerold Auerbach, *Rabbis and Lawyers: The Journey from Torah to Constitution* (Bloomington: Indiana University Press, 1990), p. 78.

   Charles Silberman, in his wonderfully controversial compendium on Jewish life in America, *A Certain People: American Jews and Their Lives Today* (New York: Summit Books, 1985), describes essentially the same phenomenon under the rubric of the Jewish obsession "with being nice" (p. 30). During the notorious Chicago Seven trial in 1968–70, the defendant Abbie Hoffman repeatedly referred to Judge Julius Hoffman — who was not related but who was also Jewish — as "a *shanda fur de goyim*."
4. Herzl, *The Jewish State*, p. 73. Even in America, we have been regarded as guests by some bigots who should have known better. Professor Talcott Parsons of Harvard — one of this country's most distinguished sociologists — wrote in the 1940s that a major cause of anti-Semitism was the "arrogance of the claim that a group who are in a sense 'guests' in a [Christian] country claim a higher status than the 'host' people." Silberman, *A Certain People*, p. 56.
5. Leonard Fein, *Where Are We? The Inner Life of America's Jews* (New York: Harper and Row, 1988), p. 47.
6. *Boston Globe*, October 28, 1986.

CHAPTER I   A Polish Jew Comes to America

1. In 1790, there were approximately 1,500 Jews in the United States. In 1826, there were 6,000 Jews; in 1840, 15,000; and in 1855 their number leapt to 100,000. By 1880, there were a total of 300,000 Jews in America. Martin Gilbert, *Atlas of Jewish History* (New York: Dorset Press, 1984), pp. 61, 81.
2. Auerbach, *Rabbis and Lawyers*, pp. 75–76.
3. An estimated 2,787,754 immigrant Jews came to America between 1881 and 1923. From approximately 300,000 in 1880, "the American Jewish population grew to almost three and one-half million by 1917, and to more than four and one-quarter million by 1927. . . . While in 1880 most American Jews were of Central European background, in 1927, 80 percent or more were estimated to have been of Eastern European origin." Chaim Waxman, *America's Jews in Transition* (Philadelphia: Temple University Press, 1983), p. 30.
4. Yehuda Slutsky, "Pale of Settlement," *Encyclopaedia Judaica* (1978 ed.), vol. 13, p. 27.
5. Auerbach, *Rabbis and Lawyers*, pp. 79, 97; Seymour Leventman, "From Shtetl to Suburb,"

in Peter Isaac Rose, ed., *The Ghetto and Beyond: Essays on Jewish Life in America* (New York: Random House, 1969), p. 35.

6. The rapid pace of Jewish immigration into the United States between the 1880s and the 1920s almost certainly would have persisted had the forces favoring restriction not succeeded in the passage of the Johnson Immigration Act of 1921 and 1924 (Waxman, *America's Jews*, pp. 29–30). Millions of Jews who were murdered by Hitler might well have been safely living in America but for these exclusionary laws.

7. Jonah Landau, "The First Yiddish Communities in America," *Der Yid*, November 9, 1979, p. 15.

8. Ibid., p. 24.

CHAPTER II   Leaving Brooklyn: Learning About Anti-Semitism

1. Justice Felix Frankfurter, in *West Virginia State Board of Education v. Barnette*, 319 U.S. 624, 646, 63 S. Ct. 1178 (1943).

2. Stephen L. Slavin and Mary A. Pradt, *The Einstein Syndrome: Corporate Anti-Semitism in America Today* (Washington, D.C.: University Press of America, 1982), pp. 39–44, 47–61.

3. This attorney, Robert S. Rifkind, wrote a letter to the *Harvard Law Record* in response to a speech I made on the subject. He stated:

> The March 11, 1983, issue of the *Record* quotes Professor Dershowitz as asserting that "barely twenty years ago blatant anti-Semitism was quite common in the legal establishment." That was not my experience, and the evidence Professor Dershowitz cites seems unpersuasive. I do not know why Mr. Dershowitz was turned down by all 32 New York Law firms to which he applied. But surely anti-Semitism is not the only possible explanation.
>
> The fact that he was turned down by all 32 of the New York law firms to which he applied suggests that something other than anti-Semitism was at work. . . .
>
> I can only report that I and many other Jews were associates at Cravath when he graduated from law school, and that many of us have become members of the firm.
>
> Robert S. Rifkind, '61
> New York, New York

I replied:

> Dear Mr. Rifkind:
>
> Just who are you trying to kid? You know, as well as I do, that in 1960, the major Wall Street firms had a double standard for hiring Jews and white Protestants. Of course Cravath would hire the bright, qualified, Jewish son of a former federal judge who was a senior partner in another major firm. But to suggest that Cravath applied the *same* standard in hiring qualified Jews and white Protestants is to blink reality. But I guess the ability to blink reality was a primary qualification for becoming a Jewish lawyer on Wall Street in those days.

4. *Hishon v. King and Spaling*, 467 U.S. 69, 77 (1984), citing *Lucido v. Cravath, Swaine and Moore*, 647 F2d. Supp. 162.

5. Justice Goldberg was so upset at the phenomenon of discrimination that he decided to go public with our story. Several years after I finished my clerkship with him, the following item appeared in the "Lyons Den," then the most widely read gossip column in New York:

> Goldberg will spend the High Holidays as usual at an Orthodox synagogue with Harvard Law School Prof. Alan Dershowitz. They met when Dershowitz came to be interviewed for the coveted job of law clerk to Goldberg, then of the Supreme Court. All went well, and Dershowitz said he felt compelled to add one vital fact, that he's Orthodox.
>
> This meant he couldn't work on Saturdays, not even answer a phone. Goldberg had him meet the young man who's to be the other clerk, Lee McTiernan. The Justice told them: "Lee can work on Saturdays, Alan on Sundays, giving me a functioning staff seven days a week."

The "Lyons Den" story made my parents heroes in the Orthodox community of New York. *New York Post*, September 5, 1969, p. 47.

6. Stephen Breyer, "Clerking for Justice Goldberg," *Journal of Supreme Court History 1990*, p. 4.

CHAPTER III   At Harvard: Quotas, Conflicts, and Honors

1. Lenny Bruce, quoted in William Novak and Moshe Waldoks, eds., *The Big Book of Jewish Humor* (New York: Harper Perennial, 1981), p. 60. Originally published by Ballantine Books in *The Essential Lenny Bruce* by Lenny Bruce.

2. Harry Austryn Wolfson, *Escaping Judaism.* Menorah Society Pamphlet No. 2 (New York: Menorah Press, 1922), pp. 1, 50–51. Quoted in Silberman, *A Certain People,* pp. 30–31.

3. See Silberman, *A Certain People,* p. 54.

4. Alan M. Dershowitz and Laura Hanft, "Affirmative Action and the Harvard College Diversity-Discretion Model: Paradigm or Pretext?," *Cardozo Law Review,* vol. I, no. 2 (fall 1979), p. 389.

5. Ibid., p. 390.

6. Ibid., p. 391.

7. Ibid.

8. Ibid., p. 394, fn. 49.

9. Ibid., p. 393.

10. Ibid., p. 394, fn. 49.

11. Ibid., pp. 394–395.

12. Ibid., p. 395.

13. Henry W. Holmes, "The University," *Harvard Graduates' Magazine,* vol. 31 (1923), p. 531.

14. Quoted in Dershowitz and Hanft, "Affirmative Action," pp. 396–397.

15. Quoted in ibid., p. 397.

16. Silberman, *A Certain People,* p. 98.

17. Ibid., p. 95.

18. Alan M. Dershowitz, "Unequal Justice," *New York Times Book Review,* January 25, 1976, p. 1.

19. Ibid.; letter from Lowell to Lewis Tolman, Esq., February 16, 1916 (Harvard Archives).

20. Dershowitz, "Unequal Justice," p. 2.

21. Dershowitz and Hanft, "Affirmative Action," pp. 413–414.

22. Douglas, quoted in ibid., p. 415.

23. "Survey after survey shows a majority of Jews endorse [affirmative action and] that a plurality even endorses 'preferential treatment,' which falls somewhere between affirmative action and quotas." Fein, *Where Are We?,* p. 258.

24. Ralph Blumenthal, "Daniel Berrigan's Speech to Arabs Stirs a Furor over Award," *New York Times,* December 16, 1973, p. 56.

25. Manuel Lopez and Jim Matthews, "Alan Dershowitz: Blacks, Jews, and Selective Morality," *Harvard Salient,* April 1985, p. 18.

26. Ross Gelbspan, "Harvard Blacks Deny Dershowitz' Charge of Antagonizing Jews," *Boston Globe,* March 6, 1985, p. 23.

27. Allison eventually resigned, under pressure, from his deanship after offering to sell corporation faculty appointments to unqualified high-roller contributors to the Kennedy School, and after bestowing a medal for "high ethics in government" on former attorney general Edwin Meese, for whose administration he served as a paid consultant.

28. James M. Markham, "Facing Up to Germany's Past," *New York Times,* June 23, 1985, p. 25.

29. Ibid.

30. James M. Markham, " 'All of Us Must Accept the Past' the German President Tells M.P.'s," *New York Times,* May 9, 1985, p. 20.

31. Associated Press, "Dutch Free 2 Nazis in Prison 43 Years," *New York Times,* January 28, 1989, p. 3.

32. Ben Zion Gold, "Guilt by Association," *Jewish Advocate,* June 11, 1987, p. 2.

CHAPTER IV   Going on Television

 1. Yehuda Slutsky, "Blood Libel," *Encyclopaedia Judaica* (1978 ed.), vol. 4, p. 1130.

 2. "Silence on Anti-Semitism," letter to the editor, Book Review Desk, *New York Times,* January 27, 1985, Section 7, p. 37.

 3. Haim Hillel Ben-Sasson, "Blood Libel," *Encyclopaedia Judaica* (1978 ed.), vol. 4, p. 1128.

 4. Thomas B. Macaulay, "Jewish Disabilities," in *The Complete Works of Thomas Babington Macaulay: Speeches and Legal Studies* (New York: Sully and Kleinteich, 1900), pp. 125–126.

 5. Ibid., pp. 120, 124.

 6. Martin Luther, from a pamphlet *Concerning the Jews and Their Lies,* quoted in *Encyclopaedia Judaica* (1978 ed.), vol. 3, p. 106.

 7. Ibid.

 8. Jean-Denis Bredan, *The Affair: The Case of Alfred Dreyfus* (Birmingham, Alabama: The Notable Trials Library, Division of Gryphon Editions, Inc., c1989), p. 352.

 9. Quoted in William Grimsted, ed., *Antizion* (Reedy, West Virginia: Liberty Bell Publications, 1976), pp. 162–163.

10. Ibid., pp. 5–6.

11. Ibid., p. 142.

12. Ibid., pp. 2, 35, 36, 40, 43–44, 78, 94, 124, 146.

13. Peter Grose, *Israel in the Mind of America* (New York: Schocken Books, 1984), p. 3.

14. Silberman, *A Certain People,* p. 48.

15. Arnold Forster, *Square One: A Memoir* (New York: D. I. Fine, 1988), pp. 68–70.

16. Silberman, *A Certain People,* pp. 337, 366.

17. Ibid., pp. 94, 339.

18. Ibid., pp. 328–329.

19. "Statement of the Colloquium," Soviet Jewry and the Rule of Law: Second International Colloquium on Soviet Jewry (London, October 1979), from *Israel Yearbook on Human Rights,* vol. 9 (1979), p. 280.

20. Glenn Frankel, "Militant Islamic Movement Upstages PLO in West Bank Uprising," *Washington Post,* December 17, 1989, p. A29.

21. Per Ahlmark, "Old-New Anti-Semitism," *New York Times,* November 13, 1989, p. A21. In a perverse twist, one of the most blatant espousers of Islamic anti-Jewish attitudes — M. T. Mehdi of the Council on Islamic Affairs — recently declared that there was "a Judeo-Christian prejudice against Islam." He failed to mention Islamic attacks on the Jewish people and repeated declarations of holy war against the Jewish nation. Associated

Press, "U.S. Biased Against Islam, Muslim Leader Says," *Los Angeles Times*, August 25, 1990, p. 15.

22. Gore Vidal, "The Empire Lovers Strike Back," *Nation*, March 22, 1986, pp. 350, 353.

23. In an editorial on September 9, 1990, the *Times* wrote: "American Jews have reason to be particularly sensitive about demonizing a Semitic people. In unthinking caricature, Arabs are portrayed either as demented terrorists or greedy oil sheiks. This is a variation of the hateful depiction of Jews as rapacious bankers or sinister revolutionaries. Anti-Semitism is anti-Semitism in both forms." Section 4, p. 24.

24. Troy A. Morgan, " 'Fairness' Amendment Defeated Amidst Rancorous Debate," *Harvard Law Record*, November 18, 1988, p. 1.

25. "Bulger's Venom Spews," *Boston Herald*, December 7, 1990, p. 40; "Closing a Code-Word Spat," *Boston Globe*, December 13, 1990; "Point of View" (television talk show), produced and hosted by Judy Jarvis, WLVI, Boston, December 16, 1990.

26. Mark Twain, *Concerning the Jews* (New York: Harper and Brothers, 1934), pp. 1–2.

27. Ibid.

28. Ibid., pp. 5, 16–17.

29. Ibid., p. 22.

30. Ibid., p. 23.

CHAPTER V   Auschwitz: The Holocaust, Justice, and Faith

1. Robert Nozick, *The Examined Life: Philosophical Meditations* (New York: Simon and Schuster, 1989), pp. 238–239.

2. My letter of nomination to the Nobel Committee in Elie's behalf made that point:

> No one in the world today deserves the Nobel Peace Prize more than Elie Wiesel. Professor Wiesel represents the survivors of the most massive genocide ever perpetrated on a segment of humankind — with the implicit approval of so many bystanders.
>
> To understand Professor Wiesel's unique and immeasurable contribution to peace, one must only imagine how it might have been without a Wiesel. It is impossible to imagine the rage that must be continually experienced by direct and indirect survivors of the Holocaust. Survivors of other mass killings and their descendants have responded by non-peaceful means — for example, the continuing violence of some Armenians against Turks. Jewish survivors have not. There has been no terrorism against innocent Germans — or even guilty Germans who live in luxury and sometimes in honor. For this alone, the Jewish survivors as a group deserve recognition for their contribution to peace.
>
> There are many excellent reasons for recognizing Professor Wiesel. But none is more important than his role in teaching survivors and their children how to respond in constructive peace and justice to a worldwide conspiracy of genocide, the components of which include mass killings, mass silence, and mass indifference. Professor Wiesel has devoted his life to teaching the survivors of a conspiracy which excluded so few to re-enter and adjust in peace to an alien world that deserved little forgiveness.
>
> . . . Wiesel's life work merits the highest degree of recognition — especially from representatives of the world that stood silently by.

3. Lon Fuller, "Positivism and Fidelity to Law," *Harvard Law Review*, vol. 71 (1958), pp. 630, 648–657.

4. See Irving Abella and Harold Troper, *None Is Too Many: Canada and the Jews of Europe, 1933–1948* (Toronto: Lester & Orpen Dennys, 1982).

5. Silberman, *A Certain People*, pp. 360–365. Not surprisingly, the Bitburg insult was orchestrated by Patrick Buchanan, about whom I have more to say later in the chapter.

6. Fein, *Where Are We?*, p. 61

7. In a recent essay in *Time* magazine (February 26, 1990), Charles Krauthammer argued

that "the double standard demanded of Israel" is a "discriminatory standard. And discrimination against Jews has a name too. The word for it is anti-Semitism."

8. Ronald C. Monticome, *The Catholic Church in Communist Poland, 1945–1985* (Boulder, Colorado: East European Monographs, 1986), p. 59.

9. Kenneth A. Briggs, "New Saint Is Inspiration for the Message of Hope," *New York Times*, October 11, 1982, p. A8.

10. John Tagliabue, "Oświecim Journal: A Place Where the Past Overwhelms the Present," *New York Times*, September 13, 1989, p. A4; Richard Cohen, "Sainthood," *Washington Post*, December 14, 1982, p. B1.

11. Cohen, "Sainthood," p. B1.

12. Martin Gilbert, *The Holocaust* (New York: Henry Holt, 1985), p. 404.

13. W. H. Lawrence, "Cardinal Puts Blame on Some Jews for Pogrom," *New York Times*, July 12, 1946, p. 1.

14. Alan M. Dershowitz, "Polish Anti-Semitism Remains a Danger," *New York Times*, July 19, 1990, p. 22; Charles Chotkowski, "Anti-Semitism Hasn't Tainted Solidarity Rift," *New York Times*, August 3, 1990, p. 26.

15. One of my anti-Semitic letters — this one from a retired U.S. Army colonel — claimed that the Kielce massacre was "fabricated . . . by Jews themselves who wanted sympathy." The pogrom in Kielce was of course no fabrication. The *New York Times* reported the incident, stating in its first-page story: "The Polish Government announced tonight that the worst anti-Jewish pogrom since Poland was liberated occurred today in Kielce." The *Times* also stated, "It is a sad and tragic fact when all shades of Warsaw political opinion are agreed that, despite the fraction of the pre-War Jewish population at present in Poland, there is more anti-semitism in Poland now than in the history of this traditionally anti-Jewish country." (Lawrence, "Cardinal Puts Blame.") A Polish committee of inquiry was formed and nine people in Kielce were sentenced to death, although the pogrom's instigators were not punished.

16. Wladyslaw Sila-Nowicki, "A Reply to Jan Blonski," translation from the Polish magazine *Tygodnik Powszechny*, February 22, 1987; handed to Alan Dershowitz in Poland.

17. Ibid.

18. Ibid.

19. Transcript of sermon by Josef Cardinal Glemp, Jasna Gora Monastery, Czestochowa, Poland, August 26, 1989.

20. John Tagliabue, "Poland's Primate Denounces Jews in Dispute on Auschwitz Convent," *New York Times*, August 29, 1989, p. 1.

21. Ibid.

22. Russell Watson, Anne Underwood, and Theodore Stanger, "Whose Holocaust," *Newsweek*, September 11, 1989, p. 35.

23. Alan M. Dershowitz, "Disquieting Interview from Carmelite Sister," *Jewish Advocate*, November 16, 1989, p. 2.

24. Tom Mathews, Rod Nordland, and Carroll Bogert, "The Long Shadow," *Newsweek*, May 7, 1990, p. 43.

25. "Polish Church Leader Cancels Visit to U.S.," *New York Times*, September 10, 1989, p. 1; John Tagliabue, "Amid Convent Dispute, Cardinal Cancels U.S. Trip," *New York Times*, September 10, 1989, p. 18.

26. James L. Franklin, "Polish Cardinal Postpones U.S. Trip," *Boston Globe*, September 10, 1989, p. 2.

27. Robert K. Lifton, "Reply to the Cardinal Glemp Affair," *Congress Monthly*, vol. 57, no. 4 (May/June 1990), p. 23.

28. Allison Kaplan, "Behind the Headlines: Meeting with Glemp Sparks Debate on How Far to Pursue Past Remark," Jewish Telegraphic Agency, December 13, 1989.

29. Chester Grabowski, letter to Derek Bok dated October 8, 1987, *Post Eagle*, October 21, 1987, p. 2.

30. Chester Grabowski, "The Onslaught Against Poland," *Post Eagle*, February 17, 1988, p. 2.

31. Chester Grabowski, "Every American Citizen," *Post Eagle*, May 4, 1988, p. 2.

32. Mark A. Stuart, "The Gospel According to St. Chester: A History of Hate," *Bergen Record*, April 25, 1984.

33. John H. Kapinos, "Prof. Dershowitz, a Jew, Slanders Polish Cardinal," *Post Eagle*, September 13, 1989, p. 2.

34. Patrick Buchanan, "Healing . . . or Awakening at Auschwitz," *Washington Times*, September 25, 1989.

35. Ibid.

36. Alan M. Dershowitz, "Pull the Plug on Buchanan's Anti-Semitism," *Union Leader* (Manchester, New Hampshire), October 9, 1990, p. 24.

37. Buchanan, "Healing." Buchanan, as usual, had his facts wrong. The Jews of Treblinka were murdered by various methods of gassing, including the use of exhaust fuels and Zyklon B. Buchanan's "facts" about the Holocaust typically come from crackpot Holocaust deniers. See note on page 163.

38. Philip Shenon, "Washington Talk: The Buchanan Aggravation," *New York Times*, February 19, 1987, p. 28.

39. Ibid.

40. "Buchanan Looks at Bush . . . and '92?" *Boston Globe*, January 20, 1991, p. 73.

41. Shenon, "Washington Talk."

42. Dorothy Bast, "Conviction Strains Relationship of Ukrainian and Jewish American," Associated Press, April 19, 1988.

43. The description of the delivery of the verdict is based on my contemporaneous observation of the event, which I related in "Ivan the Terrible Tastes Israeli Justice," *Boston Herald*, April 26, 1988.

44. Lord Denning, letter to the editor, *London Daily Telegraph*, April 28, 1989.

45. Alan M. Dershowitz, letter to the editor, *London Daily Telegraph*, May 1989.

46. Denning said that if a Nazi war criminal were now convicted, "the judge would be bound to let [him] off with a discharge or caution, after such a time." *Sunday Telegraph*, March 25, 1990. Denning has also criticized a prominent English lawyer, whose parents were Lithuanian Jews, as "a German Jew, telling us what to do with our English law." The *Independent*, August 26, 1990.

47. Alan M. Dershowitz, "The Holocaust on Trial," *Boston Herald*, April 29, 1985, p. 5.

48. John F. Burns, "Canada Puts Neo-Nazi's Ideas on Trial, Again," *New York Times*, March 30, 1988, p. 12. Current U.S. law would not permit such a prosecution.

49. Dershowitz, "The Holocaust on Trial," p. 5.

50. Ibid.

51. Robert Faurisson, *Memoire in Defense* (Paris: La Vieille Taupe, 1980).

52. Paul L. Berman, "Gas Chamber Games: Crackpot History and the Right to Lie," *Village Voice*, June 10–16, 1981, p. 37.

53. Ibid., p. 38.

54. Ibid., p. 36.

55. Ibid., p. 38.

56. Brian Morton, "The Culture of Terrorism," *Nation,* vol. 246, no. 15 (May 7, 1988), p. 651.

57. W. D. Rubinstein, "Chomsky and the Neo-Nazis," *Quadrant* (Australia), October 1981, p. 12.

58. Alan M. Dershowitz, "Chomsky Defends Vicious Lie as Free Speech," *Boston Globe,* June 13, 1989, p. 14.

59. Noam Chomsky, "Right to Speak Transcends Content of Speech," *Boston Globe,* July 4, 1989, p. 10.

60. Scot Lehigh, "Men of Letters," *Boston Phoenix,* June 16–22, 1989, p. 30.

61. William Claiborne, "Columbia Post for Kissinger Opposed," *Washington Post,* May 17, 1977, p. A1.

62. Paul L. Berman, "Reply to Chomsky," *Village Voice,* July 1–7, 1981, p. 18.

CHAPTER VI   Visiting Synagogues Around the World

1. "Patrilineal Descent" (interview with Rabbi Alexander Schindler), *Keeping Posted,* vol. 31, no. 5 (March 1986), pp. 11–12. Historically, before 1971, more Jewish men than Jewish women married non-Jews. In recent years, in our egalitarian age, women have been catching up in their rate of intermarriage.

2. Quoted in Fein, *Where Are We?,* p. 69.

3. Albert Einstein, "Why Do They Hate the Jews?" in Carl Seelig, ed., *Ideas and Opinions* (New York: Bonanza Book, c1954), p. 196.

4. The story of this case is told in my book *The Best Defense* (New York: Random House, 1982).

5. Miriam Bensman, "Crowd Jams Synagogue to Hear Kahane Debate," *Riverdale Press,* November 15, 1984, p. 1.

6. The columnist's "review" of the debate was as follows: "The debate was superior to any recently seen by Americans on national television. For two and a half hours the opponents answered the questions put to them, they did so in an honest, forceful, persuasive but graceful manner and did not resort to character defamation." Eli Kavon, "Kahane-Dershowitz Debating Democracy," *Perspectives* (Columbia's Jewish student monthly), October 1984, p. 1.

7. Ari I. Goldman, "Professor Debates Kahane on Israel," *New York Times,* November 13, 1984, p. 3. The text of the debate as given on the next few pages is from "A Debate: Alan Dershowitz vs. Meir Kahane," *Midstream,* November 1984, pp. 17–22.

8. A few years after this debate, Kahane challenged me to a rematch in Boston. This time the debate was to take place at Boston University. But the university authorities — after pressure from both Jewish and non-Jewish objectors — contrived a "security" excuse for canceling the debate. To its credit, Old South Meeting House, which had been home to some of the most contentious debates in American history, agreed to host the event. The Brahmin ghosts of this ancient church must have had some difficulty understanding the two Brooklyn-bred debaters, with their references to Yiddish and Hebrew sources. But the debate came off, with no security problems and with few agreements.

9. Babylonian Talmud, Baba Metziah, 59B.

10. Fein, *Where Are We?,* pp. 31, 196.

11. The 1973 debate with Noam Chomsky took place in a downtown Boston church. The text of the debate as reproduced here comes from my notes.

12. Debate with Norman Podhoretz, November 15, 1987, at Central Synagogue, New York City. The text of the debate as reproduced here is based on a transcribed tape recording.

CHAPTER VII   Israel

1. Thomas L. Friedman, "The Focus on Israel," *New York Times,* February 1, 1987, p. 15.

2. Leon Weiseltier, "Palestinian Perversion of the Holocaust," *New York Times,* June 12, 1988, p. 27; Leonard J. Davis, *Myths and Facts 1989: A Concise Record of the Arab-Israeli Conflict* (Near East Research, 1988), p. 273. Not much has changed when it comes to the incumbent of that office. On July 26, 1989, the current mufti issued the following statement: "Kill the Jews until the stone shall cry: 'Oh, Muslim, this Jew is hiding behind me, come and kill him. . . .' "

3. Mortimer B. Zuckerman, "The PLO as Image Maker," *U.S. News & World Report,* January 22, 1990, p. 75.

4. Michael Cernea, "Involuntary Resettlement in Development Projects," Policy Guidelines in World Bank Financial Projects, World Bank Technical Paper No. 80, 1988. Estimates of the number of people annually "displaced as a consequence only of the new dams" range "between 1.2 and 2.1 million people." Michael Cernea, "Internal Refugees and Development-caused Population Displacement," Harvard Institute for International Development, June 1990.

5. Alfred M. De Zayas, *Nemesis at Potsdam: The Anglo-Americans and the Expulsion of the Germans* (London: Routledge & K. Paul, 1977), p. 9.

6. Ibid.

7. Anthony Lewis, "Towards the Extreme," *New York Times,* April 24, 1988, p. 25.

8. Charles Krauthammer, "The Curse of Legalism: International Law? It's Purely Advisory," *New Republic,* November 6, 1989, p. 44.

9. Raymond D. Gastil, *Freedom in the World: Political Rights and Civil Liberties, 1984–1985* (Westport, Connecticut: Greenwood Press, 1985).

10. Alan M. Dershowitz, "Preventive Detention of Citizens During a National Emergency — A Comparison Between Israel and the United States," *Israel Yearbook on Human Rights* (Tel Aviv: Faculty of Law, Tel Aviv University), vol. 1 (1971), p. 317.

11. Ibid., p. 321.

12. Consul General James Kerr, quoted in Monroe H. Freedman and Alan M. Dershowitz, "Israeli Torture, They Said," *New York Times,* June 2, 1978.

13. Freedman and Dershowitz, "Israeli Torture."

14. Ibid.

15. Trial transcripts, *Ahmad v. Wigen,* 726 F. Supp. 389, 418 (1989).

16. *Ahmad v. Wigen,* 726 F. Supp. 389, 418 (1989). After Rabbi Meir Kahane was murdered, a list was found in the possession of the accused killer containing the names of the judge, prosecutor, and others associated with the extradition of Atta.

17. Alan M. Dershowitz, "Is It Necessary to Apply 'Physical Pressure' to Terrorists — And to Lie About It?," *Israel Law Review* (Jerusalem: Israel Law Review Association), vol. 23, nos. 2–3 (1989), p. 197.

18. Ibid., pp. 198–199.

19. Excerpts from the text of the debate appeared in Bill Peterson, "Jackson Talk with Jews Becomes Confrontation," *Washington Post,* March 5, 1984, p. A6.

20. Martin Luther King, Jr., Rabbinical Convention, New York City, March 25, 1968.

CHAPTER VIII   In the Soviet Union

1. See Dershowitz, *The Best Defense,* Chapter 7.

2. Letter from chairman of International Conference on Soviet Jewry (Jerusalem, March 15–17, 1983) to Alan M. Dershowitz.

3. June 13, 1977. Quoted in Dershowitz, *The Best Defense,* p. 267.

4. Laura Kam, ed., *Pamyat: Hatred Under Glasnost* (New York: Anti-Defamation League of B'nai B'rith, 1989), pp. 20–21.

5. Ibid., p. 22.

6. Morris Abram, "For Ties with Soviet Lawyers," *New York Times,* August 26, 1986, p. 17; Alan M. Dershowitz, "Equal Treatment for Soviet Lawyers and PLO," *New York Times,* September 10, 1986, p. 34.

7. Morris Abram and Alan M. Dershowitz, "The American Bar and the Soviet Bear: An Exchange," *Moment,* January/February 1987, pp. 54, 58.

8. Michael Parks, "Anti-Semitic Tide Perilous, Pravda Says," *Los Angeles Times,* July 23, 1990, p. 1.

9. Quoted in "The Intelligencer" column, *New York,* May 21, 1990, p. 11.

10. Soviet poet Andrei Voznesensky, quoted in "The Long Shadow," *Newsweek,* May 7, 1990, p. 35.

11. Alan M. Dershowitz, "President Gorbachev, Use Your 'Bully Pulpit,' " *Boston Herald,* September 17, 1990, p. 29.

12. Jan Karski, *The Story of the Secret State* (Boston: Houghton Mifflin Company, 1944), pp. 349–350.

13. David S. Wyman, *The Abandonment of the Jews: America and the Holocaust, 1941–1945* (New York: Pantheon Books, 1984), p. 316.

14. Auerbach, *Rabbis and Lawyers,* pp. 163–165.

CHAPTER IX   In Marion Prison: The Pollard Case

1. A. M. Rosenthal, "On My Mind: In the Marion Prison," *New York Times,* August 23, 1988, p. 21.

2. Pollard Plea Agreement, Letter from United States Attorney Joseph E. DiGenova, March 3, 1987, p. 3.

3. Government Sentencing Memorandum.

4. Supplemental Declaration of Caspar Weinberger, Secretary of Defense, March 3, 1987, p. 4.

5. Leon Weiseltier, on "Nightline," August 6, 1990, show #2401.

6. Alan M. Dershowitz, "The Pollards and Rosenbergs," *New York Times,* March 18, 1987, p. A23.

7. Auerbach, *Rabbis and Lawyers,* p. 111.

8. Ibid., pp. 94, 111.

9. Ibid., pp. 175, 190. See also Rafael Medoff, *The Deafening Silence* (New York: Shapolsky, 1987).

10. Ibid., p. 177.

11. Ibid., p. 105.

12. James M. Markham, "Elie Wiesel Gets Nobel for Peace as 'Messenger,' " *New York Times,* October 15, 1986, p. 1.

13. "Alan Dershowitz Receives ADL First Amendment Award," *Jewish Advocate* (Boston), November 3, 1983, p. 3.

14. Wyman, *Abandonment,* p. 325.

15. Ibid., p. 331.

16. Ibid., p. 99.

17. Ibid., p. 330. Medoff, *Deafening Silence.*

18. Ibid.

19. "The Siegman Syndrome," *Jerusalem Post,* July 9, 1990.

20. James LeMoyne, "Cuban Linked to Terror Bombings Is Freed by Government in Miami," *New York Times,* July 18, 1990, p. 1.

21. Silberman, *A Certain People,* p. 340.

22. "Dr. [Morris] Pollard credited the recent flurry of activity related to the Pollard affair in the Jewish organizational world to the involvement of high-profile attorney Alan Dershowitz in his son's case." *Washington Jewish Week,* July 12, 1990, p. 6.

23. See Dershowitz, *The Best Defense,* Chapter 3.

24. I. Leo Glasser, unpublished transcript in my possession.

25. American Jewish Congress Resolution, June 11, 1990.

26. Allison Kaplan, "Pollard Files for Divorce While in Jail," *Washington Times,* July 19, 1990, p. A4.

CHAPTER X   Jews in a "Christian America"

1. Justice Jackson in *West Virginia State Board of Education v. Barnette,* 319 U.S. 624, 642, 63 S. Ct. 1178, 87 L. Ed. 1628 (1943).

2. *Zorach v. Clauson,* 343 U.S. 306, 313 (1952).

3. In 1980, there were 5,690,000 Jews in the United States. Projections predict a *decrease* of the American Jewish population to 5,321,000 by the year 2000, in comparison to an increase in the general American population. Evyatar Friesel, *Atlas of Modern Jewish History* (New York: Oxford University Press, 1990), p. 25.

4. In the *Miranda* case, the Supreme Court cited an article about Jewish law by Rabbi Norman Lamm (president of Yeshiva University). *Miranda v. Arizona,* 86 S. Ct. 1602, 1619 n.27 (1966). A year later, Justice Douglas, writing for the Court, quoted Rabbi Lamm's article to the effect that Jewish law disallows the use of even a *voluntary* confession in court. *Garrity v. New Jersey,* 87 S. Ct. 616 n.5 (1967), quoting Jewish law and its equivalent in Lamm, "The Fifth Amendment," *Decalogue Journal,* vol. 17, no. 1 (January/ February 1967).

5. D. M'Allister, "Testimonies to the Religious Defect of the Constitution," Proceedings of the National Convention to Secure the Religious Amendment of the Constitution of the U.S., held in Pittsburgh, Pa. Feb. 4, 5, 1874 (Philadelphia, 1874), p. 41, quoting Rev. John Mason of New York. Morton Borden, *Jews, Turks, and Infidels* (Chapel Hill: University of North Carolina Press, 1984), p. 59.

6. Borden, *Jews, Turks, and Infidels,* p. 61.

7. Ibid., p. 63.

8. Ibid., p. 66.

9. Ibid., p. 63.

10. Ibid., p. 64.

11. Ibid., p. 65.

12. Ibid., pp. ix–x.

13. Arnold M. Paul, "David J. Brower," in Leon Friedman and Fred L. Israel, *The Justices of the United States Supreme Court, 1789–1969: Their Lives and Major Opinions* (New York: Chelsea House in Association with Bowker, 1969), vol. 2, p. 1520.

14. *Church of the Holy Trinity v. United States,* 143 U.S. 457 (1892).

15. Alan M. Dershowitz, "Justice O'Connor's Second Indiscretion," *New York Times,* April 2, 1989, p. 31.

16. Ibid.

17. *Zorach v. Clauson,* 343 U.S. 306, 312 (1952).

18. Dershowitz, "Justice O'Connor's Second Indiscretion."

19. *Lynch v. Donnelly,* 466 U.S. 668, 680 (1984). The Supreme Court soon modified that decision by another 5–4 vote (see note 28, below).

20. *Goldman v. Weinberger,* 475 U.S. 503, 508 (1986).

21. *West Virginia State Board of Education v. Barnette,* 319 U.S. 624, 641, 650 (1943).

22. Alan M. Dershowitz, "Yom Kippur Test Reeks of Prejudice," *Boston Herald,* October 23, 1989, p. 31.

23. Ibid.

24. Ibid.

25. *Jaffree v. Board of School Commissioners of Mobile County,* 554 F. Supp. 1104, 1118 n.24 (S.D. Ala. 1987).

26. Alan M. Dershowitz, "Hand Disgraces Federal Bench," *Boston Herald,* March 16, 1987.

27. Walter Goodman, *New York Times,* December 21, 1984, p. 10.

28. *County of Allegheny v. ACLU,* 109 S. Ct. 3086, 3096–3097 (1989).

29. Ibid., at 3128 (Brennan concurring and dissenting).

30. Ibid., at 3112.

31. Advertisement, *Jewish Press* (Brooklyn, New York), October 1984.

32. "On the Record" (television talk show), produced by Meg LaVigne, hosted by Alan M. Dershowitz, WSBK, Boston, September 19, 1988.

33. Aljean Harmetz, "Film on Christ Brings Out Pickets and Archbishop Predicts Censor," *New York Times,* July 21, 1988, p. C19.

34. Peter Steinfels, "Robertson Draws a Rebuke on Film," *New York Times,* August 24, 1988, p. 15.

35. Pat Robertson, *Pat Robertson's Perspective: A Special Report to Members of the 700 Club,* (Virginia Beach, Virginia: 700 Club, 1990).

36. Ibid.

37. "On the Record" interview.

38. "Around the Nation: School in Tennessee Bars Play About Anne Frank," *New York Times,* November 22, 1986, p. 8.

EPILOGUE   The Past and the Future

1. Alan M. Dershowitz, "About Men: Collective Adolescence," *New York Times Sunday Magazine,* May 31, 1987, p. 46.

Index

Abandonment of the Jews, The (Wyman), 282, 297
Abram, Morris, 55, 265–266
Abrams, Robert, 243
Adams, Henry, 112
Adler, Cyrus, 292
Affirmative action, 71, 76–79, 82
Afghanistan, 232
AFL/CIO, 59
African National Congress, 290, 311
AIDS, 95, 96, 202, 203, 302n
Al Haq organization, 231
All African People's Revolutionary Party, 85
Allen, Woody, 13, 16n, 42, 114, 183n
Allison, Graham, 88
Altman, Murray, 41, 300, 324
American Bar Association, 72, 264–265, 266
    anti-Semitism in, 51–56, 71
American Civil Liberties Union, 171, 231, 333
American Communist party, 81
American Friends Service Committee, 199, 219
American Jewish Committee, 293, 301
American Jewish Congress, 157–158, 159, 293, 294, 299, 301, 309
American Nazi Party, 262. *See also* Neo-Nazism
Amin, Idi, 82–83
Amnesty International, 230, 231
Annie Hall (movie), 114
Anti-Americanism, 224
Antiapartheid movement, 86
Antiblack attitudes, 83

Anti-Defamation League of B'nai B'rith (ADL), 116, 161, 231, 293, 301, 330, 338, 353
    anti-Jewish census, 113, 114
Anti-Jewish attitudes, 4, 85–86, 108, 116–121
    left-wing, 86, 111–112
    at universities, 85
    See also Anti-Semitism, Anti-Zionism
Anti-Semitic People's Party, 109
Anti-Semitism, 4, 8, 83, 311, 350–351
    anti-Zionism and, 4, 85, 117–118, 121, 178, 204, 224, 351, 352, 353
    black, 117, 301, 329, 350
    defined, 109, 113, 121
    denial of, 116–117
    historical perspective, 101–104
    Holocaust denial and, 176, 178
    institutionalized, 113–114
    international, 210, 217
    Judaism and, 14–15, 189
    political, 109, 122
    racism and, 109
    right-wing, 113, 224
    at universities, 45, 99
Antiwar movement, 86
Anti-Zionism, 81, 82, 83, 200
    anti-Semitism and, 4, 85, 117–118, 121, 178, 204, 224, 351, 352, 353
    Communist-inspired, 117, 271
    Holocaust denial and, 174, 177
Anti-Zionist Committee (Soviet Union), 310
Apartheid, 92, 231, 233, 241, 243, 265
Apartheid Bar Association of South Africa, 265

Arab nations and people, 49, 153, 198
  anti-Semitism of, 99, 119, 213–214,
    217
  Jewish population, 118, 233, 234, 319
  Palestine and, 213, 218, 223
  refugees and, 214–215, 217–219
  terrorist activities, 214, 224, 225, 247
  wars with Israel, 80, 82, 100, 190,
    191, 194, 196, 199–200, 213, 214,
    219, 221, 223, 227–230, 243–244,
    247–248, 350–351. *See also* Gulf
    War
Arafat, Yasir, 194, 220, 231
Aref (president of Iraq), 214
Argentina, 232, 233, 250
Ashkenazi Jews, 196
Asia, Jews in, 5
Association for Civil Rights (Israel), 227
Association of Soviet Lawyers, 264–265,
    266
Aswan High Dam, 215
Atheism, 183n, 189, 342
Atta, Mahmoud Abed, 237–239
Auerbach, Jerold, 79n, 282
Auschwitz-Birkenau concentration camp,
    89, 136, 140, 143–145, 147, 160,
    163, 181, 189, 248, 297
  Catholic convent at, 150–152, 153, 156
  Holocaust denial cases and, 172, 174–
    175
  postwar murders at, 146
  Weiss controversy concerning, 159–160,
    162
Austria, 103, 109, 126, 137, 138
Avineri, Schlomo, 7, 8

Bakke case, 66, 70–71
Bakunin, Mikhail, 111–112
Barbie, Klaus, 87, 163, 164–165
Barlach, Sue, 48, 57, 346
Barry, Marion, 300
Baruch, Bernard, 282
Bazelon, David, 58–59, 60–61
Beck, Bernie, 40, 41, 43, 57, 114
Beck, James, 72
Begin, Menachem, 220, 301
Beilis, Menachem Mendel, 103, 104
Belzec extermination camp, 140, 279–280,
    281
Ben-Gurion, David, 162, 189, 246
Berenkoff, George, 47
Bergen Record, 161
Bergman, Bernard, 100, 307
Berman, Paul L., 178
Bernardin, Joseph Cardinal, 154
Bernstein, Shmulka, 192
Berrigan, Daniel, 81

Bitburg, Germany, SS cemetery, 134–135,
    163, 295–296
Black Law Students Association, 84
Blackmun, Harry, 333–334
Black Muslims, 107
Black(s)
  anti-Semitic, 117, 301, 329, 350
  -Jewish relations, 78, 82, 85
Bloch, Felix, 286
Blood libel/ritual murder, 103–104, 118,
    150
B'nai B'rith, 301, 309. *See also* Anti-
    Defamation League of B'nai B'rith
Boesky, Ivan, 306
Bok, Derek, 13, 73, 74, 88
Bonner, Yelena, 252
Bork, Robert, 196
Borough Park, Brooklyn, 17, 32, 38–39,
    44
  AD childhood in/return to, 35–39,
    185, 186, 343, 349
Bosch, Orlando, 300
Boston Globe, 18, 89, 125, 125n, 142,
    156, 176
Bradshaw, Theodore W., 95
Brandeis, Louis, 47, 59, 72, 294
Brandeis University, 199n
Brennan, William, 333–334
Brewer, David, 320, 322
Brickner, Balfour, 292
Brinkley, Joel, 351n
Brooklyn College, 44–46, 53
Brown v. Board of Education, 52
Brucan, Silviu, 272
Bruce, Lenny, 63–64
Buchanan, Patrick, 98, 162–164, 165,
    166, 170, 204, 212, 224, 350
Bulgaria, 298
Bulger, William, 125–126
Burger, Warren, 332
Bush, George, 300, 317, 337n

Calabresi, Guido, 50
Cambodia, 220
Canada, 134, 171, 172, 226, 230
Capital punishment, 86, 168, 169, 170
Cardozo, Benjamin, 59
Carmichael, Stokely, 85
Carter, Jimmy, 231, 256, 259
Castro, Fidel, 231, 300
Ceausescu, Nicolae, 187, 272
Certain People, A (Silberman), 116
Chagi, Berela, 36
Chelmno extermination camp, 140
Chicago Seven, 80
Chile, 233, 254
China, 254, 257, 311

Chomsky, Noam, 173, 174, 175–178, 191, 199–201, 205, 211
Christian Nation Amendment, 320, 321–322
Christian right, 335, 336, 338, 339, 340
Christian Science Monitor, 142
Church-state separation, 313, 314–316, 325–328, 340–342
　Christian right and, 335, 336, 338, 339, 340
　historical perspective, 319–321
　Judeo-Christian tradition and, 318–320, 336
　legal basis for, 322–325, 328, 330–331
　prayer-in-school issue, 203–204, 316–318, 325, 332, 340
Chutzpah, defined, 18
CIA, 256, 266
Circumcision, 118
Civil liberties, 206, 210, 211, 212, 215, 239
　Arab-Israeli conflict and, 227, 230, 234, 237
　free speech issue, 126, 171–172, 173, 174, 177, 192
Civil rights movement, 10, 86, 242, 243
Civil War, 320, 321
Clark, Ramsey, 238
Cockburn, Andrew, 211
Code of Justinian, 102
Cohen, Carolyn, 15, 345, 346
Cohen, Mordechai, 15
Cokely, Steve, 302n
Cold War, 138
Commentary, 191, 201
Communism/Communist party, 5, 111, 112, 261, 263
　anti-Semitism and, 117, 271
　anti-Zionism and, 117
　church-state separation and, 342
　postwar, 138
　in World War II, 140, 146–147
Concentration camps and survivors, 42–43, 87, 89, 108, 131, 135, 172. *See also specific camps*
Concerning the Jews (Twain), 128n
Conservative Judaism, 38, 182, 196, 201, 202–205
Cooper, A. J., 83
Corfu, 140
Costa Rica, 228
Cotler, Irwin, 250, 251–252, 254, 255, 256–257
Coughlin, Charles, 116, 164
County of Allegheny v. ACLU, 333n
Covington and Burling, 51, 53
Cowen, Phillip, 292

Cranborne, Viscount, 216
Cranston, Alan, 243
Cravath, Paul, 71
Cravath, Swaine, and Moore, 51, 53, 54–55, 71
Crèche issue, 326, 331–334
Cuba, 254, 300
Czechoslovakia, 142, 187, 215, 272, 273
　AD relatives in, 32, 33
Czestochowa, Poland, 151, 152, 154, 157, 159

Dachau concentration camp, 135
Daniloff, Nicholas, 266
Darrow, Clarence, 47
Dartmouth College, 45, 70, 85
Davis, Angela, 81–82
Dearborn Independent, 115
Decourtray, Albert Cardinal, 152
Degas, Edgar, 113
Demjanjuk, John (Ivan the Terrible of Treblinka), 14, 161, 164–170, 178, 235, 267
Demjanjuk, John, Jr., 168
Denning, Lord, 168, 169–170
Depression, 28, 40
Dershowitz, Alan
　affirmative action and, 76–79
　birth, early life, education, 10, 17, 22, 41–47
　debates Chomsky, 191, 199–201
　debates Kahane, 191, 193–196
　debates Podhoretz, 191, 201–205
　in Eastern Europe, 271–272, 273
　group of friends, 17, 39–40, 180, 190, 343–350
　at Harvard Law School, 13, 15, 47, 54, 62, 63, 79, 93
　hate mail, 93–98, 113, 116, 122, 123, 124, 129, 160, 161–162, 291
　human rights work, 233
　in Israel, 166, 227, 235–239
　media coverage, 93, 94, 95–96, 193, 233, 237, 290, 304
　in Poland, 139, 140–142, 144–146, 147, 149, 150, 159, 272, 296
　protests anti-Semitism at Harvard, 73, 75–76, 82, 84–85, 88
　protests Nazis honored at Harvard, 90–91
　in Soviet Union, 267–271, 273–276
　support for Israel, 80–82, 177, 209, 210–212, 213, 230, 234, 244, 245
　synagogue visits, 186–188
　See also Dershowitz, Alan, cases; Orthodox Judaism, AD adherence to

Dershowitz, Alan, cases, 18, 93–94
  Demjanjuk, 165, 166
  Des Moines police, 206
  discrimination in American bar, 54–55
  JDL murder, 192
  Pollard, 7, 284, 285–292, 300, 301,
    302–305, 308–311, 312
  Reems, 86
  Shcharansky release, 250–260
  Sullivan, 153
  Weiss, 152, 153–160, 161
Dershowitz, Claire (née Ringel) (mother),
  13, 15, 22, 27, 28, 30, 34, 37, 50,
  193, 233, 247n, 327
Dershowitz, Elon (son), 139, 159, 184,
  185, 268, 269, 270, 271–272, 313–
  315
Dershowitz, Harry (father), 16, 21, 26,
  27–28, 43, 195
Dershowitz, Hymie (great-uncle), 22
Dershowitz, Ida (née Maultasch) (grand-
  mother), 13, 14, 26
Dershowitz, Jamin (son), 25, 78, 79, 185,
  328
  in Poland with AD, 139, 140, 144,
    145, 149
  in Soviet Union with AD, 273, 274
Dershowitz, Leah (great-grandmother), 21,
  23
Dershowitz, Louis (grandfather), 21, 23,
  25, 26, 32, 33
Dershowitz, Nathan (brother), 35, 38,
  305, 307
Dershowitz, Sadie (great-aunt), 23
Dershowitz, Sam (great-uncle), 23
Dershowitz, Sol (great-uncle), 23
Dershowitz, Sue (first wife). *See* Barlach,
  Sue
Dershowitz, Tsvi (cousin), 33
Dershowitz, Zecharia (great-grandfather),
  21, 22, 23–25, 26, 29, 30, 31–32,
  34, 35
Der Stürmer, 81, 104, 161
Desegregation, 82
Dewey, Ballantine, Bushby, Palmer, and
  Wood, 55
Diary of Anne Frank, The, 340–341
Diderot, Denis, 113
Discrimination
  affirmative action and, 76–78
  in American bar, 51–56, 71, 72, 73
  in clubs, resorts, 115, 116
  educational, 65–69, 74–75, 76–77, 86,
    108, 117
  geographical, 107
  housing, 115, 116
  international law and, 85

  occupational, 104–105, 107–108, 115,
    116, 117
Donahue, Phil, 96
Double standard, 119–120, 121, 122,
  135–136, 225
  freedom of expression and, 191–192
  human rights and, 256n
  for Israel, 4, 211
  terrorism and, 220
Douglas, William O., 78, 314, 323
Dreiser, Theodore, 113
Dreyfus, Alfred/Dreyfus Affair, 110–111,
  165, 284
Drinker, Henry S., 71, 72
Dual loyalty, 4, 95, 114, 120, 245, 294,
  295
  Law of Return and, 244
  Poland and, 148
  Pollard case and, 7, 285, 291, 311
Dukakis, Michael, 317
Duke, David, 122, 326n
Durham case, 58

Eastern Europe
  anti-Semitism in, 65, 118, 279
  emigration of Jews from, 23, 36, 71
  genocide in, 281
  Jewish population, 188
  postwar refugees, 215
East Germany, 138, 215
Eban, Abba, 16, 224
Eden, Anthony, 298
Edison, Thomas, 113
Edwards, Harry, 329–330
Egypt, 80, 198
  Arab-Israeli conflict and, 214, 215, 221,
    223, 229, 230
  Jewish population, 7, 187–188
Ehrenburg, Ilya, 14–15, 189
Eichmann, Adolph, 89–90, 164–165, 170,
  187
Einstein, Albert, 189, 327
Eisenstadt, Zollie, 40, 41, 43, 45
Eliezer, Rabbi, 196–197
Eliot, Charles, 66
Eliot, T. S., 113
Elkins, Michael, 131
Elon Moreh settlement, 233, 234, 235,
  242
England, 105–106, 170, 226
  anti-Semitism in, 6
  Jewish population, 319
  Palestine issue and, 213, 214
  postwar policy, 215
  security policy, 230
  South Africa and, 243n
Escobedo case, 60

Esmail, Sami, 237–238
Espionage, 7, 284, 285–291
    spy trading, 258–259, 306
Esther, queen of Persia, 244–245
Ethiopia, 250, 279, 282
Europe
    anti-Semitism in, 6, 108, 115
    Jewish population, 5, 8, 22, 23, 108,
        130, 138
Evans, Rowland, 212

Fackenheim, Emil, 188
Falwell, Jerry, 183n, 203, 338
Farrakhan, Louis, 107, 192, 193–194, 302
Faurisson, Robert, 173–174, 175–176,
    177, 178, 179, 200–201
Fear No Evil (Shcharansky), 260
Federalist Society, 124
Fein, Leonard, 5n, 132n, 135–136, 353
Fixer, The (Malamud), 103
Ford, Henry, 113, 115–116
Ford Foundation, 235
Forged in Fury (Elkins), 131
France, 87, 108, 122n, 243n
    anti-Semitism in, 6, 109, 110, 273
    Jewish population, 7, 89, 102, 140,
        187, 319
    security policy, 230
Frank, Anne, 91, 173, 179, 204, 340
Frank, Barney, 96, 243
Frank, Leo, 114
Frankfurter, Felix, 59, 64, 68, 279, 281–
    283, 295, 298
    characterization of Jews, 48, 79n, 85,
        101
Freedman, James, 53
French National Anti-Semitic League, 109
Friedman, Stanley, 100, 306
Friedman, Thomas L., 210
Front de Libération du Québec, 226
Frost, Robert, 11

Gajowinczek, Franciszek, 143
Galicia, 23–24, 26, 35, 39, 246
Gays and gay rights, 202–203, 205,
    207
Gaza Strip, 214n, 217, 219n, 220, 223,
    232, 239
Gender rights, 10, 86, 224–225
Genocide, 4, 89, 106, 130–131, 134,
    179, 180, 294, 297. *See also* Hitler,
    Adolf, genocide program; *specific con-
    centration camps*
Geremeck, Bronislaw, 19
German-American Bund, 116
Germany, 87, 89, 103, 109, 137, 243n
    Jewish population, 7, 102

    postwar, 137–138, 215–216
    war reparations, 137–138
    in World War II, 229–230
Germany Is Our Problem (Morgenthau), 137
Geyer, Georgie Anne, 212
Gilbert, Martin, 145
Glasser, I. Leo, 307, 308
Glemp, Jozef Cardinal, 150, 151–157,
    158–160, 161, 180, 273
Goebbels, Joseph, 107, 164
Golan Heights, 219n, 221–222, 303
Gold, Ben Zion, 91, 185
Goldberg, Arthur J., 14, 56, 59–60, 61,
    64, 88, 243, 310–311
Goldberg, Dorothy, 60, 61
Golden, Harry, 125
Goldmann, Guido, 88
Goldmann, Nahum, 88
Goldstein, Abraham, 37, 50
Goldwater, Barry, 100, 322, 324
Gorbachev, Mikhail, 117, 260–261, 273,
    274–276, 277
Grabowski, Chester, 161, 162
Grant, Ulysses S., 321
Greece, 233
Greenberg, Hank, 100, 324
Greenwald, Ronnie, 258
Grenada, 232
Griswold, Erwin, 64
Grynszpan, Herschel, 284
Gulf War, 16, 34, 125n, 224, 249, 351–
    352, 353
Gypsies, 107, 141, 151, 178

Ha-Am, Achad, 104
Habash, George, 218
Haganah, 285
Halakah, 181–182, 190, 196, 197
Hall, Livingston, 80n
Hamas, 119
Hand, Learned, 68
Hand, W. Brevard, 330, 331, 339–340
Harlan, John, 55–56, 73
Harvard College/University
    admissions policy, 68–69, 70–71, 75,
        76, 79, 82, 88–89, 92
    anti-Semitism at, 45, 65–69, 70, 73–
        74, 79, 82, 84, 88, 99
    honors and honors programs, 87–88, 89,
        90–91
Harvard Crimson, 75
Harvard Graduates' Magazine, 68–69
Harvard Jewish Law Students Association,
    82, 83, 353
Harvard Law School, 50, 73, 83, 91
    anti-Semitism at, 124–125
    Jews at, 63, 64, 65

Hasidism, 26, 30–31, 32, 40, 188, 196,
    198, 307–308, 331, 332, 336
Havel, Vaclav, 272, 273
Helms, Jesse, 335
Helsinki Accords, 253
Helsinki Monitors, 259
Henderson, Anne. *See* Pollard, Anne Hen-
    derson
Herzl, Theodor, 6, 8, 108n, 110–111,
    128n, 189
Hester Street, 29
Himmler, Heinrich, 89
Hitler, Adolf, 33, 42, 87, 89, 94, 95, 96,
    116, 119, 171, 188, 207, 272
    aggression, 137
    definition of Jewishness, 181
    genocide program, 4, 89, 106, 110,
        111, 130–131, 139, 146, 151, 178,
        179–180, 189, 213, 214, 220, 241,
        268
    Martin Luther as model for, 106, 107
    opposition to, 245
    Palestinian support of, 216n
    propaganda campaign, 104
    war goals, 138
Hlond, Augustus Cardinal, 146, 150
Hoar, Leonard, 45, 69–70
Hocking, William, 67
Hoffman, Abbie, 80–81
Holland, 91, 174, 175
Holmes, Oliver Wendell, 79
Holocaust, 9, 27, 29, 32, 34, 40, 42, 87,
    108, 129, 132
    analysis of, 132–134, 136–137, 138–
        139, 141
    death statistics, 140, 141n, 142, 151,
        189n, 249
    de-Judaizing of, 178
    denial, 49, 86, 90, 107, 119, 161,
        163n, 171–178, 180, 201
    Dershowitz family and, 113, 139, 144,
        167
    fear of second, 98, 207
    Jewish revenge movement, 131, 135
    Jews blamed for, 132, 146, 148, 173
    Jews influenced by, 130, 181–182, 352,
        353
    state of Israel as response to, 209–210,
        212
    world response to, 138–139
Holtzman, Elizabeth, 243
Holy Cross University, 102
Honecker, Erich, 259n
Hopkins, Harry, 215–216
"House Jew" concept, 88, 91, 310
Human rights issues, 119–120, 212, 215,
    216, 217, 231, 256, 279

AD and, 233, 236–238, 250–254
Arab-Israeli conflict and, 223, 225, 226,
    228–230, 236–239
U.S. foreign policy and, 259
Humphrey, Hubert, 61, 243
Hungary, 109, 134, 141–142, 187, 215,
    273, 298
Hurok, Sol, 192
Hussein I, king of Jordan, 352
Hussein, Saddam, 18, 230, 351
Hymers, R. L., Jr., 338

Inside, Outside (Wouk), 11n
Intifada, 81, 227, 229, 230, 234, 235,
    236n, 239
Iran, 36, 254, 257
Iraq, 83, 214, 231
    Israel and, 34, 230, 248, 263, 290,
        303. *See also* Gulf War
    Kuwait and, 218, 224
Iraqi war. *See* Gulf War
Irish Republican Army, 290, 311
Islam, 5, 118, 119, 216
Islamic Resistance Movement, 119
Israel, 4–5, 49, 81, 122n, 209
    anti-Jewish sentiment and, 111, 153,
        224
    birth, independence, history, 3–4, 16,
        131, 136, 209–210, 212, 213–220,
        245
    colonialist actions, 85, 86
    emigration from, 38, 214–215, 216
    geopolitical policy, 230, 231–232, 233
    human rights policy, 223, 225, 226,
        228–230, 236–239, 254
    immigration to, 16, 147, 182, 231,
        253, 263, 276–278
    Iraq and, 34, 230, 248, 263, 290, 303.
        See also Gulf War
    Jewish criticism of, 233–235, 240–241
    Jewish population, 5, 194, 208, 247,
        282
    Law of Return, 181n, 240–241, 242,
        244, 277, 278
    military strength, 6, 247, 248, 249,
        285
    Nazi war crimes and trials, 131, 165–
        170
    security of, 238, 239–240, 242–243,
        247, 248, 290, 350
    South Africa and, 243, 310–311
    Soviet Union and, 254
    terrorism and, 83, 220, 235–236, 239
    United States and, 117, 285, 288, 350
    wars with Arab nations, 80, 82, 100,
        190, 191, 194, 196, 199–200, 213,
        214, 219, 221, 223, 227–230, 243–

244, 247–248, 350–351. *See also* Six-Day War; Yom Kippur War
Italy, 187
Ivan the Terrible of Treblinka. *See* Demjanjuk, John

Jackson, Jesse, 193, 241–243, 244, 246, 301, 302
Jackson, Robert H., 327–328
Jacobs, Hal, 40, 41, 43, 45
Jacyk, Peter, 165
Japan, 87, 99, 228, 229–230, 243
Jaruzelski, Wojciech, 272
Javits, Jacob, 243
Jehovah's Witnesses, 48, 327–328
Jerusalem/East Jerusalem, 214, 219n, 221, 222–223
Jerusalem Post, 159, 299, 310
Jewish-black relations, 78, 82, 85
Jewish Defense League (JDL), 18, 190, 192, 310
Jewish National Fund, 213, 223n
Jewishness, defined, 181–182, 189n, 191
Jewish Press, 335
Jewish State, The (Herzl), 110
John Paul II, 143
Jordan, Barbara, 87
Jordan, 214, 218, 221, 223, 229, 352
Judaism, 6, 8, 23, 25, 182–183, 188–189, 195
    anti-Semitism and, 15, 189
    Christianity and, 183, 198. *See also* Judeo-Christian tradition
    conspiracy theory of, 108
    defined, 181–182, 189n, 191, 278
    liberal, 201, 202–205, 210
    political, 188–190
    Reconstructionist, 196
    right-wing, 335, 338, 340n
    Zionism and, 182, 189, 209, 210
    See also Conservative Judaism; Hasidism; Orthodox Judaism; Reform Judaism
Judeo-Christian tradition, 318–320, 336, 339
Judeopathy, 121, 122, 123, 350–351

Kahane, Meir, 190, 191–192, 193–196, 198, 199, 205, 235, 301, 302
Kant, Immanuel, 113
Kaplan, Mordecai, 197
Karski, Jan, 279–281, 296, 298
Kaye, Danny, 171
Kaye, Scholar, Feirman, Hays, and Handler, 53–54
Kazantzakis, Nikos, 338
Kennedy, Anthony, 333n
Kennedy, Edward, 243

Kennedy, John F., 60, 337
Kennedy, Randall, 120n
Kentridge, Sydney, 243
Kent State University, 226, 232
Kenyatta, Mohammed, 84
Keyes, Alan, 230
Khomeini, Ayatollah, 336
Kien, Abraham, 37
King, Martin Luther, Jr., 118n, 242–243
Kissinger, Henry, 15, 100, 177
Knight, Sarah, 45
Knight House, 44–45
Koch, Ed, 95, 301–302
Kolbe, Maximilian, 142–143
Kollek, Teddy, 87n
Kones, Iris, 192
Koppel, Ted, 15, 94, 95
Koufax, Sandy, 38
Kremer, Johann-Paul, 174, 175
Kristallnacht, 113, 284, 302n
Krupp armaments manufacturer, 138
Kuhn, Fritz, 116
Ku Klux Klan, 115, 122, 161, 162, 225, 268
Kunstler, William, 81, 211
Kusevitsky, Moshe, 36
Kuwait, 218, 224, 243n

Landau Commission, 239
Lanzmann, Claude, 148
Last Temptation of Christ, The (Kazantzakis), 338
Latvia, 23, 186–187
Law, Bernard Cardinal, 163
Law of Return, 181n, 240–241, 242, 244, 277, 278
Lebanon, 81, 100, 199, 200, 227, 257, 279
Lefebre, Marcel, 163
Legal positivism, 134
Lehman, Herbert, 282
Lenin, Nikolai, 261, 262
Lewis, Anthony, 227, 231
Liberty Lobby, 116, 173–174, 224, 351
Libya, 83, 120, 237
Lifton, Robert, 157–159
Lincoln, Abraham, 320
Linnas, Karl, 163
Lipner, Joe, 157
Lithuania, 23
London Telegraph, 168, 169
Los Angeles Times, 252
Lowell, A. Lawrence, 66, 67–68, 69–70, 72, 74, 89, 100
Lowenheim, Francis L., 89
Lubavitch Movement, 332–333, 335
Luther, Martin, 106–107

Macaulay, Thomas B., 105–106
McCloy, John J., 87, 88, 89, 138, 297–
  298
Macharski, Franciszek Cardinal, 152, 160n
Mack, Julian, 292
Magiera, Sister Teresa, 153
Mahoney, Paul, 125
Maimonides, 182, 198
Malachim, 31
Malamud, Bernard, 103
Mandela, Nelson, 231, 241, 299
Manes, Donald, 306
Manhattan (movie), 16n
Manhattan Project, 327
Marcos, Ferdinand, 233
Marr, Wilhelm, 109
Marshall, Louis, 292, 293
Marshall, Thurgood, 47
Marshall Plan, 138
Marx, Karl, 111–112
Marxism/neo-Marxism, 191, 199, 200
Mason, Jackie, 38, 112n
Mavens Kosher Court, 79
Meany, George, 61, 243
Meese, Edwin, 331
Meir, Golda, 60
Mencken, H. L., 112
Mendell, Clarence, 69
Mengele, Joseph, 14
Meshenberg, Carl, 39, 40, 41, 42, 43, 74,
  114, 290, 300
Meshenberg, Herman, 39
Meshenberg, Joan, 40
Metzenbaum, Howard, 243
Metzger, Tom, 116
Meyerson, Bess, 306
Michnick, Adam, 149, 272
Milgrim, Ida, 251, 253, 257
Milkin, Michael, 306
Misnagdim, 196
Mitterand, François, 273
Mondale, Walter, 243, 330
Monotheism, 183, 184
Moral Majority, 203n
Morgenthau, Henry, Jr., 137–138, 282
"Morton Downey Show," 95
Mother Teresa, 87

Nasser, Gamal Abdel, 80, 214, 218, 221
Nation, 120, 211
National Anti-Jewish Party, 109
National Conference on Soviet Jewry, 255,
  265
National Lawyers Guild, 124, 255n, 256n
National Reform Association, 320, 321
National Salvation Front (Romania), 272
Nazi Iron Guard, 272

Nazism and Nazis, 16, 27, 87, 89, 103,
  188
  collaboration with, 134, 147, 152
  genocide program, 111, 119, 147, 178,
    179–180, 294, 297
  war criminals, 131, 134–135, 136–137,
    138, 139, 163–170, 266–267
  world response to, 138–139
Neo-Nazism, 14, 107, 116, 122
  American Nazi Party, 262
  Holocaust denial and, 170–171, 173, 176
Neturai Karte, 212
Newburgh (N.Y.) *Journal*, 321
New Republic, 163n, 289
Newsweek, 152, 256, 257
New York City College, 85, 86
New York Times, 90, 96, 121, 146, 152,
  155, 164, 217n, 227, 263, 265, 285,
  300, 331
  AD writings and coverage, 193, 233,
    237, 290, 304
New York Times Co. v. Sullivan, 153
New York Times Magazine, 344–345
Nidal, Abu, 14, 238
"Nightline," 94, 95, 289
Niles, David, 282
North, Oliver, 286
North Africa, 5, 297
Northern Ireland, 226
Norway, 89, 140
Novak, Robert, 212
Nozick, Robert, 130
Nudel, Ida, 87, 263
Nuremberg Tribunal, 52, 89, 90, 131

O'Connor, John Cardinal, 163
O'Connor, Sandra Day, 322–323
Oppenheimer banking family, 108
Orthodox Judaism, 11–13, 28, 30–31,
  133, 326
  AD adherence to, 40, 56–58, 61–62,
    64, 185–186, 188–189, 198–199,
    212, 326–327, 346–348, 349
  definition of Jewishness, 181, 182
  in Israel, 194, 196, 214
Orr, William, 94

Pakistan, 290
Pale of Settlement, 23, 278, 319
Palestine, 128n, 200, 216n, 230, 244, 352
  Arab population, 298
  Jewish immigration to, 297
  refugees, 217–219
  terrorist activities, 219–220, 228
  UN resolution concerning, 213, 217,
    218, 220
  See also Intifada

Palestine Liberation Organization (PLO), 80, 86, 120, 187, 211, 223, 265, 290, 303, 351
  destruction-of-Israel program, 84, 199, 200, 350–351
  human rights policy, 230–231
  terrorism and, 220, 228, 231, 238
Pamyat organization, 92, 118, 186, 261–262, 267–270, 275
Paranaitis, Justin, 103
Paul, Weiss, Rifkind, Wharton, and Garrison, 51, 53, 54, 56
Peace Now, 235
Pearl Harbor, 221
Peel, Robert, 105, 106
Pennypacker, Henry, 67, 69
Persia, 244–245
Persian Gulf crisis, 263. *See also* Gulf War
Peterson, Chase N., 75
Philippines, 257
Pledge of Allegiance issue, 313–314, 315–316, 317
Podhoretz, Norman, 191, 201–205, 340, 342
Poland
  AD relatives in, 26, 32, 35, 139, 145, 167
  anti-Semitism in, 99, 109, 139, 146, 147, 148, 150, 151, 152, 156, 158, 160n, 272–273
  Catholic Church in, 139–140, 142–143, 146, 149, 150–152, 153–159, 160n, 163, 180n, 316n, 342
  Communism in, 149, 151, 153
  German invasion/occupation, 89, 147–148
  human rights in, 254
  Israel and, 149
  Jewish emigration from, 40, 115, 147
  Jewish population, 7, 103, 139–140, 146, 147, 149, 153, 186, 272–273, 319
  murder of Jews in, 104, 139, 140–142, 143–144, 146–148, 151, 165, 179, 180, 279–281
  Nazi war crimes and, 139
  postwar, 138n, 215
  See also Solidarity movement
Political refugee status, 276–278
Pollard, Anne Henderson, 287–288, 289, 303, 305–306, 308, 310
Pollard, Jonathan Jay, 7, 97, 284, 285–291, 300, 301, 302–305, 308–311, 312
Pollard, Morris, 304
Pol Pot, 220
Popieluszko, Jerzy, 149–150

Popular Front for the Liberation of Palestine (PFLP), 218, 237, 238
Post Eagle (Clifton, N.J.), 160, 161, 162, 224, 351
Powell, Lewis, 70, 71
Prayer in school, 203–204, 316–318, 325, 332, 340
Prisoners of Zion, 252, 253, 255, 264
Proskauer, Joseph M., 294–295
Protocols of the Elders of Zion, The, 108, 116, 119, 143, 173–174, 178, 268
Pusey, Nathan, 73, 80
Pushkin, Aleksandr, 113

Qaddafi, Muammar, 231
Quota system and geographical distribution, 65, 67–70, 71, 74, 78, 79, 92
  Jewish opposition to, 85, 202
  in World War II, 139, 148

Rabbis and Lawyers (Auerbach), 79n
"Race and Reason" program, 116
Racism, 82–85, 225
  anti-Semitism and, 109
  Zionism as, 85, 92, 96, 118, 210, 213, 247
Ransfor, Mrs. J. M., 96
Reagan, Ronald, 134–135, 164, 195, 295–296, 325, 330
Rector, John M., 97
Redgrave, Vanessa, 192
Reems, Harry, 86
Reform Judaism, 22, 23, 38, 182, 196, 331
Reform Union of American Hebrew Congregations, 182
Regents of the University of California v. Bakke, 66, 70–71
Rehnquist, William, 115, 197, 326, 328
Reich, Seymour, 159
Renoir, Pierre, 113
Ribicoff, Abraham, 243
Rifkind, Simon, 54–55, 56
Ringel, Blima (née Newman) (grandmother), 27, 47, 61
Ringel, Naftuli (grandfather), 26–27, 35
Robertson, Pat, 203, 336–339
Robinson, Aubrey, 310, 311
Rogers, William, 275
Romania, 109, 187, 215, 254, 271–272, 273, 298
Roosevelt, Franklin D., 87, 215–216, 281, 282, 294, 295
Root, Elihu, 72
Rosen, Moshe, 187
Rosenberg, Ethel, 284, 310
Rosenberg, Julius, 284, 310

Rosenblatt, Yoselle, 36
Rosenman, Samuel, 282
Rosenthal, A. M., 164, 285
Rosovsky, Henry, 89
Rostow, Eugene V., 52–53
Rothschild banking family, 108, 112
Rush, Roger M., 96
Rushdie, Salman, 119
Rustin, Bayard, 87, 243
Ruth, Babe, 100, 324
Ryan, Alan, 164

Sacks, Albert, 73–74, 89
Safire, William, 264
Sakharov, Andrei, 252–253
Santayana, George, 129
Satanic Verses (Rushdie), 119
Saudi Arabia, 214, 243n
Schindler, Alexander M., 182
Schlesinger, Arthur, 15
Scorsese, Martin, 338
Semmelman, Jack, 238
Sephardic Jews, 5, 38, 115, 196, 216
Shaheen, George T., 95
Shakespeare (Shylock character), 30, 59,
    105
Shamir, Yitzhak, 162, 220, 301
Shapiro, Susan, 316, 317
Sharansky, Natan. *See* Shcharansky, Anatoly
Shaw, George Bernard, 112, 228
Shcharansky, Anatoly (Natan), 87, 124,
    250–253, 255–260, 264, 267, 279,
    306
Shcharansky, Avital, 250, 251, 253, 257,
    259
Shcharansky, Hanna, 260
Shcharansky, Rachel, 260
Shiites, 118, 257
Shoah, 148
Sidetes, Antiochus, 101
Siegel, Bugsy, 100
Siegman, Henry, 157–159, 299
Sila-Nowicki, Wladyslaw, 147, 148, 280n
Silberman, Charles, 116–117, 301
Silverglate, Harvey, 125, 126
Silver Shirt Legion, 116
Sinai, 221
Singer, Isaac Bashevis, 28–29
Six-Day War, 16, 80, 100, 199, 212, 214,
    219n, 221, 222
Skokie, Illinois, Nazi march in, 120, 170–
    171
Slovakia, 272, 298
Smirnov, Yakov, 207
Sobibór extermination camp, 140
Sobran, Joseph, 212
Solarz, Stephen, 335

Solidarity movement, 147, 149–150, 272
Soloveicheck, Joseph, 307
Sophie's Choice, 179
South Africa, 83, 85, 87, 88, 120, 190,
    213
    apartheid policy, 92, 231, 233, 241,
        243, 265
    human rights issues, 231, 254
    Israel and, 243, 310–311
    political prisoners, 257
Soviet Union, 192, 233, 243n
    Afghanistan and, 232
    anti-Semitism in, 91–92, 109, 117–
        118, 186, 261–262, 268–271, 273–
        274, 278, 310
    anti-Zionism in, 263–264, 271
    espionage and, 284, 287, 288
    Israel and, 254
    Jewish emigration from, 36, 115, 182,
        231, 253, 275, 276–279
    Jewish population, 7, 16, 22–23, 49,
        103, 186
    Jewish refuseniks and political prisoners,
        81, 250–254, 257
    murder of Jews in, 179, 180, 268
    postwar policy, 138n
    in World War II, 146
Spain, 103, 187
Spock trial, 232
Spotlight, 116, 351
Spy trading, 248–259, 306
Stalin, Joseph, 117, 153, 268
Stanford University, 65
Status of Jews
    criticism of Israel and, 232–233
    first-class, 92, 295, 297, 313, 319, 354
    Holocaust and, 189
    legal, 313, 324–325, 342
    second-class, 101, 209, 279, 295, 315,
        319, 324, 326, 330, 336, 340
Stewart, Potter, 17–18
Stone, Alan, 79
Stone, Harlan, 71
Straus, Oscar, 292
Strong, William, 320
Stuyvesant, Peter, 115
Styron, William, 179
Sullivan and Cromwell, 53
Sussman, Helen, 243
Sweden, 89, 119, 134, 228
Switzerland, 319
Syria, 83, 216, 221, 222, 229, 303
    Jewish population, 231, 250, 279, 282

Tacitus, 113
Taft, William Howard, 71, 72
Taylor, Telford, 252

Teresa, Mother, 87
Terrorism, 187–188, 192, 193, 259
   Arab, 214, 224, 225, 247
   Israel and, 83, 220, 235–236, 239
   Palestinian, 219–220, 228, 231, 238
Third World Communities and Human
   Rights conference, 82–83
Thomson, Bobby, 202
Thornburgh, Richard, 311
Time magazine, 57, 257
Toth, Robert, 252
Touvier, Paul, 163
Treaty of Versailles, 138n
Treblinka extermination camp, 140, 163,
   165, 168, 249. *See also* Demjanjuk,
   John
Tutu, Desmond, 87
Twain, Mark, 126, 127–128, 129, 279

Uganda, 82
Ukraine, 6, 23, 165, 166
   anti-Semitism in, 99
   Jewish population, 103
   murder of Jews/war crimes, 179, 180,
      267
United Jewish Appeal, 301
United Nations, 49, 81, 85, 96, 150, 352
   Israel policy, 224, 225, 247
   Nazi war crimes and, 131
   Palestine resolution, 213, 217, 218, 220
   Zionist policy, 118, 210, 213, 247
United States
   anti-Semitism in, 6, 115, 262
   Arab-Israeli conflict and, 219
   immigration to, 3, 22, 23, 36, 115,
      147, 207, 275, 276–278, 297
   Israel and, 117, 225, 226, 246–247,
      285, 288, 350, 351, 352
   Jewish population, 5, 6, 7, 22, 23,
      115, 123–124, 127, 128, 139, 140,
      182, 232–235, 245, 250, 254n,
      293–294. *See also* Status of Jews
   Nazi war crimes and, 131, 134–135,
      138
   postwar policies, 215
   security of, 230
   South Africa and, 243n
   Soviet Union and, 224
   in World War II, 229–230, 296–297
United States v. MacIntosh, 323n
Universal Anti-Semitic League, 109
University of Massachusetts, 85

Vatican, 118n, 143, 163, 311
Vidal, Gore, 120
Vietnam/Vietnam War, 14, 81, 94, 177,
   232, 234, 242

Virgin Islands, 297
Vogel, Wolfgang, 258–259
Volkswagen Foundation, 88
Voltaire (François Marie Arouet), 112
Von Bülow, Claus, 96
Vrba, Rudolph, 297

Wagner, Richard, 113
Waite, Terry, 95
Waldheim, Kurt, 91
Walesa, Lech, 147, 272–273
Wallenberg, Raoul, 134
War and Remembrance (Wouk), 188
Warren, Earl, 43
Warsaw Ghetto, 248–249, 279, 281
Washington, George, 319
Washington Chronicle, 321
Washington Post, 143
Wasserman, Lew, 338
Watson, Thomas E., 115
Webster, William, 266
Weinberger, Caspar, 288–289, 290, 305
Weinstein, Jack, 238, 239
Weinstein, Lewis, 292n
Weisberg, Jacob, 163n
Weisberger, Josh, 40, 41, 42, 43, 45,
   46
Weiseltier, Leon, 289
Weiss, Avraham, 151, 152, 153–154,
   155, 158, 159–160, 192–193
Weizmann, Chaim, 189
Weizsäcker, Ernst von, 89, 90, 91
Weizsäcker, Richard von, 89, 90–91
Wellers, George, 175
Wells, H. G., 112–113
West Bank, 100, 218, 223, 227
   Arab control of, 214n, 219n
   Elon Moreh settlement, 233, 234, 235,
      242
   Israeli occupation, 100, 220, 221, 232
   Palestinian state in, 217
Western Europe, 23, 111
West Germany, 138, 215
Where Are We? (Fein), 5n
White American Resistance, 116
White Book, 264
Wiesel, Elie, 49, 87, 131, 141, 150, 173,
   179n, 295–296
Wiesenthal, Simon, 87
Wildman, Donald, 338
Williams, Roger, 115
Williamsburg section of Brooklyn, 21,
   24–25, 27, 32, 35, 37, 50, 192
Wilson, Woodrow, 72
Wise, Isaac Mayer, 23
Wise, Stephen S., 292, 294, 295
Wolfson, Harry A., 65

Wouk, Herman, 11n, 188
Wyman, David S., 140n, 282, 297, 298
Wyszynski, Stefan Cardinal, 104, 147,
    150, 152

Yad Vashem memorial, 179
Yale Law Journal, 48, 49, 50, 51, 57–58
Yale Law School
    AD at, 35, 36, 47, 48–49, 50–52, 55–
        57, 78, 85
    anti-Semitism and, 52–53
    exclusive clubs, 49–50
    Jews at, 64
Yale University, 45
Yeltsin, Boris, 262
Yeshiva University, 44
Yeshiva University High School, 41, 42,
    43, 44, 53, 192, 327
Yom Kippur War, 16, 100, 199, 351n

Yugoslavia, 215

Zakharov, Gennadi, 266
Zaremski, Jack, 157
Zimmerman, Barry, 39, 40–41, 42, 43,
    45, 74, 114
Zimmerman, Sam, 39–40
Zion, 29
Zionism, 6, 49, 195, 241, 285
    AD commitment to, 15, 177, 209, 210,
        213, 242
    anti-Semitism and, 111
    Holocaust denial and, 178
    Judaism and, 182, 189, 209, 210
    political, 189
    as racism, 85, 92, 96, 118, 210, 213,
        247
Zivs, Samuel, 310
Zundel, Ernst, 171, 172